THE NEW REFORM JUDAISM

THE NEW

UNIVERSITY OF NEBRASKA PRESS · LINCOLN

REFORM JUDAISM

Challenges and Reflections

RABBI DANA EVAN KAPLAN

Foreword by Rabbi Eric H. Yoffie
Afterword by Rabbi Rick Jacobs

THE JEWISH PUBLICATION SOCIETY · PHILADELPHIA

© 2013 by Dana Evan Kaplan. Foreword and afterword
© 2013 by the Board of Regents of the University of
Nebraska. All rights reserved. Published by the
University of Nebraska Press as a Jewish Publication
Society book. Manufactured in the United States of
America. ∞

Library of Congress Cataloging-in-Publication Data

Kaplan, Dana Evan.
The new Reform Judaism: challenges and reflections /
Dana Evan Kaplan; foreword by Rabbi Eric H. Yoffie;
afterword by Rabbi Rick Jacobs.
pages cm
Includes bibliographical references and index.
ISBN 978-0-8276-0934-1 (cloth : alk. paper)
1. Reform Judaism—United States. I. Title.
BM197.K375 2013
296.8'3410973—dc23   2013006648

Set in Lyon Text by Laura Wellington.
Designed by A. Shahan.

To the United Congregation of Israelites, my congregation who worships in the Sha'are Shalom Synagogue in Kingston, Jamaica—a wonderful, diverse group of Jews striving to build a modern Caribbean Judaism. May we together succeed in creating a vibrant progressive Jewish community that is scholarly, spiritual, and based on indigenous models of religious expression.

Contents

Foreword by Rabbi Eric H. Yoffie   ix

Acknowledgments   xiii

Introduction: Understanding the
New Reform Judaism   1

CHAPTER 1   In Search of a Reform Jewish Theology   15

CHAPTER 2   A Brief History of the American
Reform Movement   54

CHAPTER 3   To Observe or Not to Observe?   99

CHAPTER 4   A New Reform Revolution in Worship
and Practice   131

CHAPTER 5   A New Reform Revolution in Values
and Ethics   165

CHAPTER 6   Who Is a (Reform) Jew?   209

CHAPTER 7   On the Boundaries of Reform   242

CHAPTER 8   Seeking the Spiritual   270

Conclusion: The Promise of
Reform Judaism   307

Afterword by Rabbi Rick Jacobs   319

Timeline of Significant Events   323

Notes   333

Glossary   345

Index   353

Foreword

RABBI ERIC H. YOFFIE

Dana Evan Kaplan has become the chronicler of contemporary Reform Judaism. In this fascinating book, he takes us on a journey through the complexities of a modern liberal faith that is now confronting a period of great upheaval in American religious life—an upheaval that impacts all Jews and all religious Americans.

As Kaplan demonstrates, Reform was born in Europe as a revolutionary religious movement and soon made its way to America. Here, it discarded the theological certainties of what we now call Orthodox Judaism, and in the process set aside the heavy obligations of personal religious observance that flow from traditional belief. Committed to modernity, rational thought, and the fundamental congruence of religion and science, Reform embraced the principle of progressive revelation. This embrace turned out to be a complicated matter. A revelation that is more ongoing than fixed is liberating for both the individual and the community, but it is also unsettling. It makes the Reform revolution a permanent one, and imposes the onerous burden of informed choice on every Reform Jew, in every era.

While this volume is organized thematically rather than historically, it nonetheless gives us a complete picture of the Reform experience in America. It takes us from American Reform's early commitment to the centrality of ethical action and belief to today's far more complex reality, in which ethical principles are still important but are only one element among many in a profoundly pluralistic community. Kaplan navigates this journey wisely and astutely. He recognizes the vibrant, dynamic character of Reform but is never an apologist, and he lays out weaknesses and challenges with an admirable forthrightness.

Rabbi Kaplan is at his best in describing the difficult task of defining boundaries for modern Reform Judaism and in relating the various ways in which young Jews today, inside and outside the Reform movement, struggle to express their religious yearnings and find spiritual meaning in their lives. These chapters remind us of how difficult it is to reach these young people through established institutions, how important it is to do so, and how, at least in some instances, Reform Judaism has begun the process.

It is interesting to note that at the installation of Rabbi Rick Jacobs as president of the Union for Reform Judaism (URJ) in June 2012, the Shabbat *mincha* service included dance, meditation, and a visiting gospel choir, along with a specific commitment by Rabbi Jacobs to develop technology as a tool of outreach and to work with Reform congregations in connecting with young Jews who are outside the ambit of mainstream synagogues. Clearly, the new URJ president is thinking along the lines that Rabbi Kaplan proposes.

In a fast-changing, unpredictable religious environment, Rabbi Kaplan avoids sweeping judgments about what the future holds for American Reform Judaism. He appropriately makes no attempt to tie everything together in a neat package. At the same time, the conclusions he does reach are sensible and compelling. He observes, for example, that the "physicality" of both local congregations and the national Reform movement will be reduced in coming years. In his words, Reform Judaism in the years ahead will be "lighter on its feet." This is a significant observation and one that has not yet been fully absorbed by Reform leaders.

As recently as fifteen years ago, there was much talk of the need for synagogues to have very sophisticated—that is, expensive—physical structures and staffing patterns because in a relatively wealthy Jewish community, young Jews would not affiliate with institutions that did not reflect the "quality" they expected in all dimensions of their lives. But today, exactly the opposite is true. In financially troubled times, young

Jews are looking for congregations with modest structures, restrained budgets, and a focus on the spiritual; this is both a practical necessity and a reflection of different religious sensibilities.

I don't agree with Rabbi Kaplan on everything. He talks of a "postdenominational future," while I avoid that term. In my view, denominations will be substantially restructured but still important. I think that Professor Lawrence Hoffman has it right when he writes that "only denominations can argue our way to a viable vision of religion for the vast mass of Americans who yearn for a form of religion that is not Orthodox but is equally authentic and equally deep."

Rabbi Kaplan and I also have good-natured, long-standing differences on the role of theology in Reform Judaism. He believes, and argues in this book, that Reform needs to clarify its theology. I argue that the diverse, big-tent movement he describes so brilliantly is precisely what makes it virtually impossible for Reform Judaism to produce a coherent theology. In addition, and more fundamentally, scholars of religion have long distinguished between orthodoxy (right belief) and orthopraxy (right practice), and it is my conviction that all schools of Judaism, including Reform, unite more around shared practices than shared beliefs.

Still, these are quibbles. This is a wonderful book, and a serious one. It implicitly asks—does Reform Judaism pay a price for its revolutionary approach to Judaism and its full-throated embrace of modernity and the autonomy of the individual? And the answer Rabbi Kaplan provides to that question is yes. It does pay a price, and a heavy one. It sacrifices the sense of obligation and discipline that are to be found elsewhere in Jewish life. But it offers in its place Jewish creativity, dynamism, and a broad and essential inclusivity, not to mention a reading of Torah and tradition that is both thoughtful and exciting. This is a Judaism that, if Rabbi Kaplan's direction is followed, holds out the hope of drawing young people to its ranks—young people who hunger for a Judaism that will aid them in their spiritual search, will marry modernity to tradition, and will compete, fully and unequivocally, in the marketplace of big ideas.

Acknowledgments

I would like to thank my congregation, the United Congregation of Israelites, for their encouragement of my research and writing, which culminated in the publication of the book that you have in your hands. They are a warm and caring community who has been wonderful to me and I appreciate it greatly.

Thanks, too, to my academic colleagues at the United Theological College of the University of the West Indies, who have extended a warm welcome to me since my arrival in September 2011.

I thank Rabbi Barry L. Schwartz, director of the Jewish Publication Society. We met at a Central Conference of American Rabbis meeting, and Barry immediately took an interest in this project. His enthusiasm was infectious and his feedback invaluable. I also thank JPS managing editor Carol Hupping for her ideas on how to best present the ideas in this book and Lona Dearmont for her copyediting expertise. Also thanks to Joeth Zucco, senior project editor at the University of Nebraska Press. I am honored that this book is one of the first to be produced jointly by the Jewish Publication Society and the University of Nebraska Press.

Karen Allen helped me tremendously in the preparation of the manuscript, debating points academic and practical of all types with me. Andrew Griffin provided top-rate technical advice to keep my computers running smoothly. My thanks to Jenna Bender, Mattie Blanton, Tracy Wallace, Danielle Gibson, Sunshine Denney, April Douglas, and everyone who helped me in the technical preparation of this manuscript. Thank you, Matthew Semler, for helping with documents from the

American Jewish Archives in Cincinnati. My appreciation to Joan "Samantha" Ewan for being an inspiration of sincerity and loving-kindness.

And I thank those who read sections and commented on them. I have noted their contributions in the endnotes where appropriate.

I want to thank Rabbi Eric H. Yoffie, president emeritus of the Union of Reform Judaism (URJ), for his foreword to this book, and Rabbi Rick Jacobs, president of the URJ, for his afterword.

Many of the biblical translations are from *The Contemporary Torah: A Gender-Sensitive Adaptation of the JPS Translation*, edited by David E. S. Stein; consulting editors, Adele Berlin, Ellen Frankel, and Carol L. Meyers (Philadelphia: Jewish Publication Society, 2006).

My hope is that this book can help people of all backgrounds to understand the underpinnings of the beliefs and practices of Reform Judaism.

THE NEW REFORM JUDAISM

Introduction

Understanding the New Reform Judaism

Reform Judaism is a practical approach to religious observance that acknowledges the need to bring one's ritual practice into harmony with one's actual religious beliefs. In the pages that follow, I present some of the critical issues—both concrete and abstract—facing the Reform movement, and I provide context so that you can better grasp the complicating factors that go into the debates over the Reform understanding of tradition.

I am a Reform rabbi leading a congregation in Kingston, Jamaica. As a rabbi who has worked in congregations for most of my career, I have had to deal with the realities of Reform Jewish life. That means that my perspective is perhaps less "academic" than scholars who have spent their entire lives within the hallowed walls of academia.

Like many American-born Jews of their generation, my parents were not raised with any clear denominational orientation. But when they married in 1957, they chose Rabbi Edward Klein of the Stephen Wise Free Synagogue to perform the wedding ceremony in Manhattan. After we moved further uptown, they joined Congregation Rodeph Sholom on West Eighty-Third Street. Both of these congregations were Reform and, I guess, my parents were pretty comfortable with the general Reform approach to religious practice.

My parents had decided to send both myself and my sister to Ramaz School, a modern Orthodox day school on Eighty-Second Street and Eighty-Fifth Street. At the time, there were only two Jewish day schools in Manhattan, and Ramaz was regarded as the more liberal of the two. "Liberal" might not be the most accurate description, but at least as I remember it, they seemed to avoid teaching religious beliefs almost entirely. What they did teach was Zionism. They repeatedly emphasized how Israel was our country and we should make every effort to immigrate to the Jewish homeland. Surprisingly, their arguments were entirely secular, at least in my memory, emphasizing how we were a people and should have the right of national self-determination like other peoples. But while the school did not emphasize religion, it certainly stressed Hebrew language.

For several years, our membership in Reform temples coexisted peacefully with our enrolment in an Orthodox day school. But as my bar mitzvah grew near, I became increasingly concerned with both content and aesthetics. I participated in the Reform youth organization NFTY for a while, even going on a few weekend retreats with them, but I was dismayed by how little the other participants seemed to know about Judaism. When we would have a youth service, the counselors would call me up for the Torah *aliyah* because it appeared that I was the only one out of two or three hundred who could read the blessings in Hebrew (I do not recall there being any transliteration available, but I could be wrong).

Also, I was disconcerted by what I saw as the passivity of the congregation. I expected adults to know enough about their own worship service to be able to respond at appropriate times, and yet it seemed that most of those we saw in the sanctuary had no idea what to do and barely an idea where they were. My discomfort increased after my parents enrolled me officially in the Rodeph Sholom bar mitzvah program. One week, as we settled into our seats in the large sanctuary right before a Friday night service, the organ began playing what seemed to me to resemble a piece intended for a church funeral. I looked so distressed that my mother leaned over and asked, "Do you want to leave?" I nodded vigorously, and that put an end to my bar mitzvah plans at the temple. We signed up the next week at the Jewish Center, a modern Orthodox synagogue on West Eighty-Sixth Street led by Rabbi Leo Jung and Rabbi Norman Lamm.

This move did not mean that I believed in Orthodoxy; in fact, I have spent decades trying to reconcile my desire for an intense form of religious practice with a scholarly theoretical framework. In my senior year in high school, we had friends in Connecticut whose daughter had married a yeshiva *bocher* studying in Mir Yeshiva in Brooklyn. I went down to spend a week there and, although it was a fascinating experience, found their theology to be entirely unconvincing. Over the next several years, I slowly made my way back to Reform Judaism.

I tell you this short version of my spiritual autobiography in order to give you a bit of insight into where I come from. Every author has his or her biases, and I think it is advantageous to state them up front. It is clear to me that, while I would like to believe that my intellectual positions are drawn strictly from my scholarly arguments, much of what I say has its origins in my childhood religious experiences. Nevertheless, I believe that there is much validity to my central argument that the Reform movement needs to find a way to present a clear and compelling theology if it is to thrive in the American religious marketplace.

Opportunities and Challenges

Because the Reform movement is a theologically flexible and politically liberal American religious group, this dynamic creates opportunities— but it also presents real challenges. Foremost among these challenges is how to present Jewish religious belief in the absence of a consensus over what we believe.

Reform Judaism presents us with challenges because there is no central decision-making body that has authority to make policies that are obligatory and binding. This is because of the nature of Reform Jewish thought. Reform Jews are free to consider different ideas and make personal religious decisions based on what they find spiritually meaningful. Since people find a variety of things religiously meaningful, there is no way to build a consensus on what should be required. The very mention of the words "requirement" and "obligatory" send many Reform Jews screaming to the hills.

While this book includes a chapter on the history of Reform Judaism in America, it is not a history text. There's just enough historical back-

1. A banner hanging from the portico of Congregation Kol Ami in Flower Mound, Texas. Rabbi Geoffrey W. Dennis explains, "Beyond cute, the chief virtue of the 'Bimah Me Up' photo is that it is emblematic of many of the forces at work in contemporary Judaism: embrace of popular culture, marketing techniques, and technology in presenting Judaism to an Americanized target audience." *Photo by Michael Fripp.*

ground to enable you to make sense of the challenges that I present. In order to understand the patrilineal descent resolution, for example, it is helpful to know who Rabbi Alexander M. Schindler is. To appreciate how earlier Reform thinkers understood kashrut, or Shabbat, one needs to know something about the development of Classical Reform in the nineteenth century, and so on (see chapter 2).

The Reform movement accepts that the Torah should be interpreted to meet the needs of contemporary Jews. This is not a new approach. The sages of the classical rabbinic tradition explicitly argued that the Torah was not in heaven and that God had given the responsibility for the interpretation of that Torah to human beings. Yet the Reform movement took this idea much further than traditionalists could because they were freed from the shackles of halacha (traditional Jewish law). Not having to follow thousands of detailed laws, Reform Jews could completely reconceptualize what it meant to be a religious Jew and how Judaism could and should be practiced.

Reform Judaism rejects the concept of Jewish law as obligatory on all Jews. While selected practices may be spiritually meaningful to many, others can obstruct rather than promote contemporary religiosity. Yet there is no consensus on how to evaluate a given practice. Indeed, there is no accepted methodology for analyzing traditional texts and drawing any sort of authoritative conclusions from it. Rather, the movement evolves in response to social trends, influenced by both its leaders and its laity. While Reform Judaism has explicit principles—even if they continually evolve and therefore elude precise definition—they are complicated by the "facts on the ground."

Understanding the Reform decision-making process is especially important for a movement that has few set rules and permeable boundaries. Because of the flexible nature of the Reform approach to Judaism, policies do not remain static. Definitions evolve. This makes it hard to characterize Reform Judaism, easily leading to misinterpretations. But in order to explain what Reform Judaism is, we need to first speak of Judaism. If we have to explain the concept of "Judaism" in just a few words, how can we define it?

We could start with the following: Judaism is the religion of the Jewish people, based on ideas and concepts embodied in the Hebrew Bible and the rabbinic writings. According to Jewish tradition, the covenant between God and Abraham marks the beginning of a special relationship between God and the Jewish people. While the very earliest biblical sources may show faint residues of monolatry and/or henotheistic beliefs, Judaism has long ago definitively rejected polytheism.

Judaism is the mother religion of the Abrahamic faiths, the main monotheistic religions. In contrast to many other faiths, its central authority is vested in sacred texts and traditions rather than an authoritative religious leader or a clerical chief. In the ancient world, the high priest in the Holy Temple served as a central ritual leader, but the destruction of the Temple forced the sages to radically redesign the architecture of Jewish practice. Many of the rituals that had been performed in the Temple now had to be reconceived so that they could be practiced in new forms in either the synagogue or the home.

This revolutionary adaptation served the Jewish people well for roughly eighteen hundred years—until the emancipation, which radically changed the legal status of Jews in western society. Jews were now freed from the ghettos of Europe and given full rights as free citizens, at least in theory. This presented an entirely new situation, which Reform Judaism is attempting to address. If Judaism does not require the observance of every law written down in the Shulchan Aruch, then what is Judaism?

Contrary to the argument advanced by influential Reform thinkers of earlier generations—that there is an "essence" of Judaism—I do not think there is a single belief or practice that can be said to constitute the central and unique core of the Jewish religion. Following Michael L. Satlow's line of reasoning, I prefer to see Judaism as "a family of communities" that share a common sense of identity and participate in a discourse on a specific set of authoritative texts and ritual practices.

This definition is called a polythetic understanding, drawing its theoretical framework from a biological model. One of the benefits of this polythetic understanding is that it balances the ethnic and religious aspects of Jewish identity, which is frequently a weak point in any definition of Judaism. It is also an approach that fits in well with Reform Judaism because it allows for a flexible system of identification that does not rely on any one belief or any specific set of ritual practices.

From Scholarship to Social Justice

Reform Judaism itself has changed dramatically over the course of its two-hundred-year history. While the early, Classical Reform formulation had a clear theology and uniform ritual, the movement has become, and continues to grow, more pluralistic. Today it is an extremely diverse and inclusive religious movement. Reform Judaism has become an American religious movement and as such is subject to the vicissitudes of the American religious environment, including the American religious marketplace.

Until the end of the 1950s and even later, the Reform movement embraced a generally traditional theology, accompanied by a radical departure from Jewish observance. This shifted in the mid-1960s, when some Reform thinkers advocated radical new conceptions of the Divine, including some that were seen as rejecting a personal God and all that that implies. By the 1970s there were several competing conceptions of God that manifested themselves in the new prayer book of the Central Conference of American Rabbis (the rabbinic arm of the movement), published in 1975. This prayer book, *The Gates of Prayer*, had no less than ten separate Friday night services, the first eight of which reflected different theologies in the English parts of the service. The existence of multiple conceptions of God led to the drastic broadening of what was theologically acceptable in a Reform context.

Reform Jews strive to be theologically inclusive. Nevertheless, their starting point is the same stories in the Torah as explained in the classical rabbinic tradition. Like other Jews, Reform Jews believe that God made a covenant with Abraham that was renewed by Isaac and Jacob and later Moses. As outlined in the Hebrew Bible, God promises that if the Jews uphold their end of the contract, that God will bestow blessings on the children of Israel. According to some of the more liberal theologians, it is possible that Abraham experienced an internal vision rather than participating in an actual encounter with God.

God may be a philosophical concept rather than an all-powerful divine being. Or, if we follow the more traditional thinkers, God may indeed be omniscient and all-powerful. In Reform Judaism, one's religious beliefs are flexible. The decisive factor is what is spiritually meaningful for each individual. The Reform movement seeks to be a theological "big tent" into which almost everyone can fit.

This was not always the case. As recently as the Hebrew Union College presidency of Rabbi Julian Morgenstern (up to 1947), there was a consensus in the Reform movement that religious beliefs would be mediated by scholarship. That is to say, if historians or archaeologists discovered evidence that something was true or false, it would be incorporated into the Reform understanding of religion. Because of the influence of the cultural revolution of the 1960s and various other factors, personal spiritual meaning has become a greater force in religion. As a consequence, many Reform Jews may believe things that are not supported by scholarship and that no longer necessarily matters. Similarly, if a religious concept is supported by historical precedent but has no resonance in the culture, then the fact that it is historically accurate carries little weight.

The early Reform thinkers emphasized their belief in the mission of Israel, the Jewish duty to testify to the ethical dimensions implicit in the belief in one God. The Jewish people, according to this way of thinking, had a unique role in helping to bring ethical monotheism to the world. The belief in one God created the religious authority that was the basis for a single ethical system, binding on all human beings. Preached in its most advanced form by the biblical prophets, the belief in ethical monotheism required Reform Jews to cry out against injustice of any type. Yet the early Reform thinkers read the prophets selectively. Specifically, they ignored the national aspect of prophetic teachings, focusing almost entirely on individual ethics and the need to advocate for social justice. For several decades, the Reform movement focused on social justice as the primary vehicle for expressing ethical commitment. By the late 1940s Reform Judaism began to be closely associated with liberal politics. The connection between the two became so intertwined that for many, being a Reform Jew meant being a political liberal.

By the early 1950s the Union of American Hebrew Congregations and the Central Conference of American Rabbis were actively advocating for peace and justice. But despite all the rhetoric, there was a large gap between theory and practice. The movement passed resolutions filled with lofty expressions about what was then called *brotherhood*, while most synagogue members remained passive and largely apathetic.

Definitions and Boundaries

There are obvious difficulties that emerge from a flexible approach to religious definitions. Not only is it hard to define who is a Jew, it is also hard to delineate acceptable theological limits. Where do we draw our lines? How do we reconcile our enduring traditions with contemporary challenges? Since Reform Judaism rejects the concept that Jewish law is a central component of divine revelation, halacha is not binding. This allows Reform Jews to engage in ongoing dialogue with God as part of progressive revelation. But what does this mean in practice?

In the Reform movement we also need to be careful how we define the boundaries of what constitutes legitimate Reform Judaism. Being pluralists, we are not accustomed to identifying someone or something as authentic as compared to someone or something that is not. But as boundaries separating the different religions in the United States continue to blur, and as religious identities become increasingly multifaceted, the Reform movement will need to take a clear look at where those boundaries should be drawn.

To give you a good sense of this dilemma of boundaries, I have chosen three case studies of problematic, potentially syncretistic religious approaches (so-called Messianic Judaism, Humanistic Judaism, and Jewbuism) and look at how the Reform movement has so far reacted to them (see chapter 7). Surprisingly, many of the scholars within the movement have taken a hard line, recommending all three groups be excluded from the Reform consensus. I would argue that we need to be inclusive of people with sincere non-Judaic beliefs and deep connections with Judaism while at the same time avoiding the excessive introduction of foreign religious influences. The question is how does a nonhalachic movement determine what is just too radical to be acceptable?

The Reform movement has no universally accepted methodology for predetermining how to evaluate any particular religious issue. Many Reform Jews were resistant to any proposal that might replace the halachic system they had rejected. So there is no central authority, neither a Reform chief rabbi nor a Reform halachic system. Not only is there no mechanism for enforcement, there is not even any accepted system for determining religious policies. The best that can be achieved is ongoing discussion, which hopefully will eventually lead to consensus. Since no one has the power to force their position on others, the persuasive abilities that can be marshaled in support of a given point carry a great deal of weight.

Some believe that the Reform movement can utilize halacha in a non-binding approach that emphasizes Jewish law as religious teaching rather than authoritative legally binding rules. The Central Conference of American Rabbis created a committee that focused on issuing responsa literature, *teshuvot*, to various questions submitted to it, and these position papers have been useful for providing rabbis and congregations with a great deal of information on controversial issues and problematic questions. I contend, however, that if taken as authoritative, the concept of progressive halacha can become contrary to the entire spirit of Reform Judaism. The Reform leadership needs to be careful not to emulate the Conservative model of a quasi-halachic movement that ended up with a tremendous gulf between what should be and what is.

The earliest Reform rabbis critiqued halacha, justifying reforms from within the parameters of the Jewish legal system. This approach soon gave way to an emphasis on minor cosmetic changes that made religious services and Jewish practice generally more respectable. By the 1840s there was a critical mass of Reform-oriented rabbis in central Europe who met together three times to discuss how to develop policies on various religious questions. A consensus developed that human beings had played a significant role in the composition of the written Torah and the development of the oral law. This allowed the Reformers to introduce additional changes.

God remained an inspiration for these central religious texts, but the sages were no longer seen as having transmitted direct divine oral instructions that could not be altered in any way. The sacred texts of the Jewish tradition remained religiously important, but the specific information in them was no longer necessarily authoritative. We no longer had to follow all of the laws as set forth in the Torah and Talmud without questioning their continued relevance. Rather, Reform Jews were granted greater latitude in interpreting Jewish tradition. In recent decades, we have expanded this notion of religious autonomy, encouraging individuals to apply their own religious sensibility to various practices, accepting some as religiously meaningful while altering or even rejecting others on various grounds.

Deciding what religious practices to observe places the Reform Jew in a difficult quandary because the final decision lies squarely on his or her shoulders. Each person needs to decide what he or she is commanded to do and what they are not commanded to do. This religious autonomy creates the risk that Reform Judaism will become the religion of the least, the refuge of those seeking to justify not doing anything. This is not a new problem, but with the rapid shifts in social trends, exacerbated by the new social media, the reductionist tendency in Reform Judaism may lead to rapid alienation.

The rejection of the binding nature of Jewish law has implications for every aspect of religious life. While ritual observance can and has undergone tremendous change, the basic ethical and moral foundations of the religion supposedly remain intact. But here too, we see that little remains rigidly in place. In some cases, what was once seen as acceptable and even ethically superior is now seen as hierarchical and promoting suppression.

The Return to Tradition

Coupled with this new ethical vision, Reform Judaism has been "returning to tradition." This phrase has caused a great deal of confusion because the concept of "tradition" is understood in various and even sometimes contradictory ways. On one hand, there seems to be a constant stream of articles in the media about how Reform Judaism is becoming more "traditional." And on the other, the movement has energetically promoted new definitions of Jewish identity, including patrilineal descent (see chapter 6). Many Reform Jews are embracing previously jettisoned ceremonial practices, but at the same time, they are open to postmodern understandings that allow them to embrace radically different and even conflicting needs. How is one to reconcile these seemingly irreconcilable differences?

A significant percentage of Reform Jews have come to the realization that they need to be actively involved in "Jewish doing" in order to feel the type of spiritual connection they yearn for. While Classical Reform had stressed the theological, neo-Reform places greater emphasis on what has been interchangeably referred to as "ritual" or "ceremony." I differentiate between these two terms, defining ritual as stylized, repetitive, religious behavior that is seen as being directly commanded by God. Not only must it be done, but it needs to be performed in a specific manner and at a specific time. Ritual is efficacious, meaning that God may perform acts of whatever nature in direct response.

In contrast, ceremony is the human effort to give concrete representation to abstract religious concepts. Participants do not believe that

2. Ainsley Henriques, a leader of the United Congregation of Israelites in Kingston, Jamaica, explains a bit about the history and architecture of the Sha'are Shalom Synagogue to members of the public who attended a free reggae concert in the building as part of the "Kingston on the Edge" arts festival. Many Jewish congregations are opening their buildings to the general public to participate in the cultural exchange that is growing as invisible social barriers fade away. *Photo by Dana Evan Kaplan.*

they are directly being commanded by God, and therefore they may alter the acts that are to be done, as well as the order and timing. The purpose of the ceremony is to help people connect with their spiritual selves, however that is defined, rather than to please God in objective terms that can be checked by referring to biblical or talmudic texts.

There is also an intermediate category we could call "Reform rite," where God commands but does not require us to perform elaborate, multisequential behaviors in a formulaic manner. God retains a divine commanding voice, but the specifics of how to interpret that voice, as well as the details of how to put those commandments into practical application, are left open.

While new approaches have a great deal of potential value, some of these proposed changes seem to be in conflict with long-established expectations. Societal innovation is moving at a much quicker pace than institutional policy setting. While many congregations continue to struggle to engage worshipers on even an elementary level, individuals are creating new religious models that serve their personal spiritual needs and that are frequently outside the realm of the synagogue community.

Looking toward the Future

In the final chapter I tell of the ongoing search for spirituality among Reform Jews. A friend who read a draft of it said that almost everything in the chapter could apply to non-Orthodox Jews of any background. This is absolutely true. While most of the specifics come out of a Reform context and involve Reform Jews, the activities themselves are trends that impact the entire mainstream American Jewish community, and indeed many other Americans as well. Whether we are talking about virtual religion or spirituality through the arts or wilderness Judaism, there is nothing inherently "Reform" about these activities. We are living in a postdenominational world, and this widespread cultural trendsetting is part of that phenomenon.

Reform Judaism is a bold experiment that is just over two hundred years old, a relatively short amount of time in the context of Jewish history. No one knows how successful the movement will ultimately be. The trend toward postdenominationalism makes it harder to justify having a Reform movement that is distinct from the Conservative movement, Reconstructionism, Jewish renewal, and even Jewish humanism. Nevertheless, I believe it is critical for the future of Judaism in America for the Reform movement to remain strong.

At its theoretical best, Reform Judaism incorporates all of the intellectual challenges that have faced religion over the past few centuries, while at the same time embracing all of the spiritual trends that are so emotionally important to people. Reform Judaism therefore represents an intellectually truthful approach to religion that can meet the highest scholarly scrutiny while at the same time providing spiritual sustenance for religious seekers. The challenge is how the Reform movement can inculcate a belief in God and hence a commitment to perpetuating our approach to religious faith and Jewish identity without having a fundamentalist worldview.

CHAPTER 1

In Search of a Reform Jewish Theology

Growing up in a traditional Jewish household in Jacksonville, Florida, in the 1950s, Gail Greenfield never imagined that she would one day become an enthusiastic Reform Jew. Her family was very active in their local Conservative congregation, which at that time was leaning heavily toward the Orthodox end of the religious spectrum. At home, her family celebrated all the Jewish holidays, kept kosher, and observed Shabbat. Yet, despite her multiple involvements in Jewish religious life, she felt spiritually unfulfilled. "There was little mention of God, and somehow I felt that there was something absent from my life."

During confirmation class at her Conservative synagogue, she asked the rabbi about God, and he answered, "We don't ask those questions." Gail suppressed her spiritual yearnings for many years. "We were very involved with a synagogue when our children were young, and one day I got up the nerve to ask the *rebbetzin*, who was a friend of mine, about her beliefs in God. 'How can you believe in God after the Holocaust?' Gail asked her. To Gail's shock, the rebbetzin responded that she did not believe in God. 'I just believe in the Jewish people.'"

Gail did not find this answer satisfactory, but she had no access to an alternative approach to spirituality until much later, when she and her husband, Stanley Greenfield, moved their family to Maryland in the 1980s. "I never was inspired by attending services and found them long and boring. I never could accept the stories in the Bible as true even though they were taught as truth nor could I relate to the God of the Bible. I yearned for a relationship with God but felt no connection." Gail had many questions but few answers, and as an adult searched elsewhere while still retaining some involvement in Judaism. Yoga and Hinduism, Buddhist meditation and Reiki (a method of transmitting a healing energy through touch), are where she found a spiritual connection. And then, of course, she "felt Jewish guilt about it all."

"I continued to do my Judaism, but on my own terms. I began developing my own rituals. I put together a Tu B'Shevat seder which was meaningful and spiritual. I wrote a Purim play and even edited a Rosh Hashanah and Yom Kippur service." Gail and her friends were looking for a connection with God and a way to express their spirituality through Judaism. "I love the idea expressed by Rabbi Nachman of Bratslav, which I included in my Tu B'Shevat seder: 'Master of the Universe, grant me the ability to be alone; may it be my custom to go outdoors each day among the trees and grass, among all growing things, and there may I be alone, and enter into prayer, to talk to the One that I belong to.'"

A friend gave her a copy of *The Nature of Personal Reality* by Jane Roberts, which was supposed to be metaphysical knowledge channeled through the author. "This catapulted me into involvement with New Age interests because it answered a lot of the questions I had been looking for about the universe and how it works." Gail found that she was finally learning about the questions that had long consumed her, such as "What is the purpose of our life?" and "Why are we here?" "Fortunately, I was not motivated by a tragedy. I was just motivated by my own emotional needs—my own yearnings to find metaphysical answers. It was sort of like a search to find God, in a way, but it has just gone in many different directions."

A registered nurse, Gail became interested in healing and did a week-long training session with Louise L. Hay, the author of *You Can Heal Your Life*. Hay "talked about how we harbor resentment and anger and how it affects our bodies. Frustration can actually lead to disease. That's when I got involved in Reiki, which is a healing modality. You learn how to transmit healing energy through your hands." The next step in her spiritual evolution was to begin a Buddhist meditation practice. She began doing Vipassana meditation, a simple technique consisting of the experiential observation of mind and matter in their aspects of impermanence, unsatisfactoriness, and devoidness of self. "You really get to

3. Gail Greenfield studying *The Torah: A Women's Commentary*, published by the URJ Press. Greenfield became a member of a Reform temple after being affiliated with the Conservative movement for many years. "I consider myself a 'born-again' Reform Jew." The Reform movement has benefited in recent years from an influx of members from Conservative backgrounds. *Photo by Dana Evan Kaplan.*

learn the workings of your mind and how your thoughts cause many of the problems that you have. Eventually I learned to stop most of my negative thinking."

After their daughter bought a dermatology practice in Albany, Georgia, Gail and Stanley began spending a great deal of time there. To be with their grandchildren, Nathan and Josie, they began commuting between Jacksonville and Albany. It was at this point that they began coming to Temple B'nai Israel, the one and only synagogue in the Albany area.

At the beginning, they had to overcome a great deal of resistance to going to a Reform temple. "Somehow we were given the impression that Reform Jews were like 'half-Jews.'" When Stanley was asked by a friend to be the assistant scoutmaster at the Reform temple's Boy Scout troop in Jacksonville, "The members of our synagogue were surprised and somewhat dismayed." At an area Scout Jamboree, Stanley sent a group of Boy Scouts from the Reform temple to ask the scouts from the Conservative synagogue to join them for Shabbat services, but they refused.

Shortly after moving to Albany in 2004, the Greenfields celebrated their granddaughter's baby-naming ceremony at the temple and began attending services. "I found for the first time [that] I enjoyed attending services and felt inspired and spiritually connected. The Friday night service was short and the wording in the prayer book gave the prayers a new meaning. I could identify with God, the 'source of light and truth, Creator of the eternal law of goodness.'"

Shortly thereafter, the Greenfields began attending Torah study on Saturday morning. "It was so much more interesting to actually discuss the Torah portion than to sit through a three-hour service," part of which is the reading of the Torah. "In my adult years, I had already learned that even the Conservative movement actually acknowledged the Torah was redacted by several writers, confirming my youthful suspicion that the Torah was not dictated by God to Moses."

"At first, however, I was always questioning the truth of what we were studying, but eventually I found I could study the *parsha* as if it were fact, realizing that there were so many levels and such rich material to glean from it that it didn't matter whether it really happened. I guess that might be called Torah maturity. This could have never happened in any other setting."

For the first time in her life, Gail did not feel guilty that she was ignoring large numbers of obligatory religious acts. "I love the fact that we are freed from the commandments and can choose what is ritually meaningful. . . . Gone is all that guilt over the fact that I am not a 'good Jew.' As long as I considered myself a Conservative Jew, I measured myself against what I thought a good Conservative Jew should be—I know because I was a nurse at Camp Ramah [the summer camp sponsored by the Conservative movement] and that is Conservative Judaism at its best. Now that I am Reform, most of that guilt is gone—what a relief!"

Greenfield found that Reform theology allowed for ritual flexibility that greatly enriched her personal religious experience. The text of the prayer book could be edited in such a way as to reflect the contemporary sensibilities of the modern worshiper. "While not an ardent feminist, I very much believe in women's full participation in ritual life." She also found that the relaxation of communal religious standards allowed the temple to organize tremendously enjoyable gatherings such as potluck Shabbat dinners that had been prohibited in her Conservative congregation because the rabbi there did not trust the *kashrut* levels of the congregants.

Most of all, Greenfield enjoyed the newfound religious freedom that emphasized spiritual meaning rather than blind obedience to the law. A perfect example of that freedom was apparent this past Rosh Hashanah, which fell on Shabbat. "When I saw the shofar out, I said to my husband, 'I didn't think we blew the shofar on Shabbat.' But then we realized since it is a Reform temple, we can do what is ritually meaningful. We discussed it and decided it is much more important that the people experience those magical moments that stir our souls and link us to our generations past. What purpose would it serve not to do it?"

The Problems in Defining Judaism

Gail Greenfield's search for a spiritually meaningful Reform Judaism forced her to reevaluate everything she thought she knew about Judaism. Before we can understand the nature of Reform Judaism, I first need to impart a few words about Judaism. This is by no means an easy task. Judaism is a religion, but it is also a culture, a civilization, a way of life. There have been many books written on Judaism, but few of them provide us with a clear, understandable definition of what it is. Indeed, most authors of introductory books on the subject skirt around the issue entirely. They casually explain that Judaism is the religion of the Jewish people and then launch into a discussion of the mythological history of Abraham, Isaac, and Jacob, and Sarah, Rebecca, Leah, and Rachel.

A central idea in Jewish tradition is that God established a covenant with Abraham, beginning a special relationship between God and the Jewish people. This culminated in the giving of the Torah at Mount Sinai. Early biblical sources do show signs of monolatry, the recognition of the existence of many gods but the intent to worship consistently only one, and of henotheism, belief in and worship of a single god while accepting the existence or possible existence of other gods. But in Judaism there developed a strong belief in strict monotheism. We can therefore say that Judaism is a monotheistic religion that sees God's revelation to Moses at Mount Sinai as establishing an eternal covenant between God and the Jewish people.

In contrast to certain other faiths, the central authority is vested in sacred texts and traditions rather than in an authoritative religious leader or singular religious institution. The Kohen Gadol, the high priest, and the other Kohanim and Leviim played an important role in the ritual life in the Temple in Jerusalem, but they lost most of their influence as a consequence of the destruction of the Temple in 70 CE. The sages, who became the teachers and religious leaders of the Jewish people in the aftermath of this catastrophe, were forced to radically redesign the architecture of Jewish practice, emphasizing individual ritual performed at home and in local synagogues.

Judaism is the religion of the Jewish people, based on concepts embodied in the Hebrew Bible and Talmudic literature. But that definition is still not sufficient. In order to speak meaningfully about Reform Judaism, we need some understanding of the word *Judaism*. It has the suffix —*ism*, which appended to the noun usually indicates an ideological system such as communism, capitalism, or socialism. Accordingly,

Judaism would be the belief of the Judeans. Judah was originally the territory of the Israelite tribe of that name. Later, it became the area of the ancient kingdom of Judah, which was in the mountainous southern part of the land of Israel. The Hebrew word *Judah* became *Judea* in both the Greek and Roman periods.

Judah was one of two provinces that had originally been united under the kings Saul, David, and Solomon. Israel, the northern kingdom, was conquered by the Assyrians in 722 BCE. The conquerors took many of the local inhabitants away from their homeland, resettling them elsewhere. These people are what became known as the Ten Lost Tribes. They presumably assimilated into the host societies, although researchers, Orthodox rabbis, and Jewish adventurers periodically "discover" one or more of them in various far-flung regions of the world. There is even an organization in Israel dedicated to locating these tribes and helping them rediscover their Jewish identities. Nevertheless, the vast majority of those who had lived in the province of Israel disappeared, and most contemporary Jews are descendants from those who lived in Judea.

Some modern readers may look at the word Judaism and surmise that this word must mean the creed that the Judeans adhered to. If this were the case, then when we say that we believe in Judaism, we are saying that we follow that same creed. In order to test that assumption, we would need to know exactly what time period was being considered and what texts were being used as the basis for analysis. But even if this assumption was correct, we are not sure exactly what the Judeans believed or practiced. We can be reasonably sure that whatever they believed deviated significantly from anything that could be called modern Judaism, but it is not likely that they had definitive beliefs that could be easily characterized.

In the second book of Maccabees, the term *Judaism* appears in contrast to the term *Hellenism*. Hellenism, the devotion to and/or imitation of ancient Greek thought, customs, or styles, and more generally the Greek way of life, implies a broad approach to culture rather than a narrow creedal formulation. Therefore, Judaism would appear to have likewise referred to the Jewish way of life, which included religious beliefs alongside other cultural elements. After the rise of Christianity, religion becomes a narrower category for the construction of identity, and the term Judaism begins to be used as a reference to the religion of the Jews.

The word Judaism is, of course, an English word. The Hebrew equivalent is Yahadut, but this is a modern Hebrew word. The closest biblical term is *daat*, which literally means *knowledge* but is usually translated as *religion*. The Hebrew Bible unquestionably presents certain beliefs that the Israelites either accepted or were being urged by God to accept, but they are not formulated in a neat, tidy package. Some beliefs can seem to be at odds with others, even contradicting references to doctrines that appear elsewhere in scripture. The diversity of Jewish belief systems multiplied by the middle of the Second Temple Period. Part of the fascination with the Dead Sea Scrolls is the alternative belief system or systems they reveal. Jews in the biblical era and particularly the Second Temple Period apparently believed in all sorts of different things.

If Christianity is the religion based on the teachings of Jesus, and Islam is the religion based on the teachings of Mohammad, can it be said that Judaism is the religion based on the teachings of Moses? As with so many questions in Jewish life, the answer is yes and no. From a scholarly perspective, it is clear that Judaism has changed incredibly from the times of its origins through the various periods of its development and up to the Rabbinic Period in the early centuries of the Common Era.[1] A full account of these changes is beyond the scope of this book, and writing an authoritative account is probably beyond the capacity of even the most brilliant scholar—there is simply too much we do not know.

We know particularly little about the period from Ezra and Nehemiah, who lived in the mid-fifth century BCE, to the early sages, who apparently formed a cohesive group beginning in the first century BCE. There is a great deal of conjecture as to what may have happened, particularly concerning the possible ramifications of the Maccabean Revolt, but most of this is educated guesswork. What we do know is that the classical rabbinic tradition emerged out of a group called the Pharisees, who claimed an unbroken chain of transmission of religious tradition going back all the way to Moses himself. This is written down in the first *mishnah* of Pirkei Avot (Ethics of the Sages).

According to a contemporary understanding of this mishnah, the sages believed that God gave both the written Torah and the oral Torah to Moses on Mount Sinai. Sometimes referred to as the doctrine of the dual Torah, this belief has formed the basis for the development of rabbinic Judaism. Those who rejected this belief—such as the Sadducees in the Second Temple Period and the Karaites in the medieval period—were branded as heretics. The existence of the oral Torah was essential. Many topics were mentioned only briefly in the written Torah. There had to be an accompanying tradition to explain the full background and meaning of what could be rather obscure references. Most scholars would argue that as Judaism developed over the course of many centuries, religious leaders validated this process—which was largely unconscious—by referring to the doctrine of the oral law.

The classical rabbinic tradition is centered on the mishnah, a compilation of brief rabbinic positions redacted by Rabbi Judah the Prince in around the year 200 CE. The legal debates, which continued in Israel and Babylonia, were later transcribed and written down to form the *gemara*. Together, the mishnah and the gemara form the Talmud, which is considered the central work of the Jewish approach to religious belief and practice. The emphasis was, as we have alluded to earlier, primarily on practice. Periodically, the sages mention a particular religious belief and may make one or two comments about that doctrine, only to leave the reference hanging in the air. What could they have possibly meant by their brief reference? Sometimes it is clear but other times it remains uncertain.

Religious teachings in the Talmud are divided into halacha (law) and aggadah (homiletics). The sages were primarily concerned with halacha. While they debated many legal issues extensively, they eventually wanted to resolve each issue because the people of Israel had to know what the proper observance was. In some cases, one position might be regarded as authentic or legitimate, and another view might be seen as false and invalid. In other cases, it might simply be a situation where the sages felt that they had to establish a precedent for future practice. Here is one example from the book of Deuteronomy:

> Take to heart these instructions with which I charge you this day. Impress them upon your children. Recite them when you stay at home and when you are away, when you lie down and when you get up. Bind them as a sign on your hand and let them serve as a symbol on your forehead, inscribe them on the doorposts of your house and on your gates.
> (Deuteronomy 6:6–9)

The sages determined that the *Shema* and other biblical citations were to be written on a small piece of parchment and placed inside a container to be attached to the doorpost known as a *mezuzah*. In the medieval period, there was a debate between Rashi and Rabbenu Tam as to whether the mezuzah should be attached on the doorpost horizontally or vertically. A compromise was reached—the mezuzah was placed at a forty-five-degree angle. Halachic decisions determined Jewish law, which was the nonnegotiable standard for Jewish behavior. While not all Jews observed every halacha all the time, adherence to rabbinic law was the bedrock of Jewish society in premodern Jewish communities in both Christian and Muslim regions.

Judaism was more than just a religion, as we understand the term today. The giving of the Torah to the children of Israel on Mount Sinai marked them as God's chosen people. Living as the minority among Christians or Muslims, the Jews maintained their separate communal organizations within the broader society. The degree of cultural influence varied from place to place and from period to period. Some recent historians have argued that even during periods when Christian (and to a lesser degree, Muslim) hostility ran particularly high, there was an extensive network of not only economic but also cultural and social relationships.

The emancipation of the Jews in Europe and the Enlightenment changed the social circumstances in which Jews were isolated from the rest of the population and persecuted for denying the supposed religious truths of Christianity. Jews were now regarded as individuals required to conform to the same expectations and standards as any other citizen. While the emancipation spread unevenly throughout Europe, the principle of equality regardless of religious affiliation was accepted as the basis of American citizenship at an early stage.

As a consequence of emancipation, nationality (or peoplehood) was disassociated from religious affiliation. Some Jews felt that they needed to define their Jewish identity in strictly religious terms. Others found that they had little interest in religion but realized they had a great deal of ethnic affinity with other Jews. As modernity moved into postmodernity, it became unclear to many Jews what Judaism was and what its central religious message should be.

Michael L. Satlow argues that most efforts to define Judaism were based on the concept of essentialism. Essentialism is the position that, for any specific kind of entity, there is a set of characteristics or properties, all of which any entity of that kind must possess. Therefore, all things can be precisely defined or described, and terms or words should have a singular definition and meaning.

Essentialism holds that certain properties possessed by a group are universal, and not dependent on context. A member of that group may possess other characteristics that are neither necessary for membership nor preclude membership, but each member must possess specific characteristics without which that person would not be considered to be a member of that group.

Essentialist definitions usually have a normative dimension. Normative statements affirm how things should or ought to be. It defines which actions are right or wrong. These essentialist definitions "are created and used by a community to define itself and thus also to set its boundaries." Essentialism asserts that there is an essence which is central to the identity of the entity. An essence is fixed and unchanging. It is both the inherent, innate property of an individual object or being, and the abstract, external essence governing the type to which all examples conform.

In order to develop an essentialist definition of Judaism, it is necessary to identify what the essence of Judaism is. As Satlow explains, "Without this essence—whatever it is—it is no longer considered Judaism."[2] The problem, of course, is that there is no consensus on what might constitute the essence of Judaism. Without a clearly discernible essence, there is no basis for regarding any particular form of Jewish belief or practice as normative.

While I would strongly prefer to have an essentialist definition of Judaism, it does not seem possible. There is no single belief or practice that constitutes the central core of the Jewish religion. Indeed, the Jewish religion itself is part of an interlocking network and cannot be isolated from its related components. So where does that leave us? How can we talk about Reform Judaism in the absence of a clear definition of Judaism?

Satlow sees Judaism not as a single entity but rather as "a family of communities" in which each element shares at least some common traits with all the other elements. Not all frogs are green but all frogs will share certain characteristics. If you make a list of all of the potential characteristics that the frog family shares, you will find that each frog has some and perhaps many of those characteristics. In addition, Satlow argues that all the family members in the category that we call Judaism participate in an ongoing discourse on a specific set of texts and ritual practices. They may see these texts in different ways and they may observe or not observe various rituals. But the family of communities devoted to Judaism participate in the discourse on these religious books and the beliefs and practices described in them.

This approach to defining Judaism is what is called a polythetic understanding because it draws from numerous models. The goal is not to develop a single definition that can fit every case but rather to develop a broader comprehension of the concept, where the focus is the many commonalities that exist. We can use this approach to better understand Reform Judaism.

What Is Reform Judaism?

Reform Judaism is an attempt to redefine the Jewish religion in order to take account of modern intellectual developments as well as social changes. In contrast with traditional Judaism, Reform Judaism accepts that not every part of the written or oral Torah is necessarily divinely given in its current form. Most Reform Jews believe that there was indeed a revelation at Mount Sinai, but they differ as to what they believe actually took place. We do not need to argue over that question—no one can prove what happened at Sinai, and Reform Jews are not overly concerned with proving its historicity. What is important is that in the Reform view, the Torah was inspired by God but written down by human beings according to their understanding of God's will.

The Torah is an ancient document that records a transformative religious experience. We draw inspiring religious messages from that text, as well as from the oral Torah, which was later written down as rabbinic literature. The sanctity of the Torah derives from the awe we have of God and the wonder we experience through the miracle of our own lives. It does not depend on believing that every letter and every word of the Torah are directly from God. The traditionalists believe that the Torah is God's will, the commandments in the five books of Moses are binding on all Jews, and the Talmud elaborates on how the divine commandments can be observed according to God's will.

In contrast, Reform Jewish thinkers accept a wide variety of interpretations concerning how the revelation occurred and what the implications of that revelation are. While traditionalists hold that the theophany that occurred at Mount Sinai constitutes the normative and permanent expression of God's will, Reform thinkers believe that humans have molded the tradition to a far greater extent than previously imagined. Thus, people have control over how the religious tradition develops over the course of time. The Torah is a holy text that provides inspiration, but contrary to what you may have seen in the film *The Ten Commandments*, it is not set in stone.

All human beings are made in God's image and therefore have an infinite capacity to do good. What is important is not the performance of any specific ritual but rather the desire to imitate God's loving mercy. When people seek to know God in order to absorb the divine religious message, they become infused with the burning desire to do good works, as the prophets of the Bible urged the Israelites to do.

The prophets represent the highest and purest stage of ethical monotheism. In contrast to the Torah, which has descriptions of barbarism impossible to justify ethically, the prophets contain coherent religious messages that remain relevant for today. More than a hundred years ago, Rabbi Emil G. Hirsch of Chicago Sinai Congregation argued that the Pentateuch borrowed many of its ideas from neighboring Near Eastern "tribes and races," while the prophets represented a truly original Jewish religious contribution.

According to the Reform worldview, the core teaching of Judaism is a passion for fair and just human relations. If people can deal justly with each other, truth will triumph and peace will reign. One of the sages is cited in the mishnah as explaining that the world rests on three foundations: justice, truth, and peace. If true justice can be established throughout the world, then truth will become clearly visible and peace will follow. Such justice applies to everyone, not just Jews, because God recognizes no distinction among people on the basis of creed, race, gender, class, or handicap. All are equal in God's sight.

Despite this inherent universalism, Jews have a special obligation to other Jews. All people have a duty to look after one another. In traditional Judaism, this includes the responsibility to admonish one's fellow Jew for ritual as well as ethical lapses. That means that if I suddenly pull out my cell phone on Shabbat, my fellow Jew has the obligation to urge me to put it away immediately, since it is forbidden to use any electronic device on the Sabbath. In the Reform movement, there are no obligatory observances, and so no one is authorized to tell anyone else what to do or not do, at least in ritual matters. There are, however, general ethical principles that are binding on everyone.

According to the early Reform theologians, the Jewish people have a special role in bringing the ideas of ethical monotheism to the world. Ethical monotheism is a term describing the belief in one God who guides humanity through ethical principles. It is not dogma, doctrines, or ritual practice that are important, but rather the commitment to ethics. High ethical standards are therefore the foundation stones of the three Abrahamic faiths: Judaism, Christianity, Islam. Of course, not everyone understands their religion in this way, and so we have a constant struggle between the three major monotheistic faiths. What could and should be beautiful, pure, and loving can easily become mean-spirited, hateful, and violent.

While everyone loves the biblical stories in Genesis telling about the creation of the world and the biblical personalities who strike us as so lifelike, most of the Torah focuses on what are seen as technical laws and obscure practices. As a result, many Reform rabbis returned to the prophets, who emphasized the very same message that the modern proponents of ethics were teaching. Prophets such as Micah, Isaiah, and Hosea emphasized social responsibility, thereby fitting perfectly into the message that Reform Judaism wanted to convey. The Jews had a prophetic mission to bring an ethical vision of society to the world. The prophets had appeared to teach this same point. The ancient prophets and the American Reform rabbis thus seemed to share a common religious vision.

The reformers understood the prophets as arguing that Judaism was based on ethics, not ritual. This was an important point because if it could be shown that the ancient prophets did not accept the obligatory nature of Jewish law, then it would be far easier to argue that Reform Judaism was a direct continuation of an important stream within ancient Judaism. If the reverse could be proven, then the Orthodox could use this argument to undermine the legitimacy of the Reform movement.

Of course, prophetic words can be interpreted in different ways. Reform thinkers cited numerous statements from different prophets that seemed to support their position that ritual practice devoid of ethics was worse than complete nonobservance. As the prophet Micah asked rhetorically, "Will Adonai be appeased with thousands of rams, with ten thousands rivers of oil?" The obsession with pointless ritual is counterproductive. "He has told you, O man, what is good, and what Adonai requires of you: Only to do justice and to love mercy and to walk humbly before your God" (Micah 6:6–8).

Reform Judaism rejects the concept of Jewish law as binding on all Jews. Certainly many of the particular laws may be practiced, but only if the particular ritual inspires the individual. Each person should therefore give each ritual practice a chance, examining it and considering how it might fit into his or her daily or weekly routine. This is important because otherwise people could simply shrug their shoulders and say, "I don't find meaning in any of that." One of the challenges facing the movement is that many nominally Reform Jews do just that.

Reform Judaism holds that the Torah should be interpreted to meet the needs of the contemporary Jew. This is both subjective and relativistic. For both of those reasons, traditionalists find this approach sacrilegious. According to their way of thinking, the halachic structure of Judaism is not simply a modern, social construct but is literally based on the word of God. In contrast, Reform Judaism sees the Jewish religion as a theological system that has changed over the course of history in response to the personal and communal needs of the Jews of each generation. The central myths of Judaism are elaborate metaphors designed to help us create and transmit a sense of cosmic awe rather than convey specific information. Taking them too literally defeats the entire purpose of these myths.

Reform Jews pride themselves in their commitment to rational thought, and therefore accept scientific explanations as to how the universe came to be and how the world developed. Nevertheless, most Reform Jews believe that God created the world in some way, and continues to be involved in an ongoing process of creation. They see no conflict between science and religion since they view the laws of science as a reflection of God's will.

God revealed the divine presence not just in a one-time event at Mount Sinai but in stages over a long period of time. As former president of Union of American Hebrew Congregations Rabbi Maurice Eisendrath put it, "God is a *living* God—not a God who revealed Himself and His word once and for all time at Sinai and speaks no more." Every person can draw inspiration from God's presence in the world. This inspiration can be a force for good. The Reform movement accepts the idea that revelation is ongoing. Such progressive revelation means that all people have the potential to understand God's will.[3]

In recent years, many Reform Jews have come to a new appreciation of the importance of ritual in religious life. Classical reformers have found this trend deeply disturbing. Having been raised with the idea that Reform Judaism stood for ethics and rejected Old World ritual, they have found the "return to tradition" quite upsetting. They saw this trend as indicating a retreat from reason, an embrace of the irrational. From the other end of the spectrum, Orthodox observers were euphoric to see the Reform movement re-embracing rituals that had been jettisoned generations earlier. Some even interpreted it as an indication that the entire Reform movement was about to embrace Orthodoxy. Both were wrong.

What both ends of the spectrum need to understand is that Reform Judaism changes with the times. As people's aesthetic sense develops, Reform worship styles will change. As individuals focus more on their personal spiritual development, Reform temples will attempt to cultivate a deeper sense of spirituality. Reform Judaism will find ways to integrate new prayers and ancient practices as attitudes toward ritual and ceremony continue to shift.

Critics may argue that Reform Judaism is a religion of convenience. They see large congregations that bother to show up only two or three times a year. They note temples filled with people who can barely read Hebrew and who appear unacquainted with even the simplest facts about Jewish history and culture. They point to the high percentage of interfaith families who join Reform congregations, and argue that these families have more influence on the Reform temple than the Reform temple has on them. The list of criticisms could go on endlessly. The critics shake their head sadly and repeat the mantra they have recited for over two hundred years: the reformers have rejected the Torah, and the consequences of this rejection will be catastrophic.

The history of the future has not yet been written, and so no one knows to what extent these critics are right or wrong. What may shock the reader to learn is that these doomsayers are basing their judgment of Reform Judaism on solid grounds. If you take the classical rabbinic tradition as interpreted by the sages over the past two thousand years, you will find a broad consensus that the Torah was divinely revealed from God to Moses and that all Jews have the obligation to follow the divine laws. (If one looks further back, the historical record does not support a traditional interpretation at all, but two thousand years is apparently the limit of traditional memory). By this measure, Reform Judaism is misguided, deeply in error.

But there are other ways to look at modern religious innovation. By rejecting the central beliefs of traditional Judaism, the Reform movement has been able to fashion a more flexible set of ceremonial expectations that allow modern Jews living in an open society to continue to pledge fidelity to the ancient faith of their forebears while actively participating in the culture in which they live. By embracing modern scholarship, Reform Judaism is intellectually coherent and presents a serious contemporary approach to religiosity.

God

According to the sages, God created the world and continues to guide everything that happens on earth. Reform Judaism allows for individuals to interpret this concept in different ways. Some may accept this belief literally, while others may understand it entirely in symbolic terms. There is no list of dogmas that a Reform Jew must accept. Such theological flexibility has positives and negatives.

The Reform movement has been able to keep people with divergent theologies relatively happy. This in itself is a tremendous accomplishment. On the other hand—and this was one of the central arguments in my earlier book, *American Reform Judaism: An Introduction*—such theological pluralism weakens the religious message of Reform Judaism. If everyone has a different idea of what God is and what God can do, it is not possible to say that we need to be dedicated to our temple because of a specific religious conviction.

God is the transcendent divine being who exists beyond the limits of human knowledge. According to the sages, God is the most powerful force in the universe. The book of Genesis describes how God created the world in just six days. Reform Judaism synthesizes this text with the latest scientific knowledge. The laws of science are seen as carrying out God's will. The biblical account of creation is therefore not to be seen as an alternative theory of the world's origins competing with scientific explanations, but rather as a midrash of spiritual value. We read and analyze the text in the beginning of the book of Genesis not to understand the history of natural science but rather to see ourselves in the broader context of the history of our planet and the entire universe.

God creates the world and then interacts with Adam and Eve, Noah, and other human beings long before the first Jew appears. Abraham understands the concept that there must be one God and only one God. He circumcises himself at an advanced age, entering into the covenant that is being established between God and the Jewish people. This covenant was reaffirmed a number of times by God. God gives the Torah to Israel, presenting Moses with both written and oral instructions. The children of Israel take on the divine mission to bring ethical monotheism to the world.

When we refer to the word *Israel* in a religious context, we are not referring to the State of Israel but rather the children of Israel. Israel is a theological construct because, although we are concerned with the Jews as individuals, Jewish theology understands Israel as the chosen people who have entered into an eternal covenant with God. The word *brit* is Hebrew for *covenant* or *contract*, and was used in biblical times to refer to a wide variety of legal relationships. Yet the relationship between God and Israel was unique, requiring the Israelites to observe God's commandments in the hope of receiving divine favor. The children of Israel existed because Abraham found God and began preaching the necessity of monotheism. It was his grandson Jacob, later renamed Israel, who became the progenitor of the twelve tribes of Israel, each tribe named after one of Jacob's sons.

The centrality of God in Jewish tradition is unquestioned. While Reform Judaism historically opposed much of ritual observance, no one with even a passing knowledge would accuse the movement of being atheistic. Indeed, one of the major differences between the nascent Reconstructionist movement of the 1950s and the Reform movement was that the Reconstructionists rejected supernaturalism. By supernaturalism, the Reconstructionists meant a belief in an omnipotent God who could perform miracles. By contrast, the Reform movement avoided any conscious and deliberate rejection of traditional religious beliefs. Nevertheless, a careful study of some of the major documents of American Reform Judaism indicates a commitment to rationalism that transformed religious concepts into philosophical ones. This does not mean every Reform thinker accepted this approach; they did not. Even so, the desire to understand traditional beliefs in logical, rational terms was strong.

What is surprising is that Reform thinkers never agreed on a clear understanding of who God is and what role God plays in the world. Throughout the past 150 years, American Reform theologians have tried to present coherent accounts of what Reform Judaism stood for. The problem was that different religious thinkers came at the question from different perspectives and arrived at radically different conclusions. The results were, as you might expect, not successful. When the entire movement tried to put a consensus position on paper, the results were even less satisfactory. Each attempt to create a platform to present Reform Judaism was marred by internal dissension, which grew increasingly vocal from the late nineteenth century through the 1970s. Let us look briefly at how each of these platforms understood the concept of God.

The 1885 Pittsburgh Platform speaks of Judaism as presenting "the highest conception of the God-idea as taught in our Holy Scriptures and developed and spiritualized by the Jewish teachers, in accordance with the moral and philosophical progress of their respective ages." In contrast with the Society for Ethical Culture, which emphasized ethics independent of revealed religion, the 1885 Pittsburgh Platform began with God as the source of all being. The platform stresses that Judaism preserved this God-idea "as the central religious truth for the human race." But that does not mean that only Judaism has a correct understanding of the divine. The platform begins with a statement recognizing that every religion attempts "to grasp the infinite."

Over the next one hundred and some years, Reform theologians would clash over what was meant by God and how the Reform movement should express its beliefs. Beginning in the late 1920s, a group of Reform rabbis began advocating for a humanistic approach to religious understanding. While not rejecting the existence of God, they saw divinity as residing primarily within the person, that is, the still, small voice of conscience. These religious humanists argued that modern conceptions of science made the God of the Hebrew Bible antiquated. If religion is to speak to us moderns, it would have to present a belief system that the younger generations could embrace without a giant leap of faith.

While this approach appealed to a considerable number of Reform leaders, the consensus view was that Reform Judaism should accept

4. Rabbi Samuel S. Cohon was a leading advocate of what later became known as the "return to tradition." He believed in a transcendent God, and long before it became popular, was deeply interested in Jewish mysticism. Cohon is best known for his drafting of "The Columbus Platform: The Guiding Principles for Reform Judaism," which is seen as having reversed the anti-Zionism of the Pittsburgh Platform of 1885. *Photo by Leonard A. Greenberg. Courtesy of the Jacob Rader Marcus Center of the American Jewish Archives, Cincinnati, americanjewisharchives.org.*

a personal God. Samuel S. Cohon, professor of Jewish theology at the Hebrew Union College for more than three decades, pushed for a new platform that would emphasize a "living God." Cohon wrote the original draft of what became the Columbus Platform of 1937, officially entitled "Guiding Principles of Reform Judaism." Unlike the Pittsburgh Platform, which began with God, the Columbus Platform opened with a paragraph describing the nature of Judaism. "Judaism is the historical religious experience of the Jewish people." This approach certainly made sense to most congregants, who understood that Jewish identity had to do with ethnicity as well as religion. It was only in the second paragraph that the platform turned to God. "The heart of Judaism and its chief contribution to religion is the doctrine of the One, living God, who rules the world through law and love." The contrast with the Pittsburgh Platform could hardly be starker. The "God-idea" had now been replaced by the "One, living God." We can almost feel the emotion in the words.

Cohon explained that although he did not want the Reform movement to accept religious dogmas per se, he believed that American Reform Jews needed guidance in order to understand what Judaism stood for. "The time has come for us in this age of chaos to take our Judaism seriously and instruct our people in the way they should follow and the things they should do." Cohon felt that Reform Judaism could be seen as amorphous and confusing rather than elucidating. "We should teach them that we believe in God, in Israel, and in Torah, and show them how to revive prayer, ceremonials, and other observances, whereby we can strengthen our lives." Many complained that the Columbus Platform was not successful at presenting a vivid and compelling image of God that could capture the imagination of Reform Jews throughout the country, and that the platform's major accomplishment was the restoration of the concept of Jewish peoplehood. While this point is well taken, this limitation was probably inevitable given the increasing theological diversity of the participants and the terrible events that were then already taking place.[4]

The theological trends already apparent at Columbus continued in the decades after World War II. For those interested in the Jewish religion, the relationship between God, Torah, and Israel remained a central focus. The covenant was established for all time when God gave the Torah to Moses on behalf of the Jewish people at Mount Sinai. But what did this actually mean? The entire theological edifice depended on how one understood God. Could God still be defined as transcendent, omnipotent, and providential? If not, how could the relationship between God and the Jewish people be understood? There were no easy answers to these questions.

If Reform theologians had trouble reaching agreement in the 1930s, they had no hope of reaching consensus in the 1960s. Yet people felt that a new platform was necessary to respond to all the changes that had occurred over the preceding thirty years, perhaps the most important three decades in all of Jewish history. When a new statement was finally written in 1976, it was called a "perspective" rather than a platform in order to make clear that it was not authoritative. Nevertheless, primary drafter Rabbi Eugene Borowitz had to be very careful about what he wrote concerning belief in God. "Reform Judaism—A Centenary Perspective" therefore began with a statement that no one could refute. "The affirmation of God has always been essential to our people's will to survive." This was a reasonable interpretation of Jewish history, at least up until the modern period, but it said nothing about what Reform Judaism held about the nature of God.

The Centenary Perspective continued in this vein: "In our struggle through the centuries to preserve our faith we have experienced and conceived of God in many ways." While admitting that "the trials of our own time and the challenges of modern culture have made steady belief and clear understanding difficult for some," nevertheless "we ground our lives, personally and communally, on God's reality." If the Centenary Perspective sounds tentative, it was not because Reform theologians did not know what they believed. Rather, there were opposing groups who had dramatically different approaches to God, Torah, and Israel, and the Centenary Perspective was trying to avoid alienating any one group.

The editors of *Gates of Prayer: The New Union Prayer Book* faced the same quandary. Most agreed that the time had come to produce a new prayer book to replace the *Union Prayer Book* that had first been published in 1895. But with so much theological diversity, how would it be possible to edit a prayer book acceptable to all? The solution was to produce ten different Friday night services and six Saturday morning services, all of which followed the same structure but substituted English prayers with distinctive theological perspectives. Each rabbi or congregation could pick the service that best matched what they believed about God, Torah, and Israel.

For example, Service I presented God as omnipotent. Page 122 includes Psalm 99, which begins "Adonai reigns: let the peoples shake with awe. He sits enthroned, and the earth trembles." In contrast, Service II presented God as the still, small voice of conscience within us. Immediately after candlelighting, Service II begins with a meditation: "I harbor within—we all do—a vision of my highest self, a dream of what I could and should become. May I pursue this vision, labor to make real my dream. Thus will I give meaning to my life." Other services portray God as a mystical force, as the impetus for social activism, and so forth. By including so many different services, the liturgy committee of the Central Conference of American Rabbis (CCAR) hoped, if not to please everyone theologically, at least to placate them.[5]

By 1999, when the CCAR passed its most recent platform in Pittsburgh, many Reform Jews were open to a more forceful presentation of what God was. It was not so much that there was greater agreement. Rather, Reform Jews of different theological perspectives had grown more comfortable coexisting with others holding radically different theologies. There was an implicit acceptance that in a postmodern era, theological consistency was simply unimportant. "A Statement of Principles for Reform Judaism" begins: "We affirm the reality and oneness of God, even as we may differ in our understanding of the Divine presence."

We encounter God's presence "in moments of awe and wonder," a reference to the mystical quest, as well as through acts of compassion and justice, through loving relationships, and in our daily experiences. Emphasizing a traditional perspective that generated a great deal of controversy, the 1999 platform went on to say that we respond to God

5. Reform Jews accept other religious groups as authentic and legitimate and are interested in participating in joint activities, including interfaith ceremonies and services. In this photo, religious leaders of the three monotheistic faiths pray together for peace during a "September 11th Remembered" ceremony at Veterans Park Amphitheater in Albany, Georgia, on September 11, 2002. From left: Imam Salahuddin H. Hanif, Chaplain Stan Halstead, and Rabbi Dana Evan Kaplan. *Photo by Todd Stone. Courtesy of Albany Area Chamber of Commerce and Rachelle Bitterman.*

through prayer, study, and the performance of other *mitzvoth*. This direct reference to the commandments indicated the increasing importance of ritual in Reform Judaism.

All people were created in the image of God, and therefore, human life is sacred. Indeed, all of God's creation should be regarded with reverence and preserved and protected. We strive for a relationship with God that can fortify us through "the vicissitudes of our lives." Whether ill or healthy, hopeful or in despair, transgressing or repenting, we look to God for direction and comfort. As believing Jews, we affirm the eternal covenant between God and the Jewish people and the importance of creation, revelation, and redemption in that relationship.

The Covenant with Abraham

At the end of chapter 11 in the book of Genesis, the Torah recounts that when Terach was seventy years old, he had three sons: Abram, Nahor, and Haran. Modern biblical scholars have uncovered a great deal of information that sheds light on how the story was probably redacted, but that is not our concern at the moment. Abram married Sarai in their native land, Ur of the Chaldeans. Terach took Abram and Sarai, and Lot, the son of Haran, and set out for the land of Canaan. But they settled down when they reached the city of Haran. According to the book of Genesis, Terach died in Haran at the age of 205 years. It was at this point that God appears to Abram—whose name is changed by God to Abraham in chapter 17—and tells him, "Go forth from your native land and from your father's house to the land that I will show you" (12:1).

God makes a number of extraordinary promises to Abram. There is as yet no indication whether Abram merits these divine benefits, although later commentators explain that God's promises are in response to Abram's tremendous dedication. The midrash tells us that Abram was the first monotheist, the person who understood the central principle of Judaism that God is One.

> I will make of you a great nation,
> And I will bless you;
> I will make your name great,

And you shall be a blessing.
I will bless those who bless you
And curse him that curses you;
And all the families of the earth
Shall bless themselves by you.
(Genesis 12:2–3)

But no sooner had Abram been promised the land of Israel and reached it than a famine forced him to leave Canaan for Egypt, which had more food because of the greater fertility of the land along the Nile. When Abram was ninety-nine years old, God appeared to him saying, "I am El Shaddai. Walk in My ways and be blameless. I will establish My covenant between Me and you, and I will make you exceedingly numerous" (Genesis 17:1–2).

Let us take a look at how the commentary published by the Union for Reform Judaism Press explains these verses. While the Reform movement does not deem any particular text authoritative, *The Torah: A Modern Commentary* (revised edition) is the single-volume Hebrew-English Torah text and commentary edited and published by the Reform movement. It is widely viewed as reflecting a broad consensus on the interpretation of the Torah within the Reform movement. Therefore, its treatment of the covenant can teach us a great deal about how Reform Judaism sees the relationship between God and the Jewish people.

In *The Torah: A Modern Commentary*, the commentator asks, "Did God actually *speak* to Abram and enter into a covenant or *b'rit* built on the verbal commitment reported by the text?" The very fact that this question is being asked would surprise someone who assumes the biblical text is a literal depiction of what happened. Certainly *The Stone Edition* of *The Chumash*, to take the prime example of an Orthodox English commentary, would not think of asking such a potentially heretical question. Published as part of the ArtScroll Series under the sponsorship of the Mesorah Heritage Foundation, the *Stone Edition* accepts the Torah in its entirety as historically accurate and reflecting divine will in every word.

But in *The Torah: A Modern Commentary*, the editor is much less sure. He offers a choice: "If we take the literal view (and Jewish as well as

Christian tradition took it unequivocally), the nature of the compact cannot be in doubt. If, on the other hand, we read the story as the spiritual experience of one man who understood his God to address him in this unique fashion, the emphasis is shifted to a recounting of Abram's internal vision." The editor is trying to be theologically inclusive and not preclude any possibilities, but it is not hard to see where his sympathies lie. Abram experienced an "internal vision," an insight into what was truly important religiously. It seems that the commentator understands God as a philosophical concept rather than an all-powerful divine being who was actually present. As the editor explains, "It is through him [Abram] that God's promise is made known to us; it is through his eyes that the reality of the covenant must be viewed."

The editor emphasizes the human dimension of what is happening. "However we view the story, we are face-to-face with a remarkable human being who saw more in his environment than earth and sky, mountains and valleys." Rather than emphasizing the divine aspect of the biblical citation, the commentary explains that it is "the story of a man who looked at the world as the proving ground for human opportunities, seeing all this in the context of mutual trust and obligation expressed in the concept of *b'rit*." What strikes me in this explanation is the complete absence of God as an all-powerful, all-knowing divine being who has chosen Abram to enter into an eternal covenant with Adonai, the God of the heavens.

The commentary goes on in this vein, explaining that "the *b'rit* thus adds a new dimension to human existence, a deepening of the call that he first heard in Haran: 'Go forth!'" Abram's experiences "were the foundations on which his descendants built their house of faith and contributed their commitment to a covenant first envisioned in the dark of ancient Negev nights." The wording is inspiring. Abram is the paradigm for a man of faith who builds a "house of faith." What might trouble traditional readers is that God is perceived in completely abstract terms. In addition, unlike virtually all Orthodox commentators, who describe an active and passionate God who does not hesitate to make demands, the commentary here avoids any suggestion that God requires us to follow ritual as well as ethical laws.

The Torah: A Modern Commentary does not interpret this section in Genesis as implying that God is setting conditions on the covenant, a viewpoint that is consistent with the plain meaning of the text. The editor contrasts the many later references to the covenant as being dependent on Israel's continued faithfulness with the agreement here that God's commitment is completely unconditional. "In addition to creating a physical universe with immutable laws, God has provided for an unchanging spiritual world as well. A faithful God—faithful in natural as well as transnatural manifestations—is unlike the pagan deities whose universes were unpredictable and erratic." This particular approach is thus well suited as the basis for a Reform approach to covenant. But when the reader looks at the later agreements made, uncomfortable questions have to be asked about the nature of the Jewish people's obligations. If Jews are obligated to follow God's covenant in order to please God, then what are the precise conditions of that agreement?[6]

That need not concern us at this point. Abram threw himself on his face, and God spoke to him further: "As for Me, this is My covenant with you: You shall be the father of a multitude of nations. And you shall no longer be called Abram, but your name shall be Abraham, for I make you the father of a multitude of nations" (Genesis 17:3–4). The contemporary reader may find this promise all too ironic in the light of the loss of six million Jews in the Holocaust and population surveys that herald "the vanishing American Jew," but that seems to be precisely what God promised Abraham.

If you read the words carefully in this text, God is not promising that Abraham's descendants will be as plentiful as the stars in the sky. God does promise this, but elsewhere. Here, God is giving Abraham a new status as *av hamon*, father of a multitude, which dramatically expands Abraham's spiritual mission. It goes along with the change of his name from Abram to Abraham. As Abram, he was *av Aram*, the father of Aram, the country from which he came. As Abraham, he is now av hamon, the father of many. He is no longer a local boy charged with a local mission. Rather, he has now moved onto the world stage. This is no exaggeration—Abraham is the father of the three monotheistic faiths.

The phrase "father of a multitude" had halachic implications as well. In the book of Deuteronomy, the Torah describes how Jews bring their firstfruits to the Jerusalem Temple. "You shall take some of every first fruit of the soil, which you harvest from the land that your God Adonai is giving you, put it in a basket and go to the place where your God Adonai will choose to establish the divine name" (Genesis 26:2). Each Jew should say to the Kohen, the priest officiating at the temple, "I acknowledge this day before your God Adonai that I have entered the land that Adonai swore to our fathers to assign us" (Genesis 26:3).

The halachic question is: Can a person who converted to Judaism recite this required formula? How can a convert thank God for the land that Adonai promised to give "our fathers"? Maimonides provided the answer eight hundred years ago: "All converts are considered descendents of Abraham because the Torah calls him 'the father of . . . nations'" (Commentary to Mishnah Bikkurim 1:4). This was remarkably prescient, suggesting that Maimonides might not be shocked to see the large numbers of converts in our congregations and the vital role that they play in synagogue life. Since the traditional understanding of the text supports the modern view, we do not have to worry about reinterpreting the biblical citation or altering the practical position taken as a consequence of the traditional understanding of the text.

God then goes on to promise Abraham a glorious future. "I will make you exceedingly fertile, and make nations of you; and kings shall come forth from you." This is a direct consequence of the covenant between God and Abraham. "I will maintain My covenant between Me and you, and your offspring to come, as an everlasting covenant throughout the ages, to be God to you and to your offspring to come. I assign the land you sojourn in to you and your offspring to come, all the land of Canaan, as an everlasting holding. I will be their God" (Genesis 17:5–8).

God further said to Abraham, "As for you, you and your offspring to come throughout the ages shall keep My covenant. Such shall be the covenant between Me and you and your offspring to follow which you shall keep: every male among you shall be circumcised" (Genesis 17:9–10). God explains, "You shall circumcise the flesh of your foreskin, and that shall be the sign of the covenant between Me and you. And throughout

6. Abraham sacrificed a ram instead of his son Isaac in the biblical story of Akedat Yitzchak. In remembrance, Jews all over the world sound the shofar on Rosh Hashanah, the Jewish New Year. The seventh-grade class at Congregation Kol Ami in Flower Mound, Texas, engages in "do-it-yourself Judaism" by making their own shofars from kudu horns. *Photo by Amy McDaniel.*

the generations, every male among you shall be circumcised at the age of eight days" (Genesis 17:11–12).

Circumcision is required not only for those born as Jews but also for strangers in your midst. "As for the home-born slave and the one bought from an outsider who is not of your offspring, they must be circumcised, home-born, and purchased alike. Thus shall My covenant be marked in your flesh as an everlasting pact" (Genesis 17:12–13). In the late nineteenth century, the CCAR decided not to absolutely require circumcision under all circumstances even when it could be performed without serious medical complications. Nevertheless, most Reform synagogues expect circumcision to be practiced under normal conditions. I was privileged to accompany one of my congregants in Cape Town who decided to convert many years after marrying a Jewish woman and becoming involved in our temple. As an adult, he was required to have the procedure done in a medical facility. We read a number of prayers together as we were waiting, and although he looked terrified, he also had a glow of excitement emanating from his decision to enter the covenant of Abraham.

Revelation

The giving of the Torah was not a one-time event at Mount Sinai. Rather, God continually reveals the divine presence to those who are willing to look for divine guidance. This means that all people have the potential to understand God's Torah and what it means in contemporary terms. Revelation is progressive, continually allowing us to discover God's gifts throughout the course of history.

Reform Judaism accepts the idea of progressive revelation and therefore understands the Torah as a body of religious wisdom that can and should be interpreted and reinterpreted to meet the spiritual needs of each generation. The Torah is therefore not fixed forevermore, frozen in time. While we treasure its words, we reserve the right to reinterpret—or even reject—statements that appear in either the written or oral Torahs.

This approach has tremendous positives and substantial negatives. It is a wonderfully flexible approach, which allows us not only to reinterpret but to pick and choose when necessary. We are not stuck with a set of laws that we cannot alter—indeed, we reject the idea that Jewish law is binding on us at all. Rather, we are asked to make religious choices based on our individual spiritual needs. The problem is that this religious autonomy only works well if each person takes the time to carefully consider her religious choices. For the average American, overworked and overloaded, such careful consideration is rare indeed.

Reform Judaism holds that the Torah is a holy text, but not necessarily because God gave it to Moses at Mount Sinai. Some Reform Jews may believe that the revelation occurred exactly as described in the Torah, but scholars in the movement accept the overwhelming evidence offered by researchers over the past two hundred years that the text of the Five Books of Moses consists of at least four separate documents that have been repeatedly edited. We all accept that the Torah has important religious insights fathered by ancient Israelite redactors, and much of the Torah is extremely ancient, harkening back close to the time of Israel's origins. Most Reform Jews believe that God indeed revealed the Torah to Israel in some form, but they would certainly differ as to the exact mode that such revelation may have taken.

Rabbi Julian Morgenstern, president of Hebrew Union College from 1922 to 1947, asked, "Is the Torah, in the literal sense in which our fathers understood it, divinely revealed; that is, were its laws actually established by God and communicated whether in writing or orally, by Him to Moses and through Moses to Israel?" If the answer is yes, then all the laws of the Torah are "eternally and indissolubly binding upon all Israel." But if the answer is no, because "after careful, earnest, conservative, and reverent research" we are forced to conclude "the laws of the Torah are of altogether human origin," then what logically follows? He answers that it is "for certain, easily comprehended, historical reasons" that these texts were represented as having been given by God to Moses. As a consequence of this logic—and only once we are convinced that this sequence of arguments is correct—we are then "justified in abrogating or altering even the least of these laws."

Scholarly study brings us to "the firmly established and absolutely irrefutable conclusion that the Torah and the entire Bible are, in the literal sense at least, the result of human effort, human knowledge and human religious insight, inspiration and revelation." Morgenstern emphasizes that from a logical point of view, "reform in Judaism may only follow, and never precede, this conclusion." Academic research "tells us just what the Bible is and when it was written." If it cannot tell us "the names of the authors of the various parts of the books, it can tell quite satisfactorily what kind of men these authors were, when they lived, what religious views they held, for what purpose and under what conditions they wrote, and what value, historical, religious, ethical and spiritual, their writings have."

Biblical science, as Morgenstern refers to the scholarly study of the Hebrew Bible, also tells us "most clearly, emphatically and uncompromisingly, wherein the Bible *does differ* [emphasis mine] radically from all other books, is truly the Book of Books," and what "inspiring message and eternal significance it has for us Jews today and will have for our children and our children's children until the end of time." Morgenstern is aware that many may see the basic assumptions of biblical criticism as undermining religious belief.

He writes that this is not the case. "Contrary to the first impulsive thought, Biblical Science is not destructive at all, but thoroughly constructive." It does not "uproot the foundations of religious belief, as so many think, or timorously wish to think, but re-enforces them and builds them deeper and ever deeper, so that the religious structure resting upon them may stand securely forever amid all the tempests of doubt, superstition and ignorance." In conclusion, he answers his own rhetorical question: "No, Biblical Science has not taken the Bible from us. Rather it has given the old Bible back to us, re-interpreted and with larger message and deeper and more eternal significance than ever before."[7]

This approach is a radical departure from traditional Jewish belief. Before the Enlightenment, Judaism held that the theophany that occurred at Mount Sinai constituted the normative and permanent expression of God's will. Reform Judaism, in dramatic contrast, accepts that humans have a great deal of control over how the religious tradition develops and should develop. As it is written in the book of Deuteronomy:

> Surely, this instruction which I enjoin upon you this day is not too baffling for you, nor is it beyond reach. It is not in the heavens, that you should say, "Who among us can go up to the heavens and get it for us and impart it to us, that we may observe it?" Neither is it beyond the sea, that you should say, "Who among us can cross to the other side of the sea and get it for us and impart it to us, that we may observe it?" No, the thing is very close to you, in your mouth and in your heart, to observe it.
> (Deuteronomy 30:11–14)

The point that Reform thinkers derive from these verses is that the words of the Torah are meant to be accessible. Since the Torah is divinely inspired rather than dictated word for word by God, the religious message is fluid, subject to interpretation in each generation.

We Reform Jews revere the Torah scroll, the Five Books of Moses that are covered with beautiful Torah covers and placed in arks in our temples. It is a symbol of everything we hold dear. But for many of the earlier Classical Reformers, it was the books of the prophets that were most compelling. Core ethical teachings were found in the prophets rather than in the Torah.

Reform thinkers loved the prophets because the prophets emphasized that all human beings were made in God's image and therefore had an infinite capacity to do good. The Jewish people had a special role to play in helping to bring ethical monotheism to the world. It was the belief in one God that created the religious authority necessary to develop an ethical system of living that would be binding on all. The prophets therefore cried out against injustice of any sort.

The Jews therefore had a prophetic obligation to bring an ethical vision of society to the attention of people throughout the world. This doctrine was referred to as the "mission of Israel." That was why God had scattered the Jews throughout the diaspora and why they had to remain a distinct people. Rabbi David Einhorn, who was forced to flee his Baltimore home because of his strong antislavery position just before the Civil War, used this justification for his opposition to intermarriage. If Jews intermarried, Einhorn reasoned, they would disappear, and if they disappeared, they could no longer carry out the mission of Israel— to bring ethical monotheism to the world.

The early Reform thinkers obviously read the prophets selectively. They paid relatively little attention to the existence of a Jewish commonwealth and the hope that the Jerusalem Temple could be saved or rebuilt. Not interested in the idea of Jewish national independence, they focused on the prophetic words that emphasized individual ethics and social justice.

They also interpreted the prophets as denigrating the importance of ritual. This became a major point of controversy with Orthodox leaders, who insisted that the prophets were simply emphasizing that ritual acts without ethical behavior was anathema to God. The prophets were not, they insisted, arguing against ritual practice in its entirety. Even when Reform leaders agreed with this analysis, they tended to use these citations to justify the Reform abrogation of traditional ritual practices.

The prophet Micah made the following statement which is frequently quoted:

Wherewith shall I present myself to Adonai,
And do homage to God on high?
Shall I present myself with burnt offerings,
With calves a year old?
Will Adonai be appeased with thousands of rams,
With ten thousand rivers of oil?
Shall I sacrifice my first born for my transgression,
The fruit of my body for the sin of my soul?
He has told you, O man, what is good,
And what Adonai requires of you:
Only to do justice
And to love mercy,
And to walk humbly before your God.
Then will your name achieve wisdom.
(Micah 6:6–9)

Most biblical scholars argue that this text should not be interpreted as a rejection of the temple sacrificial system. It is, however, expressing the view that being an ethical person is more important than bringing a sacrifice to God. Specifically, it is condemning the hypocrisy of bringing sacrifices to God—and even paying great attention to making sure that those sacrifices are done exactly according to God's instructions—while at the same time mistreating others in the single-minded pursuit of selfish goals.

In the Talmud, Rabbi Simlai says that while Moses received 613 commandments—365 negative precepts and 248 positive precepts—Micah reduced them to three principles. Rabbi Simlai then quotes verse 8 from the above citation (Babylonian Talmud, Tractate Makkot 23b–24a). He explains that "to do justice" refers to the establishment of a system of justice, "to love mercy" refers to *gemilut hasadim*, acts of goodness and kindness, and "walk humbly before your God" literally means walking in funeral and bridal processions. All the commandments can be summarized as doing those things that make us better people as individuals and a more compassionate society as a collective.

Both the Torah and the prophets were to be interpreted through the lens of the oral law. The oral Torah is the verbal instructions that, according to the sages, were given by God to Moses at Mount Sinai. Moses then passed them on to Joshua, who transmitted them to the elders, who then passed them on to the prophets, who in turn conveyed them to the sages of the Great Assembly (Pirkei Avot 1:1). While most scholars today do not believe that this actually occurred in the manner described, the chain of transmission of tradition gave the sages the authority to interpret the Hebrew Bible in ways that were sometimes far from the literal meaning.

The sages believed that since God had given the oral law along with the written law, they had the responsibility of interpreting the meaning of God's verbal instructions. The practical impact of this understanding allowed for a wide spectrum of interpretation and a justification for halachic decisions that went far beyond anything written in the Hebrew Bible itself. Reform thinkers, relying on a theological perspective that reduced the direct role of God in the original religious positions, cited a number of texts to reinforce their radical deviation from traditional practice.

Reform thinkers cite a Talmudic story in the tractate Baba Meziah to show that the Torah was intended to be interpreted by the sages of each generation. Rabbi Eliezer, a proponent of unchanging tradition, was engaged in a halachic debate with the other sages concerning a technical issue relating to the "oven of Achnai." Rabbi Eliezer, called by his teacher "a well-lined cistern that doesn't lose a drop," brought a number of different lines of argument but found that the other sages remained unconvinced. "He brought all the reasons in the world," but his colleagues remained steadfast.

So Rabbi Eliezer proclaimed to the heavens, "If the law is as I hold it to be, let this tree prove it." Almost immediately, the tree that Rabbi Eliezer was looking at uprooted itself and moved a hundred *amma*. Despite this amazing feat, the other sages remained unmoved, saying, "Proof cannot be brought from a tree." So Rabbi Eliezer tried again appealing to the heavens, saying, "If the law is as I hold it to be, let these waters prove it." The water in the river that Rabbi Eliezer was looking at immediately began to flow backwards. Again the other sages were unmoved. "Proof cannot be brought from water."

Again Rabbi Eliezer appealed to the heavens saying, "If the law is as I hold it, let these walls prove it." Immediately, the walls of the *beit midrash* began to shake. Rabbi Joshua, having lost patience, scolded the walls, "When rabbis are engaged in a legal discussion, you have no right to interfere!" The walls did not know what to do so they did not collapse completely but they also did not resume their original position. According to the story, they remained in their inclined position to that very day!

Despite his repeated setbacks, Rabbi Eliezer would not give in—or give up—and he then cried out to the heavens, "Let the heavens decide!" Immediately a heavenly voice responded to the sages, "Why do you dispute the position of Rabbi Eliezer? The law is always as he says it is!" Rabbi Joshua then stood up and, quoting the Torah, responded, "It is not in the heavens!" Rabbi Jeremiah explained that while the Torah was given at Mount Sinai, the sages no longer pay heed to heavenly voices because the system of legal decision-making follows a simple principle: majority rules. Halacha is not determined by miracles or even heavenly voices but by the collective decision-making process of the sages (Baba Metzia 59B).

Of course, everything depends on how one interprets this midrash from the Talmud. While a Reform reader would likely understand the story as reinforcing the lesson that Judaism can and must change, an Orthodox reader would probably see this same story as reinforcing the authority of the sages in the halachic-making process. The Orthodox might argue that the story confirms the importance of accepting the halacha as determined by the sages and the later *poskim* (legal scholars). But for Reform thinkers, the midrash is a wonderful illustration of how Judaism has been and can be flexible. The sages are determined to advance a creative approach to solving a particular halachic problem, and they remain steadfast in that determination even in the face of miracles or the intervention of a heavenly voice. Just as the sages had to make a halachic decision based on the needs of the time, so too contemporary

Jews have to take responsibility for making religious decisions that are optimal under a given set of circumstances.

A Reform reader would likewise understand other stories in the Talmud as justifying religious evolution. There is a midrash in the Talmud brought in the name of Rabbi Yehuda, who said it in the name of Rav. When Moses passed away and went to heaven, he found the Holy One sitting and tying crowns on the holy letters. Moses said to God, "Ruler of the Universe, who is holding back your hand?" God answered, "There is a man who will appear at the end of several generations. Akiva the son of Joseph is his name. He will need these crowns, because from each and every thorn he will derive scores and scores of law."

Moses then asked God, "Ruler of the Universe, can you show this man to me?" God then told him, "Turn around," and Moses found himself in the back of Rabbi Akiva's lecture hall. Rabbi Akiva was teaching material that Moses was almost completely unfamiliar with and he could barely understand anything they were saying. But finally one student asked a question about a particular law, and the great sage Akiva answered, "That was a law given from God to Moses at Sinai." At that point Moses was relieved and asked God to bring him back up to heaven.

The point of the story in my view is that Judaism developed so much over time that even Moses barely recognized it. When Moses returned to heaven, God reaffirmed that that was the way it was intended to be. The midrash indicates that the sages understood that Judaism was supposed to evolve—that this is normal and actually beneficial. Even Moses—the greatest of all the prophets—could not be expected to know how Judaism would change over the course of time. The core of the Jewish religion is eternal, but the details are subject to contemporary cultural influences. The Reform movement is still grappling with the degree that people can change or even reject ideas, laws, or practices that are written in the Torah. Some are concerned that the Torah has a permanence which is undermined if the specifics are not authoritative. Without the legal framework, how can Judaism maintain its structural integrity?

CHAPTER 2

A Brief History of the American Reform Movement

The Reform movement developed as a consequence of a socio-legal process called the emancipation. The emancipation was a political movement designed to give the Jews, the most significant minority group in Europe at this time, rights of citizenship. The impetus for this movement began in 1781, when Christian Wilhelm Dohn published *Concerning the Amelioration of the Civil Status of the Jews*. This tract argued that once the Jews were given equal rights as citizens, they would abandon many of their more restrictive religious practices. "They will then reform their religious laws and regulations according to the demands of the society. They will go back to the freer and nobler ancient Mosaic Law, will explain it according to changed times and conditions, and will find authorization to do so in their *Talmud*."[1]

As a result of the emancipation, Jews were treated like any other citizen—at least in theory. In retrospect, it is easy to see the increasing threat that modern antisemitism posed to the physical existence of the Jews of Europe. But if we imagine ourselves living 150 or even 200 years ago, there was great reason to be optimistic. Modern European society was based on radically different notions than its medieval predecessor. Anyone could become a full citizen and participate in civic life. This was a tremendous opportunity that could potentially open up entirely new vistas.

Many Jews in Central Europe found that the easiest way to integrate into secular society was to convert to Christianity. During the eighteenth and nineteenth centuries, large numbers of German Jews did exactly that. Some were sincerely convinced by what they felt were the religious truths of Christianity, but many others saw Christianity as their ticket to social and economic advancement. We are primarily concerned with those who intended to stay Jewish but wanted to mold their Judaism into a form that would be more Germanic. They were actually embarrassed by some of the practices of the synagogue, which seemed to be rather primitive and even offensive. So they began with minor aesthetic reforms.

These early reformers set out to make changes in the synagogue service, not so much to alter beliefs but primarily to improve what we would today call the spiritual experience. The Central European synagogue was an unruly place, with people walking in and out, talking to their neighbor, and even conducting business. The early reformers responded to this situation by instituting measures to increase decorum, emphasizing that worshippers should remain silent and pay attention to the service. In order to hold the interest of the worshippers, the liturgy was abbreviated and a sermon in the vernacular was added. German prayers were read out loud alongside Hebrew ones. A mixed choir of both men and women sang religious songs accompanied by an organ.

Israel Jacobson, regarded by many as the father of Reform Judaism, introduced what is regarded as the first Reform service in his school chapel in Seesen in 1810. Along with the desire to modernize religious life, reformers such as Jacobson wanted to reconceptualize the nature and purpose of Jewish education. In pursuit of his vision, he opened a trade and agricultural school for poor Jewish boys in the town of Seesen, on the northwestern edge of the Harz mountain range. Within a few years, forty Jewish and twenty Christian children were educated together, receiving free board and lodging.

Jacobson conducted the first Jewish confirmation service on Shavuot that same year. The confirmation ceremony consisted of having the five boys answer questions on Jewish theology. Traditional religious leaders were concerned because there was little precedent for such a life-cycle event. They worried that it was based almost entirely on a Christian model. Such comparisons followed Reform innovations for generations.

Jacobson's school served as the makeshift synagogue for the students and the handful of local Jewish families. Over the next few years the numbers attending services increased, and Jacobson decided to build a house of prayer. He originally had hoped to build a domed, octagonal, cathedral-like building that would be immense, with a clock and bell tower measuring as much as eighty feet in height. The local authorities rejected the original architectural plans, and the actual building was much smaller. It did retain a small bell tower, which had little precedent in the history of synagogues.

Jacobson specifically called the building a "temple." He was not the first to use this designation. The French called all non-Catholic houses of prayer "temples," and the term became familiar in Germany as a result of the French occupation. But whereas the term had previously been simply a generic identifier, Jacobson used the word to convey a religious ideology. The Seesen temple was intended to remind worshippers of the Holy Temple in Jerusalem. He cited King Solomon, who had hoped to make the Jerusalem Temple a symbol of loving-kindness and universality. Also, the naming of the building indicated that the reformers were no longer interested in returning to the land of Israel in order to rebuild the Temple in Jerusalem.

The ghetto walls had been broken down; there was no longer a tightly controlled Jewish community. Individuals like Jacobson could do pretty much what they wanted. Whatever limitations they faced were imposed not by the traditional Jewish authorities but by the regional secular government. So long as the Central European authorities did not shut them down, reformers could run religious services that fit their sense of what was religiously appropriate. The lay people focused on what a theologian would regard as comparatively minor external changes to the worship service itself. Nevertheless, these *minor* changes created a tremendous ruckus. Shortly thereafter, small groups of reform-minded intellectuals began to consider the theological perspective of what would become known as Reform Judaism.

The Reform movement became the first modern Jewish religious denomination. They were the first to break from medieval models of religion and create something new. Many of the early Reformers in central

Europe were simply trying to adapt Judaism to contemporary needs rather than create a new movement that would have an independent identity, but that was the eventual consequence of their efforts.

Referring to Reform Judaism as the first Jewish denomination does not mean that there were not many Orthodox Jews in Germany at that time, but only that they were not yet referred to by that designation, and more importantly, Orthodox Judaism was not yet seen as a distinct subgroup within Judaism. The Reform movement became the first Jewish denomination to be so labeled because it created a new approach to Jewish theology as well as ritual practice. Accepting the scholarly understanding that Judaism had evolved over the centuries, the Reformers felt authorized to reconceptualize what the Jewish religion taught, to bring it more in line with modern ideas.

Their most radical decision was to reject the binding nature of Jewish law. It is hard to underestimate how shocking this position was. Up until that point, Judaism was virtually indistinguishable from halacha. The Reformers now intended to sever this connection. The vast compendium of the Talmud would not be thrown aside completely. Reform rabbis intended to draw on specific ideas and retain many of the practices outlined in rabbinic literature, but none of the beliefs or practices would be obligatory. Traditional Jews were horrified.

The new approach to Judaism was not something that traditionalists could classify as a completely new religion. After all, it did share the same religious themes and many of the same observances, albeit frequently in an abbreviated form. But by violating the halacha consistently and even publicly, the Reformers were, in the eyes of traditionalists, terrible sinners who needed to be admonished and convinced to repent. The traditionalists became increasingly angry as they began to realize that the Reformers were almost completely beyond their sphere of influence. These traditionalists—who were soon to become known by the designation "Orthodox"—protested to no avail. The ranks of the Reformers grew, no matter how vociferously the Orthodox objected.

The Reformers rejected the traditional understanding of halacha that Moses received two sets of teachings at Mount Sinai. According to tradition, the oral Torah is the authoritative explanation of the written Torah, the Five Books of Moses. All subsequent interpretation is simply elucidation of what had already been revealed at Mount Sinai. The reason that a verse in the Torah appeared to be incorrect or that two verses in the Torah appear to contradict one another is that God is trying to teach us something rather than revealing an error or contradiction in the text. But scholarship in nineteenth-century Germany was making the traditional view harder to justify. Reformers—some of whom were scholars—believed that they were on firm theoretical ground.

Another approach attempted to be both scholarly and traditional. Rabbi Zacharias Frankel understood the phrase "laws from God to Moses at Sinai" as referring to ancient practices that all Israel had come to accept. While their actual origins were obscure, these practices were regarded by him as if they had come from Moses at Sinai. While Frankel tried to stress the continuing validity of the halachic system, his reliance on nineteenth-century German scholarship upset traditionalists just as much as theories that abrogated the halacha. Frankel would start out as part of the rabbinical group that favored reforms but would break away during the 1845 rabbinic conference over the question of whether Jewish communal prayer should be conducted primarily in Hebrew.

By the early 1840s, a trained rabbinic leadership began to assert itself in Central Europe. In 1844, 1845, and 1846, Reform rabbinical conferences were held in Brunswick, Frankfurt, and Breslau, respectively. Most rabbis at these conferences were quite a bit more reform-oriented than Frankel, yet they understood that they had to operate within the broader Jewish community and thus maintained a strong connection with traditional rituals and observances.

Perhaps because they were obligated to uphold traditional observances they did not believe in, a number of Reform rabbis made shocking statements opposing traditional ways. For example, Rabbi Abraham Geiger, one of the most distinguished intellectual defenders of Reform Judaism, has been quoted in almost every book on this subject as expressing a visceral aversion to circumcision, allegedly referring to it as "a barbaric rite." However, the practice of these Reform rabbis remained far more traditional than their rhetoric. The vast majority of them worked to remain a part of the broader Jewish community, not fully accepting the radical Reform groups in Berlin and Hamburg who went much further with religious changes.

In Great Britain, two separate progressive movements developed: Reform and Liberal. Possibly the first call for reform was published anonymously by Isaac D'Israeli, the father of Benjamin Disraeli, who was later to become the prime minister. Published in 1833, the pamphlet argued that all the laws of Judaism—from both the written and oral Torah—were developed by people rather than God, and could therefore be changed or even annulled as necessary to meet the needs of the times. What was eternal was the "genius" of Judaism, the philosophical foundations that formed its central religious message. Nothing was done to respond to the public call, but apparently others felt the same way, and they were ready to lend their support to the creation of a Reform congregation should others initiate such an effort.

What was lacking was the social need for a new institution. After many families moved to the West End of London, they were too far from the Great Synagogue and Bevis Marks, the two synagogues that had previously served them. They needed a new neighborhood congregation and wanted to use the opportunity to introduce what they felt were long-needed changes. In 1842 they began the process of creating what became known as the West London Synagogue of British Jews.

While the congregation was quite traditional in many ways, they did abolish the second day of festivals. In the Bible, the three pilgrimage festivals of Sukkot, Pesach, and Shavuot are each observed for one day. The problem was that there was no set calendar. Since most Jews in the Second Temple Period used a lunar calendar, a person would have to see the new moon and report this sighting to the Sanhedrin, the supreme court. In the diaspora, messengers had to be dispatched on horseback to inform communities that the new month had started. If the messenger did not arrive by the start of a festival, the local community would have to guesstimate when the holiday was supposed to start. To be on the safe side, it was decreed that diaspora communities should keep two days of each festival in order to be absolutely sure they were observing the correct day. This practice was continued even after a set calendar was established. The West London Synagogue of British Jews decided to restore the original practice of observing only one day, thus rejecting the accepted postbiblical Jewish practice.

The Liberal movement came about much later. In the fall of 1901 a group of British Jewish intellectuals began holding meetings to create a new type of religious group. The Jewish Religious Union began holding services in October 1902. In contrast with the Reform movement, men did not have to cover their heads, although most did at the beginning. Men and women sat together, something that was not done in either British or German non-Orthodox synagogues. They also altered the traditional liturgy, removing references to the return to Zion, the reinstitution of sacrifices in the temple, and the resurrection of the dead. Claude G. Montefiore, who had studied the writings of the German Reformers while he was attending Oxford University, became the intellectual leader of the group. He held a number of strong convictions derived from his academic studies, including the belief that Judaism needed to be transformed from a tribal into a universal religion.

In the latter part of the nineteenth century, Reform Judaism spread to a number of other countries in Europe such as France, Denmark, and Hungary. Once there were enough potential constituents, leaders began planning for an umbrella organization. The first attempt to establish such an organization was in 1914, when the German Liberal movement invited representatives from England, France, and the United States to participate in their annual conference. World War I disrupted their plans, and subsequent political and economic events severely weakened the various European movements.

Not until 1926 was the British Liberal movement able to host a founding conference; delegates decided to call the new organization the World Union for Progressive Judaism. It was "progressive" because the two major figures—president Claude Montefiore and honorary secretary Lily Montagu—were leaders of the Liberal movement in England, and they preferred using a name that would be all-encompassing. Progressive Judaism spread to Palestine (later Israel), British Commonwealth countries such as Australia, New Zealand, and South Africa, as well as places in Central and South America and a handful of other countries throughout the world. Progressive Jews remained minorities in most western countries, where the Jewish community was dominated by the nonobservant Orthodox.

The leaders of European Reform had succeeded in developing a modern theology as well as a principled approach to ceremonial practice. But they had faced serious setbacks that had hindered their growth. There were political problems that limited the rights of Jews to full citizenship. The Reform movement's advocacy of religious change was predicated upon political emancipation. As many countries withheld political rights from the Jews and even blamed them for a variety of societal problems, the appeal of Reform Judaism declined. Indeed, governments intervened in local Jewish affairs in a number of cases to prevent the development of the Progressive movement, which they feared would serve as a counterforce against their campaigns to encourage Jews to convert to Christianity. Reactionary governments also feared that religious change could fuel the demand for social and political change.

The local Orthodox groups also proved to be effective at organizing countermeasures. Since most European countries required all Jews to belong to a *kehillah*, to which some of their tax money was directed, becoming a member of a Reform congregation meant having to pay twice. The Orthodox were able to use a variety of social mechanisms to discourage wavering Jews from affiliating with Reform temples, in some cases threatening them with a *herem*, a ban prohibiting all contact with them. Later, much of the energy that might have gone into building up European Reform was diverted to the nascent Zionist movement, which officially began with the first Zionist Congress in Basel, Switzerland, in 1898.

Although the Reform rabbinical leaders had held conferences in 1844, 1845, and 1846, the revolutions of 1848 made further efforts of this type impractical for almost twenty-five years. Finally, a new generation of Reform leaders held synods in Leipzig in 1869 and in Augsburg in 1871. The Augsburg conference was notable for passing resolutions allowing for greater religious rights for women. Despite the increased activity of the late 1860s and early 1870s, some historians see the Augsburg Synod as marking a downward turning point for the Reform movement in Europe.

Rabbi Sylvan D. Schwartzman said that in the years following the Augsburg Synod, "It became clear that Reform in Europe had spent itself." After 1871, "the movement came to a virtual standstill in most of Europe." In support of this argument, he quotes Moritz Lazarus, a philosophy professor at Berne University, who had been one of the primary leaders in both Leipzig and Augsburg. In 1886 he tried to explain why there had been no follow up to the 1869 and 1871 synods. "Several attempts at reform were made at the rabbinical conferences and synods, but these remained without any successors. The real reason why we have not continued with constant work at reforms is simple laziness."

Lazarus confessed that the Reform movement in Germany had failed to articulate sufficiently compelling reasons for the importance of Reform Judaism: "[A] religion whose teachers and leaders lack the courage to deal with the question, 'What in fact are the requirements of Judaism and what must they eventually be?'—such a faith faces the greatest of dangers, its abandonment."[2]

The Earlier Phases of the Reform Movement in the United States

When Israel Jacobson was in the process of founding his Reform temple in Seesen, the six American synagogues were still content to follow the Spanish-Portuguese Orthodox *minhag*. But fourteen years later, at around the same time that certain groups of German Jewish intellectuals were considering the possibility of reforming Judaism, a small group of Sephardic intellectuals in one particular city in the South began the first American attempt at reform.

In 1824, forty-seven members of Congregation Beth Elohim in Charleston, South Carolina, requested that the board of their synagogue consider a number of minor ritual reforms, including the introduction of some English prayers into the Shabbat liturgy. The board rejected the request. A small group broke away from the mother synagogue and founded a new congregation called the Reformed Society of Israelites. This effort failed, and the congregation disbanded in 1833, due in part to the unexpected death of one of its leaders, a Sephardic intellectual named Isaac Harby. However, less than a decade later, Congregation

7. Founded in 1749 as a Sephardic congregation, Kahal Kadosh Beth Elohim in Charleston, South Carolina, became the first American Reform temple in 1841. Their sanctuary is the second-oldest synagogue building in the United States after Newport, Rhode Island, and is the oldest in continuous use. *Photo by John P. O'Neill. Courtesy of the National Park Service.*

Beth Elohim itself moved toward Reform under the leadership of its *hazzan*, Gustavus Poznanski.

By the 1830s, large numbers of Central European Jews were immigrating to the United States. They are frequently referred to as "German Jews," although their geographic origins were quite a bit broader. Many historians have assumed that since Reform Judaism started in Germany and these immigrants were from that country, they brought Reform Judaism with them from Germany. While this may have been true in certain cases, most Central European immigrants came from small towns far away from Berlin or Hamburg, where the Reform movement was strongest. They arrived in the United States with relatively little Jewish education, but for most of them, what they knew about Judaism was traditional.

Many began peddling throughout the countryside, eventually starting dry goods stores throughout the United States. By the mid-1840s they had established many small Jewish communities along the East Coast, throughout the Midwest, and in the South. The first Jewish institution that would normally be founded would be the cemetery. Someone would die, perhaps unexpectedly, and his Jewish friends would have to deal with the question of where to bury him. If the time was right and there was a large enough group, land for a Jewish cemetery would be purchased and the first Jewish funeral would be conducted. Shortly thereafter, they might rent or buy a building for use as a synagogue. Contrary to what some of the earlier Jewish historians assumed, most of the early services were conducted along traditional lines. However, within a fairly short time, most local Jews began to adjust their practices to conform to the reality of daily life.

There were two major approaches to Reform Judaism in nineteenth-century America. Rabbi Isaac Mayer Wise, who arrived from Bohemia in 1846, became the undisputed leader of the moderate wing. Wise was interested in creating a distinctively American Judaism that would be compelling to Jews of all kinds living throughout the United States. He wrote prolifically for his own newspaper and published a number of books, but he was regarded by some of the East Coast rabbis as a self-taught dilettante who was constantly confusing concepts and warping serious theological ideas. While there may have been some truth to this impression, it was entirely beside the point. Wise was an institution builder, not a theoretician.

Wise began his rabbinical career at Congregation Beth-El in Albany, New York, where he got into a conflict with some of the members of the board. Part of the reason may have been that he was pushing for reforms that the board members felt were too radical. Yet Wise was also insisting that board members should close their stores on Shabbat, which was hardly something you would expect from a radical left-winger. In any case, the conflict escalated, and in the fall of 1850 the board sent him a letter effectively ending his employment just before Rosh Hashanah.

He refused to accept the dismissal and showed up in synagogue anyway, provoking the president, who then took a swing at Wise! The sanctuary erupted in chaos, and services had to be stopped. Wise's supporters then established a new congregation, Anshe Emeth, the People of Truth. When they were looking for a building, they found a church for sale, but it did not have anywhere they could put a women's section. As a result, Wise's congregation—and subsequently all American Reform congregations—sat men and women together.

Wise later took the pulpit of Congregation B'nai Jeshurun in Cincinnati, where he spent the rest of his life building what became the largest American Jewish denomination. That was not, however, his original goal. Like a number of other American Jewish leaders, Wise was trying to unify all American Jewry under a single banner. Already in 1847, Wise prepared a manuscript of a prayer book, entitled "Minhag America," which he intended for use by all the congregations in the country. The Hebrew *minhag* literally meant custom, but in this context it referred to a ritual style considered normative among a certain group. Wise expected his liturgy would become the American Jewish approach to prayer. He was to be disappointed.

Wise wanted congregations to adopt the same prayer book as the first step toward creating a union of congregations that could help to minimize the prevailing religious anarchy. In 1848 he issued a call to ministers and other Israelites to come together to begin planning a national union of Jewish congregations. Others had advocated the same idea but had been unable to bring together the many combative personalities, all of whom were zealously trying to guard their own turf. But Wise persevered. He established his own newspaper, the *Israelite*, in 1854 (renamed the *American Israelite* in 1874), and traveled around the country—particularly the Midwest—helping numerous congregations and performing various ceremonies. Finally, in 1873 he was able to help one of his lay leaders establish a national synagogue organization, called the Union of American Hebrew Congregations (UAHC). The name of the organization is telling—the word Reform is nowhere to be found. This omission was by no means coincidental.

In his early years in the United States, Wise was shocked at the incompetence of many of the men who claimed to be rabbis. Virtually none had actually been ordained. In those days, it is true, having formal credentials was less important than it is today. Wise himself was probably trained as a *heder* (Hebrew school) teacher and nothing more, but he claimed to be a rabbi, and later, to have a PhD as well. While he was probably neither an ordained rabbi nor a credentialed PhD, Wise was certainly a competent, energetic, and charismatic leader.

Unfortunately, many other European immigrants working as rabbis were incompetent, and a fair number were dishonest and even unstable. In addition, there was now a younger generation of American Jews who had trouble identifying with elderly German-speaking rabbis. For these reasons, Wise felt it was essential to create an American rabbinical academy. Already in 1855, Wise had made an attempt to start a rabbinical school. He established an organization called the Zion Collegiate Association to build a Jewish seminary, but the effort was premature.

After the UAHC was established in 1873, with the express goal of supporting the creation of an American rabbinical school, Wise's goal came within reach. On October 3, 1875, Hebrew Union College (HUC) opened for classes. Many of the students were too young to be rabbinical students, and many of the older students had no intention of becoming rabbis, but the institution had been established and would grow over time. As with the UAHC, the name of the school gave no indication that it had a Reform orientation.

When the first four rabbinical students were ordained in 1883, more than one hundred UAHC congregations sent representatives to Cincinnati to celebrate. The elaborate *s'micha* ceremony held at B'nai Jeshurun was universally described as religiously inspiring. Following the ordination, guests were invited to a lavish reception at the Highland House, a local catering hall. Unfortunately, the food served created a scandal that bitterly divided the American Jewish community. Despite several efforts to uncover exactly what happened, no one has been able to definitively establish who was responsible for the menu.

It appears that the local Jewish caterer had not realized that some of the guests did not eat shellfish and other nonkosher foods, and so he prepared all types of delicious—but religiously prohibited—courses. Some of the guests, particularly those from the East Coast, were scandalized. According to later accounts, two rabbis got up and stalked out, and three

MENU.

Little Neck Clams (Half Shell).
"Amontillado"
Sherry.

POTAGES.

Consomme Royal.
" Sauternes."

POISSONS.

Fillet de Boef, aux Champignons.
Soft Shell Crabs,
a l'Amerique, Pommes Duchesse.
Salade of Shrimp.
" St. Julien."

ENTREE.

Sweet Breads, a la Monglas.
Petits Pois, a la Francaise.
" Deidesheimer."

RELEVEE.

Poulets, a la Viennoise.
Asperges Sauce, Vinaigrette Pommes
" Punch Romain."   [Pate.
Grenouiles a la Creme and Cauliflower.

ROTI.

Vol au Vents de Pigeons, a la Tyrolienne.
Salade de Saitue.
" G. H. Mumm Extra Dry."

HORS-D'OEUVERS.

Bouchies de Volaille, a la Regeurs.
Olives Caviv,   Sardelles de Hollande.
Brissotins au Supreme Tomatoe,
Mayonaise.

SUCRES.

Ice Cream.
Assorted and Ornamented Cakes.

ENTREMENTS.

Fromages Varies.   Fruits Varies.
" Martell Cognac."   Cafe Noir.

8. The menu for the 1883 celebratory dinner at the Highland House following the first ordination ceremony of four rabbis who had studied at the Hebrew Union College in Cincinnati. For reasons that have never been adequately explained, the menu included various nonkosher courses. The *"Trefa* Banquet" contributed to the growing alienation between what became the Reform and Conservative movements. *Courtesy of the Jacob Rader Marcus Center of the American Jewish Archives, Cincinnati, americanjewish archives.org.*

more demonstrated their disapproval by refusing to eat. Many were utterly shocked that Hebrew Union College could host such a sacrilegious event on the very same evening that it ordained the first four American-trained rabbis. What kind of a radical religious group was this?

Some opponents accused Wise of deliberately staging what became known as the "Trefa Banquet," but this is extremely unlikely because Wise had always pushed for unity. It would make absolutely no sense for him to deliberately destroy that unity at the very moment when his dream was being fulfilled. But one dinner—however inappropriate—would not cause a permanent religious split in the American Jewish community. There were deep underlying differences that could not be papered over indefinitely. The movement Wise created was much too radical for those who, while not strictly Orthodox, leaned toward traditional views and practices. To indicate their position vis-à-vis Reform, the new group would make a mistake by calling themselves "Conservative," a name that did not reflect their core values. This unfortunate name would plague the Conservative movement throughout its history to the present day.

No longer having to worry about what the more traditional elements might say, the Reform movement moved to the left. The Americanized children of German Jewish immigrants saw the influence of liberal religion on their Protestant neighbors and wanted to embrace a Jewish version of that approach to faith. American Jews no longer lived in ghettos but in a free society. They dreamed of working together with their Christian neighbors to make the world a better place. A central part of the Reform vision was to strive for justice and peace, a recognition that people of faith had a moral imperative to work for the downtrodden. Reform leaders began using the term "prophetic Judaism" to describe the goal of following the dictates of the prophets. What was important was the commitment to ethical monotheism, in which the Jewish belief in one God was understood as necessitating the obligation to do good works.

The leaders of the Reform movement were concerned with traditionalists on the right and universalists on the left. As described in chapter 1, a group of Reform rabbis gathered in Pittsburgh in November 1885 to debate and vote on a major statement on the meaning of Reform Judaism. Written by Rabbi Kaufmann Kohler, the Pittsburgh Platform explained the central positions of the Reform movement at that time. These religious positions became known as Classical Reform Judaism, which stressed the mission of Israel—the idea that the Jews were scattered throughout the world in order to bring ethical monotheism to all.

Classical Reform temples stressed theology because understanding Jewish belief was more important than any particular ritual practice. Since both Mosaic and rabbinical laws "originated in ages and under the influence of ideas altogether foreign to our present mental and spiritual state," they could be jettisoned if they failed to inculcate the contemporary Jew "with a spirit of priestly holiness." If particular ritual obser-

9. Rabbi Isaac Mayer Wise in the midst of his colleagues—many of them his former students—at the Central Conference of American Rabbis annual conference in Atlantic City in 1898. The rabbis and a few of their wives are assembled in front of the Beth Israel Synagogue, a structure built in the Islamic Revival style, which still stands to this day. The CCAR, founded in 1889 by Rabbi Wise, now has about two thousand members. *Courtesy of HUC-JIR.*

vances were more likely to obstruct rather than advance spirituality, then they need not—actually should not—be observed.

But if ritual was not compelling, the struggle for social justice was. The final paragraph of the 1885 Pittsburgh Platform states that "we deem it our duty to participate in the great task of modern times, to solve, on the basis of justice and righteousness, the problems presented by the contrasts and evils of the present organization of society." There were numerous cases where rabbis spoke out in favor of the workers, thereby jeopardizing the position of their congregants who owned textile factories or the like. The Reform movement had more trouble deciding how to understand the prophetic vision of world peace. During World War I, the Central Conference of American Rabbis voted against a resolution endorsing Jewish belief as grounds for becoming a conscientious objector. Nevertheless, after reports of the horrors of World War I began circulating, many declared themselves to be pacifists.

In 1922 Rabbi Stephen Wise (no relation to Isaac Mayer Wise) established the Jewish Institute of Religion. Wise felt there was a need for a new rabbinical school that would be more sympathetic to Zionism and would place a greater stress on the importance of *klal yisrael*, the unity of the Jewish people. Also, by this time the New York Jewish community was by far the largest in the country, and it was felt that there should be a Reform-oriented seminary in this city. Despite these arguments, the UAHC declined to sponsor the Jewish Institute of Religion, and Wise had to bear the burden of not only running the school but also raising the operating funds. After numerous attempts, merger negotiations with HUC were finally successful in mid-1948, shortly after world-renowned archaeologist Nelson Glueck had become president of HUC. The merged institution became Hebrew Union College–Jewish Institute of Religion (HUC-JIR).

In 1900 Wise became rabbi at Congregation Beth Israel in Portland, Oregon, where he campaigned against what he perceived to be the social problems of his times. As an activist of the Progressive Era, Wise delivered fiery sermons condemning greedy industrialists and corrupt politicians. Although the Reform movement as a whole was largely opposed to political Zionism, Wise was an enthusiastic supporter from an early stage. Wise was remarkably prescient in his commitment to Zionism, campaigning tirelessly to convince the Reform movement to change its stance. Unfortunately, his reputation has been badly tarnished by criticisms that he failed to urge his close friend, President Franklin Delano Roosevelt, to do more to help the Jews of Europe during the Holocaust.

Another important Reform rabbi of this era was Abba Hillel Silver. Like Wise, Silver was a Classical Reformer who advocated for labor rights and strongly supported Zionism. After a short stint in Wheeling, West Virginia, in 1917 he became rabbi of The Temple in Cleveland and remained in that position for the next forty-six years. Silver was a Republican, which was rather unusual for a Reform rabbi, but he used his influence in the Republican Party to garner support for the creation of a Jewish state, thus putting pressure on President Harry Truman. According to a story circulating at the time, in July 1946 Silver pounded his fist on Truman's desk and bellowed at him, demanding that Truman support the admission of Holocaust survivors into Palestine. While the details of the story may be exaggerated, Silver was well known for repeatedly attacking Truman, in part to promote the presidential ambitions of his good friend Ohio senator Robert Taft.

By the late 1930s the Reform movement was rapidly moving back toward the center ideologically as well as ritually. Extreme universalism no longer made much sense under the increasingly dire political environment. The theoretical debate over whether Zionism compromised the mission of Israel seemed out of touch at a time when Nazi persecution was threatening the lives of millions of European Jews. In 1935 the CCAR decided to take a neutral rather than a negative view of Zionism. Even some anti-Zionists now began advocating resettlement plans in Mandatory Palestine. It became harder to uphold the tenet of Classical Reform Judaism that the Jews were no longer a nation but solely a religious community.

Throughout the 1940s attention shifted away from religion and toward the war, the atrocities committed against the Jewish civilian population of Europe (what would later become known as the Holocaust), and Zionism. Most Reform Jews had opposed Zionism as undermining the claim that Reform Jews were loyal citizens of the countries in which they lived. But the events of the 1930s convinced almost everyone that the Jews of Europe needed a refuge. It was no longer a strictly religious question but a matter of survival. Nevertheless, the question of whether the Reform movement should advocate for the creation of a Jewish homeland or even an independent Jewish state remained controversial. The question centered on the nature of the Jewish people and what role the land of Israel should play in their destiny.

It was through the World Union for Progressive Judaism—the international organization of Reform, Liberal, Progressive, and (in a later period) Reconstructionist Jews—that the American Reform movement became involved in what was then called Palestine. In 1959 Rabbi Solomon Freehof of Pittsburgh became the new president of the World Union. In 1960 the organization moved from London to New York, and in 1973 from New York to Jerusalem, reflecting the increasingly central role that the State of Israel played for Reform Jews.

Both the UAHC and the CCAR made statements in the early 1940s bemoaning the failure of the Reform movement to draw in new members from outside the relatively small and cliqueish German Jewish elite. In 1942 the CCAR president, Rabbi James G. Heller, called for the creation of a joint effort on the part of the various institutions of the Reform movement to evaluate why the movement was failing to attract new members and to recommend new approaches that might be directed into a campaign to expand the reach of Reform Judaism. In the difficult circumstances of the war years, nothing was done to put Heller's recommendation into action.

Reform Judaism after World War II

When World War II ended, the American Jewish community became aware that it had unprecedented responsibilities as the largest and most important Jewish community in the world. After the State of Israel came into existence in 1948, the public debate over Zionism faded away. A small group of Reform anti-Zionists continued their opposition through the American Council for Judaism (ACJ), an organization that exists even today. But there was little point in continuing to harp on the question of whether a Jewish state should have been created, so the ACJ stressed its commitment to Jewish religiosity rather than what it saw as an unhealthy preoccupation with Jewish nationalism. Eventually, even most Classical Reform Jews lost interest in the ACJ, with many joining new groups that better reflected their interests.

According to the ACJ, Judaism is a religion that stresses the belief in one God who commands us to follow the prophetic injunction to pursue justice. It most emphatically is not an excuse to engage in ethnic identity reinforcement. This focus on the religious nature of Judaism fit in well with the ethos of the Eisenhower era, and so managed to find support among a small constituency. But for the majority of Reform Jews, the idea of Jewish peoplehood was a central component of their Jewish identity.

By the 1940s the UAHC had become acutely aware that Reform Jews had lost much of the vision that had been so compelling in the late nineteenth and early twentieth centuries. Dramatic changes were needed. Rabbi Maurice Eisendrath, who became executive secretary of the UAHC in 1943 and then president in 1951, argued that the Reform movement needed to be proactive in encouraging the creation of new congregations. This had not been the case up until this point. Quite the contrary—he actually cited cases where Reform temples had actively campaigned to prevent the establishment of new Reform congregations in their geographical areas.

The problem was that many of these established Reform temples were cold, formal places where newcomers were unlikely to feel welcome. The largest, most prestigious temples also charged huge dues, preventing all but the most affluent from joining. The Reform movement consisted of a small, cliquish wealthy elite who looked down their noses at outsiders. Eisendrath wanted to reverse this dynamic, encouraging potential members to join existing congregations and groups to consider founding new Reform temples.

Beginning in 1946, the UAHC Biennial Assembly decided that, rather than wait passively for others to come to them, it would initiate programs that would help promote the growth of Reform Judaism. It launched the American Jewish Cavalcade, a program that sent nationally known rabbis on speaking tours. Many of the speakers were so dynamic that they succeeded in stirring up interest and helping to attract new members for the local Reform temples, as well as creating new congregations. The UAHC had 536 congregations in 1956 and 706 in 1970—an impressive increase. It also helped strengthen the bonds between the local congregations and the UAHC, reinforcing the awareness that Reform Judaism was more than just a single synagogue building in a particular suburb.

Eisendrath firmly believed that Reform Judaism had to change to meet the needs of Reform Jews rather than the other way around. This included being where Reform Jews lived. Since the largest Jewish population in North America was on the East Coast, Eisendrath argued that the UAHC needed to move from Cincinnati to New York City. There was, of course, considerable opposition to this plan. Reform Jews in Cincinnati and throughout the Midwest did not want the national organization being moved out of their city and region. Classical Reformers felt that this move would accelerate the shift toward a more traditional approach to Reform Judaism called neo-Reform. Despite this opposition, the UAHC voted to approve the decision. The House of Living Judaism was built on Fifth Avenue and Sixty-Fifth Street in New York City, and the move was made in the fall of 1951.

The new UAHC headquarters was right next door to Temple Emanu-El, the largest and most important Reform congregation in the country. But being physically close did not mean that Emanu-El was enthusiastic about Eisendrath's direction of the UAHC. Eisendrath had a tendency to make dramatic public statements, frequently exaggerating the actual facts of a given situation for rhetorical emphasis in line with his belief in prophetic Judaism. In 1967 the board of Emanu-El had had enough and resigned from the UAHC in protest over Eisendrath's bombastic public statements. Although this hurt the budget of the UAHC significantly, Eisendrath refused to back down.

Eisendrath died of a heart attack in his hotel room hours before his final address to the UAHC Biennial on November 11, 1973. Rabbi Alexander M. Schindler, who had already been selected to succeed Eisendrath the following year, read the announcement to the thirty-five hundred shocked delegates gathered in the ballroom of the Hilton in New York City. Schindler decided to read Eisendrath's speech denouncing President Richard Nixon for his cover-up of the Watergate break-in.

Eisendrath's speech was certainly dramatic, attacking "our ever-scapegoating president . . . so indifferent at all the obscene dishonesty and pervasive corruption that have so blackened the White House, so obsessed with 'national security' as to rationalize the most unforgivable concealment and the most blatant fabrication that have brought us within an inch of a dictatorial police state." In the face of such betrayal, "Are we still prepared to assert that religion has nothing to do with politics? Unless we Jews, conversant with the moral commands of our faith, resume our responsibilities, we will have forfeited for all time our usefulness and our reason for surviving as a people."[3]

Eisendrath was a passionate proponent of prophetic Judaism. He had started out his career as a believer in Classical Reform, but he shifted his position over the years to stay within the majority consensus of the movement. He was largely responsible for taking a small group of genteel temples, primarily in the South and Midwest, and turning it into a dynamic religious movement that shook up the American Jewish community and indeed American society as a whole. Eisendrath spoke out in favor of civil rights, opposed the Vietnam War, and showed a remarkable prescience in his public positions. As Albert Vorspan, the director of the Joint Commission on Social Action, phrased it, "Nobody slept during his tenure, for he was a disturber of sleep who brought discomfort to the comfortable."

Eisendrath, for all his dramatic excesses, could stir the emotions of his followers and provide a strong rhetorical defense of Judaism. As he wrote in his final speech, "The world needs Judaism . . . its compassion instead of the machismo of today's violence, its optimism in the face of despair, its compassion in the face of human callousness, its reverence for the life of the mind in defiance of emotionalism run riot, its love of learning and passion for justice, its hunger for peace as the apex of God's kingdom and its partnership with God in setting the world aright."

Eisendrath competed with Rabbi Nelson Glueck for primacy in the Reform movement, with each trying to outdo the other. Glueck was ordained in 1923 and began teaching at the Hebrew Union College in 1928. A dedicated scholar of the ancient Near East, he believed in using archaeology as a tool to recover as much of the history of ancient Israel as possible. In line with the academic expectations of his times, Glueck believed in incorporating scientific method into his scholarship, as part of his understanding that the acquisition of knowledge is a dynamic process discoverable for oneself, rather than something that has to be handed down as a hereditary tradition.

He became an expert in ancient pottery, matching small ceramic fragments to specific time periods and national groups. He displayed a practical ability to use his knowledge of the ancient world to help solve modern-day problems, working with the Office of Strategic Services to develop a contingency plan for a retreat from Palestine during World War II and with the Israeli government to develop an irrigation strategy modeled on that of the Nabataeans. He hobnobbed with world leaders, and was selected to deliver the benediction at President John F. Kennedy's inauguration in 1961. Many felt that he was more interested in archaeology and high society than in running Hebrew Union College, but they had to admit that his high profile brought attention and prestige to the college, particularly when he appeared on the cover of *Time* magazine on December 13, 1963.

In the years following World War II, the number of Reform temples grew, as many Americans abandoned city centers for the burgeoning suburbs. In 1940 there were 265 Reform congregations with 59,000 household units belonging to the UAHC; by 1955 there were 520 congregations with 255,000 units—an almost fivefold increase in just fifteen years. The Conservative movement grew even more. The substance of the Judaism practiced in many of these temples appears in retrospect to be rather superficial by most objective measures of religiosity, but at the time it was seen as a dramatic revival of interest in religion.

For the vast majority of American Jews, Judaism meant an ethnic identity rather than a transcendent faith. Since open expressions of ethnicity were looked down upon and religiosity was regarded as a positive virtue, many American Jews joined temples for the first time in their lives. No longer living in urban ethnic enclaves, they yearned for a way to connect with other Jews. But they were not necessarily seeking out a direct relationship with God.

They also saw temple membership as a way of reaffirming their American patriotism. The anticommunism of the Cold War years required Americans to define their values in contrast to godless communism. On Flag Day in 1954, President Dwight D. Eisenhower emphasized the connection between good citizenship and religious faith by saying, "Our government makes no sense unless it is founded in a deeply felt religious faith—and I don't care what it is."

After a campaign organized by the Knights of Columbus, Congress added the words "under God" to the Pledge of Allegiance in 1954. The following year, Congress also added the phrase "In God We Trust" to all American currency, and in 1956 it became the nation's official motto, replacing "E Pluribus Unum." While most Americans were Protestant, the president deliberately avoided using language that would exclude people of other faiths. The important thing was to be committed to the American civil religion, which was good for the individual American, American families, American communities, and the United States as a whole.

Temples affiliated with the UAHC competed with Conservative synagogues for new members. They were at a disadvantage, however, because most of those joining congregations for the first time were from heavily ethnic Jewish backgrounds who felt comfortable in the more traditional Conservative movement. The same dynamic worked in favor of the United Synagogue of Conservative Judaism when new congregations were being formed in the suburbs. If a certain number of Jews from various backgrounds had settled in a specific place, the logical decision was to establish a Conservative congregation, which was perceived as being in the middle of the religious spectrum, a form of Judaism that everyone could relate to (or at least live with).

Nevertheless, the Reform movement continued to grow. There was therefore a greater need for rabbis and other Jewish professionals who could serve the increasing numbers of Reform congregations. There was also a desire to establish Reform educational institutions in the largest Jewish communities in order to build a higher profile for the movement. In 1954 a HUC-JIR prerabbinic program was opened at the Wilshire Boulevard Temple in Los Angeles, supplementing a part-time College of Jewish Studies program that had been opened in 1947.

Rabbi Jack Skirball, who had left the pulpit rabbinate to become a movie producer and real estate tycoon, was instrumental in urging Glueck to expand the UAHC into California, which it did, purchasing a property that had been a home for asthmatic Jewish girls. In 1970 a new building was put up adjacent to the campus of the University of Southern California. The campus provided for the second and third years of the rabbinical curriculum, after which the students would transfer to either New York or Cincinnati. In 2002 the Los Angeles campus began ordaining rabbis.

Glueck had a sufficiently impressive reputation as an archaeologist that in 1963 the government of Israel offered him a ninety-nine-year lease for one Israeli pound per year on a two-acre site at 13 King David

Street in Jerusalem. The land, very close to the King David Hotel, became a prime site after the Six-Day War in 1967. The original limestone-clad buildings were designed in the International Style by architect Heinz Rau, featuring a distinctive staircase entry onto the campus. The campus was supposed to be a center for the study of biblical archaeology, but it also included a Reform synagogue, one of the first in the Jewish state.

In 1970 Richard J. Scheuer, chairperson of the Jerusalem School Committee, initiated efforts to acquire three acres adjoining the original campus. Together with architect Moshe Safdie, he developed the expansion plan for the Jerusalem campus, which encompassed a new library, classrooms, student lounges, archaeological museum, research facilities, and youth hostel. The spectacular expanded campus, with its arcades and courtyards made out of Jerusalem stone overlooking the Old City, was featured in the La Biennale di Venezia of 1991 as one of the preeminent architectural achievements of that period.

An Israeli rabbinical program was created in 1975 to train Israelis as Reform rabbis. Beginning in 1970, all American rabbinical students have studied in Jerusalem for their first year, after which they returned to one of the three stateside campuses. Eventually, most Hebrew Union College students—including all cantorial and education students—were sent to study in Israel, an educational policy that had a tremendous impact on the religious direction of the movement.

Throughout the postwar era, the Reform movement became known as the denomination that emphasized social justice concerns. Many Reform Jews became active in the struggle for civil rights. Already in 1935, the UAHC protested the cruelty of "the lynching evil" and commended those rabbis and leaders who had taken courageous positions on this crime. In 1946 the CCAR issued a statement on "Judaism and Race Relations," which called for a series of measures designed to promote equal rights for African Americans. The 1954 Supreme Court decision *Brown v. Board of Education* outlawed segregation in public education, giving Reform Jews a cause that they could commit themselves to wholeheartedly. Individual Reform Jews joined the Freedom Riders and other efforts designed to promote civil rights, such as the Mississippi Summer Project that worked to register African Americans as voters.

In March 1958 Rabbi William B. Silverman was leading the Temple Congregation Ohabai Sholom in Nashville, Tennessee, when a group calling itself the Confederate Underground dynamited the Nashville Jewish Community Center. Silverman delivered a passionate sermon on the following Friday entitled "We Will Not Yield." He began by saying, "During the course of the past week, it has been said that the rabbi should STICK TO RELIGION, TO JUDAISM AND THE BIBLE!" Silverman said that he would do exactly that, citing from the Torah, the prophets, the teachings of Isaac Mayer Wise, the Pittsburgh Platform, and even the Haggadah in an attempt to show that Judaism must devote itself to social justice, including the rights of the oppressed.

In his book *Basic Reform Judaism*, written in 1970, Silverman explained that Judaism cannot exist without ethics because man serves God through righteousness. Reform Jews are expected to understand that they must practice their religious ideals in their daily lives, whether or not it is a popular way of doing things. Ritual without ethics is a profanation of God and of life, and Reform Jews therefore must commit themselves to applying the social ethics of the Hebrew prophets. If Reform Jews are to take their religion seriously, they must mobilize themselves for a religious war against ignorance, bigotry, racial and religious discrimination, poverty, disease, and despair. The ultimate purpose is to implement the values that will enable man to create a moral society that will fulfill the commandments of God.[4]

The Reform movement also took a strong position on the Vietnam War. Already in 1964, the CCAR called for a negotiated solution to the conflict. In November 1965 Eisendrath gave a speech to the UAHC General Assembly urging them to protest against what he called the transgression of "every tenet of our faith." This was a remarkably prescient political position because it was still relatively early in the conflict, and the majority of Americans were still supportive of the war. During Hanukkah in 1965, Eisendrath had published an open letter to President Lyndon Johnson comparing him to Antiochus Epiphanes, the Syrian Greek king who persecuted the Jews in the second century BCE. The protests against the Vietnam War marked the heyday of Reform political activism, which also included working toward nuclear disarmament, for the adoption of the treaty against genocide, in favor of the women's rights movement, and other liberal causes.

Sometime between 1967 and the early 1970s, many in the Jewish community began to feel disenchanted with their fellow social justice activists. They were shocked that most liberals had failed to come to the support of Israel in the weeks leading up to the Six-Day War. A number of prominent liberal Christian religious leaders had spoken out against Israel, something that their Reform colleagues had not anticipated. Many also felt betrayed by the rise of the Black Power movement, which seemed to turn many African Americans against whites, even liberal whites who had tried to help them. Black antisemitism skyrocketed, prompting a lot of soul-searching among Jewish supporters of the NAACP.

By the late 1960s there was a striking change in focus. American Jews talked less about social action designed to help the downtrodden, and they began to focus more on the particularistic meaning of Jewish tradition. The Six-Day War dramatically increased the emotional connection that most American Jews felt toward the State of Israel. As they worried about her ability to survive in the face of Arab threats to destroy the country during the very tense three weeks preceding the war, many American Jews realized how important the State of Israel had become to them. This fear resurfaced in 1973 when Israel's physical survival was in doubt during the early stages of the Yom Kippur War. Many Reform Jews became devoted Zionists as a result of these events. Increasing numbers began to visit Israel, which likewise contributed to a stronger sense of commitment.

The disconnect between the religious doctrines outlined in the official documents of the movement and the uncertainty of the congregants grew over the course of the 1960s, one of the most tumultuous decades in modern times. As Michael A. Meyer describes it, the late 1960s was a time of "severe self-doubt and anxiety about the future." This uncertainty "displaced the ebullience that had characterized American Reform Judaism since the war. Divided and uncertain of its course, it long remained in a state of crisis."[5]

The Schindler Years

Throughout this period, the CCAR had continually discussed creating a new platform to describe the basic beliefs of Reform Judaism, but there was one central obstacle—no one could agree on what those basic beliefs were. The theological disharmony began with definitions of God, which ranged from the all-powerful God of the book of Genesis, to the humanistic conception articulated by Abraham Cronbach, who had influenced many of his students at the Hebrew Union College in Cincinnati. Despite the theological polarization, many felt that the movement needed to issue a statement on where it stood theologically.

The Reform movement had been expanding tremendously, and there were large numbers of new Reform temples. But this expansion was due primarily to sociological factors. Many felt that the central religious concepts expounded by Reform thinkers in earlier generations lacked relevance at a time of unprecedented events in American history—a foreign war had been lost and a president forced to resign. People had new expectations from their religion, and many argued that the Reform movement had to figure out a way to respond to that demand. As Eugene B. Borowitz, the HUC professor who drafted the 1976 "Reform Judaism—A Centenary Perspective" put it, synagogue life had become "stale and in need of invigoration." In order to keep American Jews in the pews, "there was a general feeling that the movement needed to rethink its directions."[6]

To address this need, the pace of liturgical change quickened. Perhaps partially as a result of the haste, the results of these liturgical efforts of the 1970s were mixed. *Gates of Prayer*, published in 1975, was deemed antiquated by critics virtually from the moment it was published. The two basic problems were that it did not use gender-sensitive language and that it put most transliterations in the very back of the book, where worshipers were unlikely to find corresponding passages in time to read them aloud.

Even worse, the theological message of the new prayer book seemed confused. Since members of the CCAR could not agree on what theology to adopt, especially in the English prayers, there were no less than ten separate Friday night services, most of which incorporated a specific approach to God, Torah, and Israel. With so much theological diversity among its ranks, it was truly amazing that the CCAR was able to sustain itself as a unified organization.

One of the primary reasons that the CCAR did not split into opposing factions over contentious issues was that the rabbinic organization allowed individual members to act on their conscience regardless of any policy positions adopted by the organization. In the case of rabbinic officiation at interfaith weddings, for example, the CCAR voted repeatedly to urge members not to participate. Nevertheless, the substantial numbers who disagreed with this policy were free to do whatever they felt was right with absolutely no restrictions imposed by the CCAR. This was in dramatic contrast to the Rabbinical Assembly, the organization of Conservative rabbis, which prohibited its members from officiating at such ceremonies and threatened violators with expulsion.

Rabbi Alexander M. Schindler succeeded Eisendrath as president of the UAHC, serving from 1973 to 1996. He was born in Munich in 1925 and fled with his family to Washington Heights twelve years later. Schindler joined the army and became a ski trooper, earning both a Purple Heart and a Bronze Star. After his ordination in 1953, he became rabbi of Temple Emanuel in Worcester, Massachusetts, and joined the UAHC in 1959, where he founded a New England regional association and served as director of education and then vice president. As UAHC president, he earned renown for his assertive support of the social action agenda of the Reform movement in the 1970s and 1980s, including civil rights, world peace, nuclear disarmament, a "Marshall Plan" for the poor, opposition to the death penalty, and women's and gay rights.

Despite his positions on the far left, he was the first leader of the Reform movement to become the chairman of the Conference of Presidents of Major American Jewish Organizations. As the *New York Times* suggested, perhaps "Rabbi Schindler's own background and distinguished bearing—his hair had long ago turned a silvery white—challenged the very notion of Reform Judaism as a heavily diluted version of the real thing." Although dedicated to the Reform movement, Schindler was the son of a Yiddish poet with roots among the German Hasidim and could use "folksy Yiddish expressions and self-deprecating humor" to befriend the more traditional.

As Rabbi Eric H. Yoffie told the *New York Times*, "The irony here is that this most reformed of reformers, someone who was politically left and a promoter of dramatic change, was also someone who was seen as possessing Yiddishkeit. He has this Jewish soul. He has this traditional manner about him. That's what made him so acceptable in the broader community. It gave him a measure of credibility."[7]

Schindler is best remembered for two issues that are intricately connected: his outreach to intermarried couples and his advocacy of patrilineal descent. In 1978 Schindler proposed that the Reform movement begin implementing a strategy to welcome the non-Jewish spouses of Jewish partners. While there had been a strong stigma against marrying outside the faith, intermarriage rates were going up. At the time, many felt that Schindler was going too far, abrogating a long-standing social policy that had worked so effectively for so long. But time has shown that he had remarkable forethought. Parental social pressure against intermarriage was in the process of dramatically declining and in the intervening years has become virtually completely ineffectual.

Addressing the UAHC Biennial at the Century Plaza in Los Angeles, Schindler said that membership numbers released the previous week showing that the UAHC had 791 affiliated congregations and approximately 1.3 million members "is nothing to boast about" because of the apathy and laxity among most Reform Jews. "For most of us, that synagogue affiliation is only marginal. It is mere form without sufficient substance," Schindler reprimanded the delegates.

Schindler called for continued efforts to instill greater religious commitment. An interim report by Rabbi Samuel E. Karff, the cochairperson of a task force created for the purpose of researching how to increase commitment, said Reform Jews do not have to believe that God is directing every life experience or that sacred texts were written by God and that this created a motivational problem. This does not mean, however, that "the presence of God" cannot be detected. Karff also argued that the Reform movement had focused too much on "ethnic" concerns rather than on issues of faith.[8]

Schindler worked alongside Rabbi Joseph B. Glaser, who was appointed executive vice president of the CCAR in 1971 and remained in that position until his death in 1994. Glaser was responsible for running the rabbinic organization for the Reform movement, which at the time had a membership of about seventeen hundred. He played an important role in the 1990 policy change that allowed gay and lesbian Jews to study at HUC-JIR and then become members of the CCAR. He also worked on behalf of various groups suffering from prejudice and discrimination, including Native Americans, Tibetan refugees, and farmworkers. Glaser led a group of West Coast rabbis in lobbying the CCAR to support the United Farm Workers of America's struggle for better working conditions, and he urged the CCAR to endorse the grape and later lettuce boycotts.[9]

Rabbi Rick Jacobs, president of the Union of Reform Judaism, later recalled how his own social conscience was developed under Glaser's influence. "My own social justice commitment began back in the late sixties when I was a camper at the Union's Camp Swig in Northern California. Rabbi Joe Glaser of blessed memory had invited Cesar Chavez to speak to us. Chavez told us about the plight of the farm workers and how eating non-union grapes or lettuce harmed their lives. Right then and there my Jewish identity was connected with social justice. Doing justly was as fundamental as saying the *shema* each day."[10]

Rabbi Alfred Gottschalk, president of HUC-JIR from 1971 to 1996 and then chancellor until 2000, focused on building the college and did not attempt to be seen as the religious leader of the Reform movement, a position that Schindler filled. Like Schindler, Gottschalk was born in Germany and fled with his family as a child. Each year on the day before he was to ordain them as rabbis, Gottschalk told rabbinic students how his grandfather took him down to the river on the day after Kristallnacht and asked him to help gather the torn pieces of the Torah scrolls that had been thrown into the water. His grandfather told him it was his job to stitch the sodden pieces of parchment back together: "One day you will put it together again."[11] According to Rabbi David Ellenson, current president of HUC-JIR, "this story provides the trope for understanding the shape and direction of his [Gottschalk's] life."[12]

At a conference on Reform Judaism and Jewish authenticity at Yale University in 1983, Gottschalk spoke of the delicate balancing act that diaspora Jews had been undertaking since the emancipation. "The hazards are great and will increase. The choice however to remain part of the secular world and to interact with it as Jews or to live in isolation from it is the quandary for a sizeable segment of modern Jewry." Gottschalk argued that while acculturation had occurred over the course of Jewish history, this did not mean that it had been a deleterious force. "There is a need for me to put an underscoring line on a reading of Jewish history which argues that this has been a millennial problem for us. The interaction of biblical Israel with Canaan, with Assyria, Babylonia, Persia, Greece and Rome and their world views, all testify to our capacity to re-form, re-construct, conserve and start the cycle again as the historical condition dictates."

Gottschalk explained, "The vast body of Jewish religious and secular literature argues for the dynamics of Reform, of restructuring, of making it possible for Jews to live and survive in changing environments. We have changed habitats, languages, customs, ceremonies, laws—we have stretched and shaped both Halakhah and Aggadah in order to exist, we have erred at times in judgment but on balance history has smiled on our survival and our capacity to assimilate while resisting—at least until the modern period—the pressure to lose our identity." He concluded by stating, "Freezing Judaism in some anachronistic time-frame is not what is asked of us."[13]

In 1972 Gottschalk ordained Sally Priesand as the first female rabbi in the United States. This was a tremendous breakthrough for women who had dreamed of becoming rabbis only to be told that girls cannot do that. Gottschalk called Priesand's ordination an action that serves as a testament to Reform Judaism's efforts at achieving "equality of women in the congregation of the Lord."[14] Priesand had grown up in Beth Israel–West Temple in Cleveland, where she became interested in becoming a Jewish professional and decided at age sixteen to become a rabbi. At the time, no one knew if her dream was achievable. Although Gottschalk willingly ordained her, many congregations refused to consider her, and she had a difficult time until she became the rabbi of Monmouth Reform Temple in Tinton Falls, New Jersey, where she served until her retirement in 2006 (see her story in chapter 5).

In 1993 Gottschalk spoke at the opening session of a symposium entitled "Exploration and Celebration" to honor the twentieth anniversary of women in the rabbinate. "It was our founders' hope that the rabbinate leadership of American Jewry would transmit the prophetic tradition of our faith through a progressive conception of Judaism reflective of, and responsive to, modernity. And it is a fundamental reality of our modern society that women are fully entitled to equal rights and equal opportunity, and equal responsibility." He then talked about his personal experience of ordaining Priesand, which is unfortunately left blank in the archival notes. He then concluded, "As a College-Institute pioneer, Rabbi Priesand opened the way for the empowerment of women in Reform Judaism and the Jewish clergy."[15]

Gottschalk also ordained Mordecai (Moti) Rotem, the first Israeli Reform rabbi, in 1980. Rotem had decided to become a rabbi in his teen years. "I searched for expression as a Jew of the 20th century," he told *People* magazine right after his ordination, "not one living 2,000 or even 500 years ago."[16] When Rotem spent six months in Los Angeles on a student exchange program when he was seventeen, he became acquainted with Reform Judaism and eventually decided to become the first rabbinical student at the HUC-JIR campus in Jerusalem. He led Or Hadash–Lyons Center for Progressive Judaism in Haifa from 1974, long before he was ordained, until 2000. From 1981 to 1986, he also served as executive director of the Israel Movement for Progressive Judaism.

Rotem found that the Orthodox monopoly on Jewish religious status made it difficult to function. He protested at the "absurdity that marriages conducted anywhere in the world, even civil weddings, are accepted in Israel—except those conducted by Reform rabbis." Rotem argued that the absence of religious pluralism had turned off many Israelis from religion. "But with our way they can rediscover their roots and cherish them," he believes. "I am bringing hundreds of youths back to Judaism because I speak their language, because I am one of them. I don't come to them in a long black coat or refuse to shake hands with a woman. In a democratic state, religion, which is a matter of the heart, cannot be enforced by law," the rabbi sums up. "Everybody has the right to his own truth."

Immediately after Rotem's ordination, Rabbi Shlomo Goren, the Ashkenazi chief rabbi, told television viewers that the *s'micha* was invalid, and called Rotem a "Purim carnival rabbi." He said that Rotem failed to observe even the most basic of Jewish laws such as the restrictions of Shabbat observance. Rotem responded, "My Shabbat is merely different. It is not based on 'Thou shalt nots' but on what I am doing: blessing the wine, praying, lighting candles, community singing and studying—in short, creating an atmosphere of being with God. My Shabbat is positive. I refuse to accept the conventional theology that proclaims, 'It is written and can't be altered.' Religion, far from being static, has progressed over the centuries" (for more on Reform Judaism in Israel, see chapter 5).

Gottschalk was fortunate to serve as president at a time when American society was prosperous and institutions of all types were expanding. He established schools of education and Jewish communal service and built a joint program in Judaic studies with the University of Southern California in Los Angeles, where he had served as dean for twelve years before becoming president. In 1979 he decided to move the New York school from the Upper West Side to Greenwich Village right next to New York University. All the campuses expanded, creating, arguably, the most important Jewish religious educational institution outside Israel. This legacy became a mixed blessing at the very end of his life when the economic downturn forced HUC-JIR to consider closing two of its three stateside campuses, a potentially catastrophic move that was only narrowly averted.

Of the three leaders, Schindler was clearly the dominant personality. And yet, for all Schindler's charisma, he devoted little time to organizational development. That became the major challenge facing Rabbi Eric H. Yoffie, who in 1996 became president of UAHC (which soon became the Union for Reform Judaism, or URJ). Yoffie's family had been members of Temple Emanuel in Worcester, Massachusetts, where Schindler had been rabbi. Yoffie led congregations in Lynbrook, New York, and Durham, North Carolina, before taking the job as director of the Midwest Council of the UAHC in 1980 and then executive director of the Association of Reform Zionists of America (ARZA) in 1983. He was promoted to become vice president of the UAHC as well as director of the Commission on Social Action in 1992.

The Yoffie Era

Beginning in 1999, Yoffie attempted to generate a "new Reform revolution," stressing the need to transform the Reform worship experience. Services in most Reform temples, he had told the UAHC leadership, had become "performance-oriented" and did not "speak to people's spiritual needs." One of his goals was to "give expression to the desire to connect with the transcendent."[17] This sentiment was widely shared throughout the movement and so it garnered much support. And indeed throughout the Yoffie years, services at Reform congregations became more participatory as well as less formal. While some Classical Reformers balked at the idea that religious services would resemble a summer camp sing-along, most temple members were pleased.

In 2007 Yoffie promoted an initiative to encourage Reform Jews to attend services Saturday mornings as well as Friday nights. The logic was irrefutable—the Sabbath runs for twenty-four hours, not just for a few hours on Friday night. Furthermore, the Reform movement should put "Torah at the center," and Saturday morning services allowed for an extensive Torah reading or a Torah study discussion. Despite these advantages, only a devout few responded to the idea.

The Reform movement had always had a reputation of being attractive to people who knew little about Judaism and had little interest in studying more about it. Yoffie initiated a Jewish literacy campaign that encouraged board members to read four books a year on Jewish topics. Soon this idea was expanded. Each issue of *Reform Judaism* magazine featured two recommended "significant Jewish books." To my delight, *American Reform Judaism: An Introduction* was selected as one of these suggested books shortly after it was published in 2003. The URJ Press began raising their profile, publishing general interest books on Reform Jewish topics that could be found not only in temple gift shops but also in large chain bookstores such as Barnes and Noble and online on Amazon.com. The URJ also initiated adult educational programs, including innovative efforts such as listservs and podcasts. Many enjoy receiving the daily e-mail "Ten Minutes of Torah."

Reform worship services gradually moved toward a more traditional approach. While they remained optional, *yarmulkes* were seen on many heads—female as well as male—whereas they had been prohibited during the heyday of Classical Reform. Enthusiastic prayer was encouraged, and music became more jubilant. Much of the influence came from the URJ summer camps, as well as the North American Federation of Temple Youth (NFTY). Cantorial music that was listened to by an audience was quickly going out of style. Instead, congregants joined together to sing simple songs that drew from folk, Hasidic, and Israeli musical styles. A new prayer book was introduced in 2007, giving the movement yet another opportunity to create new musical expressions that could accompany prayer services.

Not everyone wanted to return to traditional approaches that had been previously rejected. In order to create a vehicle for the advocacy of a Classical Reform approach to Reform Judaism, the Society for Classical Reform Judaism (SCRJ) was established on January 31, 2008. There already was an organization for Classical Reform Jews called the American Council for Judaism, but some felt it focused too much on anti-Zionism rather than promoting positive Jewish religious values. Rabbi Howard A. Berman, the longtime leader of Chicago Sinai Congregation, became the first executive director of the new organization. He began advocating strongly for the continued relevance of the nontraditional ceremonialism of Classical Reform. "For every one of the 'many people [that] had an emotional need for Judaic rituals and ceremonies,' there are hundreds for whom this is not meaningful or attractive." This is not only the explicitly lifelong Classical Reform Jews but also "a broad variety of the thousands of young Jews today who are clearly not attracted to the neo-traditionalism of either Reform or Orthodoxy." Berman emphasizes that "for every hand-clapping, tallit-shrouded, 'lai-lai-lai' chanter in our Reform pews, and for every younger *baal teshuvah* who is drawn to the cultish appeal of *Chabad*, there remain tens of thousands of Jews who will never cross the thresholds of either setting."

The leaders of the SCRJ believe that many of these alienated Jews would be attracted to "a renewed, rational, inclusive, accessible, spiritually deep, faith-centered Classical Reform option—particularly as reinterpreted in a contemporary aesthetic." They believe that their revised prayer book, *The Union Prayer Book-Sinai Edition*, is an important part of their appeal, providing "the reverential spirituality of historic Reform liturgy recast in modern—but still artful and elegant—English." In addition, contemporary Classical Reform services can offer "a balanced mix of both the great, stirring Reform music as well as contemporary musical variations that offer a forthright embrace of both Hebrew and English"[18]

In their mission statement, the SCRJ leaders explain their fundamental principles. "We are committed to the preservation and creative nurturing of the historic ideals of Classical Reform Judaism with its progressive spiritual values, rich intellectual foundations, and distinctive worship traditions." They state that among these values is "the centrality of the American experience in our Jewish identity" as well as "an affirmation of our faith's prophetic vision of peace and social justice for all people." They emphasize that "we believe that Classical Reform, which embodies its own integrity and enduring significance in the midst of the many rich streams of Jewish experience through the ages, has a continuing vitality and potential to speak to a new generation of Jews today."[19]

During Yoffie's presidency, the URJ expanded the summer camp program while neglecting NFTY. In fact, Yoffie acknowledged in a speech to the UAHC board in Memphis as early as December 1998 that NFTY was "a shadow of its former self." Founded in 1939, NFTY was established to help foster commitment to the ideals of Reform Judaism among the youth. Personal and leadership skills were to be developed in a "wholesome" Jewish environment. But as society changed in the 1980s, NFTY—as well as many other youth organizations—became less attractive. Many teenagers in particular refused to participate, dropping out completely after their bar or bat mitzvahs.

In order to build a structure that could more effectively keep youth involved throughout their high school years, Yoffie announced a reorganization of NFTY. Each of the UAHC regions would hire a full-time professional to organize youth programming in that region. It was hoped that this decentralized approach would be more effective than trying to run the entire program from New York. But the UAHC regional directors struggled to develop workable plans and then faced budgetary cutbacks that further complicated their efforts. At his final organizational presentation, Yoffie stressed the need to revamp youth programming, implicitly admitting failure in this crucial area.

The URJ summer camp programs were much more successful, due in large measure to their more intensive 24-7 social experience. Jewish overnight camps are able to give children an immersion in Jewish living that is simply not possible in their daily lives at home. While many children found temple services boring, they lit up with excitement at the prospect of *tefillot* at Camp Eisner or Camp Coleman or any of the other URJ camps. Children could develop their self-esteem in a natural setting while meeting Jewish friends from all over the country and participating in Jewish activities, both formal and informal. Beginning in the summer of 2011, the URJ opened Six Points Sports Academy, a summer camp specializing in sports located on the campus of the American Hebrew Academy in Greensboro, North Carolina. This initiative was in response to the complaint that sports-minded Jewish youth had to choose between a sports camp and a Jewish camp. Now they could have both.

The first UAHC camp in North America was Olin-Sang-Ruby Union Institute (OSRUI) in Oconomowoc, Wisconsin. OSRUI began in the late 1940s as a series of weekend retreats for young people in the Chicago area. A group of Chicago rabbis found a two-hundred-acre property in Oconomowoc and solicited three philanthropists who agreed to provide the money for purchasing the land. Rather than use the same services that were then ubiquitous at Reform temples at the time, the rabbis decided to allow the campers to have a central role in developing creative liturgy for their own worship experiences. Many of the most creative Shabbat services were edited—and sometimes even written—at one of the summer camps.

The most important impact that the camps had on mainstream Reform Judaism was their nurturing of new forms of religious song. In the early years of OSRUI, the music was mostly folk songs and civil rights movement chants. Judah Cohen, professor of folklore and ethnomusicology at Indiana University, explains that those songs, which lacked overt Jewish content, "were considered to have religious significance in that they embodied Reform principles." OSRUI eventually supplemented the political chants with classical Reform compositions, traditional Jewish liturgical works, and what became a new style of American Jewish folk music. In 1970 they hired a then unknown Debbie Friedman as a song leader. As Cohen explains, "A new genre of music was coming to the fore. It was a Reform Jewish genre of music, songs that were mainly liturgical, written by [camp] song leaders. She [Friedman] brought her tunes and her compositions to the camp and helped to empower a whole generation in this region."[20]

Friedman, called "the Joan Baez of Jewish song" by the *Forward*, began song-leading for her synagogue youth group in 1968 and then attended a songleader workshop at the Kutz Camp Institute in Warwick, New York. Soon she was writing her own songs, although she never learned to read music and had taught herself to play the guitar by copying what she heard on the records of Peter, Paul, and Mary. "I taught it [her new songs] to a group of kids who were doing a creative service with James Taylor, Joan Baez, and Judy Collins music. Not only did they sing the *V'ahavta*, they stood arm in arm. They were moved; they were crying. Here was something in a genre to which they could relate." In 1972 she recorded *Sing unto God*, an album of Sabbath songs that featured a high school choir. "I had planned to [only] make a demo tape, but when I found out it would cost only $500 more to make 1,000 LPs, I thought, why not? They sold like hot cakes at camp. That's how it started. It was a fluke."

Friedman, who never studied in cantorial school, began working as a songleader in Chicago and then as a cantorial soloist in California. She began performing concerts and recorded additional albums, which were sold at her performances. Soon her melodies began to be used in synagogue services. Perhaps her most famous creation is *Mi Sheberach*, which was composed for a *simcha chachma*, a celebration of wisdom, to honor a friend on her sixtieth birthday. The prayer is used to offer the hope of healing for those suffering. First introduced at the UAHC Biennial in San Francisco in 1993, this tune has become the most popular adopted liturgical melody in recent decades. "My friend was having a very difficult time in her life and a number of her friends were also struggling. Yet she had arrived at this age and was determined to embrace it."

Friedman herself had a neurological condition since 1988 and believed that this had inspired her to tap into the healing power of communal prayer. "Being in a community helps people deal with their pain. Oftentimes, when we're ill or depressed we feel spiritually wounded. We withdraw, we isolate, and we leave ourselves out in the cold. During healing services, individuals—sometimes hundreds of people—stand together; share time, song, and prayer; and acknowledge that we're grieving, we're in pain, and we're in solidarity." Friedman believes that the music can help sustain people in times of trouble. "We're not seeking miracles, we're not casting away our crutches—we're finding a way to deal with the fact that we might not be able to put them down. We literally take the readings and music into our bodies to sustain us through the trauma. So much singing and spirit come from the pain."[21]

Friedman emphasized congregational participation, which stemmed from her early observation that Judaism had become something that was watched rather than done. "One night I went to synagogue, and realized, sitting there, I was bored," she told the *Los Angeles Times* in 1995. "I realized the rabbi was talking, the choir was singing and nobody was doing anything. There was no participation."[22] Her music helped break down that barrier, advocating the idea that the cantor should lead congregational singing rather than perform operatic solos. But her influence was felt in all parts of the Reform synagogue service, promoting participation, egalitarianism, inclusivity, and informality.

Despite the more accessible music and greater interaction, most congregations struggled to attract congregants to services. Many members joined in order to be affiliated but attended sporadically or only on the High Holy Days. Others joined when their children needed to attend religious school but resigned after their youngest finished their bar or bat mitzvah training. After the stock market crash of October 2008, the financial condition of many congregations became precarious.

The Reform movement was struggling to attract sufficient numbers of new members and was having difficulty maintaining its financial commitments. On February 24, 2009, the Union for Reform Judaism sent out an e-mail announcing that the URJ officers had voted unanimously to recommend that the board of trustees adopt a restructuring plan. Signed by board chairman Peter Weidhorn and president Rabbi Eric Yoffie, the letter emphasized that "the Union is a congregation of congregations." Weidhorn and Yoffie explained that the restructuring plan was based on extensive studies that had been carried out over the course of several years. What they concluded was that congregational leaders did not feel they were receiving the advice that they needed in an efficient and effective manner. The restructuring was designed to better meet the needs of the slightly more than nine hundred Reform congregations in North America by, among other changes, assigning a contact person to each congregation.

Planning for the reorganization had begun in earnest in December 2008, when the October stock market crash had begun to show its full financial impact. But whereas a steady stream of letters from the URJ had emphasized the benefits of restructuring, the talk among congregational leaders was about the dire financial situation the movement was facing. The URJ was planning to close all fourteen of its regional offices, replacing them with congregational support centers in only four cities. The organization would lay off about sixty full-time employees (the number was later increased to over eighty) in order to save about five million dollars, roughly 20 percent of their annual budget.

Yoffie tried to put a positive spin on the bad news. He stated that it was "a moment to put into place a structure that better meets the needs of our congregations while also positioning us to lead a healthy, vibrant Reform movement in the years and decades ahead."[23] But many wondered whether the restructuring was an effort to make the movement more efficient or whether it was the first concrete indication that the URJ was beginning a dramatic decline.

Within weeks, the impact of the URJ budget cuts on HUC-JIR became apparent. Since its founding in the late nineteenth century, HUC had received a great deal of its financial support from the URJ. Because of de-

10. Rabbi David Ellenson, president of Hebrew Union College–Jewish Institute of Religion, awards the 2008 Roger E. Joseph Prize to Father Patrick Desbois, who "devoted his life to confronting antisemitism, furthering Catholic-Jewish relations, and preserving Holocaust memory." The award was presented during HUC-JIR Ordination and Investiture Services at Congregation Emanu-El of the City of New York on Sunday, May 4, 2008. "Father Desbois's mission reinforces our own commitment to combat all forms of racial, ethnic, and religious hatred and to advance the cause of education, tolerance, and human rights for all." *Photo by Richard Lobell. Courtesy of HUC-JIR.*

clining revenue from its congregations, the URJ had been forced to cut back the amount it was planning to send to HUC. This cutback, combined with the decline in its endowment, increasing pension liabilities, and other financial setbacks, created a potential eight-million-dollar deficit. The future looked increasingly dismal as HUC began debating the merits of closing two of the three stateside campuses. Ultimately, none of the campuses were closed, the budget was cut, but the institution was able to raise substantial revenue and continue business as usual.

In March 2010, Yoffie told the URJ Executive Committee, "I am optimistic about the future of our Movement and its institutions." HUC, CCAR, URJ, and the individual congregations will work together to build a strong movement. The leaders of Reform Judaism will "speak to the deepest needs of our members and inject our Movement with new energy, identity and purpose. We will address the future with optimism and hope. And Reform Judaism—our Judaism—will emerge stronger than it has ever been."[24]

On June 10, 2010, Yoffie announced that he would retire from his position in June 2012. A search committee was assembled and candidates were encouraged to send in their applications. Insiders have suggested that the search committee had already set their sights on Rabbi Rick Jacobs of the Westchester Reform Temple in Scarsdale, New York. This was due in part to the consensus that the next URJ president needed to be someone who already had been networking with the leaders of the New York Jewish community and had established strong working relations. They felt that someone from outside the New York area would not have the time to build the necessary connections and would be handicapped in his or her fund-raising efforts.

Jacobs had led the Brooklyn Heights Synagogue from 1982 to 1991 and had then become senior rabbi of the Westchester Reform Temple. He had served as a member of many boards and committees within the Reform movement, including the UAHC board of trustees, the editorial board of *Reform Judaism* magazine, the executive committee of the CCAR, the Governance Task Force of the CCAR, the board of ARZA, the board of the World Union for Progressive Judaism, the Joint Commission on Religious Living, and the Joint Commission on Worship.

In the broader Jewish community, he had been on the boards of a number of organizations such as the UJA–Federation of New York and the American Jewish World Service. He was also a member of the J Street Rabbinic Cabinet, a member of the board of directors of the New Israel Fund, chair of its "Pluralism Grants Committee," and cochair of its Rabbinical Council. His association with what were seen as far-left-wing organizations dealing with Israel upset a small percentage of Jewish leaders, most of whom were not affiliated with the Reform movement.

In late April 2011, a group calling itself Jews Against Divisive Leadership published an ad in the Los Angeles *Jewish Journal* and the *Forward*. "We are Reform Jews who want the Reform movement to stand with Israel." The text pointed out that Jacobs's organizational affiliations placed him outside what was seen to be American Jewish consensus positions on how best to support the State of Israel. Virtually all the leaders of the Reform movement rallied to his defense, citing his summer study at the Shalom Hartman Institute in Jerusalem and his clearly demonstrated involvement with Israel and Israeli issues. He gave a speech at the Religious Action Center in Washington DC designed to reinforce his Zionist credentials and quietly resigned from the boards of the two problematic organizations.

At the URJ Biennial in Washington DC in December 2011, Jacobs told the attendees: "We are poised at one of the most critical and dramatic crossroads in all of Jewish history. If we stay put and leave things as they are we will have failed the test of Jewish leadership. But we're not going to stay put. We are the Reform Movement and we're going to get MOVING. We're going to MOVE forward with strength and creativity."[25] He announced that the URJ, HUC-JIR, and the CCAR had formed a joint task force "to figure out the best, most effective, most fair and transparent way for us to finance our Movement's holy work." This task force will be reconsidering the structure of funding, in particular the MUM dues system used to assess each congregation based on a complicated formula.

Jacobs set three priorities for his presidency: catalyzing congregational change, engaging the next generation, and extending the circles of responsibility. Acknowledging that many congregations are struggling, Jacobs stated that the URJ would become "a catalyst and convener of best practices by sharing tools, methods and models so every one of our 900 congregations will flourish." He advocated rejecting the model of Hebrew school as a place where children are dropped off in order to absorb enough Jewishness to build a nominal Jewish identity, instead, replacing it with a family-focused educational experience where parents and children pray together and then study alongside one another. Finally, while he admitted that the URJ had "not fully figured out how to engage new members in a lifelong way, because inducing spiritual commitment is no simple matter," we do know that we need to first establish caring relationships before trying to collect dues.

The Reform movement faces many challenges in the coming years. Orthodoxy has been undergoing resurgence at the same time that the non-Orthodox have been experiencing the consequences of assimilation. The Reform movement will need to do a better job in creating attractive programs while developing a compelling religious vision that can motivate large numbers of American Jews. Specifically, the Reform movement will need to explain how it understands the relationship between God, Torah, and Israel in a nonhalachic context. In the next chapter, we look at three examples of how Reform Judaism has taken traditional practices and reinterpreted not only their religious meaning but how they might be observed.

CHAPTER 3

To Observe or Not to Observe?

Toward the end of the second decade of the nineteenth century, Hungarian rabbi Eliezer Liebermann published two small works that justified ritual reforms from a halachic perspective. He had recently moved to Berlin, where he gravitated to the recently formed Reform congregation. Little is known about Liebermann, but he appeared to have a substantial rabbinic education. This allowed him to write responsa justifying the relatively minor innovations that had already been implemented in the Berlin temple. Liebermann put together two small manuscripts, published together in Dessau in 1818.

Nogah Ha-Tsedek (The Radiance of Justice) was the first collection of responsa in favor of certain Reform innovations ever published. Liebermann collected four halachic essays, written by two Italian and two Hungarian rabbis, supporting specific practices. The two Italian rabbis argued that it was acceptable to play organ music in a synagogue. While admitting that Jews had copied this idea from Christians, one of the Italians wrote that copying a gentile custom was prohibited only when the desire to copy non-Jewish practices that was the primary purpose of the innovation. Therefore, in this case, introducing organ music was not a violation of the prohibition in Leviticus, "You shall not follow their customs" (18:3), because the main goal was not assimilation but simply to bring beautiful music into the synagogue. Furthermore, since the Levites had played musical instruments in the Temple in Jerusalem, the Christians had learned this from the Jews, and so the Jews were just restoring a practice that had originated in ancient Judaism.

Liebermann wrote the second manuscript, which he called *Or Nogah*

(Radiant Light). In this essay, he argued that some of the prayers should be recited in German because many of the Jews in Berlin could no longer understand Hebrew. This position did not violate the halacha because the Talmud clearly states that Jews can pray to God in any language. He criticized the German Jews who were putting a great deal of time and money into teaching their children secular studies but could not find the energy for the teaching of Hebrew and other Judaic studies. Liebermann noted that partially as a result, some of those attending services sat in their seats without a prayer book, not making any attempt to participate in the service. Yet Liebermann was impressed by how the Berlin temple was able to attract assimilated Jews who for many years had not been involved in Jewish religious activities. He saw the Reform temple as a moderating influence between the fervently Orthodox and the advocates of radical assimilation.

The responsa edited by Liebermann supporting specific Reform innovations began a tradition of Reform halachic analysis that continues to this day. The Central Conference of American Rabbis established a responsa committee to study specific issues such as cremation and write reports determining whether these practices would be acceptable from the Reform point of view. Nevertheless, the vast majority of Reform Jews quickly moved beyond the need to justify their religious practices. They did what they wanted, and they had little concern for how it would be seen from a halachic point of view.

Those who wanted to develop a Reform halacha hoped to undertake a scholarly investigation of historical precedents with the idea of discovering how Jews could adapt Jewish law to the demands of modernity. They saw the halacha as an ethical system that found ingenious ways to respond to the particular social conditions of each generation. Jewish law was binding but at the same time flexible, and evolved in response to a given set of circumstances.

According to this understanding of the historical process, halachic development began to fossilize in the early modern period. Therefore, the original reformers were simply presenting legal innovations that were long overdue. Changes in the halacha were based on the reinterpretation of ancient texts, employing the halachic principles upon which the system was established. The reformers, in this view, were not religious nihilists determined to destroy everything in their path, but rather, thoughtful and balanced scholars advocating appropriate innovation at a time of rapid social change.

These reformers objected to Orthodoxy's claim that the halacha was immutable, fixed for all time. They felt that the rabbinic authorities had become progressively more extreme, insisting that nothing could be changed in the halacha. It mattered not whether contemporary circumstances required new approaches or whether individual conscience compelled people to act contrary to established norms. Regardless of any other factor, the halacha could not be changed; all Jews were bound to the Torah as given from God to Moses at Mount Sinai. The progressive halachic experts wanted to create a more flexible halachic approach. Perhaps unfortunately, within a short time, this halachic approach to Reform faded away in favor of the radical rejection of the entire system of Jewish law.

As the Reform movement coalesced by the 1840s, a consensus developed that human beings had played a great role in the redaction of the written Torah and the development of the oral Torah. God was an inspiration for these central texts and remained the central focus of religious concern, but the sages transmitting the tradition did not have absolute religious authority. The sacred texts, including the Five Books of Moses, are of tremendous religious significance but do not necessarily require us to follow the laws as literally set down in them. Rather, Reform Jews have religious autonomy. They are expected to explore the tradition and come up with their own individual religious sensibility, embracing certain practices as religiously meaningful while rejecting others as redundant or antiquarian.

Referring specifically to Reform Judaism in the United States, HUC-JIR professor Eugene B. Borowitz has divided this religious freedom into two overlapping periods. He writes that from the beginning of the nineteenth century to the late 1920s, there was a period of negative freedom. During this time, "liberal Jews gloried in their right *not to do* what prior Jews had considered mandatory." From the late 1920s and especially from the late 1960s, there has been a time of positive freedom. During this phase, "liberals utilized religious self-determination *to add to* their religious observance."[1] This is obviously a gross simplification, but it makes a point. Reform thinkers want to emphasize that religious autonomy can lead to creative engagement with the tradition and not just a blanket rejection of ancient laws.

The reformers argued that if the sages had developed specific laws as responses to social conditions, then halacha could be changed as those conditions changed. Yet there was never complete agreement over how to relate to ritual observance. By the middle of the nineteenth century, opinions varied widely. If one understood Judaism as having evolved in a revolutionary manner during several key points of its history, then there was every reason to believe that such a point was upon us again.

If Jewish law was not obligatory, then what was the purpose of Judaism? Presumably, the practice of Judaism would help guide the individual toward ethical behavior. People working together could then not only improve themselves but also have a positive impact on society. What would be the source of religious instruction? Traditional religion had seen God as the ultimate giver of all ethical and moral teachings. But many nineteenth-century rationalists believed that human beings possessed an autonomous sense of ethics and morals. Immanuel Kant in particular had argued that people should use their autonomous will to choose the ethical option. The only activity that could be called pleasing to God, he reasoned, is activity that is morally and ethically beneficial in this world. But how can people determine what constitutes positive behavior? Reason. By exercising human reason, enlightened people could free themselves from the shackles of external authority. Individuals could therefore derive the principles that they needed to live ethically through the use of reason. They did not need any form of revealed religion nor any externally imposed set of religious laws.

Many Reform Jews would agree with Kant's critique of religion but nevertheless would argue that Judaism offers a great deal of religious wisdom that cannot be found elsewhere. They were, however, conscious of the need to change or even eliminate certain biblical and Talmudic laws that did not reflect contemporary understandings of ethical behavior. For example, the biblical laws concerning *mamzerut* placed restrictions on the marriage possibilities of a child born of an adulterous or incestuous union. Contemporary ethicists would find it unconscionable that the innocent victim would suffer legal consequences for the actions of his or her parents.

Despite the importance of updating certain biblical and Talmudic laws to reflect contemporary ethical concerns, the great majority of attention has focused on reinterpreting traditional ritual practices. The reason for this is that Reform Jews accept as axiomatic the idea that ethics is universal; what they need is a guide on ceremonial practice. To be sure, the Reform rabbi was expected to preach on ethics, but it was understood that the rabbi's understanding of ethics would be entirely consistent with mainstream opinion. The big question was how Reform Jews should observe daily ritual practices, sanctify holy days, and celebrate life-cycle events. Let us look at one example from each of these three categories.

Kashrut

Reform Judaism is well known for its rejection of the dietary laws, called in Hebrew *kashrut*. Rabbi Isaac Mayer Wise, the founder and builder of the early Reform movement in nineteenth-century America, used to refer to the traditionalists as practitioners of "kitchen Judaism." By this he meant they were so worried about what was going on in their kitchens that they did not pay sufficient attention to what was going on in the rest of their lives. He was not necessarily recommending that Reform Jews cease practicing all dietary restrictions. Wise himself had started off observing them all and even after he became a vigorous advocate of Reform continued to observe many of the kosher practices. Nevertheless, he and many others in the Reform movement felt that the emphasis needed to be shifted from pointless obsession with what goes into one's mouth, to greater concern over the words that come out of one's mouth.

In traditional Judaism, eating was regulated through an elaborate system of laws and customs. Many of these laws are set forth in the Torah itself and are expanded upon in the Talmud and other rabbinic writings. All fruits and vegetables are permitted because it is written in the Torah, "See, I give you every seed-bearing plant that is upon all the earth, and every tree that has seed-bearing fruit; they shall be yours for food" (Genesis 1:29). God expected humans to be vegetarians until the time of Noah, when humans were first allowed to eat meat, with the restriction that they should not consume blood (Genesis 9:3). After the children of Israel left Egypt, they were given a much more detailed list of permitted and prohibited foods (Leviticus 11:1–43).

The Torah divides animals into two categories, clean and unclean. When Noah was preparing to board the ark, God commanded him to take with him seven pairs of every clean animal and two pairs of every unclean animal. The reason why certain animals were clean and others unclean was not explained, although it appears to be related to categories of ritual purity rather than basic hygiene.

Over the past two hundred years, scholars and nonscholars alike have speculated why the Torah prohibited the eating of certain foods. Some Reform Jews believe that the entire system of kashrut was developed for health reasons, and since we no longer need to worry about trichinosis in pork or contaminated shellfish, we can eat whatever we want. Others believe that even if health was part of the original justification, there are other reasons that make the continued observance of at least some of the food restrictions spiritually worthwhile.

A four-legged animal must chew its cud and have cloven hooves in order to be kosher (Leviticus 11:3, Deuteronomy 14:6–8). The Torah lists ten animals that meet both of these criteria, including deer, goat, and sheep. The camel, hare, and hyrax chew their cud but have only partially split hooves. The pig has a completely cloven hoof but does not chew its cud.

While the Torah does not single out the pig from other nonkosher animals, pork has become a symbol of nonkosher meat, and some Reform Jews still abstain from pork although they may not observe any of the other dietary restrictions. This may be due to the fact that the Syrian Greeks tried to force us to eat pork as a way to destroy Jewish opposition to radical Hellenization. Refraining from the eating of pork became a symbol of the expression of Jewish solidarity.

The Torah likewise sets forth requirements for what constitutes a kosher fish; they need fins and scales in order to be clean and therefore

11. The Central Synagogue at 652 Lexington Avenue in Manhattan. Built in 1872 in the Moorish Revival style, the building is meant to bring to mind the golden age in Spain when Jews, Muslims, and Christians lived together in peace. The synagogue was built at a time when the Reform movement was moving into its classical phase, rejecting much of traditional ritual as spiritually empty. Virtually all congregants at the time would have eaten virtually all the biblically and talmudically forbidden foods. *Photo by Dana Evan Kaplan.*

permitted (Leviticus 11:9–12). The Torah prohibits the eating of other aquatic animals, such as seals, dolphins, sharks, and whales. Shellfish are also prohibited, including mussels, clams, and oysters, as well as crustaceans, such as shrimp, lobster, and crab.

In contrast to the laws relating to quadrupeds and fish, the Torah does not list any set of criteria for distinguishing between kosher and non-kosher birds. Instead, it simply lists twenty species that are unclean, thereby implying that all other species of birds would be kosher (Leviticus 11:13–19, Deuteronomy 14:11–18). Nevertheless, all birds of prey and birds that are scavengers are prohibited, suggesting that the Torah was following unstated criteria.

To be kosher, animals not only have to be permitted species, but they also have to be ritually slaughtered using a method called *shechitah*. It is written in the Torah, "You may slaughter any of the cattle or sheep . . . as I have instructed you" (Deuteronomy 12:21).

This was believed to have been part of the oral Torah, verbal religious instructions given from God to Moses and passed down from generation to generation. In theory, shechitah is supposed to be the most humane method of killing an animal, preventing all unnecessary suffering. The *shochet* makes one continuous deep horizontal cut with a perfectly sharp blade that has no nicks or cuts whatsoever. The shochet then examines the carcass of the animal to ensure that the major organs are unblemished, as blemishes would render the meat unfit for eating. If certain abnormalities are found, the meat would have to be declared nonkosher and sold to a non-Jew.

Even kosher animal carcasses have parts that are prohibited. Because Jacob wrestled with an angel and injured his thigh in the struggle, the sciatic nerve and its associated blood vessels were deemed to be unfit. As a consequence, it is difficult to make certain prime cuts of steak kosher. Likewise, the fat surrounding the kidneys, liver, stomach, and intestines was forbidden because those organs had been sacrificed on the altar in the Jerusalem Temple.

Kosher meat then has to be prepared for eating through a process called *kashering*, in which all traces of blood are removed by soaking and salting the meat. The Torah explains that it is prohibited to consume blood "for the life of the flesh is in the blood, and I have assigned it to you for making expiation for your lives upon the altar" (Leviticus 17:11). Alternatively, the meat can be roasted or broiled over an open flame, which would be an acceptable substitute for kashering.

The verse "you shall not boil a kid in its mother's milk" (Exodus 23:19, 34:26; Deuteronomy 14:21) was interpreted as meaning that meat could not be eaten with dairy products. Despite the obvious discontinuity between the literal meaning of the biblical verse and the rabbinic interpretation, the prohibition of mixing milk with meat became a characteristic feature of the Jewish dietary laws. Next to pork, and perhaps shellfish, eating a cheeseburger was the epitome of nonkosher dining.

The sages extended the restrictions even further, "building a fence around the Torah" to ensure that none of its core restrictions would be accidentally violated. For example, the sages were concerned that some might eat chicken with milk and then mistakenly believe that it was okay to eat red meat with milk, so they extended the restriction and prohibited the eating of chicken with any milk product. Fish, on the other hand, was seen as so distinctive that no one would mistakenly confuse it with meat, and so it remained permitted to eat fish and milk products together.

Dietary laws were one of the first ritual practices to be jettisoned by many of those breaking away from traditional society. The reason was obvious: strict observance of kashrut makes social integration much more difficult. Also, it was hard to follow all the rules, especially outside an all-encompassing Jewish society.

In the eastern European *shtetl*, everyone followed the regulations and so it was just part of life, but in a cosmopolitan city or out on the frontier, the many rules concerning diet were almost impossible to follow. *Almost* impossible. When I was a little boy visiting my grandparents in Waterbury, Connecticut, people spoke of how one family—the Gellmans—had continued to follow the kosher laws to the letter after most other people had, at the very least, relaxed their level of observance. In Albany, Georgia, one family—the Feinbergs—ordered meat from the kosher butcher in Atlanta, who put it on the Greyhound bus each week. Depending on how many stops it made, and how hot the temperature was, the meat arrived in better or worse condition.

The other reason why most Jews gave up the observance of the dietary laws was that it did not make logical sense. While it was clear to everyone why you should follow the proscription "You shall not steal," it was equally unclear why a person should abstain from eating certain foods or avoid eating them in certain combinations. American Jews were more likely to observe a particular practice if it was reinforced by the norms of the broader society. Since American Christians had no food restrictions, there was no support for those Jews who were trying to observe kashrut.

Certainly kashrut was part of a cultural system in which men and women played dramatically different roles. The women were charged with making a Jewish home, which in large part meant creating a kosher kitchen and serving kosher food that was not only ritually acceptable but also ethnically authentic. Even today, some older Jews will evaluate the food they eat at temple events based on how Jewish it tastes. Real matzah ball soup tastes a certain way, and even if you can come up with various ideas for improving the recipe, you should try to create (actually recreate) a soup that reminds the taster as much as possible of her grandmother's cooking. For cultural Jews, kosher-style became more important than actually following the dietary laws.

Most Reform Jews have ignored the traditional dietary restrictions completely. When I interviewed for associate rabbi at Congregation Emanu-El B'ne Jeshurun in Milwaukee, Wisconsin, the senior rabbi and his wife took me to their social club, where they ordered mussels for the appetizer. I was a bit shocked since I had spent the previous decade studying in Israel and working in South Africa, where such blatant disregard for the dietary laws in public would be regarded as socially inappropriate as well as religiously transgressive.

The senior rabbi ate the mussels because as a Reform Jew he felt he had the right to decide what to eat or not eat regardless of the food laws of the Hebrew Bible and the halachic restrictions of the Talmud. By eating mussels in front of me at a job interview, he was proudly proclaiming that Reform Judaism has modernized the rules in the written Torah to fit the contemporary times. This contrasted dramatically with the mentality in most of the rest of the Jewish world, where even those who no longer felt that kashrut was religiously obligatory would see a rabbi publicly flouting the rules as offensive, a gratuitous stab at the sanctity of the ancient tradition. Letting unnecessary rules gradually slip away was one thing. Deliberately rubbing other people's noses in your repudiation of the entire Jewish eating system was something else entirely.

American Reform Jews were much more radical in their rejection of kashrut than were Progressive Jews in other parts of the world. Reform, Liberal, and Progressive Jews in England, Australia, South Africa, New Zealand, and other English-speaking countries generally live in Jewish communities where the majority—and frequently the vast majority—of Jews affiliate with Orthodoxy. That does not mean they themselves are practicing Orthodox Judaism, because most are not. Nevertheless, they support the Orthodox system of synagogue life and its insistence on the centrality of Jewish law, at least in public observances. Reform Jews in these countries are judged on this basis and as a result feel tremendous pressure to conform as much as possible to communal norms.

Communal norms in the United States were and are still very different. American Jews started developing alternative religious conceptions as early as the 1820s and have a long history of accepting religious pluralism. The Reform movement allowed for individual religious autonomy, and most Reform Jews stopped keeping kosher early on. In 1885 the Pittsburgh Platform codified what became the American Reform position on kashrut and other ritual practices perceived to be antiquated: "We hold that all such Mosaic and Rabbinical laws as regulate diet, priestly purity, and dress originated in ages and under the influence of ideas entirely foreign to our present mental and spiritual state." These laws "fail to impress the modern Jew with a spirit of priestly holiness; their observance in our days is apt rather to obstruct than to further modern spiritual elevation."

This became the working assumption for the Classical Reform temple. What many forgot was that the laws regulating diet were rejected because they were believed to hinder rather than encourage spirituality. It follows that if their assumption were no longer completely true, Reform Jews might want to reconsider their blanket rejection of traditional food restrictions. And that is exactly what has happened. It took many

Temple B'nai Israel Kitchen Policy

Temple B'nai Israel is a Reform Congregation and as such does not require that members keep Kosher. There are many who have come from varied religious backgrounds other than Reform. There are also prospective members and guests who might come from backgrounds other than Reform.

The religious policy committee has made inquiries of other congregations and has consulted the Union for Reform Judaism for guidance and understanding regarding what is appropriate and what is consistent with where Reform Judaism is today.

The common thread among all sources is to have some minimal standards so that everyone is included and everyone feels welcome in our Reform Congregation regardless of their background or observance.

In order to make everyone feel welcome and comfortable, the following policies have been adopted regarding the use of the Temple kitchen and service of food in the Temple.

Whenever food is prepared or served in the Temple, a Kosher style menu is requested. However, the following practices must be observed.

  1. No pork in any form
  2. No shellfish in any form
  3. No mixture of meat & dairy in or on the same dish

Any bringing of food into the Temple should be in keeping with these clearly written guidelines. If there is ever any doubt over what these minimal standards are or any meanings, please contact the President of the Temple or the President of Sisterhood.

12. Many Reform congregations have adopted kitchen policies that restrict the consumption of nonkosher food at synagogue events. Temple B'nai Israel of Albany, Georgia, displays its kitchen policy so that everyone will be aware of what food items are acceptable. So that all members feel "welcome and comfortable," the congregation requests that "a kosher style menu" be maintained. This specifically excludes pork, shellfish, and a mixture of meat and dairy in or on the same dish. *Photo by Dana Evan Kaplan.*

decades, but increasing numbers of Reform Jews began to reevaluate their attitudes toward kashrut and to reconsider long-abandoned practices. As it is said, the grandchild seeks to recover what the grandparent sought to forget.

In 1999 the CCAR returned to Pittsburgh and passed a new platform called "A Statement of Principles for Reform Judaism." Reform Jews "are committed to the ongoing study of the whole array of *mitzvoth* and to the fulfillment of those that address us as individuals and as a community." The paragraph points out that some of these mitzvoth have long been observed by many Reform Jews. Others "demand renewed attention as the result of the unique context of our own times."

One of the "sacred obligations" that has been attracting renewed attention is kashrut. Keeping kosher is so widely seen as one of the hallmarks of Jewish practice that even those who do not observe it at all tend to remark about it. Frequently this happens right after they have ordered pork chops or lobster. "Gee whiz, I'm glad I don't keep kosher." This awareness that—while they do not follow any of the dietary rules— Jewish tradition does set forth certain restrictions is an important part of Jewish ethnic consciousness. A Jew who can eat pork chops without once thinking about how it is not kosher would be pretty assimilated.

Rabbi Richard N. Levy, the former director of the School of Rabbinic Studies at the Hebrew Union College–Jewish Institute of Religion in Los Angeles and the primary author of the 1999 Pittsburgh Platform, has urged Reform Jews to take another look at kashrut and whether it could be meaningful to them. In the third draft of what was then called the "Ten Principles," he included the clause that "some Reform Jews may" observe the kosher laws. Despite the permissive wording, many attacked this draft for pushing what they still felt was an antiquated observance. Levy professes puzzlement, citing his use of the words "some" and "may" rather than "all should" or "Reform Jews must." Clearly, even suggesting that Reform Jews might consider voluntarily following any kind of dietary restrictions still gets a lot of people worked up.

One answer may be that many people who were raised kosher felt that the kosher laws created an unpleasant environment. Everyone had to constantly be careful to avoid ruining the elaborate system of plates and tablecloths and everything else that had to be duplicated, one set for milk and one set for meat. Many of those raised in such kosher homes were determined not to repeat that in their own lives. They wanted the freedom to be able to put a fork down in either sink, left or right! For those who kept strictly kosher in and out of the house, the limitations on *where* one could eat were more onerous than the restrictions on *what* one could eat. Unless the family lived in one of the few very largest cities, there were few kosher restaurants, and hence little opportunity to eat out.

Levy understood this, but he believed that kashrut has important lessons to teach us. "Kashrut is controversial, of course, because it touches one of the most basic elements of life. Our relationship to food begins minutes after we are born, when a baby begins to cry for its mother's breast." Levy argues that since the food habits with which we grow up frequently remain with us for life, this "is one of the reasons to raise children in a kosher home." But in order to transmit positive religious values, "a Reform kosher home must be filled with love and humor and the absence of the stringent obsessiveness that led so many Jews to reject kashrut."[2]

Levy's hope is unlikely to be fulfilled, but a significant number of Reform Jews abstain from pork, the symbol of everything that is non-kosher. Smaller numbers abstain from shellfish and a few avoid eating meat and milk together. There are even some who follow most or even all the kosher regulations while continuing to identify as Reform Jews, but that level of observance is pretty unusual. Most American Jews are not going to start keeping kosher. The system is too complicated, not to mention costly. They also do not want to put themselves at the mercy of the Orthodox rabbis who certify various food products as kosher.

For some progressive thinkers, there may be alternative approaches to kashrut that emphasize contemporary values. Those who want to establish new criteria for what to eat, and what to consume more broadly, are more likely motivated by ethical considerations rather than by legal ones. Rabbi Zalman Schachter-Shalomi, the founding inspiration for the Jewish Renewal movement, has advocated a broadening of the concept of kashrut to include restrictions on consumption based on ecological factors.

Eco-kashrut is a fundamental reconsideration of what we should eat. Improving one's health is one reason. Should it be kosher to eat a diet that has been shown to cause health problems, including high cholesterol and high blood pressure, heart disease and cancer? The way that animals are treated before they are slaughtered, as well as how they are killed, would also be an important criterion. Some avoid eating veal for this reason, but we now know that cows, chickens, and other kosher animals are also susceptible to being mistreated.

The abuse of animals, as well as employees, at Agriprocessors of Postville, Iowa, forced many to confront the unpleasant reality for the first time. Agriprocessors was the largest independent kosher slaughtering facility in the entire country. Reports that the animals were being mistreated prompted Conservative rabbi Morris Allen to urge the creation of a Justice Certification, *Hekhsher Tzedek* (later renamed Magen Tzedek, a Shield of Justice) to indicate that animals were being treated humanely and workers were being employed under appropriate conditions. The Commission on Social Action of Reform Judaism submitted a recommendation that the URJ endorse the concept, which was adopted by the board of trustees in September 2008.

The impact on the environment is another important consideration. Perhaps the same food might be considered eco-kosher if it comes in a large paper box but not eco-kosher if it is wrapped up in plastic in tiny individual units. The important thing is to eat in a way that is socially responsible and reinforces the important lessons we have learned about individual ethics and environmental awareness. While the Reform movement has endorsed this approach, many Reform Jews have been reluctant to act on their principles, reinforcing the prejudices of those who believe that Reform Judaism is a "religion of convenience."

At the URJ Biennial in Toronto in November 2009, Rabbi Eric H. Yoffie spoke about this subject at his Saturday morning sermon, which is the priority-setting speech for the coming two years. He announced an initiative called "Just Table, Green Table," which would be a "commitment to ethical eating." Yoffie asked congregational leaders to "carefully, thoughtfully, Jewishly" formulate eating guidelines for their communities. The URJ published a guide setting out a five-step process that synagogue committees could use to consider the creation of new food policies to promote "healthy, sustainable, ethical eating."[3]

Shabbat

Shabbat had always been the cornerstone of Jewish observance. As the Zionist thinker Ahad Ha'Am put it, more than the Jew has kept the Sabbath, the Sabbath has kept the Jew. The Reform movement has given individual Jews the religious justification to stop observing Shabbat as understood by the Talmud and halachic codes. The movement has not been able to clearly communicate an alternative vision with sufficient detail.

The concept of Shabbat and a holy day generally has become more compelling for some Reform Jews in recent years. We work so hard that many of us have forgotten how to stop and take a moment to reflect. I travel frequently and am amazed to see all the people in airports with their smartphones furiously typing out messages with their thumbs, determined to get off that final e-mail before the flight attendants make them shut it off. We have a certain compulsion to work as hard as humanly possible. You could even call it an obsession, and in many cases, an addiction. Ten years ago if you had said that you were diagnosed with workaholism, people would have laughed, but now it is recognized as a serious problem requiring immediate psychological counseling.

And it is not only in the United States. Recently, a Toyota executive dropped dead from overwork. He was only forty-five years old, but he was putting in eighty hours of overtime per month, on top of the already long Japanese workweek. The strain on his body was just too much. Clearly, many of us need balance in our lives. We need to step back and learn to appreciate the intangibles that life offers which cannot be measured in monetary terms. But in order to do that, we need a framework. Shabbat can provide the structure within which we can stop, relax, reevaluate, and refresh.

The concept of Shabbat is embedded in the very first story of the Hebrew Bible. The Torah begins with a description of the creation of the world. Reform Judaism would not take this description as literally true, but that does not mean we have nothing to learn from it. According to

13. Since it was founded in 1854 by a small group of German immigrants as the first permanent Jewish house of worship in Tennessee, Temple Israel, located on thirty-plus beautiful acres in Memphis, has grown into a vibrant and modern Reform Jewish synagogue that now serves sixteen hundred member families as a place to gather, worship, learn, and deepen Jewish identity and commitment. The sanctuary, pictured here in 2011, is always filled to capacity for the High Holy Days, including Yom Kippur. On Shabbat, most Reform congregations draw only a small fraction of their membership to services. *Photo by Isti Bardos.*

the book of Genesis, God created the world in six days and then rested on the seventh. God blessed the day and declared it holy (Genesis 2:1–3). We, who are told to strive to imitate God, should therefore work six days and rest on the seventh. In addition to being a celebration of the creation of the world, the Sabbath, God proclaimed, should be an everlasting sign of God's divine covenant with the Jewish people (Exodus 31:13, 17).

The wording concerning Shabbat is phrased differently in the two texts of the Ten Commandments—in one version we are commanded to "observe" the Sabbath and in the other we are commanded to "remember" it. Shabbat is, according to the fourth commandment, a reminder of our having been freed from slavery in Egypt (Deuteronomy 5:15). Slaves have to work all the time, and if they do have a little bit of time to rest, it is completely at the discretion of their owner. Observing the Sabbath is a way of showing that we are free and voluntarily follow God's commandment to observe the Sabbath.

In Orthodox Judaism, Shabbat observance requires punctilious attention to a myriad of laws. While the Bible does not enumerate a complete list of prohibited activities, it does refer to field labor (Exodus 34:21, Numbers 15:32–36), treading in a winepress and loading animals (Nehemiah 13:13–15), doing business and carrying (Isaiah 58:13, Jeremiah 17:22, Amos 8:5), traveling (Exodus 16:29–30), and kindling fire (Exodus 35:2–3). In the book of Exodus (34:21), it is written that "six days you shall work, but on the seventh day you shall cease from labor." The verse continues, emphasizing that "you shall cease from labor even at plowing time and harvest time."

The mishnah lists thirty-nine prohibited categories of work, based on the types of labor related to the construction of the tabernacle in the wilderness. These thirty-nine *avot melacha* are derived by the sages from the fact that the text dealing with the tabernacle is juxtaposed to the text dealing with Shabbat. The sages therefore deduced that the acts that must be done in order to construct the tabernacle are the very same acts that must be avoided on Shabbat. In addition, the sages prohibited many additional activities in order to "put a fence around the Torah." They felt that in order to ensure the Sabbath was not desecrated, it would be prudent to abstain from activities that might lead to doing any of the thirty-nine categories of prohibited work. To give just one example, they forbade climbing trees because it might lead to the breaking of branches or the ripping of leaves.

Orthodox Jews do not use electricity on Shabbat. They may benefit from its use by setting electrical timers before Shabbat starts, but they cannot turn light switches on or off or operate any type of electric device once the Sabbath has started on Friday at sundown. In order to open their refrigerator, they will unscrew the lightbulb inside before Shabbat to avoid unintentionally "kindling a fire." They are allowed to violate any of the Sabbath restrictions in order to save a life, but otherwise are obligated to observe them under all circumstances.

The Reform movement restructured the various Jewish observances, including Shabbat, to make them easier to practice in a modern Western society. Without much debate, they dropped most of the traditional Sabbath prohibitions. They felt that such restrictions were not practical because of numerous social, economic, technological, and personal reasons, and there was no need to engage in an extensive debate on something so obvious. Rather than a process of carefully discussing the nature of the Sabbath and drawing up new rules to replace the halacha, there was a gradual evolution resulting in an informal consensus over what the Sabbath meant in Reform Judaism.

The observance of the Sabbath in Reform Judaism was discussed during the Breslau Conference of 1846. Twenty-six rabbis met for twelve days to discuss issues relating to the new religious movement they were in the process of building. Rabbi Abraham Geiger had been appointed chairman of a committee charged with researching the concept of the Sabbath and had submitted a report before the Frankfurt Conference held the previous year, but the rabbis had not had time to debate the subject. They had therefore resolved to defer discussion of this important subject until the following year.

The debate in Breslau is remembered primarily because of the position taken by Rabbi Samuel Holdheim. Holdheim argued that in a gentile society, it was no longer possible to observe the Sabbath on its historically proper day. Therefore it would be preferable to move it to Sunday. Few of the other rabbis present supported Holdheim's proposal, and instead they adopted a resolution urging Jews to celebrate the Sabbath as a day of consecration through both communal worship and home observance. They did not get into the details of what it might mean to observe Shabbat in a Reform manner. Even more troubling, they could not solve the central conundrum: how can Reform Jews observe the Sabbath when they need to work on that day?

The observance of the Sabbath faced a great many difficulties. Saturday was a workday in Germany and in the United States, and since many Jews owned businesses or worked for a business, they had to be at work on Saturdays. Whereas the Sabbath technically started on Friday before sundown and continued through Saturday until nightfall, in the Reform temple it was contracted to a single hour on Friday evening. Rabbi Bernhard Felsenthal, one of the early Reform leaders in Chicago, explained the problem: "In the Jewish world of America there exists a widespread evil, namely, that Sabbath and holidays which ought to be dedicated to the life of the spirit are also used as business days, and thereby these days miss their purpose altogether."

Felsenthal reported that some people did visit the synagogue to attend religious services for an hour during the morning, "but then they hurry into their stores or offices and attend to their business." Felsenthal wrote: "This is wrong. Throughout the week life is like a wild and restless Sambatyon [a raging mythical river with dangerous rapids]. Should there be one occasion when after the rush and turmoil of the week when rest and peace and meditation will have their turn?"[4] The goal of the Sabbath, Felsenthal explained, was to serve as an island of peace in between the busy and tumultuous workweek that was and the equally difficult week to come. But, the rabbi complained, most men refuse to stop doing business on the Holy Sabbath. He condemned this widespread practice in the strongest terms. In fact, he called it "evil." Of course, Felsenthal worked on the Sabbath as well—he was a rabbi!

The Reform temple encouraged attendance at Shabbat services as much as possible, whether members were working on the Sabbath or not. Rabbi Isaac Mayer Wise is credited with coming up with the idea of the late Friday night service. In a traditional synagogue, services would be held on Friday shortly before sunset. The afternoon prayers would be recited and then there might be a short recess. At the appropriate time, the Kabbalat Shabbat service, filled with beautiful, mystical poetry that was frequently sung, would bring in the Sabbath queen. Finally, the evening service would be recited, and the worshipers—mostly or entirely men—would go home to join their families at the Sabbath table.

This structure no longer worked effectively for most families. They were working virtually up to the minute Sabbath began and in many cases beyond, and it was very difficult for the men to get to synagogue at the appropriate time. Wise felt that if the men could not get to services at 5:00 or 5:30 p.m., especially in the winter when the Sabbath started early, why not let them go home and have dinner with their families and then they could all come together? Not only would it be easier for the men to find time for communal prayer, but it could provide a vehicle for encouraging the rest of the family to come, too. The late family service was an instant success and became very popular. Later, when the Conservative movement started to grow, many of its congregations likewise adopted the same strategy.

Wise began an abbreviated Torah service on Friday nights so that those who did not come on Saturday mornings would hear the reading of the Torah. The ark would be opened and the Torah taken out and placed on a reader's desk. The rabbi would recite the blessings and would read and perhaps translate a small selection from that week's Torah portion. Then the Torah would be returned to the ark, the doors closed, and the rabbi would deliver a sermon, which might focus on an idea from that week's *parsha*. This provided the congregation with religious inspiration from Jewish sources.

The Friday night service became the main service of the week in most Reform temples. Saturday morning services continued, but it was frequently incorporated into the Sabbath school, the religious education program for children that was sponsored by the congregation. Some rabbis kept detailed records of attendance at the Shabbat morning service, even listing the number of men and women who attended apart from the children, who were obviously required to be there. Suffice it to say that the numbers of adults coming to pray was rather modest. In Albany, Georgia, to cite one example, the temple moved the Sabbath school to Sunday shortly after the end of World War II. Without the children to provide the bulk of the worshippers, Saturday morning services were soon cancelled entirely.

Toward the end of the nineteenth century, a number of the more radical Reform congregations created Sunday services. As has been explained, the traditional Sabbath began on Friday at sunset and continued through Saturday until dark, thereby making Sunday Sabbath services nonsensical. The radicals argued that since the services on the Sabbath were so poorly attended, why not move them to Sunday? Now we have to be very careful to understand exactly what was being suggested. There were a few rabbis at the really far left end of the spectrum who actually wanted to move the Sabbath from Saturday to Sunday. If the Sabbath is a symbolic day of rest, then what real difference would it make if it was on Sunday instead of Saturday?

But most Reform Jews—even among the radicals—understood that such a unilateral move could not be implemented without severing Judaism's links with its past. What the majority of the radicals were suggesting, rather, was to supplement the Sabbath services with an additional Sunday service. In reality, they intended the Sunday service to become the best attended and therefore the most important worship service of the week. But technically—the *but* is important—they were not moving or replacing Shabbat. A number of Sunday services became immensely popular, such as Rabbi Emil G. Hirsch's at Chicago Sinai Congregation, but most struggled. Rabbis slowly began to realize that the same congregants who did not want to come to services on Friday night or Saturday morning also did not want to go on Sunday morning. They may not have been working, but it was their only day off, and they desperately wanted to stay home and relax.

Despite the low turnout for services on Shabbat, the question of observance went far beyond synagogue attendance. Those serious about Shabbat observance needed guidance. How was a Reform Jew to observe Shabbat? The CCAR had hoped to provide concrete recommendations as to how temple members should observe the Sabbath. Everyone accepted that Orthodox regulations did not apply, but it was not at all clear what was expected from Reform Jews. The CCAR established a Sabbath Observance Commission to determine what should be done, and in 1904 they issued a report, but the Reform rabbinate could not agree on even basic principles. Many rabbis wanted to give specific recommendations for how the Sabbath should be observed, while others objected to any form of religious authority. What was the meaning of Sabbath observance in a Reform context, particularly in terms of personal observance?

The Reform rabbinate struggled with this question. Shabbat observance was part of the broader question of what kinds of ritual requirements should be made on Reform Jews. Some rabbis, including those who supported an approach called covenant theology, were in favor of developing an authoritative guide for Reform Jews. Tending to be among the most traditional within the Reform movement, they emphasized that Jewish ceremonial practice was essential for nurturing the covenantal relationship with God. Others who were less traditional also felt it was important to publish specific guidelines in order to make it clear what being a Reform Jew involved. But while the vast majority of Reform Jews were interested in guidelines that might help them sort through the various ceremonial options, only a minority was interested in an authoritative code.

A number of rabbis did write guides to observance, but none of the guides were accepted as binding or were even terribly influential. Eventually, the CCAR Sabbath Committee, a successor to the Sabbath Observance Commission, published *A Shabbat Manual: Tadrikh l'Shabbat* in 1972. This was intended to be the beginning of a process that would provide clear guidelines for ceremonial behavior in all areas of Jewish religious life. The guidebook, edited by Rabbi W. Gunther Plaut, listed five purposes for the observance of Shabbat, which "represent the core of Jewish existence as expressed in sh'mirat Shabbat, Sabbath observance."

The first purpose was an awareness of the world. "The observance of Shabbat affords us a singular opportunity to reflect upon the marvel of the universe which God has created, to rejoice in the glory and beauty of creation, and to consider our part in God's continuing process of creation." The second purpose was a commitment to freedom and a "memorial of the exodus from Egypt," reflecting the fourth commandment in the book of Deuteronomy. Shabbat is a time to remember our historic commitment to freedom and justice. This means that "as God delivered us from slavery so must we strive to help all who suffer from every form of bondage and degradation in the world."

The third purpose is identification with the Jewish people. "On Shabbat, we have a weekly opportunity to remember God's covenant (b'rit) with Israel and to reaffirm our identity with, and loyalty to, the house of Israel." The guidebook explained, "It calls upon each Jew to help further the high and noble purposes of the community and to use the precious hours of the Shabbat to deepen the unique historic fellowship of the Jewish people."

The fourth purpose provides three models for the enhancement of personal life: *k'dushah* (holiness), *m'nuchah* (rest), and *oneg* (joy). K'dushah requires that Shabbat "be distinguished from the other days of the week so that those who observe it will become transformed by its holiness." Reform Jews "ought, therefore, to do certain things which contribute to an awareness of this day's special nature, and to abstain from doing other which lessen our awareness." M'nuchah "is more than relaxation and abstention from work." It is "a condition of the soul, a physical and spiritual release from weekday pressures." Oneg "is more than fun and pleasure." This is "the kind of joy that enhances our personal lives and leaves us truly enriched" so that there is a "quantity of 'free' time" during which "man can be himself and do for himself and for others what he could never accomplish during other days of the week." The final purpose is a dedication to peace. "Shabbat can become a foundation of human reconciliation, for as we observe it and remember its purposes, we—and thereby the world—will have made a turning toward peace."[5]

The manual was careful to balance the approaches of traditionalists and nontraditionalists. While it avoided suggesting that Jewish law was obligatory, the text asserted that God "offers an opportunity to introduce an 'ought' into our existence," suggesting that Reform Jews should feel a commitment to observe many of the rituals of Shabbat. While it left open the theological justification that individual Reform Jews might offer, it stressed the normative aspect of the mitzvoth, including the Sabbath prohibitions. Treading carefully, the CCAR published *Gates of Mitzvah: A Guide to the Jewish Life Cycle* and then *Gates of the Seasons: A Guide to the Jewish Year*, both of which were designed to provide Reform Jews with guidelines for recommended practice.

A Shabbat Manual was updated by the CCAR and published in 1991 with an audiotape of Shabbat music under the title *Gates of Shabbat: A Guide for Observing Shabbat*. The workbook included a hodgepodge of material, including various prayers to be recited at home as well as at synagogue, readings and meditations, excerpts from essays on religious themes, and a short section devoted to establishing the definitions for work and rest on Shabbat. The revised manual describes three Reform Jews: the Walker, the Museumgoer, and the Painter, each of whom developed his own philosophy for the observance of Shabbat. The text explains how they developed their unique approaches, emphasizing that all three "are authentic Reform Jews because the decisions they reach are made with sincerity, commitment, and a desire to draw on the resources of Judaism in order to enrich contemporary life."[6]

Since different people will want to express their individual spirituality, the Sabbath can be observed in ways that are personally meaningful. These observances do not have to conform to the traditional halachic categories and may even involve the violation of one or more of the thirty-nine *melacha*, the prohibited categories of work.

For example, if someone really enjoys knitting and finds it relaxing, she might spend part of her Shabbat afternoon making a sweater for her nephew. While this would be strictly prohibited in an Orthodox context because it breaks a prohibition, it is acceptable in Reform Judaism because it would be *menuchah*, Sabbath rest.

Rabbi Mark Washofsky suggests that activities done *li-kavod Shabbat*, in honor of the Sabbath, might be permitted even if they involve traditionally prohibited actions. It might therefore be in the spirit of Shabbat to drive to a museum and pay the admission fee because doing that would "refresh the soul." On the other hand, we might want to avoid visiting the mall because window shopping and buying commercial goods immerses us in the weekday world that we are trying to remove ourselves from on the Sabbath day.[7]

In recent years, some Reform rabbis have tried emphasizing the obligatory nature of Sabbath observance, arguing that the masses of Reform Jews need specific instructions. They fear that without better direction, huge numbers of Reform Jews are unable to articulate a rationale for Shabbat observance, and Saturday ends up becoming just another day. Without question, there is tremendous societal pressure to engage in secular Saturday activities, including organized sports, civic group meetings, and most of all, shopping.

At the 2007 URJ Biennial, Yoffie urged Reform Jews to reclaim Saturday morning for Shabbat. He urged Reform Jews to consider attending Saturday morning services and suggested that congregations might focus their attention on how to build effective Saturday morning worship and study experiences. Yet when I met with him in Savannah in late 2008 at a regional biennial, he cited this particular initiative as one of his least successful efforts. Most Reform Jews continue to prefer restricting Shabbat to a narrow window on Friday night. This attitude has no historical precedent and it is difficult to believe that it can be transmitted from generation to generation.

It is important for the Reform Jew to consider historical norms before rejecting traditional practices or adopting new approaches. *Gates of the Seasons*, a short guidebook to Reform observance of the Holy Days, says, "In creating a contemporary approach to Shabbat, Reform Jews do not function in a vacuum. Although we may depart from ancient practices, we live with a sense of responsibility to the continuum of Jewish experiences."[8]

Marriage and Divorce

Family life has always been of essential importance in Judaism, and the Reform movement has done what it could to reaffirm this centrality. In *Gates of Mitzvah: A Guide to the Jewish Life Cycle*, it is written, "In Judaism the decision to marry implies a willingness to enter wholeheartedly into a sacred covenant with another person." The text emphasizes that it is "a mitzvah for a Jew to marry and to live together with his/her spouse in a manner worthy of the traditional Hebrew designation for marriage, *Kiddushin*—set apart for each other in a sanctified relationship."[9]

The legal term for entering into marriage is called kiddushin, a form of the Hebrew word *kadosh* (holy). Marriage is a sacred union and therefore the institution reflects the relationship between God and the children of Israel. The book of Genesis quite early in its narrative describes the process of getting married: "So it is that a man will leave his father and mother and cling to his wife, and they become one flesh" (2:24).

In the early rabbinic period, the process that led to Jewish marriage included three stages: *shiduchin* (engagement), *erusin* (betrothal), and *nisuin* (nuptials). Although the standard translation of the word *shiduchin* is engagement, the procedure carried with it a far greater commitment than what we would associate with the contemporary concept. Shiduchin included the signing of *tenaim*, a legal contract stipulating the obligations of the two parties and a penalty for the violation of the terms set forth. While most Reform rabbis ignore this part of the traditional Jewish marriage process, the Orthodox continue to issue tenaim.

Erusin was a formal betrothal ceremony at which the groom gave a ring to the bride and recited the traditional words that constituted kiddushin, the sanctification of the relationship: *harei at mequdeshet li betabaat zo kdaat Moshe veIsrael* (Be consecrated to me with this ring as my wife in keeping with the heritage of Moses and Israel). While the couple would not yet cohabit, the bride would be forbidden to any other man from that moment. Nisuin normally took place a year after erusin. Bride and groom would be brought together under a *huppah*, and the *Sheva Berachot*, the Seven Benedictions, would be recited. However, later rabbinic authorities felt that the elapse of so much time between erusin and nisuin was asking for trouble and integrated the latter two stages into the modern Jewish wedding ceremony.

While the combination of erusin and nisuin is a standard feature of all modern Jewish weddings, including Orthodox ones, there are a number of Reform innovations. The *ketubah* is egalitarian, speaking in terms of what the couple promise each other rather than what the man promises the woman. Likewise, there is an exchange of rings during the Reform wedding service. In the traditional ceremony, the groom would give his bride a ring as a concrete indication of *kinyan*, the halachic category of acquisition. These and other changes were instituted to reflect the values of Reform Judaism in ritual terms. While this symbolic representation of equality seems basic to us today, it took many decades for the Reform movement to embrace the idea.

The question of whether it was permissible to exchange rings was discussed at the Augsburg Synod in 1871. A group of Reform-oriented rabbis had come together to discuss religious issues and attempt to build a policy consensus. In the discussion about the marriage ceremony, Rabbi Joseph Aub of Berlin made a motion that the bride should be permitted to present the groom with a ring while saying the words *Ani ledodi, vedodi li* (I am my beloved's, and my beloved is mine.) Aub explained that many of the young brides he had recently met with in Berlin had requested that they be allowed to present a wedding ring to their husband-to-be.

"These ladies stated that they did not wish to be completely passive at the marriage altar, as if they were objects and as though the marriage ceremony could be performed without their equal participation."[10]

Whereas in traditional Judaism the husband was the dominant figure in the family, feminism has changed family dynamics in virtually all non-Orthodox households. Marriage is still seen as establishing a holy bond between two people, but they could be two men or two women as well as a man and a woman, and the commitment is seen as mutual and equal. In recent years, most Reform rabbis have come to accept the idea that sexual orientation is something we are born with or develops as a result of the complex interplay between a number of genetic, hormonal, and environmental influences at a young age. They are therefore inclined to officiate at the wedding of gay or lesbian couples who are committed to Judaism, whereas a somewhat lower percentage of Reform rabbis are willing to officiate at the weddings of heterosexual couples who do not share a religious commitment to the Jewish religion.

In traditional circles, it is expected that both men and women will get married and have children. The mitzvah of having children is biblically required only for the man, but obviously he would need the assistance of his wife in order to fulfill God's requirement! In Reform Judaism, there is a more open approach that is accepting of different types of alternative lifestyles.

In addition to accepting gays, lesbians, and transgendered Jews, the Reform movement has become more accepting of permanently single people. In the Torah, God says, "It is not good that the man be alone" (Genesis 2:18). The sages add, "One who has no wife lives without goodness." In fact, the rabbis were such strong proponents of marriage that they urged even those who were too old or unable to have children to marry anyway, since procreation was not its sole purpose.

Most Reform rabbis balance their belief that marriage is preferable with tolerance for those who choose to remain single. Washofsky, for example, writes, "Many human beings are quite happy alone, leading lives of fulfillment and contentment. We do not condemn them for their decision to live as singles."[11] He does go on to state that he nevertheless believes that marriage is ideal for human beings.

All the innovations pioneered and the changes accepted pale in comparison to the subject of intermarriage. According to Jewish law, a Jew is only permitted to marry another Jew. This was for religious reasons, since someone of another religion would have conflicting beliefs. Furthermore, it would be much more difficult for the Jewish partner to practice his or her religion in a home not devoted entirely to the Jewish ritual system. In most American Jewish families, the reason was more tribal than religious. Children were urged to marry someone Jewish so that the ethnic identity of the group could continue into the next generation.

In the 1970s the Reform movement shared the feeling held by most others in the American Jewish community, that intermarriage should be discouraged. Partially because it was the least traditional and partially because it was the most tolerant, the Reform community found that it had the highest percentages of intermarried couples of all the American Jewish denominations. This was not a major issue in the early 1960s, when intermarriage rates were still in the single digits, but it became much more serious as intermarriage rates increased dramatically throughout the 1960s and 1970s. In 1977 Harvard demographer Elihu Bergman made the controversial extrapolation that, based on available data and likely trends, the Jewish population in the United States would decline precipitously.

In December of the following year, Rabbi Alexander M. Schindler, president of the Union of American Hebrew Congregations, gave a dramatic speech calling for a vigorous effort to reach out to the unaffiliated and particularly the intermarried. Schindler argued that just because a Jew married a non-Jew, it did not mean the couple was necessarily lost to the Jewish community. The Reform movement could take steps that would have a significant impact on the religious direction of intermarried couples, potentially influencing many to gravitate toward affiliation with a Reform temple. While the movement would continue to encourage conversion to Judaism, it would also welcome intermarried couples in which the non-Jewish partner had not formally converted.

Many interfaith couples approach rabbis with a request that they officiate at their weddings. Some want the rabbi to be the solo officiant, while others want the rabbi to co-officiate with a minister, a priest, or on rarer occasions, an imam or other religious clergyperson. Since the CCAR has a policy of allowing for individual rabbis to follow their consciences, there is no penalty for breaking with the majority opinion. While the CCAR has repeatedly passed resolutions urging rabbis not to officiate at interfaith ceremonies, the organization has allowed its members to do what they felt was right. Chief executive Rabbi Steven Fox is currently promoting ways for the Reform rabbinate to dialogue productively on this issue while avoiding what was becoming an increasingly bitter debate. At the CCAR conference in San Francisco in March 2010, a resolution was endorsed that further opened up the spectrum of acceptable possibilities.

In traditional Judaism, it is relatively easy to get married. All a couple has to do is declare their intentions in front of two witnesses and then enter a private space to consummate the relationship, and presto, they are now married. It is almost easier than flying to Vegas to have Elvis marry you! Getting divorced, however, is another matter. The writ of divorce needs to be a carefully constructed document handwritten with great care by a rabbinic scholar with special expertise in *gittin*, or divorce documents. The husband then has to deliver the *get*, or divorce document, to the woman personally or arrange for a *shaliach*, a reliable messenger, to do so, all the while following specific rules and regulations.

The husband must give the *get* voluntarily. If he refuses to do so, the wife is left in legal limbo. She then becomes an *agunah*, a woman who is prohibited from remarrying because she has not been granted a *get*. She is prohibited from remarrying or even having sex with another man because she is technically still married. If she has children with another man, those children would be classified as *mamzerim*. They would theoretically only be allowed to marry other mamzerim, thereby carrying the stigma of adultery into the next generation. The Reform movement rejects this idea because the child would suffer from the sins of his or her parents.

No longer committed to the observance of the minutiae of the halacha, it made no sense for the Reform movement to require such an elaborate process to be followed in the case of divorce. The Reform movement did not require any *get* in order to be religiously divorced. Rather, most Reform rabbis told their congregants that it was sufficient to acquire a civil divorce. The main reason was that the Reform movement did not want to interfere in legal matters under the jurisdiction of the secular authorities.

In 1843 Holdheim argued that divorce in Talmudic law was a civil process rather than a ritual act. The sages of the Talmud did not distinguish between the two because there was no significant differentiation between civil and religious law. But Holdheim argued that this was certainly no longer true for most Jews in Central Europe, who conducted their civil affairs according to the laws of the state. As a consequence, contemporary Jewish religion should not meddle in what is entirely a civil issue. The Philadelphia Rabbinical Conference of 1869 adopted this idea. "The dissolution of marriage is, on Mosaic and rabbinical grounds, a civil act only which never received religious consecration. It is to be recognized, therefore, as an act emanating altogether from the judicial authorities of the state. The so-called ritual Get is in all cases declared null and void."

Rabbi David Einhorn, the most prominent theologian at the Philadelphia Conference, drew a distinction between marriage and divorce. The Reform movement felt that marriage should continue to be sanctified by a rabbi in a religious ceremony because marriage is an act of sanctification. The process of divorce, on the other hand, should be handled entirely by the civil authorities since it represents the destruction of the sanctity that was created at the time of the wedding ceremony. This may have been a sensible policy in 1869, but in recent years, many Reform Jews have felt the need for a spiritual process to help them cope emotionally with the stress of divorce. People have come to understand that religion can play an important role in people's lives not only in happy times but in sad times as well. Judaism has always marked death as well as birth and so why not divorce as well as marriage?

In response to this perceived need, a number of new ceremonies for divorce have been written. Some of them focus on providing an alternative document to the traditional *get*, which is seen as inappropriate because of its unequal treatment of the wife. The Reform text of the document of divorce can provide one or both partners in a failed relationship with a concrete statement pronouncing the marriage ended. It can also contain various statements designed to encourage each partner to accept the finality of the divorce and begin to move on with their lives.

In recent years, some Reform Jews have begun using a Reform divorce document written by Rabbi Simeon J. Maslin and published by the CCAR in 1983. Termed a *Seder P'reidah*, a ritual of release, the document was designed to give one or both parties a way to understand their divorce in a religious context. The CCAR hoped to create a sacred space in the divorce process to provide divine sustenance and a mechanism for spiritual healing. Of course the fact that it is an innovated response to contemporary needs means it would not be halachically valid, a point Maslin has emphasized.[12]

A text of this Seder P'reidah is printed in the *Rabbi's Manual* published by the CCAR in 1988. There are two versions, one for a situation where both divorcing parties are present and the other, which is probably used more frequently, with only one of the parties present. The *Rabbi's Manual* recommends that the ceremony take place in the presence of witnesses. Participants, the manual suggests, "might invite their children, family, or close friends to be present." In the opening section of the service, the rabbi explains that since earliest times Judaism has allowed for divorce when a woman and a man "no longer experience the sacred in their relationship."[13]

Many of the Reform objections to specific Jewish laws are "protests of conscience." Laws that violate our ethical sensitivities are not acceptable even though they may be codified in Jewish legal works. This is particularly true in cases where Jewish law treats the Jewish woman in an unequal manner. The same ethical consideration can be extended to a myriad of other laws and regulations. But where does this ethical sensitivity come from? Are we allowing liberal assumptions to trump religious values?

CHAPTER 4

A New Reform Revolution in Worship and Practice

On May 26, 1999, the Central Conference of American Rabbis met at the historic Rodef Shalom Congregation in Pittsburgh. This was the same congregation that had hosted the 1885 Pittsburgh Platform symbolizing the rejection of Jewish tradition that was seen as the hallmark of Classical Reform Judaism. At 11:30 a.m., the rabbis voted to adopt a new platform called "A Statement of Principles for Reform Judaism" by a vote of 324 to 68, with nine abstentions. It was the culmination of almost two years of intense and acrimonious debate that began when Rabbi Richard N. Levy, then president of the CCAR, made public an initial draft of a proposed new platform. The draft advocated that Reform Jews consider trying out and perhaps adopting many ritual practices that had formerly been regarded as unacceptable in a Reform context.

The platform that Levy proposed would be the fourth comprehensive statement of beliefs to be passed by the American Reform rabbinate in its history—the first being in Pittsburgh in 1885, the second in Columbus in 1937, and the third being a statement rather than a platform in San Francisco in 1976. During the course of 1998 and the first half of 1999, the proposed document went through six drafts. During this process, most of the references to specific ritual acts were removed in order to placate the 20 to 25 percent of the movement's members who were attached to greater or lesser degrees of Classical forms of Reform Judaism. The suggestion that Reform Jews might consider eating kosher food, taking ritual baths in a *mikveh*, and even wearing *tefillin* was shocking

14. The cover of *Reform Judaism* magazine showing Rabbi Richard N. Levy with yarmulke and tallit, which upset many supporters of Classical Reform. Levy can be seen holding one of the tzitzit, specially knotted ritual fringes, between his index finger and thumb. The photo suggested an embrace of traditional ritual that dramatically contrasted with the less ceremonial approach practiced by Classical Reform Judaism. "Why are you destroying the religion I grew up with?," one congregant asked him. *Photo by Rose Eichenbaum. Courtesy of* Reform Judaism *magazine.*

to some Reform Jews who considered such proposals as an attack on their entire approach to religious life.

Reform Judaism magazine, the official organ of the Reform movement, published the third draft of what was then called the "Ten Principles for Reform Judaism," with a cover photo of Levy with a tallit and a yarmulke. While many people applauded the tone as well as the substance of the proposed platform, many others were distressed and saddened by what they felt was an abrogation of the historical positions of the Reform movement. There were letters that attacked Rabbi Levy personally, suggesting that he would feel a great deal more comfortable in the Conservative or even the Orthodox movement. Others stressed the fact that because Levy had spent most of his career working for the Hillel Foundation, a Jewish university campus organization, he could not possibly understand the mentality of the congregational Reform Jew.

For those who associated tradition with medievalism, Levy's proposals struck a raw nerve. Some of the responses were very harsh. A woman from Mequon, Wisconsin wrote, "Abandonment, hurt, outrage, violation, betrayal. These are just a few of the first words that came to mind after I read Rabbi Richard Levy's proposal."[1] Another reader wrote sarcastically: "It was quite a surprise to read the contents of Rabbi Levy's article. . . . I did have to check the cover to make sure it said Winter 1998 and not Winter 1698."[2]

In response to the large volume of comments, and because of their intensity, Levy, working with other CCAR and UAHC leaders, produced a fourth draft, which was discussed at the December 1998 UAHC board meeting. This draft was more moderate in tone than the original draft had been. Yet there were still a number of phrases that caused difficulties for certain members of the UAHC board. The primary issues included the urging of the reading and speaking of Hebrew, and the encouragement to consider making aliyah—moving to Israel—which many found excessively Zionist. But Judge David Davidson summed up the general response when he stated: "The issue generated a lot of apprehension, some heat, and even some dismay, but after hearing Rabbi Richard Levy's very personal and very open presentation yesterday, the apprehension is largely dissipated and most of the heat is gone."[3]

From that point on, the process leveled out. Although an announcement was made that no vote would be taken at the Pittsburgh conference, this decision was rapidly reversed and a new announcement went out to declare that the platform would be brought to a vote. Further, the leaders of the CCAR now united behind Levy in support of the new platform. They urged that it be passed as a way to show people that the Reform movement was moving forward and that the platform could stimulate discussion and further study. While many found this a rather weak argument for passing a platform, by the time of the vote, there were very few who truly opposed the ideas in the statement, at least among those in attendance at the conference.

Most of the general press initially reported that the platform was a "radical" move toward traditionalism. The *New York Times*, in a front-page article the day after the vote, wrote that the principles would "encourage the observance of traditional rituals . . . that were set aside at the movement's founding." This was typical of the reporting done by the American news media, which emphasized the concept of the return to tradition and referred only in passing to earlier drafts of the platform having specifically mentioned many of the traditional rituals Reform Jews might consider readopting. Ten days after the vote, *Time* magazine published an article on the platform, entitled "Back to the Yarmulke."[4] There was of course no mention of the yarmulke in the platform, a fact that the *Time* magazine reporter certainly knew. Yet the article seemed to convey the impression that the Reform rabbis had published the platform primarily in order to urge the re-embracing of traditional practices.

An Associated Press wire report said that the CCAR had "approved a return to traditional values such as the wearing of yarmulkes, keeping kosher and praying in Hebrew." While this may have been true to *some* degree, the emphasis on a "return to tradition" created a spin that could be seen as misleading, even inaccurate. Later newspaper accounts, however, such as one by reporter Stacy J. Willis, published by the *Las Vegas Sun* three weeks after the conference, stated that the platform was far more of a compromise than an unambiguous and dramatic move to the right, and that it reflected pushes and pulls in different directions.[5]

Writers for many of the regional and national Jewish newspapers, in contrast, were much more likely to stress the fact that the final draft was "watered down" compared to the original proposal. The *New York Jewish Week* wrote: "The new Platform is seen as a victory for the Classical wing of the movement, which rejected attempts by Reform leaders to inject more tradition and observance into daily practice."[6]

Some actions were open to being interpreted as reactions to the Platform when they were not necessarily so. Shortly after the platform was passed, Rabbi Harry Danziger wrote an article for his synagogue newsletter announcing to his congregants that he would start wearing a yarmulke at services. He wanted to make it clear, however, that this decision was not a direct result of the platform: "Timing requires a disclaimer: What I share here has nothing to do with the much-publicized 'Declaration of Principles of Reform Judaism.'" Danziger stated, "What is here was my intention long before that document was born. The place of the *kippah* or yarmulke has changed enormously in Reform Jewish life. For years, few American Reform Jews wore head coverings. It was virtually a symbol of being Reform to wear one no longer!"[7] Danziger explained that over the past several years this has changed, and noted that a number of rabbinic interns have worn yarmulkes on the bimah during services and that the rabbis and cantor have worn yarmulkes at weddings and other ceremonial occasions when requested. He said that although he had not worn a kippah during regular services for some years, he has now found renewed religious meaning in wearing one, and so would begin to do so.

The Revival of Traditional Practices

The New Reform Revolution, which began to bring back abandoned and rejected ritual practices, had its roots in trends that began long before 1999. Seeking to explain the changing atmosphere in the postwar period, Rabbi Solomon B. Freehof told the CCAR in 1950 that "there has been a general shift in the world atmosphere from classicism to romanticism." Freehof explained that romanticism leads to an interest in more ritual because it is based more on emotions than intellect. As a result, there is a greater need for ways to express feelings. This change in sentiment has impacted all the American religious groups, not just Reform Jews. The Church of England, for example, has seen "a shift from Protestantism to a sort of ritual Catholicism, the drama without the doctrine." In terms of specifically Jewish influences, Freehof credited both the Zionist movement and a nostalgia for the lost eastern European past with helping to broaden the range of viable options for religious expression. He explained that we have "added a folk-feeling to our theology."

Freehof also knew that much of the impetus for greater ceremonialism came from newly suburbanized Jews from eastern European backgrounds who had only recently joined Reform temples. Most had relocated from urban enclaves where they had lived in heavily ethnic neighborhoods. While they may have had little religious background, they felt very Jewish and wanted to express that Jewishness in concrete ways. They may have joined a Reform temple but wanted nothing to do with what they saw as the sterile, "church-like" formalism of Classical Reform. The question was whether this interest in ritual would express itself only as sporadic and inconsistent observances or whether the Reform movement could channel it into a system of religious thought expressed in concrete religious behavior.

As the number of synagogues grew in the years after World War II, the approach to ceremony increasingly emphasized "traditional practices." This somewhat nebulous term referred to anything that made the Reform temple look and feel more like a shul from the old country. While adding "tradition" to a skeletal service structure was a meritorious concept, most of these newly rediscovered traditional practices were rather superficial changes. More Hebrew was used, for example, but the congregants did not make any effort to learn or understand the Hebrew, so the net effect was a service that appeared to be more traditional but did not actually transform the fundamental religious experience. Likewise, there was an interest in greater participation but an unwillingness to fundamentally change patterns of socialization that would make that involvement meaningful. Congregants wanted to appear to be involved without actually making a religious commitment.

Despite this superficiality, or perhaps because of it, the congregational membership of the UAHC grew from 300 to 656 between 1943 and 1964. This increased the number of families affiliated from about sixty thousand to two hundred thousand. Many people were moving to the suburbs, and new Jewish suburbanites needed congregational homes. But the growth was short-lived. By the late 1960s the membership rolls of the UAHC hit a peak and flattened out. Michael A. Meyer writes that the Reform movement began suffering from "severe self-doubt and anxiety about the future." This malaise replaced the ebullience that had been easily sensed just a few years earlier. The Reform temple "long remained in a state of crisis" because of "uncertainty over how to respond to the social upheavals occurring in American society during this period."[8]

While everyone was dissatisfied with the inertia of the Reform movement at that time, no consensus emerged about how to reorient Reform Judaism to meet the needs of American Jewry. There were many ideas; specifically, two ideologically motivated groups were pushing in opposite directions—one to the right and one to the left. In 1972 Theodore Lenn published a study entitled *Rabbi and Synagogue in Reform Judaism*, which found that fully 42 percent of rabbis perceived a "crisis" in American Reform Judaism. An almost identical number—43 percent—wanted to incorporate a greater degree of traditional practice into Reform Judaism, while 29 percent wanted to move toward Jewish humanism.[9]

By the early 1970s it was becoming clear that many people had an emotional need for Judaic rituals and ceremonies. There was something about the physical experience of holding and making blessings over ritual objects that could not be replaced by sitting in the pews listening to the rabbi pontificate on the dogmas of ethical monotheism. Theological consistency became less important than the freedom to experiment with different types of ceremonies and ritual acts.

This shift away from Classical Reform came at a heavy price, theologically speaking. Regardless of what one believes about God and religious truth, it is beneficial for a religious movement to have a carefully worked out theological system that can be explained step by step. The environment in the 1970s precluded the creation of such a coherent theology, leading the movement into the acceptance of theological pluralism, the mutual coexistence of a number of different theologies. With the possible exception of radical humanism, all types of Judaic theologies were acceptable in the Reform movement. While the freedom to explore alternative religious beliefs was liberating, it undermined the argument that Reform Judaism was *the* ultimate form of rational religion, *the* purest type of ethical monotheism.

In my view, the theological consistency necessary for coherency has been lost in contemporary Reform Judaism. This worries me a great deal, but it does not seem to overly concern the leadership of the movement. When Rabbi Eric H. Yoffie, then president of the Union for Reform Judaism, wrote the afterword to one of my previous books, *American Reform Judaism: An Introduction*, he agreed that I had a legitimate concern. "Who can deny that Kaplan is correct when he says that theological clarity is desirable, and that it is easier to pass along one's beliefs when one knows what they are?" But Yoffie suggested that I overstated the problem. "Theological struggle is to be encouraged, but the absence of theological consistency has rarely been a major problem in America for Jews of any stripe."

Yoffie emphasized that he continued to believe "the major task for Reform Jews is to build on the religious revival now occurring in our ranks, to encourage Jewish study and the observance of both the ethical and the ritual *mitzvoth*, and to strengthen our ties with the Jewish people in the Land of Israel and throughout the world." He argued that "we need to immerse ourselves in Jewish *doing*, guided always by our liberal principles, and if we do so, appropriate theological formulation will be developed afterwards."[10]

I fear that we may never fully immerse ourselves in the religious acts Yoffie sees as a first step and so will never even begin the theological process I believe is essential. The legacy of the sixties, I fear, will haunt us for decades to come.

By the early 1970s the changing religious landscape had fundamentally overturned the basic assumptions of not only Classical Reform Judaism but every mainline Western denomination. Filled with doubts about what they could believe religiously and what they could accept socially, members of Reform congregations seemed to distance themselves from the temples that had once meant so much to their parents.

A generation gap opened up, with many young people seeing the synagogue as a dull and old-fashioned institution where their parents went primarily to socialize. In the absence of any satisfactory explanation from their parents as to why going to temple was important, the younger generation was left to find their own spiritual path without significant parental guidance.

In the same year that Lenn released his report, Leonard Fein published a study of the UAHC membership entitled *Reform Is a Verb*, in which he found that most Reform congregants had little emotional investment in their temple. More than a third of those surveyed told Fein that the synagogue was not an important institution in their lives. One gets the impression that others felt the same way but were perhaps embarrassed to admit it. Many seemed simply apathetic, lacking the passion necessary even to criticize the direction of the movement.[11]

Fein recommended that the Reform movement begin a process leading to "a revolution of rising Judaic expectations." The most important prerequisite for this revolution would be the creation of a sense of community. "No single conclusion registered as strongly as our sense that there is, among the people we have come to know, a powerful, perhaps even desperate, longing for community." In spite of this problem, Fein found there was a considerable amount of energy in the movement. What members needed were opportunities to explore Judaism in both the cognitive and experiential realms.[12]

What Reform Jews began realizing was that they needed to be actively involved in religious ceremony in order to feel the type of spiritual connection they yearned for. Classical Reform Judaism had stressed the theological, rejecting halacha and actively discouraging most forms of Jewish practice. By the 1960s and certainly the 1970s, my impression was that the Classical Reform approach was failing to capture people's imaginations, leading to emptier synagogue services. When I attended services at Temple Israel in Waterbury, Connecticut, between 1975 and 1978, I saw a declining congregation that came only on the High Holy Days and special events. There were so few people attending that I became extremely concerned about the future of Reform Judaism in America. Based on what I saw there, I began believing that there was a desperate need for a new approach that could help make Judaism feel more alive, more relevant to people's lives. Many American Jews begin to believe that Judaism needed more content, more structure.

As a consequence, the already developing trend toward more traditional ceremony gained speed. This raised a number of questions. If Reform Judaism was now going to embrace many customs that had previously been ignored or rejected, how would it differ from Conservative Judaism? Also, if the Reform movement began embracing a great deal of tradition, would it be rejecting its Classical Reform roots? These issues were discussed and debated for years. No consensus emerged. What was clear was the fact that many Reform Jews eagerly embraced ancient rituals and newly created ceremonies, reveling in what had once been an almost forbidden realm of religious behavior.

On a theological level, Reform Judaism does not hold that a commanding God gave the Torah and requires punctilious observance of the commandments as developed in the classical rabbinic tradition. Therefore, Reform Jews were not and are not required to observe any specific Jewish practice, such as keeping kosher, observing the Sabbath, or following the Jewish laws of prayer. During the Classical Reform era, the thinking was that most traditional rituals inhibited true spirituality and should not be performed. An alternative system of thought and (minimalistic) practice was developed to replace the halachic system. Reform Jews became known for what they did *not* do.

Many—but by no means all—Reform Jews were finding its principled antinomian approach to be increasingly sterile. Perhaps because of all the emotion generated by the political and social events of the 1960s, many Reform Jews wanted to feel more connected to the tradition. Also, there were increasing numbers of Conservative and even Orthodox members who had switched over to Reform, and they usually wanted more ceremony. The end result of the "return to tradition" was a movement that re-embraced selected aspects of that tradition. It may not have made sense intellectually, but it felt right.

Particularly noticeable to the casual observer were the changes in the worship service. There was a great deal more Hebrew, although many in the congregation read it using transliterations. Substantial numbers of women as well as men wore previously rejected ritual garments, including yarmulkes and tallitot. Congregants were much more likely to participate actively in the services, no longer relegated to the sidelines as observers. The music became much more upbeat and the sense of excitement palpable.

Ceremonial observance was clearly on the upswing when Rabbi Sanford Seltzer, then director of research for the UAHC, published comments about a 1989 survey of worship practices in Reform congregations. "Where custom and ceremony were once marginalized and the use of Hebrew negligible, heightened ritual involvement will, in all likelihood, be characteristic of the Reform synagogue of the 21st century." Despite his confident prediction, Seltzer did hedge a bit by including the words "in all likelihood." He understood that predicting the future was a perilous undertaking. Today things are changing so quickly that it is even harder to predict the trends of even the next five years. Because the clientele that the Reform movement caters to is highly acculturated, they are easily swayed by sociological trends and cultural shifts.

The most prominent ceremony to be reintroduced was the bar mitzvah, which marked the passage of a young man from childhood to adulthood at age thirteen. After preparing for at least a year, the boy would participate in services by reading a selection from the Torah scroll as well as chanting the prayers before and after the reading. This was a difficult task because the Torah text did not have either vowels or punctuation.

In the second half of the nineteenth century, Classical Reform had done away with the bar mitzvah in favor of confirmation. The rationale for replacing bar mitzvah with confirmation had been that students could better understand the theology of Judaism when they were fifteen or sixteen, and that it was important to teach them the principles of the religion and not just have the students repeat words they had memorized in a foreign language they did not understand.

Confirmation also served the goal of egalitarian education. Girls as well as boys studied with the rabbi and other confirmation teachers for a number of years, thus providing young people of both genders with an equally rich Jewish education. This was a revolutionary social development. Girls in Orthodox and even Conservative congregations could not

15. Confirmation ceremony at Temple B'nai Israel, Albany, Georgia, May 2009. In Reform Judaism, young men and women have always received the same Jewish education and participated fully in the confirmation ceremony. The Reform movement has become pluralistic, allowing members to embrace greater ritual if they find it meaningful, or alternatively, remain faithful to the tenets of Classical Reform. Note that Phyl Fralich, on the left, is wearing a yarmulke and a tallit while Davidson Goldsmith, on the right, is not. *Photo by Stanley Greenfield.*

dream of acquiring the same level of education that the boys received, and girls had no ceremony to mark their entry into young adulthood.

While the confirmation service was intended as a progressive innovation that would provide young people with a deeper knowledge of Judaism, many of the new Reform Jews saw it as a shameless copying of Christian models that were inappropriate for a synagogue. They demanded the right to hold bar mitzvah ceremonies for their thirteen-year-old sons. Since feminism had already established that women deserved the right to participate equally in religious activities, these tradition-minded parents expected their daughters to become bat mitzvahs. In 1922 Rabbi Mordecai M. Kaplan, the founder of Reconstructionist Judaism, had introduced and conducted the first bat mitzvah ceremony for his daughter Judith at the Society for the Advancement of Judaism thus establishing a precedent. When Reform congregations began considering the reintroduction of the bar mitzvah, they naturally included the bat mitzvah as well.

There was certainly opposition from Classical Reform advocates who felt that the bar mitzvah overly emphasized rote ritualism and was therefore contrary to the spirit of Reform Judaism. Confirmation was preferable because it marked the communal acceptance of the Torah at Mount Sinai, a connection reinforced by its celebration on or around Shavuot. Classical Reformers believed that the bar mitzvah was a throwback to a tribal rite that had originated in an earlier period in the development of Judaism and lacked the essential elements necessary for proper religious devotion.

This rejection of the bar mitzvah concept set the stage for what could sometimes be a bitter conflict. At Temple B'nai Israel in Albany, Georgia, Rabbi Martin Hinchin introduced the ceremony after his arrival in 1946. Those families that wanted their sons to become bar mitzvah could have the ceremony in the temple, as long as they committed to also continuing their son's Jewish education through confirmation. But when Rabbi Joseph H. Freedman from Waterbury, Connecticut took the pulpit in 1958, the temple board voted to prohibit bar mitzvahs entirely. From that point on, those families who wanted their sons to become bar mitzvah had to travel weekly to Tallahassee, Valdosta, Atlanta, or even New York City for lessons and the ceremony itself. This situation continued into the early 1980s, until well after Freedman retired and moved to San Francisco (of all places!).

Seltzer's 1989 study also found that many temples had reintroduced the Saturday morning service. In fact, 384 out of 425 congregations surveyed stated that Saturday morning had become the preferred time for conducting bar and bat mitzvah ceremonies. In addition, more than half held Saturday morning services regularly even when there was no bar or bat mitzvah. The constant stream of bar mitzvah ceremonies did not sit well with the regulars at the Saturday morning minyan, as virtually the entire service was focused on the thirteen-year-old child, and the guests were there to celebrate with the family rather than to pray. Most of the regulars therefore preferred to hold a separate service even when there was a much larger bar or bat mitzvah service taking place simultaneously.

The increase in popularity of the Saturday morning service was offered as evidence that the Reform movement was re-embracing tradition, and in one sense it supports that conclusion. In contrast to the Classical Reform temple, where confirmation was held once a year, the neo-Reform congregation now has frequent bar and bat mitzvah services on Saturday mornings throughout the year.

However, it is important to note that the movement has embraced only one aspect of Sabbath observance. Unless and until large numbers of Reform Jews take the entire Shabbat experience seriously, it is difficult to see how the "return to tradition" really changes anything.

Promoting Specific Ritual Behavior

One of the problems with practicing Reform Judaism was that the movement did not prescribe specific ritual behavior. This had been discussed by the CCAR repeatedly since its founding in 1889, but no consensus had emerged and the CCAR was therefore unable to provide much direction. Without a clear message concerning what should and should not be done, most Reform Jews did very little. This quickly became the default religious setting for Reform Jews and Reform Judaism in the late nineteenth and early twentieth century. But by the 1930s, at the latest, sentiment reversed course.

In 1950 the Committee on Reform Practice did a study that found "widespread and increasing acceptance by congregations and their members of ritual practice and ceremonial observance." In his report to the General Assembly of the Union of American Hebrew Congregations, Rabbi Morton Berman stated that the study "demonstrates that Reform Judaism is determinedly engaged in helping to meet a fundamental need of every human being for symbolism and ceremonialism in his religious life."

Berman cited statistics from the study as "striking evidence" that "our movement has undertaken to correct a most costly error made by the early anti-ritualistic Reformers." Berman announced that the study showed that the majority of the members of Reform temples had a "new attitude" toward observance. They understood that disciplined practice has "the power to restore in the Jew a sense of kinship with God, because they are the reminders of the providential role that He filled in His people's life throughout the ages."

The question that both supporters and opponents of the new interest in ceremony asked is: Why was the Reform movement moving toward greater ceremonialism? The early reformers were so intent on emphasizing the theological principles of Judaism and the ethical implications of those principles that they felt there was no place for the rituals and ceremonies of traditional Judaism. Berman told the delegates that "the early builders of our movement failed to recognize that man cannot live by reason alone, that he needs to sate his emotional hunger for the poetry and beauty, for the mysticism and drama which are to be found in meaningful symbolism and ceremonialism."[13]

There were certainly periodic attempts to rectify the situation, but each effort was stymied by opponents, some of whom objected to traditional practice and others who opposed the establishment of any criteria. But the radical changes taking place in American society in the period immediately following the assassination of President Kennedy—which in retrospect marked the beginning of "the sixties"—created the momentum needed for reconsideration. In 1965 Rabbi W. Gunther Plaut called on the CCAR to produce a guide to Reform Jewish practice. He specifically proposed that the CCAR create a guide to Sabbath observance, since this seemed to be the greatest need at the time.

During his heartfelt speech, Plaut explained the reason why such a guide was desperately needed. "We have failed to give direction to our people. How can they know what is expected when we steadfastly refuse to tell them? Vague pronouncements about 'observing the spirit of the Sabbath' are about as efficacious as talking about 'being good.'"[14] Plaut argued that the solution was to revive halacha in a Reform context, an effort that Rabbi Solomon Freehof had been undertaking for many years. Paraphrasing Mordecai Kaplan's Reconstructionist dictum that "the past has a voice, not a veto," Freehof called for guidance rather than governance. In a 1975 interview, Freehof explained, "I'm struggling for a philosophy which will allow us to have a kinship with the greatness of the Jewish spirit. The problem is how to have loyalty and freedom—and it's a problem. The purpose of my response is not governance, but guidance."[15]

While Plaut and some others were enthusiastic about this approach, many thought it was directly contrary to the core principles of Reform Judaism. The CCAR allowed Plaut to move his projects forward, but the inherent fact that the movement allowed for total freedom and complete autonomy meant that Plaut could only influence those who were already interested in the Freehofian approach. The gap between the different parties became a gulf.

Plaut's speech led to the creation of a Sabbath Committee that published *A Shabbat Manual* in 1972. The very idea of the Reform movement publishing a guidebook on what to do and what not to do struck many as exceedingly strange, but others understood that it was an essential element of the reorientation of a movement that was at risk of self-destruction. An interesting debate took place between Plaut and Rabbi Eugene Mihaly, an HUC professor from Cincinnati, at the 1975 CCAR Conference. While both seemed to support providing greater guidance to congregants, Plaut wanted the Reform movement as a whole to provide that guidance while Mihaly believed that the responsibility should be left with individual rabbis.

Plaut argued that the Reform movement needed to teach its members that there were many opportunities for performing ritual and ceremonial acts. He was careful to soft-pedal the idea that the movement might embrace the concept of mitzvah as an obligatory religious act, stressing that "we cannot accept the Halacha of tradition, but we must relate to it."[16] He debated with himself over what term should be used, *mitzvah* or *hovah*. Mitzvah might be translated as commandment, while hovah would probably be best understood as obligation. Both words implied that the halacha was obligatory, an idea that was anathema to most Reform Jews. He eventually settled on the former term since most American Jews were familiar with the word mitzvah. Plaut emphasized that he was interpreting the concept in a specifically Reform understanding, which encouraged individuals to consider practicing specific rituals but did not make anything obligatory.

The Sabbath Committee then expanded the scope of their interest. Taking a new name, the Committee on Reform Jewish Practice, they prepared a concise but comprehensive guidebook entitled *Gates of Mitzvah: A Guide to the Jewish Life Cycle*, published in 1979. In his introduction to *Gates of Mitzvah*, Plaut observed that Judaism "was never meant to be merely an institutional religion." He was referring to the fact that by this time, most Reform Jews associated the practice of Judaism with what they did in the temple. While they understood and accepted their obligation to be ethical people at all times, they did not necessarily associate that commitment specifically with Judaism. Plaut was trying to gently point out that Judaism had always been a religion that one practiced all day, every day.

Therefore, he explained, the volume "aims at helping each individual Jew to make Jewish decisions in his or her life." His wording was clear: each Reform Jew has the right and indeed the obligation to make his or her own personal decisions. In order to make authentic Jewish decisions, they need to have certain basic religious knowledge. While a 166-page guidebook is not going to provide a deep wellspring of religious wisdom, it could at least provide Reform Jews with basic information. *Gates of Mitzvah* "sets out guideposts for making such decisions; the rest is up to each person."[17]

In 1983 the Committee on Reform Jewish Practice published an updated and expanded version of *A Sabbath Manual* entitled *Gates of the Seasons: A Guide to the Jewish Year*. As the title suggests, the new guidebook included not just the Sabbath but all the Jewish holidays, including ones that had generally been ignored by virtually all Reform Jews. In his introduction, Rabbi Simeon J. Maslin jokingly begins by asking "What? Another book on Jewish practices from the Reform movement?" Maslin admits that many Reform readers might be wondering, "What is happening to the Reform movement?" He answers that in order to answer this question properly, it is necessary to understand "what Reform Judaism really is."

Maslin explains that Reform Jews do not believe that revelation happened at only one moment in the distant past. We Reform Jews are not bound by the way that the ancient sages, who lived in a prescientific civilization, may have understood the concept of revelation. Rather, we see revelation as progressive and can therefore embrace the performance of certain customs and ceremonies while rejecting others. Maslin quotes from the *Union Prayer Book*, which emphasizes that we should "welcome all truth, whether shining from the annals of ancient revelation or reaching us through the seers of our own time."

Maslin states in both *Gates of Mitzvah* and *Gates of the Seasons* that some "ancient practices" are recommended while others are not. In addition, certain completely new practices are included for the first time ever in a Reform context. Just as it is our right as Reform Jews to "discard practices which have lost meaning for contemporary Jews and which lack an aesthetic dimension," so too "it is our duty also to find new and contemporary modes for the expression of inchoate spiritual feelings." The practice of the commandments, Maslin concludes by quoting from a well-known blessing, has "kept us in life, sustained us, and brought us to this moment."[18]

By the 1980s the use of the word mitzvah was generally accepted as normative within the Reform movement. However they defined it, Reform thinkers were increasingly comfortable using the term. Some understood the concept to refer to the divine commandments that are obligatory on all Jews. Others saw the word as simply indicating that Reform Jews were being called upon to do good deeds, as in the use of the term "Mitzvah Day" during which the members of a temple organize several good-works projects to be done on a single Sunday. Either way, the acceptance of the term was a victory for those promoting greater ritual observance.

A New Reform Revolution

By the second half of the 1990s, UAHC president Rabbi Eric H. Yoffie came to the realization that the movement faced an unprecedented challenge. Arguing that dramatic changes were urgently needed, he suggested that the status quo would lead to disaster. In 1997 Yoffie said, "This is the single most momentous hour in the history of our movement. We must now decide whether our Reform heritage will be permitted to wither, or if it will be handed over to generations to come." He empha-

16. Rabbi Eric H. Yoffie participating in a prayer service on a mission of Reform Jews to Israel in 1998. The previous year, Yoffie had warned, "This is the single most momentous hour in the history of our movement. We must now decide whether our Reform heritage will be permitted to wither, or if it will be handed over to generations to come." At that time, he had emphasized the urgency of the situation. "We have a few years, a decade at most, to respond to the spiritual emergency that threatens to engulf us." *Courtesy of URJ.*

sized the urgency of the situation. "We have a few years, a decade at most, to respond to the spiritual emergency that threatens to engulf us."

Speaking at the 1999 UAHC Biennial Convention in Orlando, Florida, he outlined some of the problems. Yoffie explained that statistics indicated about 40 percent of all Americans attended some form of congregational worship at least once a week, but less than 10 percent of American Jews participated in weekly synagogue services. "We joke about two-day-a-year Jews, but we know in our hearts that the fault is not entirely theirs. We need to ask ourselves why so many of these Jews feel religiously unsatisfied in our synagogues."

Yoffie proposed "a new Reform revolution," which would include a series of initiatives designed to stimulate religious activity. First and foremost was the continuing effort to transform the worship experience.

Yoffie explained that the early Reform religious service was a reaction against the "mechanical mumbling" of the Orthodox. The German Jews who created the modern Reform temple wanted choral singing accompanied by organ music that could inspire worshippers by its dignity and solemnity. But this type of worship experience, inspiring or at least impressive to earlier generations, now came off as dull and old-fashioned.

Yoffie was careful not to engage in any bashing of Classical Reform Judaism. He made it clear that whatever their faults, Classical Reform Jews had always attended services regularly and took worship seriously. He stated that it was overly simplistic to blame the Classical Reformers for all of the problems in the Reform movement. The truth was that the Classical Reform approach had worked remarkably well for generations.

The problems began as American society changed suddenly and radically in the 1960s. The Classical Reform approach became a relic of an earlier age, antiquated and almost prehistoric. Yet the congregants who had been indoctrinated with the Classical Reform approach were highly resistant to change. They had been taught that Reform Judaism *was* Judaism, and any other approach was either primitive or inauthentic. If that was so, the reintroduction of traditional practices was nonsensical, diluting and even distorting what had been a pure form of ethical monotheism. Many were profoundly alienated.

Those who had been raised in Classical Reform temples wanted to continue to experience the type of worship service they had been accustomed to when they were growing up. They objected to the concept of looking at the contemporary religious scene and designing a new type of religious service based on those observations. While traditional religious symbols were important to many of those raised with them, as well as to others who had come to appreciate their spiritual value, the supporters of Classical Reform saw these symbols as representing all that was wrong with the contemporary synagogue.

This fundamental disagreement caused conflicts that Yoffie dubbed "the worship wars." This led to a clash between two aesthetic sensibilities that were seemingly irreconcilable. In an organization that placed a premium on cooperation rather than authoritarianism, the conflict over how to run a service threatened its equilibrium. Rabbis and temple boards accused each other of usurping each other's authority, while cantors struggled to find an appropriate sphere of influence. With so many forces pushing for innovation, leaders became fearful of making too many changes too quickly. There was what Yoffie described as a "paralyzing fear of change" in many temples, even in some that had been regarded as more dynamic.

In his address at the UAHC Biennial in 1999, Yoffie said that Reform Jews were rediscovering the power and purpose of prayer, but he implied that we needed to do a lot more. He proposed that the entire movement focus its energies on creating a worship experience that would no longer be "a bit too cold and domesticated." We needed to sing to God, "to let our souls fly free." He reassured the leaders present that this did not mean Reform Judaism was abandoning the rationalism at the foundation of Reform Jewish belief for close to two hundred years. Judaism, he reiterated, had always advocated for emotional as well as intellectual pathways to God.

The key change required was the use of inspiring music in religious services. He explained that every congregation that had successfully revived its worship experience had introduced music that was "participatory, warm, and accessible." Whereas the Classical Reform temple had stressed decorum, the successful neo-Reform congregation had found ways to get their members to sing. Listening to beautiful music may be an enjoyable experience, but it is primarily passive. In order to touch people's hearts, it was absolutely necessary to transform them from an audience into participants. "Many of us have lost our voices. The music of prayer has become what it was never meant to be: a spectator sport."

Yoffie made a series of specific recommendations to realize this vision. First, congregational boards should devote a major portion of two upcoming board meetings to "defining a worship agenda" for their congregation. Second, congregations should reorganize their Ritual Committees to better work with rabbis and cantors on worship renewal. The reorganized Ritual Committees should study the history and theology of Jewish prayer with their rabbi or cantor and then should undertake an in-depth self-evaluation of worship in their congregations. As part of this process, synagogue evaluation teams should visit at least four other Reform congregations to see what sister congregations are doing in the realm of worship.

Third, Yoffie proposed that the UAHC initiate an online movement-wide dialogue on prayer. He hoped that hundreds of temple presidents, ritual chairs, rabbis and cantors, and many others would join this online discussion. Fourth, the UAHC, HUC-JIR, CCAR, and the American Conference of Cantors should cosponsor worship retreats for rabbis and cantors to "develop the scholarly and professional dimensions of worship reform, and examine successful models from across the country." I attended one of these worship retreats organized by the Southeastern Region of the URJ outside Atlanta, Georgia. The leaders of the retreat modeled several different styles of worship, presenting traditional as well as innovative modes that the participants could take back to their home congregations.

Finally, Yoffie inaugurated a program of adult Hebrew literacy. He expressed understanding with those who argued that the increased use of Hebrew in prayer was contrary to the principles of Reform Judaism but gently said that he disagreed with them. Even with much more Hebrew, "every Reform service contains an ample number of English prayers so that all worshippers can pray with comprehension." Nevertheless, it was important to understand that Hebrew is not just a vehicle for expressing prayers to God but "part of the fabric and texture of Judaism, vibrating with the ideas and values of our people."[19]

The problem, of course, is that few Reform Jews know very much Hebrew. If they were raised in the Reform movement, they likely attended a religious school that met once or twice a week for a few hours. It is obviously difficult to teach very much of any foreign language in just a few hours a week, especially in an after-school or Sunday-morning format. The teachers may very well be volunteers and the students are likely to be tired and cranky. Even under optimal conditions, the number of hours allotted is simply not sufficient.

The difficulty of teaching Hebrew was one of the reasons the Classical Reform leaders had decided to eliminate the bar mitzvah in favor of confirmation. The restoration of the bar mitzvah as well as the establishment of the bat mitzvah requires students to learn enough Hebrew so they can read from the Torah as well as some of the prayers. They will not be able to converse in modern Hebrew and may understand only a very small amount of what they read.

Part of the solution has been to introduce transliterations. The 1975 *Gates of Prayer: The New Union Prayerbook* introduced transliterations of some prayers in the back of the book, but most worshipers found it awkward to keep referring to a different page whenever they had trouble reading a Hebrew prayer.[20] Along with the desire for gender-sensitive language, the lack of transliterations is what prompted the CCAR to publish a small, gray hardcover version of *Gates of Prayer* in 1994. So when the movement began planning the creation of a new prayer book, it was clear that a version with transliterations would be made available. It was also understood that a version without transliterations would also be published. Why? Some rabbis felt that the presence of transliterations dramatically reduced the incentive to learn Hebrew. If all the prayers were transliterated, there was no need to break one's teeth learning the Aleph-Bet. With two different editions, rabbis could choose the style that suited them and everyone was happy.

Mishkan T'filah: A Reform Siddur was published in 2007 after many delays. The new prayer book featured the Hebrew prayer on the right-hand page with a transliteration on the facing page and a literal translation directly below it. On the left-hand page, there would usually be two creative prayers in English. This structure allowed for a tremendous amount of flexibility. Rabbi Peter S. Knobel, the chair of the CCAR editorial committee, told the *New York Times*, "This is a way of having the best of both worlds. You have the possibility of doing, if you want, an entire service in Hebrew, as traditional as you can be within the Reform movement. At the same time, you can do something extremely creative."[21]

Unlike most of the previous prayer books that dictated when congregants should stand or sit, and when they should read responsively or together, the new prayer book omitted stage directions. This gave the rabbi or worship leader the maximum flexibility to determine the contours of a particular prayer experience. While laypeople that I spoke to did not object to this change, they expressed trepidation over the possibility of having to lead a service with *Mishkan T'filah* precisely because of this innovation. But once they become familiar with the prayer book, they will learn how to find their way around it. Along the edge of each page is a list of the prayers in that section of the service, listed in blue, with the prayer on that page bolded in black. While this requires some familiarity with the structure of the prayer book, it can be extremely useful.

While the *Gates of Prayer* had ten different Friday-night services, most of which focused on specific theological themes, *Mishkan T'filah* only has two. Since the second service is primarily a shortened liturgy designed for ease of use, there is essentially one main Friday night service. Rather than creating entirely separate services to reflect different theological perspectives, the new prayer book tries to include prayers that can be interpreted in different ways. What struck me looking through the book was that many of the prayers focused on what spirituality can do for the individual. For example, one of the creative readings at the beginning of the T'filah for Shabbat evening reads:

Prayer Invites

God's Presence to suffuse our spirits, God's will to prevail in our lives.
Prayer may not bring water to parched fields, nor mend a broken bridge,
nor rebuild a ruined city.

But prayer can water an arid soul, mend a broken heart,
rebuild a weakened will.[22]

The prayer, adapted from the writings of Rabbi Abraham Joshua Heschel, was brought over with minor editorial changes from Service II of *Gates of Prayer: The New Union Prayerbook*, the immediate predecessor to *Mishkan T'filah*.[23] Service II in *Gates of Prayer* was the most humanistically focused of the ten Friday-night services. The text in the earlier prayer book reads:

Prayer invites God to let His presence suffuse our spirits, to let His will prevail in our lives. Prayer cannot bring water to parched fields, or mend a broken bridge, or rebuild a ruined city; but prayer can water an arid soul, mend a broken heart, and rebuild a weakened will.[24]

Mishkan T'filah changes the phrase "God to let His presence" to "God's Presence" in order to eliminate the gendered pronoun "His," but it also eliminates or at least reduces the direct reference to God as an active agent. The reading is made more acceptable to a person who does not believe that God acts in history but who might be willing to accept that God's presence, perhaps understood in a symbolic sense, can be experienced through prayer. Also, in the earlier version, prayer *cannot* bring water to parched fields, whereas in the new version, prayer *may not* bring water to parched fields.

The reading is written to be easily understandable by anyone, not requiring any training in Judaic studies or theology. All you have to do is pick up the prayer book and read the prayer. For those expecting the traditional *tefillot* in Hebrew or in English, the right-hand pages provide a fuller text of the traditional *siddur* than previous prayer books published by the CCAR. For those looking for creative expressions of personal spirituality, the English readings on the left-hand pages provide a plethora of material.

Perhaps the editorial committee's most controversial decision was whether to reintroduce the prayer for the resurrection of the dead. What most concerns me here (and elsewhere) is not so much the final decision but rather the methodology used (or not used) to reach it. If we want to present a vibrant religious faith to our community and the outside world that can draw in believers and hold them with a religious intensity, our prayer books need to be well thought out. Our approach to understanding "tradition" should blend scholarship with spirituality, and we need to be willing to stand up against popular trends that cater to the trivial and simplistic. It is fine to offer worshipers options as long as the central theological message remains undiluted. If we are to build a strong and enduring Jewish Reform movement in the United States, Americans need to know what Reform Jews believe in and stand for.

Instead of clarity, the committee process seems to have led to indecision and ambiguity. The committee studied the relevant text and went back and forth several times. In the end, they decided to insert the Hebrew word representing the concept of physical resurrection as an option: "*Baruch atah, Adonai, m'chayeih hakol (hameitim)*." The blessing without the word in parentheses would read, "Blessed are You, Adonai, who brings life to everything." If the word in parentheses is substituted for the final word, then the blessing would read, "Blessed are You, Adonai, who brings life to the dead."[25]

However, the English text on the right-hand page—where the literal translation is supposed to be—reads, "Praised be the God whose gift is life, whose cleansing rains let parched men and women rise again." In contrast to the normal practice of the prayer book, this is not a literal translation of the text. In the commentary at the bottom of the page— another innovation of *Mishkan T'filah*—the editor explains that Classical Reform prayer books replaced the expression "who resurrects the dead" with more generalized language "expressing the hope for a spiritual immortality." This represented the mainstream theological thinking of the Reform movement for over one hundred years and was based on rationalism and scientific scholarship. Nevertheless, the editor explains that *Mishkan T'filah* provides the original (traditionalist) wording as an option, "acknowledging its metaphorical power." Neither intellectual consistency nor rational inquiry apparently can stand up to postmodern metaphors.

Rabbi David Ellenson, the president of HUC-JIR, told JTA that "there is no question that this represents a move towards tradition in the Reform movement." The reporter did not ask Rabbi Ellenson what he meant by the word "tradition." I would argue that since the traditionalist belief of physical resurrection is only restored as an option in parentheses and even then is pooh-poohed in the commentary, what we have is not a restoration of traditional Jewish theology but rather ambiguity, contradiction, and doctrinal confusion. Jonathan Sarna gave a historical perspective. "Certainly to the 19th century reformers, the idea that Judaism believed in resurrection of the dead seemed to them the antithesis of the kind of rational Judaism that they thought most Jews wanted and expected." Sarna is certainly correct. So why would the committee insert that single word in parentheses? Rabbi Elyse D. Frishman, the editor of *Mishkan T'filah*, explained the methodology that led to this significant theological shift. "For a number of people in our movement, reclaiming traditional language feels very meaningful, and when that language resonates positively, people want it."[26] I would have hoped that the prayer book would reflect sound Jewish theology and not just popular sentiment. Unfortunately, that may not be a reasonable expectation in the current environment.

The Creation of New Ceremonies

None of the ceremonial adaptations discussed here are unique to Reform Judaism. Rather, they can be found among many groups of non-Orthodox Jews (and a small number of liberal-leaning modern Orthodox as well) throughout the United States, Israel, and a handful of other countries. What they share in common is a self-emancipation from rigid notions of what must be done. Freed from the necessity of conforming to the halacha, the more creative non-Orthodox have experimented with different types of ceremonial innovations.

In certain cases, even devout Orthodox Jews can develop new ceremonial practices. As long as it does not violate the halacha, there is no reason that ceremonial innovation is necessarily prohibited. One case in point is Miriam's Tambourine, which Vanessa L. Ochs found in the homes of Chabad-Lubavitch Hasidic women. "Owning them, decorating them, or just having them around channeled anxiety, released creative energy, and mobilized the community of Lubavitch women worldwide."[27] The tambourine helped these women identify with Miriam, Moses's sister, who had played an important (if somewhat behind-the-scenes) role in the liberation of the Israelites from Egyptian bondage.

Many of the original ceremonial innovations were designed to raise Jewish feminist consciousness. Significant numbers of Reform temples initiated *Rosh Hodesh* services monthly to mark the coming of the new moon. Talmudic literature had mentioned that Rosh Hodesh had special meaning for women, and Jewish feminists seized on this reference to justify the creation of a new type of religious service. The traditional tefillot had always included a special prayer for the new month, but now an entire service was developed around this date which focused on feminist themes. Since many feminists felt excluded from the rituals being performed in the synagogue, they had the strongest motivation to create new ceremonies that helped them express the spiritual freedom they sought.

The most influential source of new ceremonial behavior is the innovative corner of American Jewish religious life. These individuals and groups are not necessarily tied to a specific denomination. In fact, their iconoclastic nature made it more likely than not that they would be independent of any narrowly defined school of thought or religious movement. Nevertheless, leaders of the early Reconstructionist movement pioneered ceremonial innovation and then later Jewish Renewal developed new approaches to ceremony that transcended standardized categories.

Jewish Renewal developed out of the counterculture of the 1960s. Groups of mostly young Jews began forming *havurahs*, small fellowship associations that prayed, studied, and sometimes lived together. Others experimented with new approaches to Judaism that stressed emotion more than intellect and broadened the boundaries of what could constitute Judaism. Numerous individuals and groups eventually coalesced around the charismatic figure of Rabbi Zalman Schacter-Shalomi, affectionately called Reb Zalman. Reb Zalman has created an entirely new approach to Jewish prayer that he calls *davenology*.

Members of Reform temples were initially quite cold to these bold efforts at revitalizing Jewish spirituality through ceremonial innovation. The Classical Reform temple was an austere place, formal and forbidding. The goal was to instill a sense of awe by creating a grand cathedral effect with majestic architecture, beautiful stained glass windows, and a high church style of worship. The rabbi performed the ritual according to a strictly defined set of directives, mimicking the role of the Kohen in the Jerusalem Temple. It was only when this approach to Reform Judaism began crumbling that it became possible to consider allowing Reform Jews to find individualized ways to mark what might be spiritually meaningful to them.

There is no consensus on how or under what circumstances one should go about creating a new ceremony. If the goal of creating a given ceremony is to meet the spiritual needs of the people participating, then the type of ceremony created would depend on the emotional state of the individuals involved. The desire is to sacrilize meaningful events in the lives of the individuals or their family members. While many people have little interest in even well-established rituals such as the bar mitzvah, pressuring all concerned to emphasize the party at the expense of the religious content, others seek to bring religious meaning into even the most mundane aspects of daily life.

The ceremonial innovators explained that traditional ceremonies were experimental and variable in their early stages. Contrary to what some believe, the practices traditional Jews observe were not given by God to Moses at Mount Sinai in the exact format they appear in today. The traditional prayer book, for example, contains many psalms, liturgical poems, and other material added in the medieval and even early modern periods! *L'chah Dodi*, the beautiful poem sung as part of the Kabbalat Shabbat service on Friday nights, was composed by Shlomo Halevi Alkabetz, a sixteenth-century Kabbalist from Safed.

But while the medieval rabbis tinkered around at the edges, adding a few new things here and there, the sages in the period immediately following the destruction of the Second Temple in 70 CE had to recreate Jewish practice in its entirety. Prior to the cataclysmic Great Revolt against Rome, Jewish religious life had been centered on the Temple. After the Romans set it on fire, how could Judaism continue to function? The sages, led by Rabban Gamaliel and Rabban Yochanan Ben Zakkai, built an academy in a small town called Yavneh, which became the center for tremendous ceremonial innovation.

With the Temple gone, the entire sacrificial system was no longer possible. The sages adapted traditional ceremonies originally practiced in the Temple to new settings, primarily the home and the synagogue. While it was no longer possible to offer sacrifices, the synagogue liturgy edited at this time included frequent references to what had been done in the Temple. Likewise, home observances were modeled on what had been done by the Kohanim in the Temple. The classic example of this is the Passover Seder in which a shank bone is placed on the Seder plate as a remembrance of the Passover sacrifice in the Jerusalem Temple. The sages were responding to a radically new situation. They created new ritual that would preserve the memories of what had been done while allowing for the flexibility necessary to meet the practical needs of the survivors of what was the greatest catastrophe in Jewish history up until that point.

In the second half of the twentieth century, the State of Israel created new days of commemoration to mark the remembrance of the Holocaust, Yom HaShoah, and the creation of the state of Israel, Yom HaAtzmaut. Many traditional Jews—primarily Haredim—objected, maintaining that it was prohibited to unilaterally declare the creation of new days of mourning or rejoicing without the authorization of a Sanhedrin, a Jewish religious supreme court. But the Israeli leaders felt that they needed to remember these events in a formalized manner and that they could not wait for the religious authorities to reformulate the procedures allowing for innovation.

In the United States, commemorations for these two events were also organized. The focus, however, was on individual religious expression rather than communal remembrance. This was part of a broader societal trend in the United States toward individualized spirituality. So while Yom HaShoah and Yom HaAtzmaut were acknowledged, there was more focus on how religious innovation might help each of us deal with the challenges and rewards of life. American Jews were looking for ceremonies that might help them through the transitions that were becoming increasingly noticeable, both for good and bad.

One type of ceremony that has been adapted and expanded for contemporary needs is the healing blessing. In the traditional synagogue it is customary to give a *misheberach* blessing to each man after he had recited the blessings for the Torah reading. This practice was curtailed and largely eliminated in the Reform temple because there were no longer multiple aliyot being called up to bless the Torah during the reading. Instead, if there was any Torah reading at all, the Classical Reform rabbi would take the Torah out of the ark himself, pronounce the opening blessing, read a short selection from the scroll, pronounce the concluding blessing, wrap up the Torah, and return it to the ark. Since there was no one called up for any of the honors, there was no opportunity to bless anyone.

Another reason for the elimination of the misheberach was that the Classical Reform temple emphasized that God was concerned with cosmic issues. The Lord was certainly capable of healing Aunt Matilda in Omaha but was unlikely to break the cycle of nature unless there was an absolute need on a broad scale. God wanted human beings to work together to make the world a better place, but He never promised to alleviate all of our individual problems, whether psychological or physical. Our duty was to honor and praise God for being the architect of the universe rather than see God as our personal change agent.

But in recent decades, the need for a blessing for not only physical health but also emotional wellbeing has become much greater. This need has been addressed in a number of ways, including healing services which focus on spiritual responses to hurt and damage of various types. There have been new liturgical works written specifically for the purpose of helping people to cope with pain and injury.

Perhaps the best known is Debbie Friedman's *Mi Shebeirach*, a healing prayer written in Hebrew and English, which was originally composed for a *simchat chochma*, a ceremony devised by the composer-singer to celebrate wisdom. Friedman, who had become the best known Reform Jewish composer and singer, created this ceremony in honor of a friend who was celebrating her sixtieth birthday. "My friend was having a very difficult time in her life and a number of her friends were also struggling. Yet she had arrived at this age and was determined to embrace it." After Friedman's death, it became known that she had long suffered from a debilitating neurological disease, and this likely also played a role in her determination to pray for healing.

She introduced the new liturgy with a beautiful melody at the UAHC (now URJ) Biennial in San Francisco in 1993, hoping the prayer would offer worshippers a sense of "spiritual connectedness."[28] Friedman took some of the Hebrew wording from the traditional Mi Shebeirach but rephrased parts and integrated English into the prayer to form an organic whole. The second verse focuses specifically on the theme of healing:

17. Debbie Friedman performing with alumni of HUC-JIR's School of Sacred Music at a tribute concert at Central Synagogue, November 12, 2009, to support student scholarships at the school, now renamed the Debbie Friedman School of Sacred Music in her memory. She is best known for her *Mi Shebeirach*, her version of the traditional prayer for healing, which is recited weekly by many if not most Reform congregations. *Photo by Richard Lobell. Courtesy of HUC-JIR.*

Mi she-bei-rach i-mo-tei-nu
M'kor ha-bra-cha-l'a-vo-tei-nu
Bless those in need of healing
With r'fu-a sh'lei-ma
The renewal of body
The renewal of spirit
And let us say, Amen.[29]

Before a congregation begins the song, it is customary to ask those who have a relative or friend who is in need of healing to rise and say the name of their loved ones so we can all keep that person in mind.

This practice of praying for healing might suggest that we believe that God intervenes in the daily affairs of human beings and that God is capable and willing, for example, to cure cancer or reverse heart disease. When I first heard about this prayer and similar practices, such as rabbis praying in hospital rooms for the recovery of a sick patient, I was rather taken aback. It seemed to be an antirationalist approach to religion that was, as I understood it at the time, contrary to Reform Judaism.

I changed my mind after I saw how strong an impact these practices made on people. I witnessed how rabbis dispensed personal prayers to their congregants, and I observed the appreciative faces of the recipients. I could have pointed out that Maimonides, the famous twelfth-century rationalist Jewish philosopher, might have been rather distressed. But the prayers seemed to create so much hope and love that any intellectual objection would have been beside the point.

Understood symbolically, it is certainly possible to reconcile the new healing prayers with a rationalist approach to Judaism. Rabbi Lawrence Hoffman, a professor at the Hebrew Union College–Jewish Institute of Religion in New York and the cofounder of Synagogue 3000, explains that he and his colleagues see healing "as embedded in a culture that honors the humanity of others; that looks for the best, not the worst in everyone; that helps people succeed, not fail; and that eliminates the cultural aggravations that drive up blood pressure, cause embarrassment, promote guilt, and chase people away."[30] Since the concept of healing can be a positive spiritual force, most Reform Jews welcome its

18. Rabbis Batsheva Appel and Dana Evan Kaplan co-officiate at a pet blessing ceremony outside of Temple B'nai Israel, Albany, Georgia. Many Reform Jews are experimenting with new ceremonies designed to acknowledge important relationships, significant milestones, and dramatic transitions in their lives. Since pets are frequently beloved members of the family, it seems logical to acknowledge their emotional importance in our lives. *Courtesy of Dana Evan Kaplan.*

reintroduction into the liturgy irrespective of their theological positions, if they have any such positions.

There are many other ceremonial innovations, including baby-naming ceremonies for girls, gay and lesbian commitment ceremonies, ecological Passover seders, and ceremonies to mark the onset of first menstruation, to give just a few examples. There are also quirky—some would say outlandish—ceremonies that remain on the fringes, ranging from mezuzah-placing ceremonies for automobiles, "bark" mitzvahs, rain dances, and Hebrew tattoo initiations. Over the course of time, some will go mainstream and others will fade out of view. With the easy accessibility of documents on the World Wide Web, all it takes to create a new ceremony is a word-processing program and an Internet connection.

CHAPTER 5

A New Reform Revolution in Values and Ethics

Sally Priesand became the first American woman to be ordained as a rabbi, helping to establish the concept of equality as a paramount value in American Reform Judaism. "I always wanted to be a teacher of whatever was my favorite subject," she told JointMedia News Service in 2012. "In the end, I decided to become a teacher of Judaism." She was the first woman to achieve this goal but not the first to have attempted it. There had been a long process of debate spanning several decades. But now the time was right. Hebrew Union College–Jewish Institute of Religion president Rabbi Nelson Glueck supported her candidacy. After Glueck's death, his successor, Rabbi Alfred Gottschalk, continued to support her ambition. Perhaps most importantly, Priesand's parents "gave me one of the greatest gifts a parent can give to a child: the courage to dare and to dream."[1]

In her book *Judaism and the New Woman*, she writes, "On June 3, 1972 I was ordained rabbi by Hebrew Union College–Jewish Institute of Religion in Cincinnati, Ohio. As I sat in the historic Plum Street Temple, waiting to accept the ancient rite of s'micha, I couldn't help but reflect on the implications of what was about to happen."

Priesand's ordination would put an end to a long history of rejection. "For thousands of years women in Judaism had been second-class citizens. They were not permitted to own property. They could not serve as witnesses. They did not have the right to initiate divorce proceedings. They were not counted in the *minyan*." Even in Reform Judaism, women "were not permitted to participate fully in the life of the synagogue.

19. Rabbi Sally Priesand holding a Torah at her ordination ceremony on June 3, 1972. She was the first woman ordained as a rabbi by the Reform movement in the United States and has become a symbol of the feminist struggle for equality in American Judaism. After her ordination she served first as assistant and then as associate rabbi at Stephen Wise Free Synagogue in New York City and led Monmouth Reform Temple in Tinton Falls, New Jersey, from 1981 until her retirement in 2006. *Photo by Garrett Cope, for the* Jackson (Michigan) Citizen-Patriot. *Courtesy of the Jacob Rader Marcus Center of the American Jewish Archives, Cincinnati, americanjewisharchives.org.*

With my ordination all that was going to change; one more barrier was about to be broken."

Looking back three years after her ordination, she wrote, "When I entered HUC-JIR, I did not think very much about being a pioneer. I knew only that I wanted to be a rabbi." With the support of her family, she was willing to spend eight years preparing to enter a profession "that no woman had yet entered." Her decision to do this was "an affirmation of my belief in God, in the worth of each individual, and in Judaism as a way of life."

Her years as a rabbinical student were certainly not problem-free. "Though Reform Judaism had long before declared an official religious equality between men and women, Reform Jews still believed that a woman's place was in the home." Fortunately, the Reform movement "no longer insisted that men and women sit separately during worship service. They allowed women to be counted in the *minyan*, to conduct the service, to serve as witnesses in ritual matters. They demanded that girls receive a religious education equivalent to that provided for boys." Reform temples permitted women to become voting members of the congregation and they "even permitted them to be elected to offices on synagogue boards. But they were not yet ready for the spiritual leadership of a woman."[2]

Priesand was by no means the first woman to study at the Hebrew Union College. In fact, founder Rabbi Isaac Mayer Wise had accepted women from the very beginning in 1879. But none had ever been ordained as a rabbi. In the interviews she did at the time of her retirement in June 2006, Priesand repeatedly told of how she was perceived. "I think at first they thought I came to marry a rabbi rather than be one."[3] She was not joking. Most female students had specialized in education, using the opportunity to meet and eventually marry rabbinic students. The Judaica skills acquired would prove useful to these women in their role as rebbetzin, the rabbi's wife. Being a rebbetzin was a full-time job. The rebbetzin taught religious school, helped run the sisterhood, and served as a role model for the women in the congregation. But the influence of feminism was encouraging younger women to aspire toward their own career rather than just helping out their husband's.

"As my eighth and final year drew to a close, I was faced with finding a job. Some congregations refused to interview me. I was disappointed and somewhat discouraged by these refusals." As the first American woman ever to be ordained as a rabbi, she knew that the path would not be easy. "Since I had not expected everyone to welcome me with open arms, I had prepared myself for this possibility. I knew that I needed only one acceptance and I never really doubted that I would find one synagogue ready to accept me." Several synagogues interviewed her "for my public value, so they could say they were first."[4] Eventually, the Stephen Wise Free Synagogue offered her a position as assistant rabbi. She was the last candidate in her class of thirty-six to be offered a rabbinic position. Priesand speculated recently that she was probably offered the job because it opened up so late that all of her classmates had already committed themselves elsewhere. She worked under senior rabbi Edward Klein, the same rabbi who coincidentally had officiated at my parents' wedding. Rabbi Klein, Priesand recalls, loved "to be introduced as the first equal opportunity employer in the American rabbinate."[5]

She reported that she performed the standard rabbinic duties, conducted worship services, gave sermons, taught adult education courses, and supervised the youth group. In her early memoir, she wrote, "The only area in which people have shown any real hesitancy has been that of my officiating at funerals." Recently, she explained what caused this concern. "Very often people would say, 'My father was traditional—how can I have a woman rabbi at his funeral?'" But Rabbi Klein told everyone, "Rabbi Priesand is the rabbi, and she will do the funeral. If you don't take her, you're not going to get anybody from this synagogue."[6] After working at Stephen Wise for seven years, she took a part-time job at Temple Beth El in Elizabeth, New Jersey, and became chaplain at Lenox Hill Hospital in Manhattan. A two-year search culminated in a 1981 offer to become the solo rabbi at the Monmouth Reform Temple in Tinton Falls, New Jersey, where she served for twenty-five years until her retirement in June 2006.

Rabbi David Ellenson, the president of HUC-JIR, told CBS News, "Sally Priesand was a genuine innovator in American Jewish life and in Jewish history. Her decision to study for the rabbinate paved the way for the inclusion of half the Jewish population."[7] Priesand is important as a symbol of equality. While most traditional Jews would view the ordination of women as violating halacha and therefore prohibited, for most Reform Jews it is an issue of correcting a historic injustice. Women were excluded from Jewish religious leadership for at least two thousand years. The Reform movement therefore had to act on a moral imperative to right a wrong. Any other course of action would have been shirking our responsibility.

Eugene B. Borowitz explains that the unequal status of women in society was a challenge to the ethical sensitivities of Reform Jews. "No issue is more deeply troubling to the modern Jewish conscience than the treatment of women in our society and in our religion. The special disabilities people face merely because they were born with female gender extend beyond our ability to specify them." Borowitz, who was born in 1924, is old enough to remember how things were in the old days. "How strange it now seems that until recently single women, even those with good jobs, could not get bank loans or that married women had to have their husbands sign their loan applications." Women were eligible for "a few, relatively marginal jobs but not ones with power or administrative control, even over large numbers of other women. Of course, there were some few exceptions to these rules but they were just that, exceptions."[8]

Borowitz argues that Jewish attitudes toward women's rights were historically relatively enlightened. "A case can be made for the *relative* [italics in original] humaneness of the Jewish tradition. When compared to other religions and cultures in similar periods, the status of the Jewish woman was higher and legally much more secure. She had an honored, stable, significant position in community and family life and a distinct if separate role in observing God's law."

Borowitz wants it clearly understood that while he is not criticizing the rabbinic approach to the role of women from a historical perspective, he does not believe that policies established fifteen hundred years ago or more can be ethically justifiable today. "Viewed as human creation, Judaism's law concerning women reflects the universal prejudice of premodern mankind somewhat alleviated by the humane sensitivities of Jewish faith. But seen traditionally, as God's own dictates, Jewish law and custom concerning women are unacceptable to the modern conscience." From a Reform religious viewpoint, God could not possibly want half of all the people on this earth to be treated as inferiors.

Summarizing the halachic regulation for determining one's eligibility to lead others in the performance of various commandments, Borowitz writes, "Simply put, Judaism made women a different category of persons than men and this differentiation rationalized their subordination to men. Men set the terms under which women were to operate, the classic sign of discrimination; Jews have no difficulty recognizing when Christians do the same thing to them."[9] Borowitz's point is clear—Reform Jewish ethics requires a reevaluation of historic norms in the light of contemporary values.

Ethical Behavior

When people casually talk about the concept of ethics, they usually think of the instinctual human capacity for choosing good over evil.[10] While we may absorb ethical lessons from our parents and teachers, we believe that people can sense what they should do in a given situation. When we see an elderly person struggling to put her groceries into their car, we just know that the right thing to do is to stop and help her. It is not necessary to study ancient texts in order to be a good person. All we need to do is to allow our internal value system to operate and pause long enough to see opportunities all around us.

This is not the biblical view of ethics. According to the Torah and the prophets, it is God who determines what is right and what is wrong. Both good and evil are present in the world that God created. God, of course, wants us to do the right thing but leaves the choice up to us. This is called free will. In the Torah, God promises to reward the Israelites if they follow the divine commandments and to punish them if they do not. That is not the only reason—or even the primary reason—why people should choose to do good. We should desire to imitate God, who is good. If we successfully emulate God, we bring greater holiness into the world and bring redemption that much closer.

Reform Judaism drew its ethical inspiration primarily from the prophets. At a certain point in the late nineteenth century, some believed that the prophetic books would supplant or even replace the Torah itself. Many referred to their faith as prophetic Judaism in order to emphasize how important the prophets were for them. Perusing the books of the prophets, Reform rabbis were able to draw on a wealth of material that emphasized the obligation to feed the hungry and clothe the naked, defend the widow and orphan, and behave compassionately toward the stranger and the slave. In the book of Amos it is written, "Hate evil and love good and establish justice in the gate" (5:15). In the prophetic understanding of ethics, the Israelites need to do good because that is what God demands of them.

In the book of Micah it is written, "What does Adonai require of you? Only to do justly, to love mercy, and to walk humbly with your God" (6:8). Rabbi Leo Baeck commented that "what we owe to God is to be paid first and chiefly to His children." The good person can be properly described only by using these two adjectives, "just" and "loving." We must act in this manner toward every person on this earth because he is our "fellow man." This is "by God's appointment," not the result of "our good will, nor our kindness, nor is it any social convention or legal enactment that makes him so." Rather, every person alive is our compatriot "by the appointment of the One God, and therefore no man must deprive him of his standing or reduce its meaning." Baeck explained that "to the Hebrew mind there can be no religion without our fellowman."[11]

The prophetic call to make ethics the most important concern of humankind resonated with Reform thinkers of all types. Looking for a way to justify Judaism as a modern religion that promoted peace and harmony, they found the primary source material that they were searching for in the prophets. This was in dramatic contrast with much of the narrative in the Torah itself, where God commanded the Israelites to slaughter some of the indigenous inhabitants of the land of Israel and do other things that would normally be regarded as not only immoral but criminal. In contrast, the prophets appeared to teach a pure form of what became known as ethical monotheism, stressing that both the individual and the group have an obligation to God to uphold the highest ethical standards under all circumstances.

Reform theologians found much of the Torah overly concerned with the building of the tabernacle in the wilderness and then the minutiae of the sacrificial system in the temple. The sages spoke of 613 mitzvot, but many of them could no longer be observed without a functioning temple in Jerusalem. Yet Reform theologians certainly did not want to see the temple rebuilt because that would allow for the resumption of the temple cult, which they saw as primitive and lacking moral purpose. Thus they turned to the prophets for ancient models of Jewish behavior, which emphasized what was truly important.

One of their central concerns was how the powerful treated the powerless. The prophets attacked the ruling class of Judea, blaming them for the suffering of the masses. In the book of Micah, for example, the prophet addresses "you rulers of Jacob, You chiefs of the house of Israel!" Micah admonishes them, "for you ought to know what is right, but you hate good and love evil." Rather than trying to treat the poor with respect and insist on justice, the economic and political elite have done terrible evil. "You have devoured My people's flesh; You have flayed the skin off them, And their flesh off their bones." After breaking their bones to bits, "You have cut it up as into a pot, like meat in a caldron" (3:1–3).

For those interested in both Judaism and social revolution, the words of the prophets were an inspirational message from the world of the ancient Israelites. While they were not necessarily eager to take on their prophetic responsibilities, the prophets were bold and fearless. Nathan, for example, stood up to King David, who had sent an innocent man to his death so that he could consort with the man's wife. Reform rabbis hoped to follow this model of condemning all unethical behavior, even that of the rich and powerful.

Many of the early Reform thinkers cited specific quotations from the prophets to support their position that ethical behavior was far more important than ritual observance. For example, in the book of Isaiah we find: "When you come to appear before Me, who required this from you, that you should trample my courts? Offer vain sacrifices no more, incense is an abomination to me." Holy days observed by people who were behaving unethically repulsed God. "New moon and Sabbath, the holding of convocations—I cannot endure iniquity along with solemn assembly."

God tells the people that their prayers will not be heard as long as they refuse to commit themselves to social justice. "When you stretch forth your hands, I will turn My eyes away from you; when you increase prayer, I will not hear, for your hands are full of blood." God tells the Israelites what they must do. "Wash yourselves, be clean, put away the evil of your devices from before My eyes; cease to do perversely. Learn to do good; seek justice, relieve the oppressed, uphold the orphan's rights, defend the widow's cause" (Isaiah 1:12–17).

Some reformers saw these prophets as proto-reformers who, writing more than two thousand years ago, were already anticipating the direction of the modern Reform movement. Orthodox leaders, of course, rejected this idea as preposterous. They explained that while these prophets were certainly condemning ritual behavior that was not backed up by ethical concern, none of the prophets ever suggested abrogating the system of ritual commandments.

Many Reform theologians not only argued that ethics were more important than ritual but went so far as to suggest that prophetic ethics were the essence of Judaism. While the rituals and practices of Judaism might change over the course of history, Jewish ethical teachings remained the unchanging core.

The Reform approach to Judaism emphasizes not only that a great many things have changed but also that things can and should change. Does that include ethics? Are there certain behaviors we might have considered ethical three thousand years ago that we now consider unethical and vice versa? This would certainly be the case. We now have knowledge in many fields that the ancients had absolutely no awareness of. As a consequence, it is not only possible but actually obligatory to reevaluate many of the ethical teachings of the Tanakh. While we are aware of the dangers of relativism, there is no intellectually honest alternative.

While most Reform theologians have focused on the ethical teachings of the prophets, it is important to emphasize that they also drew ethical teachings from the Torah itself. While some stories in the Torah shock the ethical sensitivities of modern readers, there is also a great deal of ethical wisdom. There is no single word in biblical Hebrew that conveys the meaning of the English word *ethics*. The word *mussar* eventually came to mean something roughly similar, but its use is restricted in the Tanakh to methodology employed by a father to teach his children (Proverbs 1:8). The central reason for this was that since ethics were an integral part of the religious demands that God placed on the children of Israel, there was no need to differentiate ethical commandments from the others.

The Torah clearly teaches that we have an obligation to try to help others, even when it might appear that they are not worthy of being helped. In the book of Genesis, God decides to destroy the cities of Sodom and Gomorrah because of their extreme wickedness. But when the angels came to tell Abraham what was to be done, he begged that the people of Sodom and Gomorrah be spared. Why? For the sake of the righteous who might be among them. "Shall not the Judge of all the earth act justly?" (18:25). A lengthy negotiation then takes place with God offering to spare the city if a certain number of righteous can be found. Abraham accepts the premise of this concept but argues that the number of righteous should be lower than what God insists upon. Eventually, Abraham gets God down to ten righteous people, but unfortunately even this number is lacking, and God then destroys the two cities. The lesson we learn from Abraham's position is that we can never give up on society. No matter how bad we have gotten, we have to struggle to set ourselves right.

Reform theologians pointed out that while other ancient Near Eastern cultures may have also expressed concern for ethical conduct, the Torah places ethics in a position of unparalleled importance. In the book of Deuteronomy it states, "For what great nation is there that has a god so close at hand as is our God Adonai whenever we call? Or what great nation has laws and rules as perfect as all this Teaching that I set before you this day?" (4:7–8). Israel is unique in both its God and the commandments that were given to them. The two are directly connected and, in fact, inseparable.

Reform thinkers emphasized that Jewish ethical teachings were part of a religious system that stressed actual human behavior over abstract theological concepts. In traditional Judaism, ethical behavior was governed by the same halacha that determined all other aspects of how

Jews should live their lives. Since Reform Jews rejected the binding nature of the halacha, they had much greater freedom to address ethical dilemmas. The added flexibility could enable the Reform movement to respond creatively and compassionately in ways that would be outside of or even in contradiction to the halachic system.

Social Justice

The commitment to social justice has long been a cornerstone of Reform Judaism. The Reform commitment is based on the belief that we are all made in the divine image of God. Reform Jews believe that our religion requires us to work for the betterment of society. God is a God of righteousness who wants human beings to be holy just as God is holy. As the Adoration (Alenu) prayer from the *Union Prayer Book* puts it: "O may all, created in Thine image, recognize that they are brethren, so that, one in spirit and one in fellowship, they may be forever united before Thee."[12]

God inspired the prophets of Israel to urge all Jews to pursue justice, seek peace, and establish brotherhood and sisterhood among all. Because of this, we all have an obligation to do what we can to help others. As Albert Vorspan and Rabbi David Saperstein write, "Indifference to the problems that confront society is the unforgiveable Jewish sin."[13] The Reform movement has fought for the equality of all people as well as the responsibility of government to help those most in need of assistance.

According to Saperstein, "the belief that human beings can improve themselves and can create a better world is one of the fundamental distinctions between Judaism and Christianity."[14] Saperstein argues that "normative Christianity" has limits on the theoretical ability of human beings to improve their world. The Jewish view, in contrast, emphasizes that "we would create the messianic world through the work of our own hands." His point is that Reform Jews believe that people have the ability to create a better world. Judaism rejects the idea that people can give the responsibility for solving social problems to God. Rather, we are partners with God in the building of a more just society.

The leaders of the Reform movement believe that they are following the legacy of the Hebrew prophets, who applied the ethical insights of

Judaism to the social problems of their generation. Just as the prophets urged the ancient Israelites to create a society guided by God's compassion for all people, so too we today need to work for the betterment of the world. The reason for this is that Judaism stresses the sanctity of each individual. Every single man and woman is equal because they were created in the image of God. As the book of Numbers states, "One law and one ordinance shall be both for you, and for the stranger that sojourneth with you" (15:16). Every Jew has the obligation to God to respect the civil rights of all people. It is written in the Talmud: "What is hateful unto thee, do not do unto thy neighbor" (Shabbat 31a).

In the book of Deuteronomy it is written, "Justice, justice, you shall pursue" (16:20). This is, of course, only one of many biblical commandments. But for those dedicated to social justice, it encapsulates the primary purpose of the entire Torah. Seeking justice can take many forms. In the late nineteenth century, Reform rabbis campaigned against the excesses of the factory system created by the Industrial Revolution. In the early twentieth century, they spoke out against the sweatshops that mistreated vulnerable immigrant employees. At the end of World War I, the CCAR passed a resolution proposed by the Committee on Synagog (their spelling) and Industrial Relations that called for a more equitable distribution of the profits of industry. During the Great Depression, they pushed for government intervention to help those suddenly impoverished.

After World War II, the Union of American Hebrew Congregations became more proactive in advocating for social justice. From the 1870s until the 1930s, the congregations had generally expressed socially conservative positions reflecting the predominantly business-focused laity. There had always been a commitment to social justice, but it was tempered by the economic interest of the majority of the membership. For various reasons, this political orientation began shifting in the late 1940s and early 1950s. Reform Judaism began to be associated with liberal politics. The connection between the two became so tight that for many, being a Reform Jew meant being a political liberal.

While the UAHC passed numerous resolutions dealing with social justice issues, the first comprehensive statement on the subject was not issued until 1955. The "Statement of Basic Principles on the Synagogue and Social Action" stressed that the ethical ideals of Judaism need to be applied to the economic processes of society. While it is perfectly acceptable for some to earn more than others, every worker should be able to achieve a decent standard of living. It is an intolerable situation if people cannot earn enough to provide for themselves and their families.[15]

This position in support of economic justice was quite daring at the time since individual rabbis had gotten into trouble over this issue. Condemning rich industrialists for abusing their factory workers was risky if the largest contributors to the temple were those very same industrialists.

The model for an independent rabbi unafraid of speaking the truth about economic justice was Rabbi Stephen Wise. Wise had turned down the plum position as senior rabbi of Temple Emanu-El in New York because the board insisted on approving his sermons in advance. They knew he would condemn businessmen who paid low salaries to workers suffering under terrible working conditions, and they were determined to prevent outbursts that would alienate some of their members. Wise then established his own congregation, which he called the Free Synagogue, not because members did not have to pay any dues but rather because the rabbi was free to speak on issues of conscience.

By the early 1950s the Reform movement was speaking about the need to actively work for peace and justice. Despite all the rhetoric, there remained a large gap between theory and practice. The UAHC wanted to avoid a situation in which the synagogue was filled with lofty expressions of fellowship, love, and peace while synagogue members did nothing to actually make the world a better place.

The implementation of successful social justice programming could bridge the gap between "confession and commitment." In order to create a mechanism for political activism that could help Reform Jews act on their abstract principles, in 1962 the UAHC established the Religious Action Center (RAC) in Washington DC. The RAC allowed the Reform movement to engage in lobbying in favor of universal issues of moral and ethical concern, at least as the leadership understood those concerns. The RAC acted on resolutions approved by the UAHC, now the URJ. They

20. Under the leadership of sixteen-year-old activist Gabrielle Flaum of Short Hills, New Jersey, the URJ Eisner and Crane Lake Camps represent the Reform movement's youth during the "Free the Soldiers Rally" on July 16, 2007, at Dag Hammarskjold Plaza at the United Nations in New York City. *Courtesy of URJ Eisner and Crane Lake Camps.*

took clear political positions on controversial social issues ranging from capital punishment to the Brady bill to cigarette advertising.

While not every Reform Jew in every congregation agreed with all the Religious Action Center's positions, they could respect the fact that the Reform movement was trying to put the ethical ideals of Judaism into a concrete form. The fact that Reform Jews had something important to say about the pressing controversies of the day emphasized that the Reform movement saw Judaism as a living faith. Religion existed to provide guidance to individuals so that they could take collective action to address the needs of contemporary society.

A bit later, the RAC further expanded the scope of its activities, lobbying on behalf of various Jewish causes and in favor of American political and economic support for Israel. This too could be a big problem, because how one interpreted support for Israel could vary depending on one's political perspective. The Religious Action Center generally tried to follow the consensus on what constituted support for Israel and was usually able to take positions that most Reform Jews felt were in Israel's

best interest without becoming mired in the distinctions between left and right. The RAC performed its most valuable work in helping Reform Jews focus on the social justice activism that was seen as being so important.

A number of political and social causes caught the attention of Reform Jews, but the most compelling was, without a doubt, the struggle for civil rights. The involvement of the Reform movement in this struggle was extensive and multifaceted. Rabbi Maurice N. Eisendrath, president of the UAHC in the postwar era, responded aggressively to the pressing issues of the day. This was at a time when there was a great need for religious leaders to intervene in political affairs. The civil rights movement was in the process of formation, and most Reform Jews were sympathetic to the plight of the American Negro.

Even before the crucial U.S. Supreme Court decision *Brown v. Board of Education* of 1954, the Reform movement had taken a clear position in favor of equal rights. In 1946 the CCAR issued a statement entitled "Judaism and Race Relations," which called for an end to discrimination. The statement supported the establishment of a Fair Employment Practices Commission, which would make sure that equal opportunity was actually practiced, as well as for the elimination of all types of segregation. Within a few months of the Supreme Court decision, the general assembly at the UAHC Biennial voted in favor of implementing the decision immediately throughout the country.

This inaugurated a period of enthusiastic support for civil rights. Reform Jews joined the Freedom Riders, activists who rode on interstate buses into the segregated South to test the Supreme Court decision *Boynton v. Virginia*, which had outlawed racial segregation in the restaurants and waiting rooms of interstate bus terminals. Others volunteered to help in the Freedom Summer, also known as the Mississippi Summer Project, a campaign launched in June 1964 to register African American voters, who had been almost completely excluded up until that point. In August 1963 seventy Reform rabbis took part in the March on Washington for Jobs and Freedom, during which Dr. Martin Luther King Jr. delivered his "I Have a Dream" speech.

Some Reform Jews exposed themselves to the risk of arrest and even violence. After King was arrested on June 11, 1964, on the steps of the Monson's Motor Lodge Restaurant, he wrote a "Letter from the St. Augustine Jail" to Rabbi Israel Dresner to urge him to recruit rabbis to help out. The result was the largest mass arrest of rabbis in American history. On June 18, 1964, Albert Vorspan and fourteen rabbis were arrested for praying in an integrated group in front of Monson's, and two others were arrested for sitting down at a table with three African American youngsters in Chimes Restaurant.

In a letter they released, the rabbis wrote, "We could not pass by the opportunity to achieve a moral goal by moral means—a rare modern privilege—which has been the glory of the non-violent struggle for civil rights." In a separate incident, Rabbi Arthur Lelyveld was attacked with an iron bar by two pro-segregationists in Hattiesburg, Mississippi. While some Southern Reform rabbis risked their careers (and potentially their lives) by taking strong positions in favor of civil rights, others pretended that the issue did not exist.

Rabbi Milton Grafman of Birmingham, Alabama, has become the best-known Reform rabbi to have taken a position dramatically at odds with the CCAR and UAHC. Grafman was one of the eight signers of "A Call for Unity," an open letter that provoked King to write his "Letter from Birmingham Jail." The white clergymen urged an end to the demonstrations, suggesting that African Americans living in the area could negotiate privately with local government officials and take their cause to the courts. King responded by arguing that forceful, but still peaceful, civil action was necessary. Civil disobedience in the face of unjust laws was justified and indeed necessary. "One has a moral responsibility to disobey unjust laws."

While most northern Reform Jews deeply sympathized with King's position, virtually all southern Jews—including members of Reform temples—wanted to stay away from the controversy. Among other reasons, they were afraid that southern whites might boycott their stores, destroying their livelihoods. They were even afraid of the possibility of antisemitic violence, remembering all too well the lynching of Leo Frank in Atlanta. After several Reform rabbis flew in from New York and posed in front of the local courthouse for a photograph protesting segregation, Rabbi Joseph H. Freedman of Albany, Georgia, quipped, "It's nice to know that the Northern Reform rabbis are willing to fight to the death of the last Southern rabbi."

The Reform movement also became actively involved in many of the other political and social causes of the 1960s and 1970s. In 1966 Eisendrath took an early stand against the Vietnam War, writing an open letter to President Johnson. The UAHC passed a resolution in 1967 urging President Johnson to reject the counsel of those calling for an intensified military engagement. The UAHC and CCAR also involved themselves with numerous other issues ranging from drug abuse to censorship and child care to religious symbols on public property.

In recent years, the Hebrew expression *tikkun olam*, the repairing of the world, has become associated with the commitment to work toward social justice. The term is originally a kabbalistic concept in which vessels were broken and scattered throughout the universe, and the mystics were trying to bring these broken shards back together again in order to redeem the world.

The Reform movement and other non-Orthodox organizations that became involved in tikkun olam activities used the expression in a simpler way. The world is broken when children in Africa are dying of

21. For over twenty years, the HUC-JIR soup kitchen at the New York campus has provided a nutritious meal weekly for homeless neighbors in the Washington Square area.
The student-run soup kitchen creates a comforting atmosphere and demonstrates the
role that social justice plays in the life of the college-institute. It is a tangible way that
Reform rabbinical students fulfill Isaiah's prophetic call to share bread with the hungry
and bring the homeless into one's house. *Courtesy of HUC-JIR.*

malnutrition. The world is broken when African American children in American ghettos are being deprived of the education they need for success as an adult. The world is broken when governments slaughter their own civilians or allow private militias to do so.

Despite the attempt to link the meaning of tikkun olam to the contemporary world situation, it was a strange choice of wording for a movement that had put such a strong emphasis on rationality. In a time when mysticism was becoming popular, it probably became the identifier for social justice simply because people began to remember its Hebrew wording. Perhaps the link with mysticism is central to its popularity, but this has not been conclusively demonstrated. If the intellectuals had chosen the best name for this ideological agenda, it might have been *tzedek chevrati*, which literally means social justice and has no mystical implications.

Some Reform leaders believe that the interest in social justice activism is declining. In some of the congregations that I visit as a scholar in residence, people reminisce about how their temple had once been a center for the struggle for civil rights, a sanctuary for Central American refugees, the headquarters for the local pro-choice movement, and the like. The story always ends the same way: they had done heroic and almost unbelievable things in the 1970s but in recent years had found it more difficult to motivate themselves and were currently doing very little.

Many congregations focus on doing good things on one day of the year—Mitzvah Day. This is a large-scale operation designed to get everyone in the community involved in several social justice projects planned for a Sunday. While these Mitzvah Days are usually very successful, they can sometimes become a substitute for an ongoing social justice commitment. Some blame the increasing emphasis on ritual for the decline in the involvement in social justice.

While there is some truth to this argument, there is no reason that Reform Jews could not simultaneously be active in social justice while increasing their level of ritual observance. Speaking to the UAHC Executive Committee in February 1998, Rabbi Eric H. Yoffie reemphasized that the Reform movement remains committed to social justice. "Even

22. HUC-JIR students demonstrating on behalf of freedom of religious expression in New York. Social justice is an essential component of Reform Judaism. To be a Reform Jew is to hear the voice of the prophets in our head; to be engaged in the ongoing work of tikkun olam; to strive to improve the world in which we live; to be God's partners in standing up for the voiceless and fixing what is broken in our society. *Courtesy of HUC-JIR.*

as Reform Jews embrace ritual, prayer, and ceremony more than ever, we continue to see social justice as the jewel in the Reform Jewish crown. . . . A Reform synagogue that does not alleviate the anguish of the suffering is a contradiction in terms."

When Rabbi Rick Jacobs spoke to the URJ Board of Trustees upon his election as president in June 2011, he was amused that the meeting was held close to his first pulpit, where he had done so much social justice work. "My rabbinate began just a few blocks from here in an old, rambling brownstone building with a small, diverse congregation of all ages and backgrounds seeking to build a community of meaning and purpose. I was hired to be the part-time rabbi and educator of the Brooklyn Heights Synagogue."

His warm and spirited sacred community grew steadily with a willingness to experiment with every aspect of congregational life. "It was exciting to build a congregation with a group of lay leaders who hungered for more than they had known."

On his watch they opened one of the first homeless shelters in New York City to be housed in a synagogue. "That holy work in the 1980s led us to join an interfaith, interracial coalition of faith communities and what would turn out to be one of the earliest community organizing projects within our Movement." This led to specific projects. "Our passion for justice led us to build 1200 affordable housing units not far from here in a neighborhood that had only known decline. Commercial banks wouldn't give our coalition a construction loan so we created our own bank for social responsibility called Community Capital. It was here in Brooklyn that I learned that congregations with purpose and imagination can do great things!"[16]

Zionism and Israel

Support for Zionism has been a cornerstone of the American Jewish civil religion for decades, ever since the establishment of the State of Israel in 1948. While Reform Judaism in the late nineteenth and early twentieth centuries had held largely negative views on the Zionist political movement, virtually all rallied around the idea of a Jewish homeland in the face of Nazi persecution in the 1930s and mass murder in the 1940s. However, in recent years, the American Jewish community has become openly divided on what it means to support Israel politically. Though most Reform Jews tend to be liberal, there is a huge gap between the political views of the leadership and that of the multitudes in local congregations.

Leaving aside the sometimes bitter dispute over how Israel should relate to its Arab neighbors (and residents), there is a major problem for the Reform movement. It is not fully accepted on equal terms as a legitimate expression of Jewish religiosity. The crucial battleground for the future of the movement is in the State of Israel, where the Israel Movement for Progressive Judaism (IMPJ) is fighting the entrenched, institutionalized Orthodoxy and widely held negative perceptions about the Reform movement.

The IMPJ is part of the World Union for Progressive Judaism (WUPJ). As described in chapter 2, the World Union is the international umbrella organization for Reform, Liberal, Reconstructionist, and all other types of Progressive Jews, founded in London in 1926 to maintain and strengthen existing progressive movements and to initiate efforts to build new ones whenever possible. While the Union for Reform Judaism is by far the largest of the World Union's nearly forty constituent groups, the IMPJ may be the most important.

The stakes are high. Because of the central position the State of Israel holds in the Jewish world, building a strong Reform movement there is the highest priority for the World Union. Israel is the world center of Judaism and Jewish tradition. The ability or inability of the Reform movement to establish itself as a legitimate player in the Israeli Jewish religious world will have tremendous implications for the future of Reform Judaism. If Reform is unable to fight its way into the Israeli societal structure, it will always be perceived by Jews in Israel and throughout the Jewish world outside North America as a passing fad popular only in the United States.

With such a diverse population expressing such a multiplicity of views and practicing religion in so many different ways, one might expect the Reform movement to find a ready niche in the Israeli religious marketplace. This has not proven to be the case. Since Israel's rabbinate controls all issues of personal status, non-Orthodox rabbis in that country are not able to perform legally binding marriage ceremonies, divorces, or even most burials. Reform and Conservative conversions are accepted by the Jewish Agency, thus allowing such individuals to immigrate to Israel under the Law of Return. Such converts, however, will not be recognized as Jews by the chief rabbinate and may therefore have problems once they settle in the country.

Complex and multifaceted problems face the Reform movement in Israel. The early Jewish settlers came from countries that lacked the pluralistic religious environment that would have allowed alternative forms of religious expression to develop. The settlers arrived in a Palestine ruled by the Turks, who likewise did not encourage Western liberal cultural or intellectual developments. The early Zionist pioneers included few Western immigrants, and most of those who did settle in Israel adapted themselves to the prevailing social and religious norms.

The Reform movement is not recognized as a legitimate Jewish expression of Judaism in the Jewish State on an equal footing with Orthodoxy. In the Israeli context, Jewish religion has meant Orthodoxy. Orthodoxy is linked directly to the state through a number of important institutions, including the chief rabbinate, the rabbinical courts, the state religious educational system, and the local religious councils. In addition, an Israeli civil religion has emerged that accepts Orthodoxy as an integral part of the identity of the state, so that even most "secular" Israelis accept Orthodox Jews and Orthodox Judaism as representing the Jewish religion.

Most Israelis tend to see religion in black and white terms. Although each individual may or may not practice it, the only true religion is Orthodox Judaism. Reform Judaism—and all other forms of non-Orthodox Judaism—are seen as inauthentic. In addition, only recognized Orthodox rabbis are accredited by the chief rabbinate to perform official functions including marriages, divorces, and burials. Orthodox synagogues are planned, designed, and built by the state whereas Reform congregations need to solicit their own funding and buildings without government support, either financial or political. And yet, without Israeli government recognition, the Reform movement risks being seen as less legitimate than Orthodoxy, little better than a "cult."

As WUPJ executive director Rabbi Richard Hirsch bluntly stated in 1999, "If Progressive Judaism can develop and thrive only in a non-Jewish environment, if we cannot succeed in impacting on the lives and values of Jews living in the Jewish state, then the charges of our critics may be substantiated. Therefore, the ultimate test of Jewish authenticity for Progressive Judaism lies in our efforts in Israel. If we succeed in Israel, we pass the test. If we fail in Israel, then doubt is cast on the authenticity of our Diaspora movement."

The Reform movement has poured effort and money into building up the Progressive presence in the State of Israel, yet the government could simply pass new laws to bypass any legal gains achieved through future rulings by the High Court of Justice. Shas and other Haredi political parties have indicated their determination to do just that, if the need should arise. Until the movement can achieve official recognition and equal legal status with the Orthodox, it will remain a small, struggling, barely tolerated denomination on the fringes of Israeli life. The marginalization of the Israeli Progressive movement threatens to undermine the legitimacy of the Reform movement in the United States and throughout the world.

Whether the Israeli Progressive movement is fully accepted in the State of Israel or not will have an impact on the legitimacy of the Reform movement throughout the world.[17] As Ephraim Tabory puts it, "While the personal identity of many Reform Jews on the micro level may not be affected by developments in Israel, Reform Judaism on a macro level is under attack."[18] That attack is not only political. Anat Hoffman, the executive director of the Israel Religious Action Center, argues that "the incitement against us has reached such a fever pitch that if a Reform synagogue were to be blown up tomorrow I would not know whether an Orthodox Jew or a Palestinian perpetuated the act." She believes there is "an ocean of hatred" against Reform Judaism in the Jewish State.[19]

During the decades when the Jewish national home was being built, the Reform movement was preoccupied with other concerns and, to the extent that Reform philanthropists gave to the Zionist cause, they prioritized general societal institutions such as hospitals, schools and so forth. A few Progressive congregations were established to serve the religious needs of the small number of Reform Jews in the nascent state but only a few produced significant achievements. Little was said in the 1930s and 1940s about the emerging status quo, which gave exclusive religious authority to the Orthodox. After the creation of the State of Israel, the leadership of the Reform movement began to realize the negative implications of the religious status quo and began taking measures to try to change the situation. New congregations were established to build a movement inside the country. Later, lawsuits were filed with the Israeli supreme court in an effort to overturn the legal structure that perpetuated the Orthodox monopoly over religion in the state. While both courses of action saw some significant gains, neither accomplished anything dramatic enough to radically alter the prevailing situation.

Because of the centrality of the State of Israel in the Jewish world, the building up of a strong Reform movement in Israel has been the highest priority for the World Union for Progressive Judaism. Since most countries with Jewish populations had Orthodox majorities, the leaders of the World Union felt it would be more diplomatic to respond to indigenous requests for assistance rather than to send advocates into Jewish communities that had no Reform constituency. Palestine was simply one of many countries with small and struggling Reform Jewish groups and did not merit special attention until much later.

In 1960 the organization moved from London to New York, and then in 1973 the headquarters for the World Union for Progressive Judaism was moved to Jerusalem, indicating the high priority that the Reform movement placed on Israel. The World Union was built adjacent to the Hebrew Union College, establishing a center for Progressive Judaism in a high-profile section of the city. The movement later built Beit Shmuel, an educational facility, and Mercaz Shimshon, a cultural center. In 1987 the movement established the Israel Religious Action Center, a political advocacy arm of the Progressive movement in Israel modeled on the Religious Action Center in Washington DC. According to their website, IRAC stands for the goals of "advancing pluralism in Israeli society and defending the freedoms of conscience, faith, and religion."

23. Celebrating Simchat Torah at Kehilat Birkat Shalom on Kibbutz Gezer. The congregation was founded in 1997 for residents of the Gezer Regional Council communities in the Ramla-Rehovat area between Jerusalem and Tel Aviv. Like all Progressive congregations in Israel, leaders welcome visitors from abroad for Kabbalat Shabbat services and offer tours of neighboring Pinat Shorashim, a Jewish educational park rooted in Jewish sources. Their goal is to strengthen the Jewish identity of all visitors by exploring the role that Eretz Yisrael plays in the lives of diaspora Jews. *Courtesy of AZRA.*

It was only in the late 1960s that the WUPJ began to develop an Israeli movement. Although a number of German Reform rabbis had emigrated to Israel in the 1930s, and a successful school under Reform auspices was founded in Haifa, there was no Reform movement to speak of until the late 1950s, and even then, it was embryonic. Kehilat Har-El was founded in Jerusalem in 1958, attracting a primarily anglophone immigrant clientele. This remained the pattern as more congregations were established throughout the country. The movement has experimented with different types of structure. In 1976, Yahel, the first Reform kibbutz, was established in the Arava Valley, and in 1983 Kibbutz Lotan was founded nearby.

While Rabbi Maurice Eisendrath had argued in favor of the creation of an Israeli Reform movement as early as 1953, it was only in 1968 that the World Union first held a biennial conference in the country. Since that time, the World Union has devoted much effort into building up the Israel Movement for Progressive Judaism, which was incorporated under Israeli law in 1971. The Israeli leadership of the IMPJ chose to refer to themselves as the movement for Yahadut Mitkademet (Progressive Judaism), avoiding the use of the term "Reform." By doing so they hoped to minimize the negative associations that many Israelis had of the American Reform movement. Particularly damaging was a video replayed on Israeli TV showing a Reform rabbi and a priest co-officiating at a wedding ceremony. At the time, many Israelis, including some secularists, found this to be a shocking and offensive sight.

On the other hand, many non-Orthodox Israelis have been positively impressed by the accomplishments of the Israeli Reform movement, especially Beit Daniel in North Tel Aviv. A few years ago, a number of leading Israeli writers and intellectuals called on the Israeli public to sign up as members of the Reform movement to protest against the Orthodox monopoly on life-cycle ceremonies. Orthodox spokesmen responded by renewing their attacks on the legitimacy of Reform Judaism, and unknown individuals suspected to be from the Haredi community vandalized buildings associated with Reform institutions.

The UAHC established the Association of Reform Zionists of America (ARZA) in 1978 inspired by the vision of Rabbi Roland Gittelsohn and guided by the ideological formulations of Rabbi David Polish. According to their website, ARZA "sees Jewish nationalism as a seamless aspect of 21st century Reform Jewish identities, and through instrumentalities such as ARZA's Institute for Reform Zionism, seeks contemporary understandings of Zionism and of Jewish peoplehood." Through rather verbose language, it is saying that the Reform movement embraces Zionism and encourages identification with the Jewish people.

The Reform movement has built an impressive complex on King David Street in Jerusalem; it includes the Israeli campus of Hebrew Union College and Mercaz Shimshon, the WUPJ's cultural center, which opened in October 2000. Designed by world-famous architect Moshe Safdie, the fifteen-million-dollar facility was built adjacent to Beit Shmuel, WUPJ headquarters. Both centers offer panoramic views of Jaffa Gate, David's Citadel, and the walls of the Old City.

24. "Freedom of Religion in Israel" was the message on two of the signs held up by supporters of the Israeli Reform movement at a demonstration in front of the office of the
Israeli Chief Rabbinate in Jerusalem. Anat Hoffman, the executive director of the Israel
Religious Action Center, appears in the center left. Rabbi Rick Jacobs (wearing a tie)
held up a sign saying, "There is more than one way to be a Jew." *Courtesy of IRAC.*

Beit Daniel was built in 1991 to serve the non-Orthodox Israeli population of North Tel Aviv. The Daniel Centers for Progressive Judaism
now include three branches: Kehilat Halev, Mishkenot Ruth Daniel in
Jaffa, and Beit Daniel itself. They oversee seventeen preschools and kin-
dergartens, filling a niche that is not covered adequately by the state's
school structure. Many "secular" Israelis come to Beit Daniel to celebrate life-cycle events, particularly bar and bat mitzvahs.

Perhaps due to changing Israeli patterns of thinking and living, the
Israeli Progressive movement has increased its number of congregations from twenty-six in 2009 to thirty-five in 2011. According to one
government research report, forty thousand Israelis define themselves
as Reform. While this is still a tiny percentage of the population, and
many of them may have rather eccentric notions of what it means to
be a Reform Jew, nevertheless this is a major step forward. In addition,

the Reform movement has for the very first time begun receiving land grants and limited public support for the building and maintenance of Reform synagogues.[20]

Recently, the Israeli attorney general's office announced a plan where non-Orthodox rabbis serving in rural areas will receive their salaries through the Culture and Sports Ministry. The recommendation by Attorney General Yehuda Weinstein was in response to a 2005 petition to the High Court by American-born Miri Gold, the Reform rabbi of Congregation Birkat Shalom at Kibbutz Gezer, and the Israel Religious Action Center (IRAC). The funding was arranged through the Culture and Sports Ministry rather than through the Religious Services Ministry, which funds Orthodox rabbis, in order to prevent the resignation of minister for religious services Yaakov Margi of the Haredi Orthodox Shas party. In any case, it is potentially a major step forward since the Reform movement has up to this point been denied public funding for rabbinic salaries.

IRAC executive director Anat Hoffman stated: "I think we are alive in a historic moment. The first *olah* from Detroit [to become a rabbi] . . . the first non-Orthodox rabbi to be recognized by the state of Israel—Miri Gold—has made history. And it is high time that the state recognized that its citizens have a diversity of religious needs that cannot be met only by Orthodox Judaism." Hoffman explained: "Every Israeli citizen pays for religious services from his tax money; there is no reason why Reform or Conservative Jews should have to pay privately for something that should be paid from public funds. And Israelis hate to be suckers."[21]

In the English edition of the Israeli newspaper *Haaretz*, URJ president Rabbi Rick Jacobs wrote a response to the recent advances. "This is a clear example of something we all value: the strength of Israel's democracy. It is also a signal that the structures of our Movement inside Israel today are strong and bold and inevitably moving in the direction of making Israel a more open and representative society. The tireless work of our Israel Religious Action Center and of our Reform synagogue movement has paid off, but as we all know, this is only a first step toward legalizing—and sanctifying—liberal Judaism in Israel."

Jacobs wrote frankly that Reform Jews are expecting equality everywhere in the world, including the Jewish homeland. "The Reform Movement, both in Israel and around the world, feels a deep commitment to Israel. But that commitment will be hard to maintain if we are not equal in Israel. We teach our young people about the miracle of the Jewish state, about the promise of a future that can unify all Jews, no matter where they live and no matter how they practice their Judaism."

But he added, "It has always been a puzzle to our members that in a state that lives in our heart and in our lives, we, as Reform Jews, are considered second-class citizens at best. Now, thanks to Rabbi Miri Gold, who has devoted so much of her life to creating the type of change that will sustain the Jewish people and Israeli democracy into the future, we have begun a new era."[22]

These successes please the leadership of the American Reform movement who support the State of Israel but hope to help mold it into a pluralistic and tolerant society. However, with the Haredi population increasing dramatically, there is unfortunately little hope that the Israeli society of the future will be more open-minded than it is today. Israel's Central Bureau of Statistics is predicting that the Haredi population will make up nearly a third of the country's population within fifty years. Since the Orthodox have held the balance of power in every coalition government since the founding of the state in 1948, it is almost certain that they will become far more important politically over the coming decades. But history can bring us surprises, and we will have to wait and see what happens.

Inclusivity

One of the major contributions of Reform Judaism has been its advocacy of inclusivity. While traditional Judaism put people in categories and dictated specific ritual obligations for each category, Reform Judaism held that everyone was equal before God. Orthodoxy did not dispute this notion, but it limited ritual accessibility based on lineage (being born of a Jewish mother), heritage (whether the paternal line descended from Kohanim, Leviim, or Israelites), gender, and other factors. The Reform movement swept away virtually all the distinctions that had formed an integral part of the halachic system. It no longer mattered where you came from or what your family background might have been. The only thing that counted was who you were. If you were a sincere person with a thirst for knowledge and a desire to integrate the lessons of Judaism into your life, then you should not be limited in any way.

This inclusivity is a hallmark of the modern Reform movement. Women, GLBTs (gays, lesbians, bisexuals, and transgendered), and in some conceptions non-Jews practicing Judaism without formal conversion are three groundbreaking categories of people who have been promised complete religious equality as part of this commitment to the value of inclusivity.

In traditional Judaism, women as well as men were obligated to perform the mitzvot. Nevertheless, women were exempt from one particular category of mitzvot. That category was *mitzvot aseh she-ha-zman gumrah*, or positive, time-bound commandments. The reason for exempting women from that particular category of commandments was that positive, time-bound mitzvot needed to be done at particular times of the day. This might not be possible for women who had the responsibility of taking care of children and performing other vital household tasks.

The rabbis were particularly concerned about the possible conflict between a woman's obligations to her children and the requirement of praying three times a day. While these prayers did not have to be done at a specific time, there was a limited time frame within which the obligation needed to be met. For example, the morning prayer needed to be recited within four halachic hours of sunrise. This might translate in practical terms to anywhere from 5:45 to 10:45 a.m., to take just a hypothetical example. In addition, the obligation to pray was best fulfilled in a minyan, a quorum of ten.

The sages made the decision not to require women to observe this set of obligations, and as a result women were excluded from one of the key areas of religious life. Since women were not obligated to perform that particular mitzvah, they could not be counted as part of the minyan that was necessary to hold public prayers. Furthermore, they could not lead such prayers since it would not be acceptable for someone who is not obligated to perform a particular mitzvah to lead others who were obligated.

While this was and remains a problem for modern Orthodox women who want to take a more active role in prayer services, it was never a major controversy in the Reform movement. Since Reform Judaism rejected the authority of the halacha, there was no problem in simply ignoring the restriction. Women could be granted equal access to leading prayers, just as they could be given equality in every other aspect of religious life. That was the theory, at least. In reality, Reform temples were dominated by men. Only men could become rabbis, and rabbis were the ones who led services. Despite the lack of a religious justification for limiting the ritual role of females, women were relegated to the sisterhood, effectively shut out of leadership until the 1970s.

The problem in earlier generations was social rather than halachic. American Reform Jews were used to seeing men lead prayers, and men serve in positions of religious authority. Women helped the congregation through their voluntary activities for the temple sisterhood. This was the way that men and women behaved in bourgeois society in the late nineteenth and early twentieth centuries. As long as Reform Jews saw their Christian neighbors following this division of labor between the genders, it seemed normal and appropriate.

That is certainly not to say that no changes were made. One of the daily blessings in the traditional prayer book has men thanking God for "not having made me a woman." Women thank God for "making me according to thy will," which hardly seems like a dignified equivalency. The editors of the early Reform prayer books changed the wording of this blessing and that was the end of that. The fact that the blessing was many hundreds of years old did not matter; if it offended contemporary sensibilities, it was history. In *Mishkan T'Filah*, the new version of the blessing reads as follows: "Praise to you, Adonai our God, Sovereign of the universe, who made me in the image of God."[23]

Many Orthodox women defend the traditional versions of this prayer, explaining that men are thanking God for having been given the obligation to observe positive, time-bound mitzvot. I find this apologetic response baffling. If a man wanted to thank God for having given him more mitzvot to observe, the prayer could have been worded that way. One of the liberating aspects of being part of a separate religious movement is that we Reform Jews no longer have to fight it out with the Orthodox. We make the changes that we feel are necessary in the prayer book and in all other aspects of Jewish religious life, and the Orthodox reinforce whatever practices they want to continue observing regardless of contemporary social values such as inclusivity or any other criteria.

Some Orthodox leaders earnestly argue that women are spiritually superior to men, whether because they give birth to children or because of certain purported innate characteristics. These spokespeople argue that women simply do not need to pray as often or perform as many mitzvot as men. They cite the fact that the Hebrew word for womb, *rehem*, has the same root as the Hebrew word for compassion, *rachamim*. They present stories from the midrash and mystical traditions to support this view, designed to make women feel affirmed in their role in the Orthodox Jewish home. Research done by Debra Kaufman has shown that a significant number of women do feel more comfortable living in an Orthodox environment. While they may not be able to climb the pinnacle of political power in the Orthodox community, they have a secure and respected position in Orthodox society.

Most women, however, clearly prefer the egalitarian route. They want to be equal in educational and employment opportunities and they want to be taken seriously in religious life. The Reform movement has been able to respond to their demands because Reform Judaism accepted the principle of gender equality since the Central European Reform rabbinical conferences of the 1840s. Nevertheless, it took until 1972 for the Reform movement to actually ordain a woman as a rabbi. There had been a German Jewish woman, Regina Jonas, who had studied for the rabbinate in the liberal seminary in the 1930s, but the Berlin rabbinical school refused to ordain her at the end of her studies and she had to be ordained privately. While the earliest women rabbis in the United States of the 1970s faced special challenges, women today are easily accepted as rabbis, cantors, synagogue presidents, and so forth.

While the issue is complex, some critics believe the problem that Reform temples are facing today is not that women are being excluded or discriminated against, but rather that they are dominating temple life, driving out many men. This is part of a broader pattern sometimes referred to as the feminization of American religion. It may be that men participated in religious activities and volunteered for leadership positions not so much because they were dedicated to Judaism but because they were looking for a way to express their masculinity.

If my male readers have ever participated in an Orthodox minyan, they understand immediately how much of a male bonding experience it can be. Once that is taken away, many men may no longer feel the desire to participate. Likewise, becoming temple president or taking on any of the other major leadership positions used to be a way that a man could demonstrate his social status and also his economic success, since these positions tended to go to the more affluent men. But once leadership roles were being routinely filled by women, many men no longer felt that those particular positions were worth striving for.

If full gender equality turns out to be a highly beneficial arrangement for both sexes over the long term, then there will be a great deal of positive energy produced by and for the Reform temple. But if there are indeed unresolved gender-related issues, the Reform movement may need to launch strategic campaigns to encourage men to reengage. The Union for Reform Judaism has already undertaken a limited number of initiatives to promote male spirituality and to encourage men to engage in some of the same gender-specific activities that women have been doing over the past thirty years. We will just have to wait and see if inclusivity can be reconciled with males' continued synagogue involvement.

In the case of women, the Reform movement has taken a group that is recognized as a legitimate category in Jewish law and eliminated restrictions on that group. In the case of gays and lesbians, however, the Reform movement is legitimizing a group that had never had any sanctioned status in Jewish law. Homosexual behavior was prohibited in the halacha, and gays and lesbians were not recognized as a category of Jews. From a traditionalist perspective, legitimizing these sexual sinners was a far greater step than expanding the ritual eligibility of women. The transgressive had become normative and even praiseworthy.

In the Torah, there are three direct references to homosexuality. "Do not lie with a male as one lies with a woman; it is an abomination" (Leviticus 18:22). "If a man lies with a male as one lies with a woman, the two of them have done an abhorrent thing; they shall be put to death" (Leviticus 20:13). "No Israelite woman shall be a cult prostitute, nor shall any Israelite man be a cult prostitute" (Deuteronomy 23:18). Each of these statements is interpreted as prohibiting homosexual acts between men.

Various non-Orthodox thinkers have tried to explain away these three statements, arguing that the Torah had only specific types of acts in mind or that the concept of homosexuality was entirely different in the ancient Near East and that the Torah had no intention of prohibiting the type of loving homosexual relations that are common among American gay men. These efforts are interesting in that they show just how committed their authors are to reach a conclusion that will be pleasing to the gay community. Unfortunately, there is no definitive evidence that these arguments have any real historical validity.

That is not to say that Reform Judaism needs to retain the traditional bias against male homosexual behavior. Rather, I just think that it is preferable to honestly state that we are radically deviating from twenty-five hundred or more years of Judaic opposition to homosexual behavior and that we are setting a new course because of the radical reappraisal of sexual identity and sexual behavior that has been happening in the western world over the past three or four decades.

Once a consensus developed that gays and lesbians (bisexuals were not included and transgendered individuals were not yet thought about) deserved equality, the Reform movement moved rapidly in support of gay rights. In 1977 the Union of American Hebrew Congregations General Assembly passed a resolution at the Biennial in San Francisco deploring discrimination against gay men and lesbians. That same year, the CCAR passed a resolution stating that they have "consistently supported civil rights and civil liberties for all people, especially for those from whom these rights and liberties have been withheld." Since "homosexuals have in our society long endured discrimination," the CCAR resolved "that we encourage legislation which decriminalizes homosexual acts between consenting adults, and prohibits discrimination against them as persons."

Ten years later, the UAHC passed an additional resolution calling on member congregations to accept gays and lesbians into all facets of congregational life. The preamble to this resolution provides part of the religious justification for this position: "God calls upon us to love our neighbors as ourselves." The prophet Isaiah "charges us further: 'Let my house be called a house of prayer, for all people' (Isaiah 56:7). . . . We Jews are asked to create a society based on righteousness, the goal being tikkun olam, the perfection of our world."

Each of us is created in God's image. We therefore have "a unique talent which can contribute to that high moral purpose; and to exclude any Jew from the community of Israel lessens our chances of achieving that goal." The UAHC resolution explained that what this meant was that "sexual orientation should not be a criterion for membership of or participation in an activity of any synagogue." Thus, all Jews should be welcome, however they may define themselves.

In 1993 Rabbi Alexander M. Schindler, then president of the UAHC, urged the Reform movement to support the right of gay and lesbian couples to adopt children, to file joint income tax returns, and to be eligible for health and death benefits. In a resolution that same year, the UAHC pointed out that "committed lesbian and gay couples are [still being] denied the benefits routinely accorded to married heterosexual couples." A resolution was passed arguing that full equality under the law for lesbian and gay people requires legal recognition of lesbian and gay relationships.[24]

Some Reform rabbis, particularly those interested in Reform halacha, remained concerned that certain religious concepts were being blurred in the rush to support gay rights. In 1997 the CCAR Committee on Responsa addressed the question of whether homosexual relationships can qualify as *kiddushin*, the sanctification of a holy union. By a vote of seven to two, the committee concluded that "homosexual relationships, however exclusive and committed they may be, do not fit within this legal category; they cannot be called kiddushin. We do not understand Jewish marriage apart from the concept of kiddushin."

The following year, the CCAR Ad Hoc Committee on Human Sexuality issued a report that went completely against the spirit, although not necessarily the letter, of that responsum. Almost unanimously, they voted that "kedushah may be present in committed same gender relationships between two Jews and that these relationships can serve as the foundation of stable Jewish families, thus adding strength to the Jewish community." It is interesting that the wording is careful to exclude interfaith gay relationships and focuses on the argument that recognizing gay Jewish marriages will strengthen the American Jewish community rather than making a statement on equality as a social justice issue.

In March 2000 the CCAR approved a resolution supporting the rights of Reform rabbis to officiate at gay and lesbian commitment ceremonies. In line with the long-standing policy of the CCAR to respect differing viewpoints, the resolution stated that "we recognize the diversity of opinions within our ranks on this issue. We support the decision of those who choose to officiate at rituals of union for same-gender couples, and we support the decision of those who do not." Rabbi Shira Stern of the Women's Rabbinic Network said: "This is not a woman's issue, or a gay or lesbian issue. This is a human rights issue." For those Jews "who have no choice in the matter of sexual identity, we as leaders of the movement must provide them with the religious framework in which to celebrate their union."

As President Barack Obama told the Seventy-First General Assembly at the Biennial in Washington DC on December 16, 2011, "And as all of you know, standing up for our values at home is only part of our work. Around the world, we stand up for values that are universal—including the right of all people to live in peace and security and dignity." The audience applauded enthusiastically. "That's why we've worked on the international stage to promote the rights of women—to promote strategies to alleviate poverty—to promote the dignity of all people, including gays and lesbians—and people with disabilities—to promote human rights and democracy."

The Green Revolution

The Reform movement has long been committed to environmental responsibility. Protecting the environment is an important priority, first and foremost, because if the ecological system of our planet is destroyed, we will all perish. Even if we do not destroy our environment entirely, the loss of various species and habitats will be a tragedy that cannot be reversed and one that will have serious negative consequences for humankind. While this concept might seem self-evident, environmentalism was not explicitly discussed in most religious discourse prior to the 1960s. Even afterward, it is not always clear what forms the religious basis for a position in favor of ecological preservation.

In order to support the environmental cause, the leaders of the Reform movement had to deal with the anthropocentrism that is emphasized in certain biblical and rabbinic texts. Specifically, in the book of Genesis, God instructs humanity to hold dominion over nature. The most obvious understanding of this is that the world is created for the benefit of human beings. One could extrapolate from this that humankind can therefore do what they want with the world. The Reform movement, of course, rejects this line of thinking, arguing that the Torah's words should be interpreted as giving humans the responsibility of protecting the world rather than a license to despoil it.

The book of Genesis states, "God then blessed them, and God said to them, 'Be fruitful and multiply; fill the earth and tame it; hold sway over the fish of the sea and the birds of the sky, and over every animal that creeps on the earth'" (1:28). Some theologians have interpreted this verse to mean that God was giving humankind the right to use nature at will. According to one group of Protestant theologians meeting to address a "Theology of Survival" in 1970, "any solution to the current environmental crisis would require major modifications to current religious values."[25]

Lynn Townsend White Jr. presented a paper at the American Association for the Advancement of Science in 1966 on "The Historical Roots of Our Ecological Crisis" in which he argued that the Industrial Revolution marked a critical turning point in our ecological history. The mentality that underlay the Industrial Revolution was that the earth was a resource for human consumption. White traced this approach back to medieval Christianity, which drew its exegesis on the book of Genesis from ancient Jewish sources.

He argued that Judeo-Christian theology led to a modern attitude that accepted the exploitation of the natural world because the Torah was understood as asserting man's dominion over nature, establishing anthropocentrism as a central religious value. Christianity makes a fundamental distinction between humans, who are formed in God's image, and all other forms of life, which have no souls and are therefore inferior. White's ideas set off an extended debate about how religion may have encouraged the nonchalantly destructive attitudes toward the environment that dominated western societies until the 1960s.

Most Reform Jewish thinkers, along with many others, however, take issue with this interpretation of Judeo-Christian perspectives on environmental responsibility. These scholars and activists align more closely with the interpretation from *The Torah: A Woman's Commentary* that states the words "hold sway" are "not a mandate to exploit nature" but rather an exhortation to be good stewards of our resources, which are on loan from God to humanity.[26]

Following this line of reasoning, the human domination of the earth is a misinterpretation of text that actually requires us to protect and nurture the planet rather than allowing us to exploit and destroy. Humanity may have a special role in the order of life, but that role is one of extra responsibility because of our ability to think abstractly and engage in long-range planning.

The creation stories in the book of Genesis and reflections throughout the midrash demonstrate that we are an integral part of and dependent on nature rather than apart from it. Rachel Cohen, senior legislative assistant at the Religious Action Center of Reform Judaism, refers to Genesis Rabbah 13:3 as a Judaic source emphasizing our place in the natural order. Rabbi Shimon Bar Yochai said, "Three things are of equal importance: earth, humans, and rain." Rabbi Levi ben Hiyyata explained that Bar Yochai's comment meant "to teach that without earth, there is no rain, and without rain, the earth cannot endure, and without either, humans cannot exist."[27] The Torah and its teachings remain relevant, even when the discussion focuses on environmental issues that could not possibly have been envisioned thousands of years ago.

Rashi explains that the verses in Genesis 1:28–31 indicate that humanity has a mandate to dominate the world but that this mandate is given to them by God on the strict condition that they will show themselves worthy of this responsibility. By this interpretation, if human beings misuse their dominant position in the natural order to destroy species and harm the natural environment, they would be violating the terms of their mandate from God. Many Reform Jews are sensitive to this understanding and work to protect the environment and show that they are doing all that they can to be ecologically responsible.

On their web page, the Union for Reform Judaism has an explanation for "Why is Greening Jewish?" They write that the most important citation determining the Jewish relationship with the environment is Genesis 2:15: "The Lord God took the man and placed him in the Garden of Eden, to till it and tend it." In Ecclesiastes Rabbah, the sages imagine what God might have told Adam: "Look at My works! How beautiful and praiseworthy they are! And everything I made, I created for you. Be careful [though] that you don't spoil or destroy my world—because if you spoil it, there is nobody after you to fix it" (7:13). The URJ web page adds that as modern stewards of creation, we too must be especially careful not to destroy this earth beyond repair.

The URJ Biennial that took place in Toronto in November 2009 placed an emphasis on environmental responsibility. "Green is the color of choice," the press release stated. Several learning sessions focused on environmental themes including "Save Green by Going Green: Greening URJ Synagogues, Camps, and Homes" and "Green Advocacy: Going Beyond Greening Your Actions." The URJ vowed to make the 2009 Biennial the most sustainable ever, taking steps to reduce energy, water, and paper use. It was held at the Metro Toronto Convention Centre, one of the most environmentally friendly meeting places in North America, with energy-efficient lighting, a multi-acre green roof, and ultra-efficient heating and air conditioning systems. The URJ worked with Convention Centre staff to provide "green tours" of the facility to allow Biennial participants to see firsthand its sustainable features, emphasizing the location as an exemplar of environmental responsibility.

Delegates were urged to *travel justly* by taking whatever steps possible to reduce their environmental impact and offset the carbon footprint of the Biennial. In order to fund this effort, the URJ created an Environmental Sustainability Fund. Money raised will be earmarked to counter-act carbon emissions by funding renewable energy, reforestation, and other greenhouse gas reducing projects in Israel and around the world. The North American Federation of Temple Youth passed a similar recommendation on carbon offsetting in 2010.

The delegates also voted to adopt a "URJ Resolution on Climate Change and Energy" that urged Reform Jews to "take action toward integrating an ethic of environmental stewardship into every aspect of Jewish life." The resolution authorizes the Religious Action Center of Reform Judaism, the lobbying arm of the Reform movement, to take an active role in the political debate on the appropriate global response to climate change. Yoffie made sustainable food systems a focus of the Biennial by announcing an initiative on environmentally responsible and sustainable eating choices. He encouraged congregations to take on the environmental impact of food choices by planting community gardens, starting community-supported agriculture (CSA) programs and implementing other sustainable food system programming. The 2011 URJ Biennial held at the Gaylord National Hotel and Conference Center in Washington DC continued these environmentally friendly policies.

The UAHC first dealt with the question of protecting the environment way back in 1965, when the delegates called for the conservation of natural resources. In the following decades, the Reform movement came back to this issue periodically. In 1969 they passed a resolution against environmental pollution. In 1979 they called for an environmentally sound energy policy. In 1983 they supported a resolution protesting against the widespread use of dangerous industrial toxins.

In 1984 the CCAR Responsa Committee published a responsum on Judaism and the environment. The issue was of increasing importance, and the Responsa Committee wanted to address the roots of environmental activism in traditional Jewish sources. Unfortunately, they could not find very much. The responsum mentions the biblical ordinance against destroying fruit trees while besieging a city, pointing out that the regulation "has been reinterpreted far more broadly to include any purposeless destruction during siege." They mention environmental concerns dealing with the city of Jerusalem, including garbage removal, the existence of dung, and remnants of animal carcasses left over from ritual sacrifices.

The CCAR Responsa Committee pointed out that much of the Talmudic and post-Talmudic references fall under the category of the principle of *baal taschit*, which they translate as to "cause no wanton destruction." They mention the need to be compassionate to animals and under what circumstances it would be permitted to kill them for food. They conclude by making a brief reference to the fact that "many benedictions regularly thank God for the wonders of nature." In conclusion, the responsum states, "Judaism has emphasized an appreciation of the environment and nature since the Biblical period. These issues do not play a dominant role in Jewish life, but they remain important."[28] The responsum lists these subjects but seems unable to explain how they are directly relevant to contemporary environmental concerns. The core problem with the responsum is that the writers focus exclusively on halachic material, ignoring midrashim that would function much better in explaining a Jewish theology of environmentalism.

The CCAR, however, did take note of a crucial midrashic source when they adopted a resolution on the environment at their annual convention in Seattle in June 1990. They cited Ecclesiastes Rabbah (previously mentioned above) that God said to "humanity" in the Garden of Eden: "See My works, how beautiful and praiseworthy they are. Everything I have created has been created for your sake. Think of this, and do not corrupt or destroy My world; for if you corrupt it, there will be no one to set it right after you" (chapter 7, section 13). The resolution goes on to explain that "we are heirs of *Bal Tashchit*, an environmental ethic that ever commands us to preserve and not to destroy God's world." Since "economic, industrial, and governmental forces have combined to create an international society blinded to such an environmental ethic, to the point that has come to threaten our physical security." The resolution then lists various measures that the CCAR recommends that institutions, congregations, families, and individuals undertake. They also encourage rabbis, religious school educators, and social action committees to disseminate "the wisdom of our tradition pertinent to the preservation of God's world in order to foster and nurture a Jewish environmental ethic."[29]

In 1991 the UAHC passed a resolution at its Biennial in Baltimore that broadly called on the U.S. and Canadian governments to take various measures to protect the environment. This included helping to protect endangered plants and animals, to create protected wilderness areas, to take measures against air pollution, and to help ensure the continued supply of clean water. The resolution also called for government policy to respond more forcefully to emerging environmental threats such as global warming. The UAHC called on the government as well as various organizations and institutions to establish recycling programs as one concrete way to reduce environmental impact. The UAHC also urged governmental authorities to prevent environmental injustice to the poor and minority communities in North America and around the world who most often bear the brunt of environmental degradation. Finally, the resolution called on the UAHC and other Reform organizations to provide specific guidance to congregants and congregations in terms of how to modify their behavior in order to preserve the planet.

The 1991 resolution explained, "The Jewish community's mandate to cultivate, protect, and nurture the environment is deeply rooted in our tradition." The resolution explained that the biblical commandment of baal taschit enjoins the children of Israel, "Do not destroy things from which humanity may benefit" (Deuteronomy 20). While the resolution does not cite a specific verse, it would appear to refer to the following scriptural passage:

> When in your war against a city you have to besiege it a long time in order to capture it, you must not destroy its trees, wielding the ax against them. You may eat of them, but you must not cut them down. Are trees of the field human to withdraw before you into the besieged city? Only trees that you know do not yield food may be destroyed; you may cut them down for constructing siegeworks against the city that is waging war on you, until it has been reduced.
> (Deuteronomy 20:19–20)

The 1991 resolution on the environment continues with one additional biblical reference. "The warning against idolatry founded [sic] in Deuteronomy reminds us that if we abuse the environment, displaying contempt for the integrity of God's creation, purse [sic] rain will cease to fall and the ground will cease to yield its produce." Again, the resolution provides no chapter or verse, but the reference is in the book of Deuteronomy:

> Take care not to be lured away to serve other gods and bow to them. For Adonai's anger will flare up against you, shutting up the skies so that there will be no rain and the ground will not yield its produce; and you will soon perish from the good land that Adonai is assigning to you.
> (Deuteronomy 11:16–17)

The Reform movement has also advocated in favor of other ecological issues, including improving biodiversity and decreasing global warming. Many Reform Jews support the concept of "a sustainable society," even though that would require us to radically change our style of living. It is our obligation to protect the world and to work toward the literal fulfillment of tikkun olam, the repairing of the world.

CHAPTER 6

Who Is a (Reform) Jew?

Laurel Snyder was born when her Irish Catholic mother from California "got knocked up when she was twenty-two, and rather than have the abortion (though she did name me after the Laurel Clinic, when she decided 'not to go through with it') she married my dad, a Jewish Socialist from Baltimore. Accidental. Haphazard."[1] Later, reflecting on her parents' relationship, she wrote, "They were young and they didn't really understand each other. My mom was a lovely little hippie and a closet Anglophile. My dad was a severe young politico, both a stoic and a skeptic. They didn't get along very well. But they weren't stupid or mean or faithless, and they loved me. I'm very lucky."

When Snyder was a little girl, religion seemed to be a nonissue for her parents. "My mom didn't go to church and my dad didn't go to temple, but at some point early on, my parents decided to raise me Jewish, and my younger brother and sister too." She was led to understand that this was a practical measure, a direct consequence of the fact that they lived in Baltimore, and since her grandparents in that city were Jewish, that would "make things easier at the holidays."

Snyder attended a Reform religious school on Sunday mornings at a huge temple in the heart of the Baltimore Jewish community where many of her classmates lived. Girls with names like Rachel Goldstein and Rachel Cohen wore fancy clothes and did not talk to her. Nevertheless, she writes, "I loved Hebrew school. I loved learning the strange histories, bloody stories, and foreign traditions, which were largely absent in my own home and neighborhood. I love stringing apples in the *Sukkah* and dressing up for Purim."

Snyder began living what she calls a "Half/Life," by which she means living in simultaneous worlds or homes. She began alternating attending services at the Bolton Street Synagogue one weekend, and the Corpus Christi Church the next. "It was abundance, and I never felt the two religions to be in any conflict, because nobody ever really asked me to pick one." In contrast to some of the contributors to *Half/Life*, the collection of spiritual autobiographies from interfaith homes that she would later edit, Snyder always felt that she was unambiguously Jewish. "I was Jewish, and I never questioned that fact. I had been *bat mitzvahed* and I knew the prayers I was supposed to say. When I sat in the pew with Susan [her best friend] or my mom I never took communion or said the creed. I never crossed myself. That wasn't me, or any part of what I expected. But I had a place there too. I watched."[2]

She was fascinated by Susan's Catholicism, "which made my mom's Catholicism fascinating too." She was amazed at the ritual practices. "I was in love with the incense and the candles. I was in love with the Christmas tree and the smell of the soup kitchen. I played hide-and-seek with Susan in the church rectory, and in the church itself, where I got tangled, literally, in the robes hanging inside a vestment closet, and felt at home."

After she went to college in Tennessee, she began to study Judaism more seriously. She took Jewish studies classes, taught Hebrew school at the local synagogue, and studied in Israel for a semester. On summer break back in Baltimore, she decided to undergo an official conversion to Judaism and immersed herself in the *mikveh*. As I read her story, I was surprised at how she continued to express an affinity with Catholicism—even after her conversion.

Snyder hammered out "an intentional religious life, a Half/Life full of very particular choices but rooted in my haphazard beginnings." She had grown up with a Christmas tree so she continued to put one up in her adult life. She stopped eating pork and shellfish but did not claim to be kosher since strict observance of the laws of Kashrut would involve far more. "I read Jewish novels and collected Catholic religious art. I went to Italy, but once I'd visited the Florence Synagogue and the Venice Ghetto, I headed for Santa Maria Novella."

A few years ago, Snyder was invited to her local Jewish Community Center to do a reading of her picture book *Baxter, the Pig Who Wanted to Be Kosher*. "*Baxter* isn't really a book about being kosher. It's about wanting to be accepted into a community. But I always like to make sure my listeners know what the word *kosher* means before I read it, since the joke at the center of the book depends on that." Snyder then asked the crowd if they could define the word. Before anyone else could answer, her own son Mose, who was five at the time, jumped up and shouted out, "I know! I know! Kosher is *us*! *We're* kosher!" Then he sat back down again, beaming proudly. Snyder thought, "I might have been proud too. Only, you see, we're not kosher."

On the drive home, Snyder tried to figure how to explain to Mose that to be kosher, one must live by a rigid religious daily dietary code. She wanted him to respect the practice but also needed him to understand that they were not practicing the kosher food laws. Should she simply blame her parents, who had not raised her that way? Snyder reflected that it is difficult to explain how you behave religiously to your child when you have not figured it out yourself.

Snyder lit candles each week and said the blessings, belonged to a *havurah*, and had a cohort of local Jewish friends who got together for monthly potluck dinners and to go to services at the synagogue. Her children made her want to be a better version of her Jewish self and to pass something special on to them, something more than "You're Jewish because I'm Jewish." But she realized that sometimes the opposite was true. Sometimes her children exposed the limits of her faith. She admitted she did not keep kosher and did not really want to. Her husband was not Jewish, although they were raising their family to be. They ate tacos for Shabbat dinner most weeks and regularly skipped Friday night services. Lying to her children about her religious life was no way to model the value of faith.

Snyder decided to write another picture book, *Good Night, Laila Tov* (*laila tov* means "good night" in Hebrew), to paint an honest portrait of her largely secular household so that her children could recognize the family in her story as Jewish but also like their own family—not exactly kosher. She found herself "a little afraid that, in attempting to write a picture book for everyone, I was letting the Jewish particularity go. Aren't family, nature, and environmentalism tenets of faith beyond the Jewish world, in every religion? What did it say about me, my choices, my household, that the Jewish life I was choosing to depict looked like it could be any household at all?" Snyder recalled that moment with Mose, the moment she realized she had somehow misled him because of whatever she was unsure of or did not know about faith, and concluded: if it was not honest, it would not count.

The purpose of faith "is to infuse life with greater meaning. To make it more real. Not to dress it up. Not to pretend. My kids and I are on a journey together. We're setting out for parts unknown. And while we may find ourselves changing as we trek along, there is a sacred quality in simply being who we are today. Of stopping on the trail and taking a deep breath. It's enough, I think, to be exactly who we are, kosher or not."[3]

Defining Who Is Jewish

Snyder is an example of a child of mixed religious parentage who chose Judaism and has continued that pattern into her own marriage. The leaders of the Reform movement want to do everything they can to attract people like her. This should not be that hard. Reform Judaism is widely perceived to be the most cutting edge of the major American Jewish denominations. Those who have followed the dramatic religious transformations of the last few decades have noted the central role that the Reform movement has played. Many of the most vibrant congregations are affiliated with the Reform movement. In addition, Reform Judaism has an attractive approach to Jewish practice that stresses religious autonomy. This fits well with the contemporary interest in personal spirituality. As a result, people from many different backgrounds have developed an interest in Reform Judaism and have asked the question, "How do I join?"

According to tradition, Abraham was the first Jew. He rejected polytheism and was therefore chosen by God to be the founding father of the Jewish people. Along with his wife Sarah and many followers, Abraham migrated from Ur of the Chaldees to Canaan, later to be known as the land of Israel. While there is an extensive scholarly literature on the origin of the Jews, there is no consensus regarding where the Jews came from, what they believed at the beginning of their coalescence into a distinctive group, or many other questions of the historical development of Jewish identity.

Historically, Jewish status was determined in one of two ways: birth or conversion. A Jew could be defined as anyone who is a member of the Jewish people, an ethno-religious group emerging from the Israelites of the ancient Near East. Unlike many other ethnic groups, however, ethnicity and religion are intertwined. The Jewish people and the religion of Judaism are inseparable. While there are many Jews who identify themselves as ethnically Jewish but religiously uninvolved, they risk losing their right—from the mainstream Jewish community's point of view—to identify with the Jewish people if they embrace another religion. That is a significant difference from an Asian American or an Italian American, both of whom can continue to identify with their ethnic group regardless of their faith.

Today there are a new set of questions. Some of these issues deal with conversion to Judaism, but others involve how to define Jewish identity in a multicultural world. Largely a result of the widespread acceptance across religious and ethnic boundaries, many people have parents who believe in and/or practice different religions. How does having a Christian mother or a Buddhist father affect one's Jewish status? What about someone who was raised Jewish but became a Sufi or began practicing another type of spiritual practice? Are they still Jewish? Can they participate in a synagogue service or even lead it? There are dozens of such questions that can be asked.

The traditional source for answering these types of questions was the halacha, Jewish law. Various classical works provide the detailed theory, and more recent codes explain these laws in great detail. Orthodox Jews can refer to these sources in order to determine "who is Jewish." The basic answer, however, is quite simple. In Jewish law, a Jew is someone born of a Jewish mother or someone who was converted to Judaism according to the halacha. But the Reform movement does not accept halacha as obligatory and therefore does not see itself obligated to follow

25. Nigel Chen-See prepares for immersion at Rockfort Mineral Bath in Kingston, Jamaica, as part of his *giur* process. Discovered in the aftermath of the Great Earthquake of 1907, the waters of the bath flow from coldwater springs in the surrounding mountain range, thereby meeting the halachic requirement of immersing in running water. Immersing in a mikveh is one of a series of formerly jettisoned traditions relating to the conversion process that are being brought back. Some Reform Jews believe that immersion should even be a requirement in order to become a Jew. *Courtesy of Dana Evan Kaplan.*

its dictates. The question therefore becomes "who is Jewish according to Reform Judaism?"

The Reform movement is an independent religious group that makes its own policy decisions without having to answer to other Jewish denominations. In contrast, most Orthodox Jews do not believe that anyone has the right to make decisions that deviate from the halacha as defined by Orthodox authorities. While the Reform movement has made many decisions that have offended traditionalists, the redefinition of Jewish identity is seen by most as the most egregious. The reason they see this decision as particularly offensive is that as long as all Jewish groups had the same definition of who is a Jew, the integrity and unity of the Jewish people was preserved. Once the liberal denominations developed different criteria for defining who is a Jew, the minimal basis for maintaining a common commitment to *klal yisrael*, the unity of the Jewish people, was destroyed.

One problem was that the concept of conversion differed. The Reform movement broke away from tradition by changing certain practices and soon began developing justifications for those changes by explaining how Reform Judaism differed from traditional Judaism in theology as well as ritual. Once these differences were established, conversions done by Reform rabbis would logically follow the Reform approach. Men or women converting to Judaism through a Reform temple would not be required to believe that both the written and oral Torahs were given from God to Moses word for word, and that the halacha was the direct consequence of that revelation. They would therefore not be required to follow the halacha, but rather would be allowed to decide on their own what rituals and ceremonies held religious meaning for them.

But it was not just Reform conversions that distinguished the Reform conception of Jewish identity. Patrilineal descent became an even bigger obstacle to Jewish unity. Already in the nineteenth century, the Reform movement was accepting the children of Jewish fathers and non-Jewish mothers into religious school. After studying for many years, these individuals—now young adults—would be confirmed with their classmates, accepting the yoke of the Torah upon themselves. Eventually this informal practice was officially endorsed by the Reform movement as the patrilineal descent resolution of 1983. Traditionalists vehemently objected, arguing that the Reform movement was undermining the very basis of the Jewish religion. Even sympathetic outsiders could not help but express concern for the unexpected consequences that were sure to follow.

Patrilineal descent is relevant to those who still believe in clearly defining who is a Jew. Increasing numbers of Americans have rejected this and other definitive classifications in favor of more nuanced and flexible understandings of identity. Some Reform congregations have taken this postmodern sensibility to its logical conclusion, rejecting all traditional criteria for establishing who is a Jew. They argue that as long as someone is involved in the congregation and has no conflicting beliefs or practices, they are happy to accept such an individual as a full member with all rights and privileges regardless of religious background or whether the person has formally converted. A significant number of loyal members of certain Reform congregations were not born Jewish nor have they undergone a formal conversion. Nevertheless, some congregations accept these individuals as Jews in every way, allowing them to participate in services, bless the Torah, and do anything that any other Jew might do ritually or communally.

This is not, however, accepted Reform practice. In his book *Jewish Living: A Guide to Contemporary Reform Practice*, Rabbi Mark Washofsky argues that "Jewish identity . . . is not determined purely by the individual, exclusively as a matter of personal belief or a feeling of attachment."[4] Washofsky argues that a person cannot become Jewish simply by making a declaration to themselves or to their friends. Rather, a person who was not born Jewish should go through an educational program leading to a rabbinically supervised religious ceremony. Otherwise, there is no oversight by the community, and anyone can claim anything, potentially leading to chaos.

Washofsky explains that Jewishness is partially analogous to citizenship. To become an American citizen, a person must either be born in the United States or must go through a naturalization process, which he compares to conversion to Judaism. Just as an individual needs to be born in the United States in order to immediately be an American citizen, Washofsky writes that a person needs to be born of a Jewish mother in order to automatically be Jewish. Likewise, a person who wishes to become naturalized needs to follow the procedures set down in the regulations, whether the civil laws governing American citizenship or the religious regulations determining Jewish identity.

Some object to this approach, arguing that identity has become so transitory that it is no longer possible to put individuals into clearly definable categories. Even more to the point, increasing numbers of people are going to resist authority figures who claim exclusive rights to determine other people's spiritual identity. Many Reform Jews reject Orthodoxy precisely because they want a flexible approach to religion that stresses spirituality rather than law. Of course, it is also true that other Reform Jews want the opposite—a coherent set of religious policies that can be universally applied so they can present Reform Judaism as a holistic system. Because of such fundamental disagreement, it is never going to be possible to state *the* Reform position on this (or any other) issue.

Whether one argues for more structure or greater freedom, most agree that Reform Judaism has a great deal of spiritual wisdom that can inspire Americans from many types of backgrounds. The Reform movement has pioneered Outreach, a campaign to educate interested non-Jews and offer them the possibility of converting to Judaism. Rabbi Eric H. Yoffie, the past president of the Union for Reform Judaism, argues that Outreach represents a theological principle central to the Jewish mission to the world. Yoffie writes that the starting point for Outreach must be the same as for all of Jewish thought: "our unique destiny as a religious people, tied to God in a covenant that we trace back to Abraham and Sarah." While some are born as Jews, and therefore "Judaism speaks the language of fate," the Jewish religion "speaks as well the language of choice."[5]

Conversion to Judaism

Conversion to Judaism is a topic near and dear to my heart. As a college undergraduate and later as a rabbinic student, I spent a great deal of time thinking about the problems facing the American Jewish community, and I hit upon what seemed at the time to be the optimal solution—to encourage hundreds of thousands of non-Jewish Americans to convert to Judaism. I began to realize that most other religious groups put a great deal of emphasis on proselytization. In contrast, none of the Jewish denominations made the slightest effort. On the contrary, their attitudes seemed to range from apathy to belligerence. I thought this should change.

The Torah does not have any formal mechanism for converting people to Judaism. There are scattered references that seem to indicate that individuals and even groups began practicing Judaism, but it is not always clear whether they actually became part of the Jewish people or remained in a liminal state, no longer non-Jewish but not yet quite Jewish. The most famous convert in the Hebrew Bible is Ruth, who converts herself. After Ruth's husband dies, her mother-in-law, Naomi, urges Ruth to return home to Moab. Ruth refuses, explaining that "your people are my people; your God is my God." With this simple declaration, she becomes a Jew.

Conversion actually goes back much further than Ruth. Abraham was the first convert in a sense, since it was he who discovered the one true God and spent the rest of his life trying to spread the truth of ethical monotheism. In the book of Genesis, there is a reference to the "souls gotten in Haran" by Abraham, and this idea was embellished in the midrash. Abraham tried to serve as a model for the new faith, doing his best to live up to the high ethical standard demanded by the one God. It is not at all unlikely that his charisma, combined with deep devotion, could attract a substantial group of followers quite quickly. There does not seem any reason to assume that Abraham intended the new faith to be a tiny group forever. That was the way that history played itself out, but that was not necessarily the original plan.

Many scholars now believe that Judaism was a missionary faith until Christianity became the official religion of the Holy Roman Empire, which banned Jewish proselytization. It seems that Judaism made a positive impression on large numbers of pagans who lived throughout the Mediterranean. Some actually converted to Judaism, but many others became demi-proselytes, adopting many of the religious beliefs of Judaism and practicing selected customs, but not formally converting. One of the reasons many stopped short of full conversion was that Israel was an ethnic group, to use a modern term for an ancient status. This meant, in practice, that you could not just convert to Judaism as a religion; you had to join the group in a social, political, and even an economic sense.

Another problem was that male proselytes had to undergo circumcision, which was not commonly done at that time. Indeed, converts were expected to observe all of Jewish law, which imposed considerable demands. If Judaism had been able to proselytize more successfully in the immediate pre-Christian era, Christianity might never have spread beyond a small group in a handful of cities in the land of Israel. As it happened, Christianity and later Islam made millions of converts by preaching a religious message that was based on the theological concepts of early Judaism.

Once Christianity entrenched itself as the official state religion of the Holy Roman Empire, laws were passed making it illegal to convert anyone to Judaism. From the fourth century on, Judaism adopted a new policy of nonproselytization. External political events influenced an internal debate that had been going on for hundreds of years. Almost a thousand years before, Ezra had returned from Babylon and ordered the many Jewish men in Israel who had married non-Jewish wives to send their wives and children away. Many, if not most, of these wives and children presumably would have been happy to convert to Judaism, but Ezra did not want that to happen. At around the same time, the book of Ruth was written to glorify a particular convert, obviously suggesting that conversion should be encouraged. King David himself was supposed to have been a descendent of Ruth, and since the messiah is to be of the House of David, the messiah will have a female proselyte ancestor.

While some of the sages wanted to encourage conversion, others did not. Once the new Roman laws made Jewish proselytization illegal and sometimes punishable by death, the debate was effectively ended. It seemed to justify the position of those who had opposed conversion all along. The already difficult requirements for a prospective proselyte were made even more restrictive. Nevertheless, the Talmudic requirements were minimal in comparison with Orthodox expectations today. The sages required the convert to accept "the yoke of the commandments," demanding that the rabbinic supervisor teach the convert a few of the "heavier commandments" and a few of the "lighter" ones.

Thus, the overseeing rabbi had a great deal of discretion. Unfortunately, later rabbinic authorities tried to eliminate most of this flexibility, insisting that the convert commit themselves to the observance of all the commandments in their entirety. Even worse, some rabbis developed a profound prejudice against potential converts. The consulted rabbi was even required to refuse to convert an interested candidate three times, rejecting their appeals and sending them away. Some historians argue that there developed an almost pathological unwillingness to admit any outsiders into the Jewish covenant, and hence the Jewish community. This negative attitude persisted for many hundreds of years, throughout the medieval period and even into modern times.

The Reform movement was founded in large part in order to redefine the relationship between the Jewish people and the outside world. It is therefore not a surprise that Reform leaders were more sympathetic to those seeking to embrace Judaism. The Reform movement was not bound by halachic precedents and could, therefore, develop independent policies. Reform congregations were much more open to visitors and were willing to take in new followers, whether or not they came from Jewish origins.

Even so, conversion was not high on the list of priorities in the early decades of Reform Judaism in Germany. It was not one of the religious issues that were extensively debated in the first four decades of the nineteenth century. In Central Europe during this time, Judaism was not likely to appeal to large numbers of people, even though intermarriage rates were slowly rising, and not all Jewish partners converted to Christianity. There was substantial antisemitism, even before the rise of the Nazis. Converting to Judaism was not a socially acceptable thing to do, even for those without prejudices of any kind. Christianity opened many doors that were closed to Jews, and probably for that reason most conversions were from Judaism to Christianity rather than the other way around.

In the United States, however, things were different. There was a commitment to social egalitarianism and an acceptance of the various religions on an equal basis. Nevertheless, for a long time the numbers converting to Judaism were relatively small. Intermarriage rates were low, and only a fraction of the non-Jewish spouses in interfaith relationships converted to Judaism.

The Reform movement welcomed these converts and saw them as a positive sign for both Judaism and America. Rabbi Isaac Mayer Wise, the founder of the major institutions of the American Reform movement, traveled around the country during the latter half of the nineteenth century performing conversion ceremonies for students who had been prepared by the local congregation. He would then write up and publish a report in his newspaper, the *Israelite* (later renamed the *American Israelite*). The conversion ceremony was modeled on the confirmation service with the convert being expected to answer theological questions during the service. This was strictly a formality; the questions and answers had been prepared beforehand and were memorized or read at the service. Nevertheless, it emphasized that the Reform congregation saw the embrace of Judaism as essentially theological.

During the twentieth century, there were sporadic efforts to start a missionary campaign of one sort or another, either from within the Reform movement or through an independent organization. While some of these groups are sociologically interesting, none of the efforts really amounted to much. But in the 1970s, Rabbi Alexander M. Schindler, the president of the UAHC, announced the inauguration of a campaign to reach out to non-Jewish Americans who might be interested in converting to Judaism. The major targets were non-Jews married to Jews, but he also spoke of trying to reach unchurched gentiles, a controversial proposal that landed him on the front page of the *New York Times*. The reason he spoke of reaching out to unchurched gentiles as opposed to gentiles as a whole was that he did not want to give evangelical Christians an excuse to begin openly proselytizing Jews. Thus, in interfaith discussions, Jews could say to their Christian counterparts, "We don't try to convert Christians and so you shouldn't try to convert Jews."

When Outreach was implemented as a UAHC program, the emphasis was entirely on the encouragement of non-Jewish spouses to convert rather than unchurched gentiles as a whole. This in itself was potentially controversial because the sages had insisted that a person wanting to convert to Judaism should have no ulterior motive.

Being romantically attached to a Jew was certainly regarded as an ulterior motive. Nevertheless, I have found that converts married to born Jews were more likely to stick with Judaism than strictly ideologi-

26. Rabbi Alexander M. Schindler, president of the Union of American Hebrew Congregations, came to the realization that the Reform movement needed to openly endorse patrilineal as well as matrilineal descent. He initiated a process that led to the Central Conference of American Rabbis voting in favor of what became known as the patrilineal descent resolution. *Courtesy of George Kalinsky.*

cal converts with no Jewish family connections. It is much easier to develop the Jewish ethnic identity so necessary to fully integrate into the Jewish community if one has a Jewish spouse and Jewish in-laws. Connecting the convert to the Jewish community as a people and not just a religion remains a challenge facing those who work with potential converts.

The movement generally prefers the term "Jew by choice" instead of the word "convert." In many people's minds, the word convert carries a negative stigma, partly because it is seen as a specifically Christian act. When I look up "conversion" in the index of books, I would find a category entitled "conversion to Christianity" but nothing similar to "conversion to Judaism," which would sometimes be listed under "Jewish proselytization." Also, the words convert and conversion implied a conversion experience. In Christian conversion testimonies, the convert suddenly sees the light. They undergo various tests and are uncertain of their way until there is a precise moment when everything suddenly becomes clear. They now suddenly understand what they need to do and why. This was not the Jewish model of embracing Judaism, which stressed learning how to observe Jewish ritual in one's daily life. I prefer the Hebrew word *giur*.

The numbers of non-Jews converting to Judaism hit its zenith in the 1970s and declined somewhat after the "The Status of Children of Mixed Marriages" resolution of 1983 (which will be discussed later in this chapter). Some blame the patrilineal descent resolution itself, a reasonable supposition, since many intermarried couples had sought the non-Jewish wife's conversion so the children could be regarded as Jewish. If the children could be Jewish without the mother being Jewish, then it was no longer necessary for her to convert. But it is important to note that societal attitudes were changing, largely as a result of the influence of feminism, and it was becoming acceptable for women to decline to follow the religious lead of their husband. So the Reform movement should not be blamed for the decreasing number of conversions.

Today, virtually every Reform synagogue has many active members who were not born Jewish. Some of them have formally converted to Judaism while others—many others—have not. In Temple B'nai Israel in Albany, Georgia, there is a high level of social acceptance of many of the non-Jewish spouses of Jewish people who have been active in temple life over the years. Several unconverted spouses have served with distinction as sisterhood presidents as well as members of the board of directors of the entire temple (although not as temple president). Yet at the same time, a few older people will say to me, "You know so-and-so? She is so devoted to the temple. You know she never officially converted?" Attitudes change slowly. Whereas twenty years ago there was still considerable skepticism about converts who had no Jewish background, today there is only a slight uncertainty about active members who never formally converted.

Since each Reform rabbi is autonomous, he or she can set any requirements for conversion they wish. There are rumors of the existence of a few Reform rabbis who require virtually nothing and will convert almost anyone willing to pay their fee within a very short amount of time. One rabbi in Florida (who is not a graduate of the HUC-JIR but rather was ordained by his father) even advertises a single-day conversion program! A candidate can come to his office at nine o'clock in the morning and leave with a conversion certificate by five o'clock in the evening. It is easy to make fun of these types of rabbis, but they are catering to a significant segment of the community. If couples face a united rabbinate who uniformly insists on what it sees as unacceptable standards, many of those couples will choose to walk away.

Most Reform rabbis require the conversion candidate to complete an introduction to Judaism course that covers the basics of Jewish beliefs and practices. They also expect regular attendance at synagogue services so the conversion candidate can see what Jewish prayer is like and how the community functions. These programs take between six and twelve months to complete. In smaller congregations, the rabbi may tutor an individual if there are not enough candidates to form a study group.

A uniquely modern dilemma has arisen when one member of a non-Jewish family wants to convert but the rest of the family does not. In traditional Judaism, this would be impossible, since rabbis would never agree to essentially create an intermarriage where none existed before.

But today, most Reform rabbis would be sympathetic, since we are always on the lookout for people who have a sincere interest in studying about and practicing the Jewish religion. As long as the conversion is not going to exacerbate marital discord, most Reform rabbis will encourage the conversion of one-half of a couple.

The traditional requirements for conversion included circumcision for men and immersion for both men and women. If the man is already circumcised, he is required to undergo *hatafat dam brit*, in which a small needle is inserted into the place on the penis where the foreskin originally was, and a drop of blood is extracted. Immersion would usually take place in a mikveh, a specially constructed place where people can dunk themselves in a body of running water. They could also use a river or the ocean, although since they have to be completely nude, there might be issues of privacy. In the Reform movement, rabbis did not require immersion in a mikveh for practicing Jews, so they could hardly require it for converts. The issue of circumcision was more sensitive because circumcision had been such a central Jewish ritual for thousands of years. In the early 1890s, Rabbi Henry Berkowitz, then of Kansas City, had a member come to him with the following dilemma: the father said that his daughter was planning to marry a young non-Jewish gentleman. The non-Jewish future husband was willing to convert, but adamantly refused to undergo circumcision.

Berkowitz wrote an open letter to the Reform rabbinate, stating that he personally would be willing to officiate at the conversion under those circumstances but that he wanted to bring it to the Central Conference of American Rabbis first so they could deliberate and reach a decision as a group. Berkowitz felt that it was important to make religious decisions by consensus rather than to unilaterally introduce such a radical innovation. The issue was discussed at great length during the early 1890s, and a decision was reached in 1893 to allow conversion without circumcision at the discretion of the officiating rabbi. Since the 1960s, many rabbis have been imposing more traditional requirements.

At the 1996 CCAR conference in Philadelphia, the Committee on Conversion held a meeting, with an overflow attendance, at which it decided to draw up a new comprehensive set of guidelines to give Reform rabbis recommendations for conversion procedures. This new set of guidelines would replace a document that had been written in 1980–81. According to the final draft of what became known as *Dibrei Giur: Guidelines for Rabbis Working with Prospective Gerim*, "The overwhelming consensus of those present was that the single most important issue that the Committee could address was the need within the Conference for a comprehensive set of guidelines to assist rabbis in their work with prospective gerim." Under committee chairs Rabbi Jonathan Adland and later Rabbi Richard Shapiro, the committee presented the document at the CCAR conference held in Monterey, California, in 2001.

The new guidelines called for rabbis to consider bringing conversion candidates before a *beit din*, having them immersed in a mikveh, and encouraging and possibly even requiring circumcision. "We recognize today that there are social, psychological, and religious values associated with the traditional initiatory rites, and therefore recommend that the rabbi acquaint prospective converts with the halachic background and rationale for berit mila, hatafat dam berit, and tevila and offer them the opportunity to observe these rites."

Many saw these guidelines as a further step toward re-embracing tradition, a trend that had come to public attention during the controversy over the 1999 Pittsburgh Platform. Julie Wiener, a reporter for the *Jewish Telegraphic Agency*, wrote, "In another break with its past, the Reform movement is poised to adopt new guidelines that embrace traditional rituals for people converting to Judaism."[6]

While the new guidelines do refer to the various rituals involved in the conversion process, the document stresses how to improve the conversion process. For example, it recommends that rabbis require potential converts to actively participate in synagogue life for at least a full year prior to their conversion. Shapiro told *j.*, the northern California Jewish weekly newspaper, "We're trying to improve the quality of the attention we give to people who are considering conversion."[7]

HUC-JIR president Rabbi David Ellenson agreed that the guidelines reflect "the general trend towards a greater receptivity to tradition." Nevertheless, Ellenson pointed to the conflicting patterns that were emerging at the same time. "The irony is on the one hand we have an ever greater turning towards traditionalism—reflected across the board in all the denominational movements—and simultaneously we have a community that is on the whole more highly acculturated than ever before in American history." Ellenson stated, "We have a renaissance in Jewish life and at the same time have record numbers of people who do not participate."[8]

Patrilineal Descent

On March 15, 1983, patrilineal descent became the official policy for the entire Reform movement in the United States. The CCAR passed the resolution entitled "The Status of Children of Mixed Marriages," the final text of the CCAR Committee on Patrilineal Descent. As the opening sentence of the resolution read, "The purpose of this document is to establish the Jewish Status of the children of mixed marriages in the Reform Jewish community of North America." Progressive, Liberal or Reform movements in other parts of the world were free to make their own religious policies, and most chose to stick with the traditional definition of Jewish identity. In the United States, the patrilineal descent resolution reaffirmed the Jewish identity of tens of thousands of children in mixed-marriage families and has been widely seen as a tremendous success.

Although the Hebrew Bible determines Jewish lineage in patrilineal terms, the mishnah reverses that position, stating that the offspring of a Jewish mother and a non-Jewish father is recognized as a Jew while the offspring of a non-Jewish mother and a Jewish father is considered a non-Jew. While historians have attempted to explain why the sages reversed what appears to have been a long-standing precedent, the fact remains that the Talmudic position became normative in the halacha.

Orthodox groups have insisted that no change be made. Redefining who is a Jew, they argue, would split the Jewish people into groups that could no longer marry each other. A number of Orthodox writers stressed that this decision marked the end of Jewish unity, threatening to divide the Jewish people into two separate factions. They begged and pleaded with Reform leaders to reconsider before they did something that would be so grave and so final that nothing would ever be able to repair the damage. But their apparently heartfelt protests should not be taken completely at face value. Their vociferous objection to the patri-lineal descent resolution was hyperbole, because the Orthodox did not accept Reform or Reconstructionist conversion either. Therefore, even if these liberal movements had insisted on full conversion, it really would have made little difference.

The Reform movement's desire to accommodate intermarried cou-ples was nothing new. It had long accepted the children of Jewish fathers and non-Jewish mothers into religious school.[9] But the numbers were relatively small, and there did not seem to be any need to formalize a policy regarding the children of Jewish fathers and gentile mothers. But by the early 1980s, the children involved had increased manyfold, and the majority within the Reform movement felt that a more explicit pol-icy would be helpful.

Schindler decided that the Reform movement needed to act, and he urged his fellow Reform rabbis to pass a resolution accepting patrilineal children as Jewish. "The Status of Children of Mixed Marriages" stat-ed that its purpose was "to establish the Jewish status of the children of mixed marriages in the Reform Jewish community of North America." The rabbis wrote, "We face, today, an unprecedented situation due to the changed conditions in which decisions concerning the status of the child of a mixed marriage are to be made."[10]

Advocates argued that it could no longer be assumed that the child of a Jewish mother will be Jewish or that the child of a non-Jewish moth-er will not be. Therefore, it seemed logical to them to declare that the same requirements should be applied to establish the status of a child of a mixed marriage, regardless of whether the mother or the father was the Jewish partner. They declared that "the child of one Jewish parent is under the presumption of Jewish descent. This presumption of the Jewish status of the offspring of any mixed marriage is to be established through appropriate and timely public and formal acts of identification with the Jewish faith and people."

If a child was born of either a Jewish father or a Jewish mother, and was raised Jewish, that child would be regarded by the Reform move-ment as Jewish. The child was, however, expected to participate in the various Jewish life-cycle ceremonies that usually mark the life stages of a Jewish person. Someone who had a Jewish parent (even a Jewish mother!) but had not been raised as Jewish and had not had any public religious acts of identification such as a Jewish baby-naming ceremony, a bar or bat mitzvah, or a Jewish confirmation service could theoretically be regarded as a non-Jew despite their lineage. Under such circumstances, the Reform movement would be defining Jewish identity more strictly than even the Orthodox.

The Reform movement was harshly criticized from certain quarters for changing the rules of the game. But it was American society that had been changing, and the Reform movement was simply trying to adapt to the new realities of contemporary society. Jewish identity was now something one chose rather than something one simply was. Children with one Jewish parent were choosing to identify themselves as Jewish. They were being asked to voluntarily undergo significant religious acts of identification as a way of showing their commitment to Judaism and to the Jewish people. While Jewish children had always been asked to prepare for their bar and bat mitzvahs (or confirmation in the Classical Reform temple), their Jewishness was never contingent upon successful completion of that ceremony or any other. The emphasis had now shifted from birth to conscious choice.

Not surprisingly, conversion rates began to fall. Some non-Jewish mothers had converted out of sincere belief, but many others had become Jewish in order to please their spouse or their spouse's parents. This type of Jew by choice no longer had to convert in order for her children to be raised Jewish. Nevertheless, as I mentioned earlier, it would be erroneous to attribute the entire decline in conversion rates solely to the patrilineal descent resolution. The significant shift in attitudes during the 1970s and into the 1980s had a tremendous impact on the rates of conversion. In contrast to the conformity expected in the immediate post–World War II period, American society began to emphasize that people could and should choose the spiritual path they found most meaningful and comfortable to them as individuals. Most Americans now believed that converting to any religion should be done only if it was what the person really wanted to do. Otherwise, converting would be insincere and negate one's own spiritual identity.

Each spouse was much more likely to pursue his or her own religious interests rather than conforming to a single model for the entire family. If one partner felt strongly about religion, the other might accommodate him or her by allowing the children to be raised in that faith. They themselves would nevertheless be more likely to remain connected to the faith of their birth or the religion that they had chosen, rather than simply following their husband or wife. With attitudes changing so dramatically, the patrilineal descent resolution probably came along at just the right time.

Not everyone was happy. A small number of Reform rabbis, most of whom were socially and religiously more conservative than the movement as a whole, opposed the patrilineal descent resolution. They were accorded a respectful hearing at the various deliberations at the CCAR conferences at which the subject was discussed, but the issue affected too many people for their arguments to be accepted as policy, even if some others may have agreed with them in theory. While the Reform movement allowed rabbis (as well as any Reform Jew) to have a belief or position that differed from the official policy of the Union of American Hebrew Congregations (now renamed the URJ) or the CCAR, patrilineal decent became such an important part of Reform policy that virtually every congregation embraced it almost immediately.

Many Orthodox leaders expressed shock that the Reform movement unilaterally implemented such a radical change in the definition of who is a Jew. Most Reform leaders dismissed Orthodox objections as unreasonable. If the Orthodox rabbinate had agreed to accept the validity of Reform conversions, then perhaps a case could have been made that the patrilineal descent resolution was unnecessarily harming the relationship with the Orthodox and undermining mutual recognition of each other's conversions. However, since the Orthodox rejected the validity of Reform conversion, the vast majority of Reform Jews felt that they had no choice but to implement a daring but necessary innovation. Whether the Reform movement was filled with the children of women converted by Reform rabbis or women who had not converted at all was not going to make the slightest bit of difference to most Orthodox.

Also, over the past twenty or thirty years, social relations between Orthodox and Reform had lessened considerably. Reform families were more likely to have non-Jewish relatives than to have Orthodox relatives. The number of close friendships between Reform and Orthodox had declined. The connection between Reform Jews and the State of Israel had weakened. The result was that Reform Jews cared much less about what the Orthodox might think.

But while there was general satisfaction with the gist of the policy, people had lingering concerns about some of the technical details of the resolution. In particular, many felt that the patrilineal descent resolution was poorly worded, so poorly worded that it was hard to understand what it actually said. Others felt that the title of the resolution was misleading and that this was causing confusion. So, while virtually no one was interested in repudiating the policy, many were in favor of tweaking the specifics of this important determinant of Jewish identity.

In 1996 the CCAR created an eleven-member task force to interpret and develop guidelines for the successful implementation of the patrilineal descent policy. Some complained that the phrase "under the presumption of" was vague and that the entire resolution was difficult to decipher. Others argued that the reference to patrilineal descent was misleading because the resolution accepted descent from either the mother or the father. In response to these criticisms, the task force suggested that the resolution be referred to as "equilineal descent" or simply "Jewish descent" rather than patrilineal descent, and it issued a series of recommendations for the successful implementation of the policy. But despite complaints about the name of the resolution and its convoluted wording, there was widespread acceptance of the policy itself. As Dru Greenwood, then director of Outreach for the UAHC, put it, patrilineal descent is "totally accepted" by most Reform congregants.[11]

The patrilineal descent resolution provided a viable solution for some couples who felt comfortable with their personal religious differences but wanted to raise their children with a single religious faith. It also proved a godsend for Jews with strong ethnic identities married to non-Jews in which neither partner had strongly held religious convictions. Because of their faithlessness, they would have felt hypocritical asking their partner to convert. But now, because of the patrilineal descent policy, they could now arrange to have their children raised as Jews.

The pluralistic nature of American society increased acceptance of interfaith marriage in which each partner followed his or her personal religious faith and ceremonial observances. In such households, it became increasingly likely that the children would develop multiple identities rather than committing themselves to a single religious or ethnic self-definition. In recent years, many half-Jewish individuals have begun to talk of their experiences growing up, sometimes caught between their Jewish and Christian identities, but more often comfortable with multiple self-definitions. The patrilineal descent resolution has little meaning for such multiculturalists and is not helpful in defining their children as Jewish. So while the patrilineal descent resolution was useful in responding to a particular social trend, at a particular moment, it is unlikely to be sufficient to guarantee the Jewish identities of children born in twenty-first-century America.

The Non-Jew in the Synagogue

The halacha did not envision any role for a non-Jew in Jewish ritual. One of the basic premises of the sages was that Jews were the chosen people and as such had certain religious responsibilities, namely the performance of mitzvot. Since a non-Jew was not a member of the children of Israel, he or she was not part of the covenant and therefore performing mitzvot would not make any sense. Actually, the non-Jew would be completely exempt from mitzvot that were ritually based. However, they are obligated to observe certain ethical commandments.

The sages pointed out that Noah had been given a set of commandments that he and his family had to observe in the aftermath of the flood. After the dove returned to Noah with an olive branch, he waited another seven days and then sent the dove out again. When the dove failed to return, he knew that the flood waters had receded. The earth began to dry and on the twenty-seventh day of the second month, the process was complete. God blessed Noah and his sons and told them they were prohibited from doing certain things, most notably committing murder.

In total, God gave seven laws to Noah. The sages stated that God was supplementing concepts that had been given to Adam and Eve earlier, when they were still in the Garden of Eden. Since Noah and his family were now allowed to eat animals—something that had not been permitted to Adam and Eve—God added the prohibition of cruelty to animals. Specifically, God prohibited Noah and his family from tearing flesh from an animal while it was still alive. In addition, there were prohibitions against idolatry, murder, theft, adultery, and blasphemy. They were also required to set up an effective judiciary to enforce the laws fairly and equitably.

The sages held that a non-Jew who keeps the Noahide Laws could attain the same spiritual level as the Kohen Gadol. Such a person would be considered a righteous gentile and would earn a place in the world to come. There would be no reason for a righteous gentile to convert because he would achieve all the possible merits anyway. Converting to Judaism would only bring upon him a large number of new obligations with no corresponding increase in potential reward. That is why it is frequently said that Judaism does not encourage conversion. Any non-Jew can go to heaven as long as she is a good person.

Jump ahead two thousand years. The situation is now very different, and Reform temples are only one of many houses of worship in cities, towns, and suburbs throughout the United States. Jews and non-Jews mix freely, not only in social situations but in religious environments as well. The synagogue attracts spiritual seekers as well as people with Jewish ancestry and those married to Jews. Religious meaning is a much looser term than an obligation to observe the commandments, and so it could be argued that a new set of guidelines is needed. In a postmodern world, the traditional categories of Jew and non-Jew are no longer as clear or as distinct as they once were.

Our congregations certainly have many people who fall into the liminal space between Jew and non-Jew. One man I know, for example, was raised as a Lutheran but has been married to a Jewish woman for about thirty years. He attends services virtually every week and demonstrates an emotional connection with Judaism. He does not want to convert while his father is still alive, but he is clearly a deeply committed and fully practicing Reform Jew, certainly by the standards of our congregations. Should he be allowed to open the ark during a Friday night service? Would it be religiously permissible to ask him to be one of the readers on the High Holy Days? If he can do all these things, does it make any sense to exclude him from the recitation of certain specific prayers, such as the blessings before and after the reading of the Torah?

Other situations are even less clear cut. A woman I know is a devout Catholic who attends church services every week. She has been married to a Jewish man for about thirty years and has raised three children as devoted Jews. She attends synagogue services frequently and feels a strong emotional connection with the congregation. She identifies herself as a Catholic rather than as a Jew, and has no plans to change her religion. Yet she is one of our more active members, and it seems only fitting to recognize her in some way. What kind of honors can we give her without compromising our religious principles?

Inclusivity is one of the most important positive characteristics of a contemporary congregation. We want to convey that we really do want to include everyone, especially people who have been part of our congregations for many years. How would a longtime devoted congregant feel if I refused to call her up for an English reading about the beauty of the world and then ask a Jewish-born person who almost never comes to temple to do the reading?

At this point, a traditional person may be losing patience with me. "Rabbi, I'm surprised at you. Rules are rules. All religions have rules and we just have to follow our rules." The problem with that sort of thinking is that Reform Judaism does not really have rules. The halacha is not accepted as binding and no alternative "Reform halacha" has ever been broadly accepted. Considering that fact, it is truly amazing to me how Reform congregations throughout the country seem to have developed a remarkably consistent consensus. But that consensus is simply based on a common perception of what seems reasonable. And what is reasonable can change over the course of time. In today's fast-paced environment, change can occur very rapidly.

I wrote above that the idea of a "Reform halacha" has never been accepted as binding. Nevertheless, the American Reform movement has engaged in analyzing Jewish law from its earliest stages. The responsa written are not authoritative but do provide an interesting look at how a certain segment of the Reform rabbinate has viewed various legal issues. In 1979 the CCAR Responsa Committee under the leadership of Rabbi Walter Jacob wrote a responsum on the question of "to what extent may non-Jews participate in Jewish public service?"

They wrote that from the medieval period onward, Christians and Muslims were considered in Jewish law as monotheists rather than pagans. They cite the opinion of Hiyya bar Abba, a Talmudic sage who stated that non-Jews outside the land of Israel were not to be considered idol worshippers but rather people who were following ancestral practices. Maimonides went even further, categorizing Christians and Muslims as children of Noah who were helping to prepare the world for the coming messianic era. The Responsa Committee cited additional cases where Jews respected Christian and even pagan practices and even accepted their prayers specifically. For example, if an idolater recited a prayer in the name of God, Jews who heard it were to respond with "Amen."

The responsum stated that in modern times, Jews had gone several steps beyond the established precedents. For instance, many of the names of people read on the kaddish list are not Jewish. In many of these cases, they are the relatives of people who have converted or married into the congregation, but others are Christian (and perhaps occasionally Muslim, Hindu, or from another faith). "We have, therefore, gone much further than any generation before our time by permitting non-Jews a larger role in our public services." The Responsa Committee attributes this to the "more open and friendly interreligious attitude which the Reform movement has encouraged and led."

However, the committee stressed, the steps taken have remained "within definite limits." The Reform movement has not allowed non-Jews, "no matter how friendly," to lead any of the "essential elements of the service." Therefore, Christians, Muslims, and other non-Jews who are categorized as "children of Noah" can participate in anything that does not "require specific statement from them." They could recite a general prayer, particularly if it was at a nonliturgical, communitywide service or a special family occasion such as a bar or bat mitzvah. According to the committee, it would not be appropriate to lead any of the central prayers attesting to a specifically Judaic religious commitment.[12]

Each Reform congregation is in an ongoing process of defining the role of non-Jews in congregational life. There are few precedents for the contemporary situation, and leaders have had to use their common sense, making decisions on the basis of what would be most effective and appropriate under a given set of circumstances. The congregations have to mediate between two partially conflicting goals. On one hand, they want to encourage non-Jewish spouses to raise their children as Jews and be as active as possible in synagogue life. On the other hand, the congregation has to maintain its Jewish identity, preventing the introduction of non-Jewish ideas and practices that could potentially threaten the religious integrity of the institution.

Virtually all Reform congregations allow non-Jews to be members as part of a family unit. As long as the family has a Jewish member, a non-Jewish spouse is part of the family membership unit. In addition, many accept anyone who identified with the Jewish people and followed the Jewish religion as his exclusive faith, even if he had not formally converted. While congregational constitutions differ, most Reform synagogues still expect their most important lay leaders not only to identify themselves as practicing Jews but also to have a clear and definitive claim on Jewish identity. Therefore, someone born and raised in another religion who had never formally converted to Judaism would be highly unlikely to become a temple president, no matter how dedicated they were to the congregation.

The boundary lines that have been drawn are unlikely to remain in their current places forevermore. The dramatic increase in intermarriage has forced Reform temples to reevaluate their previous policies, broadening and loosening their definitions. Those compromises have worked quite well for the past two or more decades. But the younger generation has been raised in a multicultural environment filled with postmodern conceptions. As they become the Reform Jewish leaders of the future, it is unlikely that they will be satisfied with the current status quo. Many congregations may do away entirely with rigid definitions of who is a Jew. Others may come up with entirely new perspectives, seeking to synthesize American liberal conceptions of self with traditional definitions of Jewish identity.

The Current Situation

In June 2001 the Central Conference of American Rabbis adopted new guidelines for conversion, called "Guidelines for Rabbis Working with Perspective *Gerim*," or *Divrei Giur*. *Gerim* is the plural for *ger*, a convert to Judaism.

The document was the most detailed rabbinic statement ever prepared on how rabbis should handle the entire topic of conversion to Judaism, from the initial contact through the final ceremony. While the numbers converting to Judaism had been declining somewhat due to changing cultural norms and possibly because of the patrilineal descent resolution, there were still significant numbers converting. One positive by-product of the new mentality toward religious identity is that since people felt it was inauthentic to convert in order to please one's spouse, the commitment of those choosing conversion is much greater.

Divrei Giur recommended that the UAHC (now URJ) "Introduction to Judaism" curriculum should be the core curriculum for conversion programs. This course should include a minimum of thirty-six hours of instruction spread over at least eighteen weeks. The Introduction to Judaism course should not, the document warned, be presented as a "conversion class" but rather as a part of the adult educational offerings of the synagogue. "It is beneficial for there to be a variety of students taking the Course: Jews renewing their knowledge of Judaism, other non-Jews simply learning about Judaism for better interfaith understanding," and other types of people from a variety of backgrounds studying for a variety of reasons.[13]

In November 2005 Yoffie proposed a Biennial Initiative to invite conversion. He urged congregations to find concrete ways to honor non-Jewish members who are raising Jewish children, while at the same time encouraging them to convert to Judaism if they are willing and able to do so. Yoffie admitted that fewer non-Jewish spouses were converting to Judaism. "In the early years of outreach, Alex Schindler often returned to this topic [conversion]. Alex told us: 'We need to ask. We must not forget to ask.' And for a while, our Movement actively encouraged conversion. Many of our congregations began holding public conversion ceremonies during regular worship services, but such ceremonies are far rarer now." He suggested the reason: "By making non-Jews feel comfortable and accepted in our congregations, we have sent the message that we do not care if they convert. But that is not our message."

In his address to the delegates, he emphasized that "it is a mitzvah to help a potential Jew become a Jew-by-choice." Perhaps sensing that many Reform Jews had begun seeing their congregations as not only multicultural and multiethnic but also multireligious, he told them, "The synagogue is not a neutral institution; it is committed to building a vibrant religious life for the Jewish people." Yoffie reiterated what he felt was the optimal result: "We want families to function as Jewish families, and while intermarried families can surely do this, we recognize the advantages of an intermarried family becoming a fully Jewish family, with two adult Jewish partners." Yoffie stated, "Conversion first is always desirable." He hedged just a bit to prevent criticism. "Judaism does not denigrate those who find religious truth elsewhere; still, our synagogues emphasize the grandeur of Judaism and we joyfully extend membership in our covenantal community to all who are prepared to accept it."[14]

On its web page, the URJ went out of its way to reassure members that encouraging conversion is not trampling on an individual's right to determine her own identity. "Asking someone you care about to consider conversion is simply an invitation. It is not coercion or pressure. It is an expression of valuing the individual and a desire to share a tradition that you consider precious." Inviting conversion "is a loving proposal that is offered when a relationship has been established either between two individuals or between an individual and the Jewish community. Conversion involves a solemn covenant where one party makes a commitment to Judaism and the other party (individual or community) makes a commitment of acceptance and support."[15]

Not everyone liked this push for conversion. One of those offended was Rabbi Samuel N. Gordon, the founding rabbi of Congregation of Sukkat Shalom of Wilmette, Illinois, which bills itself as "a unique and innovative congregation celebrating diversity" and "welcoming the intermarried, the unaffiliated, and those searching for a meaningful Jewish life." Perhaps unsettled by the front-page headline in the *New York Times* "Reform Jews Hope to Unmix Mixed Marriages," Gordon wrote a response on InterfaithFamily.com. "My primary objection to Rabbi Yoffie's stand is that it sends a terrible message to people just beginning to enter the Jewish world." Gordon explained, "When a young couple approaches me concerning their engagement and plans for their wedding, they are seeking a rabbi to officiate at their ceremony, and they are beginning to address issues of how they will define the religious identity of their family and home."

He agreed that a Jewish clergyperson is an advocate for Judaism. "I see my role as rabbi to welcome them into the Jewish world and help them begin to make informed choices about identity, values, and traditions. I am certainly not a neutral party in my counseling and advice. I believe that Judaism has much to offer the new family in terms of values and meaning." Nevertheless, Gordon felt that advocating for conversion would somehow make it appear that he was trying to manipulate them. "But the truth is, this is a most delicate moment in the life of the engaged couple making their marriage plans. If the rabbi is perceived as having a hidden agenda of conversion, that plays into whatever fears of manipulation the couple might feel."

Gordon argued, "I need to be a person of integrity without a hidden agenda when I am beginning to counsel young couples who come to me at the time of engagement."[16] Obviously, different rabbis have different ways of approaching different situations. That said, it seems strange that Gordon cannot simply explain to these couples that if the non-Jewish partner is interested in embracing Judaism and has no other religious entanglements, he would be thrilled to study with them with the optimal goal being the embrace of Judaism.

The change in approach, if there is indeed any change at all, is quite subtle. The *New York Times* spotlighted the Larchmont Temple in Westchester County, an eight-hundred-family congregation that is supposedly pioneering a more proactive approach. Senior rabbi Jeffrey J. Sirkman told reporter Michael Luo that he wanted to move conversion "from the back burner to the front burner." Continuing the analogy, he added, "It's always been in the pot that's simmering. Maybe now this gives us a little bit of the O.K.—in Hebrew, *hescher*, which means the validation or the stamp of approval—to elevate for discussion, or at least put it out there in a way that says this shouldn't be something we are afraid to do or talk about in a public setting."

I heard Sirkman speak on a panel on the role of clergy in conversion and shaping congregational culture at a Gerecht Institute conference in January 2012 on Long Island. An amicable soul with a friendly face, he repeated many of the same points that were made in the *New York Times* article six years earlier. "I have the inherent Jewish struggle. It's that inner struggle of knowing that we want to reach out there as much as we can. At the same time, we don't want to appear to be the Lubavitch."

That hits the bull's-eye. Perhaps the Reform movement needs to adopt a more aggressive proselytization policy. As Jonathan D. Sarna told Luo, "The truth is, not more than about a third of the products of mixed marriage identify Jewishly. There is a great fear that if a small Jewish community simply acquiesces to a situation of high intermarriage, that pretty soon, do the math, that a small community, which is really an endangered religious species, will simply disappear."[17]

In March 2012 Rabbi Rick Jacobs, the then incoming president of the URJ, wrote an opinion piece for the *Jewish Telegraphic Agency* titled "Synagogues Must Reach Out to 'the Uninspired.'" He recalled seeing a scene from the film *Money Ball* in which Billy Beane, the legendary general manager of the Oakland Athletics, tells his scouts that they must "adapt or die." Jacobs told his readers, "These words haven't stopped echoing in my head."

His argument is familiar. "In this new era of Jewish life—an era defined for many by the abundance of choices we face in every aspect of our lives—our synagogues must adapt or risk becoming ossified." So far, Jacobs's argument sounds like hundreds of others, but then he shifts course. "Synagogue life is too important to be entrusted solely to those who already are within congregational walls. We must, emphatically, expand the notion of what a synagogue means. That's the path being blazed by the Union for Reform Judaism and others seeking to widen the embrace of Jewish life." The shift from the Reform temple as a membership organization to Reform Judaism as a religious movement is a quantum leap.

Jacobs argues that since the fastest-growing group in the Jewish community is what we call "the unaffiliated," the Reform movement needs to find a way to engage them. Jacobs starts by changing the terminology. Rather than calling them the unaffiliated, Jacobs prefers the term "the uninspired." It is our job, he argues, to inspire them. How does one do that? "By reorientating our synagogues to address the needs of this group." Whether this is possible remains to be seen. Jacobs says that "synagogues must speak to the soul; they must challenge and educate." That sounds like good advice for recruiting new members of virtually any type. But then he gets more specific. "Synagogues must be places where we extend ourselves to people we don't know. It is easier to associate only with those who are just like us, but being part of a sacred community makes us responsible for those who think, earn, practice and vote differently than we do. That is how our souls get stretched beyond their narrow reach."

Jacobs believes that "our web of mutual responsibility doesn't end with those in our congregation. Rather that's where it begins." Synagogues, he argues, must reassess their focus on their own membership to the exclusion of "what happens outside their walls." He warns, "Young Jews on the outside are not knocking on the door. It is our collective responsibility and challenge to reach them by breaking down the synagogue walls and engaging them, wherever they may be."[18]

CHAPTER 7

On the Boundaries of Reform

Most Jews feel that the most egregious violation of traditional norms is the integration of Christian elements into Jewish practice. We will be looking at what is broadly called Messianic Jewish groups in the next section, but let's begin by meeting Moishe Rosen, the founder of Jews for Jesus, an organization whose very mention infuriates many otherwise placid American Jews. Even though he was born to a Jewish mother (and a Jewish father) and would therefore be regarded as Jewish by halachic standards, his religious beliefs would make him ineligible for membership in a Reform temple—any Reform temple.

Rosen grew up during the Great Depression in a Jewish neighborhood in Denver. According to Rosen, his mother's parents were "Reform Jews from Austria," his paternal grandfather was Orthodox, and although his father attended an Orthodox synagogue, he was "not religious" and viewed religion as a "racket."[1] As he writes in his testimony on the Jews for Jesus website, he grew up in a neighborhood where "if you walked into a grocery store, or the shoemaker or the barber, you expected to hear Yiddish."

He recalled that there was one Conservative congregation and one "Reformed" temple, but they were for upper-class people. "Orthodoxy was the way that most of us went, even though we didn't particularly follow doctrines. We didn't particularly work at being observant." He began dating Ceil Starr, a young Jewish girl who had moved from Boston to Denver. Her family was *frum*, strictly observant. When Moishe and Ceil were married, the wedding was held in an Orthodox synagogue.

By that time, Moishe was an agnostic and Ceil an atheist. "God didn't have a place in our lives. Prayer meant talking to yourself, and miracles were like magic fairy tales."

During her first pregnancy, Ceil began searching. When she was still in high school, she had begun pondering the question of whether Jesus might hold meaning for her. "I was 16 years old, and it was the night of our school Christmas pageant. I was one of many Jewish girls who had sung the words to these songs without giving them a second thought. But now, as we glided across the stage in slow, dance-like rhythm, singing, "O come / O come Immanuel / And ransom captive Israel," something stirred within me. I suddenly realized that Jesus was Jewish and it made me wonder for just a moment if he could be for us after all."

Over the next few years, she was strangely affected by casual exposure to Christian influences. Moishe and Ceil went to see *Quo Vadis*, a 1951 movie about the Christians in the Roman Empire. "We didn't go out of a particular interest in Jesus. We went because this was an epic film in full color, which was something special in those days. And it was playing in a plush downtown theater, which was also a treat. The two of us slid down in the velvet seats, glued our eyes to the screen and ate our popcorn as though this was just any movie . . . and I think to Moishe, that's all it was. But the movie left a lasting impression on me. Something about Jesus captured my attention."

In December 1951 Rosen bought an album of Christmas carols for his wife.

He knew I enjoyed the music and to us there was no religious significance in listening to these seasonal songs. But when I listened to the words to "O Little Town of Bethlehem," it was as though I was hearing them for the first time: "Yet in the dark street shineth / The everlasting Light." I remembered my high school Christmas pageant and the sudden realization that Jesus was Jewish. Just as suddenly, I prayed, "God could it be possible that what these Christians are saying about Jesus is true? I'm ready to go back to Orthodox Judaism and keep all the laws if that is what you want—or I am willing to believe in Jesus if he is really our Messiah."

Ceil began studying the gospel with a Christian missionary who knocked on their door one day. When Rosen found out, he told the missionary she was not welcome in their home, but Ceil continued to study with her over the telephone. "One day, Moishe came home and found me engaged on one of our telephone Bible studies. My husband, who ordinarily would not deny me anything, became so infuriated that he ripped the phone out of the wall!" As her faith deepened, he confronted her about her beliefs, and she told him, "Please don't make me choose between you and God. If it were anything else, you know I would choose you. But if you give me an ultimatum about this, I'll have to choose God."[2]

While this story makes it appear that it was Ceil who initiated their involvement with Jesus, Rosen had also shown an interest in Christian belief as a teenager. Seventeen-year-old Moishe started becoming interested in the gospel when a Christian named Orville Freestone started talking to him on a street corner. Recalling the encounter much later, he remembers thinking, "What he says makes sense. So that means that I must be one dumb Jew because Jesus couldn't possibly be the Messiah. And I'm not going to read this book [the New Testament], because if I read it, I might believe it. And I don't trust my own judgment. No, I'm not going to have anything to do with this. If the rabbis ever get together and decide that Jesus is the Messiah, maybe I'll go along with them."

Now, four years later, he found himself married to a Jewish woman who was in the process of becoming a believer in Jesus. He went to see the rabbi who had married them but did not find any of the rabbi's arguments against Jesus to be persuasive. On one particular Saturday night, he started reading some of his wife's pamphlets with the intention of ridiculing them. He came across one pamphlet entitled "What Is Heaven Like?" He got partway through the text when he suddenly "discovered that faith was there. I really did believe in Heaven, believed in the Bible, believed in Christ, and was ready to say so."[3]

Rosen went on to found Hineni Ministries, better known as Jews for Jesus, in 1973 in San Francisco. According to their mission statement, "We exist to make the Messiahship of Jesus an unavoidable issue to our Jewish people worldwide." Jewish people, they explain, tend to dismiss evangelistic methods and materials that are couched in Christian termi-nology because it reinforces the assumption that Jesus is for non-Jews rather than for Jews. Jews for Jesus has pioneered new approaches to break down that barrier, including creative evangelistic literature that stresses the Jewish roots of Christianity, witnessing campaigns that high-light the conversion stories of Jewish-born people, including Holocaust survivors, and innovative methods of communication that they hope will reach Jews who have heretofore been resistant to the gospel.

Is Rosen upset or at least disappointed that no Reform synagogue would possibly accept him as a member? His daughter Ruth told me, "My dad grew up believing it was his duty as a Jew to reject the possi-bility that Jesus was for him. Coming to believe that Jesus truly is the Messiah foretold by Jewish prophets shifted his sense of duty radically, but he remembers exactly how he once felt—so it's been no shock that he's not welcome to join any synagogue, Reform or otherwise."

Whereas chapter 6 dealt with individual Jewish identity, this chapter will look at ideological groups that may or may not be acceptable within the parameters of Reform Judaism. We will look at three such groups, each of which identifies with what they see as Judaism as well as an ad-ditional ideological or theological system. It goes almost without saying that these three groups are very different from one another and that I am not trying to imply that they share fundamental similarities. Rath-er, they are being grouped together here for one reason and one reason only—Reform thinkers and leaders need to decide whether they are in or out. Our first test case, that of "Messianic Judaism" of which Moishe Rosen's Jews for Jesus is one organization of many, is the clearest and easiest of the test cases.

"Messianic Judaism"

Jesus was born and died as a Jew. He never became a Jewish Christian and certainly not a Christian. His followers may have regarded him as a likely messiah. After his death, many continued to follow him, and a number of factions developed. They shared a commitment to the teach-ings of Jesus, but they differed on a number of important theological and halachic points. While the vast majority of Jews in Israel at this time did not accept the teachings of Jesus, the various Jewish Christian groups were part of a large and variegated Second Temple Judaism that included not only Pharisees, Sadducees, and Essenes but also dozens and perhaps hundreds of other religious sects, many of which have been lost to history.

Paul and other missionaries took their nascent faith and began proselytizing among the gentiles, in the process turning a Jewish sect into a new religion. Belief about Jesus evolved from seeing him as a messianic contender to theological conceptions of him as the son of God, part of the Trinity. While Jewish Christian groups continued to practice Judaism for some period, they eventually disappeared, either merging into mainstream Christianity or returning to Judaism. Most Jews, who never accepted any of the beliefs about Jesus, were never part of this process and encountered Christianity as a challenge to their religious system. "Why don't you believe in Jesus?" The simple answer was that Jesus was not and had never been part of Judaism in any way, shape, or form.

Over the course of the centuries, many, many Jews converted to Christianity. The majority were coerced. Christianity was the dominant faith in Christian countries while Judaism was a barely tolerated minority religion. Christian rulers could and did demand that all Jews in their land either convert or leave. This was done in England in 1290, France in 1306, and Spain in 1492. Other countries such as Portugal did not offer any choice, simply forcibly converting all Jews in 1497. In some cases, such as during the Crusades, Christians offered Jews the choice of conversion or death. Nevertheless, there were an unknown number of Jews who were attracted to Christianity and converted voluntarily. In medieval times, such an apostate was scorned and labeled a *meshumad* (destroyed one).

In modern times, however, and certainly over the last forty years, Americans have developed a much more open and tolerant approach to people who switch religions. American Reform Jews went along with this change in attitude and have become broadly tolerant of people born as Jews who have decided to embrace another faith. The question that Reform Jewish leaders need to ask is how to view the multiple groups that claim to be of Jewish ethnic background while holding some form of belief in Jesus and simultaneously maintaining Jewish ceremonial practices.

"Messianic Judaism" is a broad term referring to numerous groups that share a desire to practice at least some of the rituals of Judaism, while simultaneously believing in Jesus as the messiah and, in some cases, the son of God. While they differ significantly in their approach toward Jesus, whom they refer to as Yeshua, they agree that he was much more than a charismatic teacher and failed revolutionary. There are even some who believe they should observe halacha, since Jesus himself was presumably an observant Jew.

Many Messianic Jewish groups observe Jewish practices, including celebrating Shabbat and other Jewish holidays, abstaining from the eating of some or all nonkosher food, and praying in Hebrew as well as English. Because of the diversity of the different groups, it is difficult to generalize. While the various messianic congregations are ostensibly composed of Jewish believers in Jesus, apparently as many as 80 or 90 percent come from non-Jewish backgrounds.

While the original Christians of the first century were obviously Jewish, Gentile Christianity became the dominant form of the new religion, and Jewish Christians were eventually forced into either merging into the new Christian movement or returning to normative rabbinic Judaism. The idea of embracing Jesus without abandoning all traces of Jewish identity reappeared in the Hebrew Christian movement in the nineteenth century. In 1866 the Hebrew-Christian Alliance of Great Britain was organized, eventually establishing branches in several other countries including the United States. A number of similar missionary organizations were created, frequently funded by evangelical groups and usually led by Jewish-born converts to Christianity.

Many of the current groups that constitute Messianic Judaism began in the 1960s. One of the earliest, and certainly the best known, of the Messianic Jewish groups is Jews for Jesus. They claim that belief in Jesus as messiah is a fulfillment of the prophecies of the Hebrew Bible itself. Unlike some of the other messianic groups, they are not interested in promoting traditional Jewish practices for their own sake. They do argue, however, that there is a need for a specifically Jewish mission because most Jews are not receptive to what they see as religious truth if it is regarded as Christianity. An evangelical outreach campaign that explains why they believe Jesus to have been the Messiah will be most effective if it can justify their claims from within the Jewish tradition.

The Union of Messianic Jewish Congregations, an umbrella body formed in 1979 by nineteen independent Messianic Jewish groups, states that Messianic Judaism is "a movement of Jewish congregations and groups committed to Yeshua the Messiah that embrace the covenantal responsibility of Jewish life and identity rooted in Torah, expressed in tradition, renewed and applied in the context of the New Covenant." They write that Jewish life is a reflection of the history of the community, and that they aspire to be an active player in that community. Therefore, they argue that Messianic Jewish groups should "be fully part of the Jewish people, sharing its history and its covenantal responsibility as a people chosen by God. At the same time, faith in Yeshua also has a crucial communal dimension. This faith unifies the Messianic Jewish community and the Christian Church."

Since Reform Judaism is perceived as being open-minded and regards inclusivity as an important value, it may surprise some readers to learn that virtually no one within the Reform movement is willing to accept Messianic Judaism as a legitimate form of Judaism. Along with virtually everyone else in the organized Jewish community, Reform Jews argue that Messianic Judaism is a contradiction in terms if the messiah that is being referred to is Jesus. In fact, they argue that the term itself is a deliberate misrepresentation since it suggests that they are the Jews who believe in the concept of the coming of a messiah. This is completely false. Almost all Jews believe in the eventual coming of a messiah or the dawning of a messianic era. What they do not believe is that Jesus is that messiah. For most in the Jewish community, anyone who claims that Jesus is their savior is no longer a Jew.

Rabbi Mark Washofsky, in his book *Jewish Living: A Guide to Contemporary Reform Practice*, states categorically that "the religion of these 'Jewish Christian' groups is *not* Judaism but Christianity and that a Jew who adopts their doctrine becomes an apostate," and furthermore, "we should do everything in our power to correct the misapprehensions they preach and to maintain strict separation from them." Messianic Jews should not be allowed to become members in any Reform temple nor should they be treated in any way that would give the impression that they are accepted as part of the broader Jewish community.

The CCAR Responsa Committee dealt with issues related to Messianic Jews on a number of occasions. In 1983 they published "Status of a 'Completed Jew' in the Jewish Community," in which the committee answered a question posed by Rabbi Arnold S. Task of Greensboro, North Carolina. Task explained that there were a number of individuals in his community who were born and raised Jewish but now accept Jesus as their savior. How should the congregation view such individuals?

The Responsa Committee searched historical precedents and found many sources that discussed how to react to Jews who had converted to Christianity. It is not certain that these cases actually apply to Messianic Jews, most of whom do not see themselves as having converted. However, the Responsa Committee believed that these precedents were applicable, explaining that the Jewish tradition has regarded a Jew who converted to another religion as still Jewish, even though they had sinned. They could return to Judaism through a process of *teshuva* (repentance).

The 1983 responsa took a radical position, suggesting that messianic Jews were not Jews at all. Jews who apostasized under duress could be seen as Jews who had sinned and were eligible for readmission. "Outside pressures played a major role in the lives of the individuals involved. This is not the case with the 'Completed Jew.'" Because the Messianic Jew is a willing apostate, the Responsa Committee would "be stricter with her than with individuals who were forced into a position of becoming Christian." They concluded, "For us such [a] modern willing apostate is a non-Jew."

The Responsa Committee was thus taking a contrarian position that goes against precedent. Indeed, the Responsa Committee emphatically writes, "We would disagree with the *Talmud* and later [medieval and early modern] tradition." In this particular responsum, the Reform rabbinate was taking a stricter position than the sages of the classical rabbinic tradition! Perhaps aware that this position was untenable, the

Responsa Committee has not repeated this view in subsequent publications. According to Washofsky, the Responsa Committee has "tend[ed] to modify" their position in recent years.[4]

The consensus position was summarized by Walter Jacob in the responsum "An Apostate Proselyte" in 1980: "Judaism does not recognize a permanent change in status away from the Jewish people. A convert reverting to another religion would be considered [merely] an apostate."[5] Therefore, a Messianic Jew should not be excluded from attending services, classes, or other activities because "we always hold the hope that they will return to Judaism and disassociate themselves from Christianity." Apparently, the committee was not worried that such a person could have a negative religious influence on others in the congregation. However, the Responsa Committee stressed that "they should be seen as outsiders who have placed themselves outside the Jewish community."[6]

Washofsky urges rabbis to refrain from officiating at marriages of Messianic Jews. This specific issue was analyzed by the CCAR Responsa Committee in 1981 under the leadership of Walter Jacob. A Messianic Jewish man wished to marry a Jewish female. What should the local rabbi do? The responsum begins by assuming that a Messianic Jew would probably be considered a non-Jew. If that was the case, they explained that the Reform movement has opposed rabbinic officiation at mixed marriages. The CCAR passed resolutions in 1909, 1947, and 1973 stating that mixed marriages are contrary to the tradition of the Jewish religion, and therefore should be discouraged. Even though more than half of all Reform rabbis will officiate at interfaith marriages, most will not get involved with a wedding that involves a Messianic Jew.

The committee then asked what the policy would be if the Messianic Jew was regarded as an apostate, meaning a Jew who now practices Christianity. After reviewing the traditional rabbinic literature on how apostates were to be treated, the committee concluded it was clear that "an apostate stands outside the community in all but relatively few matters until he has repented." As a consequence, the Responsa Committee recommended that rabbis refuse to officiate at the wedding of a Messianic Jewish male with a Jewish female.

The question was then posed by the committee if it was possible to classify the Messianic Jew as still being Jewish. They quickly rejected this possibility since the young man had said he believed that Jesus of Nazareth is the messiah who has come to fulfill the messianic promises. "By making these assertions, that individual has clearly defined himself as a Christian." They concede that he may be different from normative Christians but point out that a number of Christian groups, such as the Seventh-Day Adventists, observe some Jewish customs as well, and no one would seriously suggest that a Seventh-Day Adventist should be regarded as Jewish.

The committee did not hide their fear that Messianic Jews might blur the difference between Judaism and Christianity. While virtually all American Jews understood that mainstream Christianity was not their religion, they might become confused with Messianic Judaism because of the preponderance of Jewish practices mixed with Christian theology. The Responsa Committee expressed dismay that many Messianic Jews have "presented themselves as Jews rather than Christians through misleading pamphlets, advertisements, and religious services." Therefore, rabbis should not officiate such a marriage. Indeed, "we should be much stricter in our relationship with 'Messianic Jews' than with other Christians."[7]

On the basis of the responsa issued by the CCAR Responsa Committee, Washofsky recommends additional sanctions. Reform Jews and Reform congregations should not do anything that would imply that Messianic Jews are part of the American Jewish community. We "may" refuse to bury them in our cemeteries. Washofsky uses the word "may" rather than "should" only because it is not acceptable in Reform thinking to phrase anything in a required form. Nevertheless, he clearly believes—and most Reform leaders would agree with him—that Reform congregations absolutely should avoid providing any religious services for Messianic Jews. Extrapolating from this, I would add that we should not invite them to communal functions or do anything that would seem to suggest that we accept their religious beliefs as within the boundaries of acceptability.

In my opinion, Washofsky goes too far. Let me quote the precise wording from his book *Jewish Living* lest zealous readers accuse me of misconstruing the text. Washofsky writes, "We should offer no support to their religious activities. Our synagogue gift shops, for example, may refuse to sell religious items to them. Should refusal to serve them be construed as a violation of civil law, the staff of the gift shop may attempt to discourage members of these groups from purchasing Jewish religious articles."[8] I find this suggestion bizarre. In response to my comment, Washofsky retorted, "Really? Is it 'bizarre' to recommend to Jews that they not assist these Christians in the distortion of our religious symbols? That strikes me as an eminently reasonable suggestion. One can disagree with it, but to call it 'bizarre' is surely to go over the top."[9]

I remain unconvinced. Messianic Jews are going to get Judaica from any number of sources, whether or not Reform temple gift shops sell to them. Such a refusal begins to create a cycle of hurt and bitterness that would seem antithetical to religious devotion. In the United States, every American has the right to choose the religious beliefs they want to hold and the religious groups they want to affiliate with. In a postmodern world, people are combining divergent—and even contradictory—systems of thinking.

We Reform Jews find it sad that some of those born as Jews have rejected Judaism as we understand it. I think that the most appropriate response is to reinforce our efforts to teach our philosophy to all who might be receptive. While we should not do anything to suggest that we accept Messianic Judaism as a legitimate form of contemporary Judaism, we should not be rude to them either. There is little to be gained in initiating a petty "turf war."

One poster on RJ.org wrote of being told by a born-again Christian that his Jewish friend had accepted Jesus and was now "completed as a Jew." The poster responded that perhaps the friend was completed as a Jew from the Christian's perspective, but from our point of view, as a Jew he was finished.[10] That feeling has been and remains the dominant one in the Jewish community. Nevertheless, as increasing numbers of nonpracticing Christians who have not converted to Judaism and even practicing Christians married to Jews enter into Reform congregations, the potential for syncretistic influence grows exponentially.

Jubus

American Jews interested in Buddhism have come to be called Jubus, or less frequently, Bu-Jews. Likewise a Hindu Jew can be called a Hin-Jew, a Sufi Jew a JuFi, and so forth. According to one estimate, American Jews are six to eight times more likely to become Buddhists than other Americans. Celebrities including Orlando Bloom, Robert Downey Jr., Adam Yauch of the Beastie Boys, Jeremy Piven, and many others have told interviewers that they are Jubus, Jewish Buddhists. There are many types of Jubus, some of whom would be more suitable as members of Reform temples than others. While the term can be used in a number of ways, we will restrict our discussion to Jubus who are not just Jewish by ethnicity but regard themselves as believing in and practicing some form of Judaism. The question is whether such individuals can be accepted as members of Reform congregations.

Most Jubus maintain that their practice of aspects of Buddhism enriches their spiritual life and is not contradictory with Judaism. Songwriter and singer Leonard Cohen told the *New York Times* that he could practice Zen meditation and also be an observant Jew who keeps the Sabbath: "In the tradition of Zen that I've practiced, there is no prayerful worship and there is no affirmation of a deity. So theologically there is no challenge to any Jewish belief."[11]

The first case of an American Jew expressing serious interest in Buddhism goes back at least as far as the 1893 World's Parliament of Religions held in Chicago. Charles Strauss declared himself a Buddhist at a public lecture, later becoming a public advocate for Buddhism in the West. Much later, the Beat generation influenced many to explore Buddhism, a trend that continued with the coming of the 1960s. Most who became involved with Buddhism at that time felt they had to choose between Buddhism and Judaism.

In the early 1970s, four American Jews founded the Insight Meditation Society, which began offering meditation retreats to cultivate awareness and understanding. They also established the Barre Center for Buddhist Studies, which focused on integrating scholarship with meditative insight. Many of the early teachers of Eastern philosophies were from Jewish backgrounds, including Richard Alpert, Norman Fischer, Jack Kornfield, and Sharon Salzberg.

The term Jubu became well known through Rodger Kamenetz's description of a Jewish-Buddhist encounter in his book *The Jew in the Lotus*. Kamenetz credits Dr. Marc Liberman, a San Francisco ophthalmologist, with being the first person to describe himself as a Jubu.[12] Kamenetz wrote about an October 1990 meeting between the Fourteenth Dalai Lama of Tibet and a group of Jewish religious leaders. Meeting in Dharamsala, a remote hill town in northern India where the Dalai Lama has been in exile, the discussion brought out new insights on the meaning of spirituality and the role it could play in national as well as personal identity and destiny.

Sylvia Boorstein, one of the founders of the Spirit Rock Meditation Center in Woodacre, California, is one of the best known Jubus in the country, largely due to her popular book *That's Funny, You Don't Look Buddhist: On Being a Faithful Jew and a Passionate Buddhist*. While she is not affiliated with the Reform movement, her spiritual journey and approach to spirituality has served as a model for many Reform Jews. She wrote a book about her experiences, in part to "replace emphasis on religious identity with the idea of the importance of religious aspiration." Boorstein hoped that by telling her story and the stories of some of her friends, she could change the questions she asked herself from "Am I compromising myself as a Jew?" to "How am I progressing toward my goal of becoming a fully loving and compassionate person?"[13]

Because of her familial background, she needed to figure out a way to be both a "faithful Jew" as well as a "passionate Buddhist." She explained, "I was no longer limited by attachment to parochial viewpoints." While she had no intention of repudiating her Judaism, she thinks she was mistaken to have focused excessively on her ethnic identity. "I have Jewish lineage. It began with my birth in a Jewish household that nourished it with stories and song and prayer and tradition that seem to have written themselves into my neuronal fibers. They are the language of my heart. I am thrilled to be able to tell my grandchildren stories I heard as a child. And I expect they will pass on to their grandchildren the stories I tell them about my grandparents."

But being a "faithful Jew" was not enough. Boorstein was desperate for a spiritual discipline that could help her deal with her existential angst. She suffered from feelings of despair to the point where she had given up all hope. But then in 1977 she was introduced to Buddhism "at a time in my life when I was frightened by my sense that life was too hard, too fragile, to accept without despair. I doubted it could be otherwise." She went on her first Vipassana retreat, which focused on what the Buddhist masters call mindfulness. "I think what most excited me . . . about Buddhism was that it offers a succinct explanation for suffering."

Boorstein learned that in Buddhism, there are no beliefs that have to be accepted. Rather, there is a spiritual practice that needs to be taken on and tested out. That suited her personality quite well. She was even more pleased to hear that while pain is a given in life, people can learn to end their suffering through spiritual practice. The first of the Four Noble Truths is that life is fundamentally unsatisfying because of its fragility. Since life is temporal, by definition nothing lasts. "It was such a relief! My reading of how life is was not a personal melancholy misperception. My response to it was melancholy, but here were teachers who said that it was possible to cultivate wiser responses."[14]

If the Reform movement is willing to accept people like Boorstein on the assumption that they are embracing a spiritual discipline rather than a religion, the next question would be, Is there any specific aspect of Buddhism that would not be permissible? Are there certain types of Buddhist practice that violate the prohibition against idolatry? The Ten Commandments prohibit Jews from worshiping idols. Indeed, Judaism prohibits the worship of any other deity other than Adonai. Is the statue of the Buddha that so many tourists to Thailand bring home with them just a memento or is it a replica of an idol?

It is prohibited for a Jew to embrace another religion, whether it was instead of or in addition to Judaism. Therefore, it is important to determine whether Buddhism should be regarded as a religion or simply a philosophy of life. The status of the Buddha himself becomes significant. Was the Buddha a prophet or even a god—or just a wise man? Many argue that Buddhists do not worship the Buddha but simply revere him, expressing gratitude for the Buddha's compassionate teachings. By teaching the Dharma, that which supports the regulatory order of the universe, others might be released from their suffering and achieve Nirvana, the profound peace of mind that is acquired with liberation.

Some Jubus avoid specific Buddhist practices so as to ensure that they do not violate the prohibition against idol worship. David Grotell explained that "although I have a meditation spot in my home, as a Jew, I just can't allow myself to put a statue of Buddha there."[15] Others argue that placing a Buddha figure in one's home is not prohibited because the Buddha never considered himself to be a god. Orthodox rabbi Akiva Tatz disagreed, arguing that the core of the difference between Judaism and idolatry is that "true service understands that God is everything, I am only to serve; idolatry understands that I am everything, and my gods are to serve me."

Tatz has coauthored a book entitled *Letters of a Buddhist Jew* in which a "Zen Jew" named David from Chicago writes to him, at the urging of two Orthodox rabbis, for counsel and direction. David writes that Zen has "helped me to awaken spiritually for the first time in my adult life." He continued his study at a Zen Buddhist center in Evanston, where he was undergoing lay ordination, which in his words meant that he "accepted the basic Buddhist precepts (quite similar to the Ten Commandments) as a code for living." Yet this spiritual joy has created family discord. His wife has told him: "David, your practicing Buddhism is a knife in my heart."[16] Tatz supported the wife, arguing that an Orthodox Jew has no business dabbling in Buddhism.

One might expect the Reform response to be more tolerant and accepting, but not all Reform rabbis are sympathetic. In 1992 the CCAR Responsa Committee was asked by a temple president whether it would be acceptable to allow a couple who practiced Buddhism as well as Judaism to join the congregation. The wife, an ordained priest in the Zen tradition, was born Jewish, while the husband converted to Judaism as a teenager. The husband explained that "by adding Tibetan Buddhist practices to his life, he has enhanced his Judaism."

At the time of the inquiry, they were members of a Conservative synagogue where their involvement in Buddhism was apparently unknown.

The couple wanted to switch to a Reform temple because they believed the religious education program to be superior. They held that Reform Judaism was more compatible with their personal approach to religion. The couple considered their Buddhist practices nontheological, "permitting synchronous religious practice."[17]

The Responsa Committee wrote that there is no conflict between Judaism and meditative practices. However, the fact that the wife was a Buddhist priest would make her ineligible for membership. They added that the husband might qualify, but "as a family the couple does not." Even assuming that the word "priest" (like the word "rabbi") means "teacher," the Responsa Committee was concerned that being a priest demanded a special type of devotion. They thought it reasonable to assume that becoming a priest meant that the disciple had not only mastered certain teaching practices but had integrated the underlying philosophy into her being. This assumption was based entirely on the question submitted, since the Responsa Committee did not feel it necessary to contact the couple and speak to them directly.

In their responsa, the committee pointed out a fundamental difference between the worldviews of the two religions. "Judaism clearly affirms this world and does not, as the majority of Buddhist traditions do, denigrate its importance." Judaism, they explained, is a "deed-oriented" religion while Buddhism has a "contemplative" approach. "While the merits of the latter are great," Buddhism has a different approach to everyday life. The differences were so great that Rabbi Leo Baeck argued that Judaism and Buddhism are "two religious polarities."[18] I personally disagree with this position. Baeck's comment was not meant to exclude. Even if the gross stereotypes in the responsa are true, these polar approaches would seem to be complementary rather than in conflict.

The committee added that public perception must be taken into account. The Jewish community and especially members of that particular temple "would be confused by what they would see as [an] experiment in religious syncretism and a watering down of Jewish identity." While the couple may have found a spiritual approach that meets their personal needs, "it does not fit the needs of a congregation." No evidence for this opinion was offered.

The committee did take note of the fact that the couple "want to be Jewish and do, in fact, practice on some levels." Therefore, "we must be sure not to push them away." But if they are truly unsuitable to be members, then the congregation has no choice but to reject them. And there is no way to make that rejection painless. Of course the couple will feel pushed away—that is, after all, exactly what happened. The Responsa Committee suggested that the rabbi should counsel them and "help them find their way." Without knowing the couple, I cannot say for sure, but it certainly seems to me that they had already found their way. They were simply a little ahead of their time.

Writing on About.com, Rabbi Jeffrey W. Goldwasser, then of Congregation Beth Israel of North Adams, Massachusetts, tried to soften the responsum a little bit. "There are streams of Buddhism which clearly practice a polytheistic religion that is entirely incompatible with Judaism." However, "other streams of Buddhism are better understood as non-theistic contemplative practices that offer practitioners ethical systems and paths for self-improvement." Goldwasser concludes that "these latter forms of Buddhism may not even be 'religions' in the Western sense of the word, as they lack any teachings about God or gods (or lack of gods) in the universe."

Unfortunately, he concludes by reverting to the hard line of the Responsa Committee: "My personal opinion is that when 'Jewish Buddhists' ask to be part of the Jewish community, the answer often should be 'no.' It's hard to live in two houses at the same time." He then closes by softening his stand yet again. "If I believe that Judaism has something to teach the other peoples of the world, it also is possible that Judaism can learn from other spiritual practices that are compatible with our own."[19]

On the Reform Judaism blog RJ.org, William Berkson takes a slightly more accepting tone. He writes that Buddhism has a lot to offer, particularly for a person who is skeptical about providence but hungers for a sense of holiness. Such a person may respond positively to the lack of an interventionist God who commands and judges. Buddhism stresses compassion, which resonates with Jews looking for *rachamim* (mercy), one of the core values in Judaism. It offers disciplined approaches for achieving peace of mind in a troubled world, something that virtually everyone is yearning for.

However, Berkson argues that Buddhism has "critically different views and goals" than Judaism. Buddhism is a religion of detachment in general and detachment from suffering in particular. Judaism, on the other hand, is a religion of commitment. Being committed inevitably produces some anxiety. The Buddhist ideal is "of an impoverished monk, detached from worldly cares, meditating on a mountain retreat." The Jewish ideal is "of a family, after the week's labors, around the table at Shabbat— praying, discussing matters of family, of Torah, and arguing about how to better the world, all with love." He concludes, "While we can learn from Buddhism, and even incorporate some ideas from it in Judaism, we need to be aware that it is a radically different approach to religion, and to life."[20]

I appreciate the theological problems and sincerely believe that the Reform movement needs to find a way to inspire "spiritual searchers" who have turned to Buddhism or other Eastern philosophies after failing to find existential meaning in Judaism. Let us take one of many possible examples. Growing up in a Reform temple, Karen Kissel Wegela said she felt an "ethnic connection" with other Jews but no "personal connection" with her religion. It was through Buddhism that Wegela found personal meaning, helping her cope with the pain she felt when her best friend passed away at age thirty-two.

Much later, she reconnected to Judaism through Rabbi Zalman Schachter-Shalomi, the spiritual leader of the Jewish Renewal movement. "He talked about Judaism in a way that, for the first time in my life, actually made some sense." Without her encounter with Schachter-Shalomi, she would have not reconnected with Judaism.[21] Like Wegela, most Jubus are hungering for an intense connection with God and very much want to absorb the religious teachings of Judaism. The Jewish establishment—including the Reform movement—would be well advised to focus on how we can make the great religious wisdom of the Jewish tradition accessible to a generation that wants to connect with its teachings, rather than wasting time and energy developing rationales why we need to drive them away.

We still need to determine how high the boundary with Buddhism will be erected and how strictly it will be maintained. At present, most congregations would accept Jewish people who want to be members of their congregation, barring any obvious impediment that cannot be ignored. Most Jews with an interest in Buddhism would be accepted as members enthusiastically with no one expressing any objection. That might change if the Union for Reform Judaism were to begin urging congregations to check whether potential members were associated with Buddhism, but such a policy shift is almost inconceivable.

Judaism with a Humanistic Perspective

If you are not currently a member of a Reform temple, you may be wondering what criteria congregations have for accepting new members. The one sure way to find out is to request a membership application and see what kinds of questions are asked. Since it is normally expected that a member will be Jewish, one would anticipate some questions to determine whether the applicant was born Jewish or converted to Judaism. But the constitutions of some Reform synagogues do not specifically require the applicant to be Jewish, according to any criteria, but only to feel an affinity with the Jewish people and believe in Judaism, however defined. The one condition is that the applicant cannot believe in or practice any other religion in addition to Judaism. The key point is that usually, nothing is said about an individual being required to believe in God.

What about a congregation that wants to join the Reform movement? Are there any requirements for a temple that wants to become a part of the Union for Reform Judaism? This question arose in the early 1990s when Congregation Beth Adam applied to join what was then called the Union of American Hebrew Congregations, now the Union for Reform Judaism. Beth Adam had been formed in the fall of 1979 by a small group of humanistic-oriented Jews living in Cincinnati, Ohio. To the surprise of many, their application was rejected.

This nascent group had a series of discussions with Robert Barr, then a rabbinic student at the Hebrew Union College–Jewish Institute of Religion, and decided to engage him as a rabbinic intern through the Society

27. Rabbi Robert Barr of Congregation Beth Adam in Cincinnati, Ohio, fought for years to see his congregation allowed to enter the Union of American Hebrew Congregations, now the Union for Reform Judaism. Despite the UAHC's decision to refuse their membership application, the Congregation Beth Adam has thrived and membership has increased. It is known worldwide for its sponsorship of the online congregation, OurJewishCommunity.org. *Photo by Alan Brown.*

of Humanistic Judaism (SHJ). They sponsored High Holy Day services and organized a religious school for their children. The congregation was incorporated as a nonprofit organization the following year and elected its first board of trustees. In the spring of 1981, Barr was ordained and was elected as Beth Adam's founding rabbi.

Barr had been influenced by Rabbi Sherwin T. Wine, an HUC-JIR-ordained rabbi who taught a philosophy that he called Humanistic Judaism. In 1963 Wine founded the Birmingham Temple, the first Humanistic Jewish congregation, and established the Society for Humanistic Judaism the same year. Wine is best known for writing *Judaism Beyond God: A Radical New Way to Be Jewish*. The Society for Humanistic Judaism remained small, but a devoted group crystallized around Wine, allowing him to play the role of mentor and senior spiritual guide for his fledgling movement.

Wine believed that Jewish culture and history should be the primary sources of Jewish identity rather than belief in God. This assumption was probably true for most Reform Jews, but they masked it because being openly agnostic or atheistic was not considered respectable. Wine believed that bringing one's true beliefs into sync with one's practices was beneficial, and he dedicated the new movement to this task. The Jewish Humanistic movement included services and religious ceremonies but excluded any and all mention of God.

Judaism was defined as the historic culture of the Jewish people. Religion was only one part of that culture, and Wine was willing to adopt certain aspects of religious ceremony to help his congregation express their connection with the historic practices of the Jewish people. But he wanted it understood that Jewish history is a purely natural phenomenon. Being a rationalist, he clearly explained that biblical and other sacred texts, no matter how ancient, were the result of human activity.

Barr agreed with Wine that it was possible to follow Judaism without believing in God. Many Reform Jews did not believe in the traditional conception of God, but they retained many of the references to God in the prayer book because they found it consistent with the historical presentation of Jewish liturgy. It helped them to justify their continued commitment to Jewish identity in religious terms, an identity that they found beneficial in the United States, a country where most people identified themselves as religious. Barr felt that retaining language referring to God was inconsistent if one did not believe in an "interventionist deity" of any type, so he edited a prayer book for his congregation that removed all overt references to God in both Hebrew and English.

When Beth Adam began, the Society for Humanistic Judaism was an organization of individuals. A number of influential members of Beth Adam joined the SHJ, and an informal relationship with the congregation was forged. When the SHJ shifted from individual to congregational membership, they approached Beth Adam, but the congregation decided not to formally affiliate. Barr became increasingly uncomfortable with the SHJ. In his view, it placed too much emphasis specifically on Wine's theology, which stressed a rejection of traditional beliefs. In contrast, Barr wanted to develop a liturgy that would be an "affirmation of a Jewish identity that valued personal choice and decision."[22]

As a consequence, Beth Adam had been an independent congregation since its founding. After deciding not to affiliate with the SHJ, it decided to apply to join the UAHC. No less than three Beth Adam members had served on the HUC-JIR board of governors, a high honor reserved for loyal and generous supporters. Beth Adam fit the mold of the typical Reform congregation—with the exception of their theological perspective.

Barr argued that Beth Adam should be accepted into the UAHC because the congregation was "already making a contribution to the Jewish future." While he admitted that some might object to their creation of a liturgy that was not dependent on terms directly referring to God, he pointed out that his congregation's theology might change direction over the course of time. He described his congregation as "on a religious journey" and argued that acceptance into the UAHC would have a tremendous impact on how they saw themselves and how they saw Judaism. He delicately stated that it was ludicrous for the UAHC to be considering the recruitment of irreligious gentiles—a project that UAHC president Rabbi Alexander Schindler had enthusiastically endorsed—while excluding an already organized Jewish congregation ready and willing to join the Union.

While Schindler did not officially support the acceptance of the application, he told delegates at the 1991 UAHC Biennial that the application would "generate a boon to our community" by opening a debate on what beliefs, if any, should be required of a UAHC member congregation. Normally, a congregation like Beth Adam would be rubber-stamped, but here there was an issue because the congregation excluded God from its liturgy. The congregation's literature stated that members did not recite either the Shema or the Kaddish because prayers "which presume a god who intervenes or manipulates the affairs of the world" would be inconsistent with its humanistic religious message. The congregation had edited their own prayer book, which removed not only the word "God" from English prayers but also all synonyms such as "the Creator," "Source of Life," or "the One who is exalted." They did not believe they should pray to God as a congregation because "the use of prayer in services would be incompatible" with the humanistic affirmation of "our right and responsibility to control our own destiny based upon ethics and morals arising out of the human condition." This is not the same as atheism. In response to my comments on this subject, Barr noted that some people find their concept of God in Beth Adam's liturgy despite the term "God" never being used.

The response to the application was largely negative. In 1990 a majority of the CCAR Responsa Committee voted against recommending that the congregation be allowed to join the UAHC. Chairperson Rabbi W. Gunther Plaut wrote that the congregation's "elision of God" meant that Beth Adam "does not admit of Covenant or commandments."[23] The majority felt that while the Reform movement could certainly accept individuals that might be agnostic or even atheist, it could not admit congregations whose declared principles contradicted the religious beliefs of Reform Judaism. Three members of the Responsa Committee disagreed, arguing that accepting Beth Adam into the UAHC was an organizational question that did not mean that the Reform movement endorsed their theology.[24]

A special meeting of the UAHC Midwest regional board was held in downtown Cincinnati immediately preceding the UAHC regional biennial, and it voted not to recommend that Beth Adam be admitted. Despite the lack of local and national support, the congregation decided to appeal to the National New Congregations Committee and the national board.

In June the UAHC board of trustees devoted an entire day to hearings on the question of the admission of Beth Adam into the UAHC. Many of those from small Jewish communities were more tolerant, arguing that the UAHC needed to extend its hand to virtually every Jewish congregation that wanted to affiliate. Judith Sherman Asher of Santa Fe, New Mexico, for example, argued that Beth Adam's views on religion were similar to that of many Israelis. She favored admitting Beth Adam because many American Jews turned to all sorts of spiritual paths, and the UAHC should welcome as many of them as possible. I would tend to agree, but it is necessary to decide where the boundaries are. Some spiritual paths may be legitimate Jewish avenues for spiritual expression and yet may be incompatible with Reform Judaism.

Doris Finkel-Peltz of Portage, Indiana, then the chairperson of the UAHC's Small Congregations Committee, agreed, emphasizing that it was important to accept all Jews. "I don't go around asking, 'What kind of Jew are you?' The Holocaust taught me not to." Living in a small city of about thirty thousand people, Finkel-Peltz strongly believed that inclusivity was a more important value than theological consistency. She was ignoring the fact that the Reform movement is intended to be logically based on certain religious beliefs or at least positions. No one in the UAHC was denying the right of the members of Beth Adam to call themselves Jews. The question was whether the congregation could be admitted into the organization of Reform temples. To do that, the congregation would have to meet certain religious expectations.

The UAHC board voted 115 to 13 to reject the application. The board felt that their rejection of Beth Adam did not mean that they were being arbitrarily exclusionary. As John Hirsch of Temple Beth El of Great Neck, New York, who had fought for the inclusion of gay and lesbian Jews, stated, it is "Beth Adam that is being exclusionary. It's one thing to come into synagogue and choose not to say a particular prayer, or any prayer, for that matter—or to join and try to change the traditional prayers to better reflect our beliefs, our lives, or our identities. Beth

Adam does not give Jews the right to make that choice." Hirsch found the idea that they would not let him say certain prayers in public to be offensive. "I cannot go there and say the Kaddish for my mother. I cannot go there and say the prayer that our ancestors said on their way to the gas chambers."

The Beth Adam decision made it clear that the Reform movement had theological limits on the left. Schindler explained that "some common understanding is necessary to give us the kind of ideological cohesion which a religious movement . . . requires to retain its distinctiveness and to secure its continuity." He said that he hoped that the members of Beth Adam "will come to recognize 'that the genius of Judaism is best expressed in the declaration that only God is God and there is none else,' though God can never be known."

Today, the Beth Adam website has a statement about the congregation's concept of God. It states, "Because Beth Adam's services do not incorporate traditional prayers, many falsely assume that a humanistic approach to Judaism is atheistic. As acknowledged in our Mission Statement and reaffirmed in our educational philosophy, Beth Adam's liturgy 'gives expression to Judaism's ever evolving religious experience and promotes humanistic values of intellectual honesty, open inquiry, and human responsibility.'"

The explanation, written by Barr, goes on to state that whether an individual member accepts any of a number of different conceptions of God "is not the central issue." What is important at Beth Adam "is our agreement upon a philosophic system that is based upon human reason and experience." The liturgy, which was developed by the Ritual/Life Cycle Committee, is designed to reflect the theological viewpoints enunciated by Barr. The website states that some people respond to their first service by immediately finding it to be an "articulation of their own long-held worldviews." Others, even some who agree with Beth Adam's approach to theology, "are uncomfortable with the unfamiliar liturgy. Yet with time our liturgy becomes a natural expression of their philosophic beliefs."[25]

The leaders of the UAHC felt that the Reform movement needed to set parameters or else it risked becoming a generic association of congregations that did not share any common religious perspective or values. As Plaut put it, "Reform Judaism cannot be everything, or it will be nothing."[26]

Blurring of Boundaries

The Reform Movement is known for being liberal and open-minded. We value tolerance and pluralism, holding that there are many different ways to be a good person and that one does not have to be a believer in Judaism in order to go to heaven. Likewise, Jews do not have to practice Reform Judaism in order to be good Jews. Nevertheless, every religious movement has to have some set of boundaries, delineating what is acceptable and what is not.

In an article written for *Commentary* titled "What Does Reform Judaism Stand For?," Jack Wertheimer—a traditional Conservative Jew— asks, "What of red lines to the religious left? Are there any limits there?" He argues that the Reform movement has grown, not because of what it stands for, but because it does not stand for anything. This same criticism had previously been applied to the Conservative movement, but Wertheimer is pointing out that it has become increasingly applicable to the Reform movement, which in many ways has supplanted the Conservative movement as the umbrella denomination.

Wertheimer admits that the Reform movement does set some boundaries, placing the Society for Humanistic Judaism (because of their denial of a personal God) and of Jews for Jesus (because of their belief in what Jews believe to be a false messiah) outside the parameters of Reform Judaism. But he criticizes the Reform movement for accommodating too many other types of belief systems and ceremonial innovations "under the rubric of legitimate Jewish expression." Even worse—in his view—the movement "has been remarkably silent on what it would consider beyond the pale."[27]

While outsiders may have the impression that the Reform movement has no limits whatsoever, this is not the reality, as the three cases in this chapter clearly demonstrate. The problem is that the Reform movement has no clear methodology for predetermining what is kosher and what is not. Having rejected the traditional halacha, the Reform movement emphasizes freedom—the freedom of choice, the freedom of not having to do specific ritual acts that are dictated to them by legal authorities. Reform Jews are resistant to any proposal that might replace the yoke of the Commandments, which they had been able to remove, with an alternative system. In addition, there is no intellectual approach to the creation of a new system of liberal guidelines that is universally compelling.

Mark Washofsky explains that "perhaps the only method (if you can call it that) for locating our boundaries is through the experience of ongoing argument, in which the various stakeholders contest the answers to questions such as those you pose here." In an argument, Washofsky continues, "nobody has the power to *declare* the right answer; the 'right' answer must be arrived at, over time, by way of emerging consensus." The purpose of argument is to persuade, and "arguments carried out within self-identified communities of interpretation are attempts at mutual persuasion." This process is "neither as neat nor as final as an authoritative pronouncement from on high, but it *is* the way that a liberal and pluralistic community can locate its parameters."

Washofsky is an advocate for the writing and reading of Reform responsa literature. In traditional rabbinic practice, a person writes to a halachic scholar with an intricate question of Jewish law. The scholar analyzes the sources and gives a definitive answer. Some Reform thinkers believe that this approach could be used by the Reform movement, albeit in a nonbinding variation. Washofsky explains that each Reform responsum is "itself a sustained argument—based upon the interpretation of the Jewish textual tradition by a group of Reform rabbis—in favor of drawing a particular boundary in a particular place." In contrast with the Orthodox approach, decisions reached in a particular responsum are not authoritative and Reform Jews are not obligated to adopt them. "The point, though, is that each of these texts is an argument, an effort at sustained persuasive discourse, that invites argument in return."

The argument on a given issue will end "if and when the community arrives at a consensus understanding of its position on the specific issue under discussion."[28] Of course, the same open discussion and vigorous debate can be held in a broader context, allowing all different types of

Reform Jews to participate in the decision-making process. In my view, one of the weaknesses of the Conservative movement was their over-reliance on the Committee on Jewish Law and Standards (CJLS) in the Rabbinical Assembly. Dominated by an intimidating Talmudic scholar who had little appreciation for the sensitivities and sensibilities of the masses of Conservative Jews who cared little about the halacha, the CJLS issued rulings that were wildly out of synch with the clientele that the Conservative movement was supposedly trying to cater to. The Reform movement needs to avoid falling into this trap.

The notion of "reform" is that of a dynamic force constantly seeking the meaning of progressive revelation for our lives today. We have changed, and we continue to change. In fact, the only constant is change. That is why we use the word "Reform" rather than "Reformed." the word "Reformed" would indicate that we changed and now we are all set. The Reform movement does not believe that. Even if Reform Jews wanted everything to stay the same, they are aware that society is evolving at a rapid pace.

According to Wade Clark Roof, American religious institutions across the spectrum are undergoing transformations in both form and style, "encouraged by a democratic, highly individualistic ethos and rapid social and cultural change." As a consequence, "boundaries separating one faith tradition from another that once seemed fixed are now often blurred; religious identities are malleable and multifaceted, often over-lapping several traditions."[29]

As American Jews embrace a variety of spiritual approaches that they find religiously meaningful, there is inevitably going to be a blurring of boundaries and a violation of traditional norms. Reform Judaism will need to cultivate a sophisticated "discourse of disagreement" in order to meet this challenge.

CHAPTER 8

Seeking the Spiritual

Patrick Aleph, lead singer of the punk band CAN!!CAN and a Jewish blogger from Atlanta, blends his newly embraced religious commitment with other interests that might surprise most older middle-class Jews. "When I'm on stage screaming, hitting my face with a microphone and pouring beer on my head, at least I'm singing about the Torah," Aleph told CNN.[1] On his web page, PunkTorah.com, Aleph invites the alienated to reconnect with the Jewish sense of spirituality. "If you love G-d, Torah, and the Jewish People . . . but are REALLY tired of the crap that goes along with it, then keep reading."[2]

Along with Michael S. of Aravah Design, Aleph has designed PunkTorah for "scene kids, metal heads, old school punks, atheist Jews, college students, 30-something hipster parents . . . anyone who feels disconnected from the Jewish World of summer camps, Holocaust guilt trips, and overpriced High Holiday tickets." In contrast to the establishment's concept of Judaism, Aleph wants to present a noncoercive, non-guilt-inducing, relaxing Jewish spirituality that can help people enjoy themselves and make a connection with the Jewish experience.

In contrast to the image of the synagogue as a boring institution that caters to the older generation, PunkTorah.org wants to think of Jewish houses of worship as nightclubs, places "where you go and relax for the first time all week. Take a load off, make a new friend, sing, drink, dance . . . whatever moves you! Somewhere along the way, the Jewish People lost sight of that. We're here to bring it back." PunkTorah was designed to cater to people who feel that they are "too indie" for temple. Rather than losing touch entirely, they can study the *parsha* of the week and connect with Judaism in a myriad of ways through PunkTorah.

Aleph is an example, albeit not a typical one, of what has been called "Emergent Jews," "New Jews," or "pancultural Jews." Members of the X, Y, and millennial generations, they take an interest in selected aspects of Jewish culture but resist being defined by any formalized identity. Whereas older generations saw themselves as "Jewish," the younger cohorts move from interest to interest without feeling the need to define themselves in any specific manner.

American Jews no longer feel that they are in exile, in *galut*. They feel accepted in American society and recognized as an influential voice in its culture. There is no longer—if there ever was—a single Jewish community that can speak with one voice. The United Jewish Appeal, which has since merged with the Council of Jewish Federations and the United Israel Appeal to become the United Jewish Communities, no longer uses the slogan "We are one." The reason for this is simple—it no longer reflects an attainable aspiration.

The concept of "the Jewish people" has come under attack from numerous directions. After World War II, the American Jewish community overwhelmingly endorsed a Jewish civil religion that encapsulated the self-understanding of what constituted Jewish identity. As explained by Jonathan Woocher in his book *Sacred Survival*, the Jewish civil religion enabled American Jews to give meaning to their Jewish identity by connecting them to the historic drama of destruction and rebirth that had played itself out between 1939 and 1948.

American Jews dedicated themselves to the survival of the Jewish people as their sacred cause. Religious belief or disbelief was regarded as being beside the point. What was important was helping to promote the survival of the Jewish people. Primary among the causes that needed to be supported was the State of Israel; American Jews gave generously to any charity that represented an Israeli institution. I visited the home of one family that had certificates of recognition framed all over their living room from the Weizman Institute of Science, to which they had donated tens of thousands, and perhaps even hundreds of thousands, of dollars. To my surprise, they told me they had never even visited the campus. For them, it was enough that it was a recognized Jewish academic institution in Israel.

But what resonated for those old enough to remember the news reports of Nazi atrocities or the miraculous victory of Israel over the Arab armies in June 1967 does not necessarily move those who were born after 1980. This has created a generation gap that threatens to undermine Jewish communal institutions, including those of the Reform movement. As the denomination that has catered to the less traditional elements of the community, the Reform movement needs to reach the X, Y, and millennial generations if it is to remain vibrant in the coming years. This is an enormous challenge because, among other reasons, many within these cohort groups have radically reinterpreted concepts formerly regarded as sacrosanct.

Some go so far as to entirely reject the concept of Jewish peoplehood. On the website Jewcy, a play on the words Jew and juicy, then senior editor Joey Kurtzman debated Jack Wertheimer on the question "Is it true that American life has annihilated Jewish peoplehood?" Kurtzman answered in the affirmative. "Modern American life is the most corrosive acid ever to hit the ghetto walls." This is a reference to walls that were built around Jewish neighborhoods in early modern Europe, physically keeping the local Jewish communities separated from the general population. Kurtzman suggests that though the actual walls were torn down by Napoleon's army, the American Jewish establishment has kept parallel psychological ghetto walls in place to this day.

Using the ancient nation of Moab as the symbolic representation of the broader non-Jewish American society, Kurtzman urges the American Jewish leadership to "jettison the language and ideology of peoplehood." Young American Jews "are whoring after Moab so fervently that the boundaries between Israel and Moab are being washed away. We're not merely influenced by the non-Jewish world—we're inseparable from it."[3] How such a policy shift would help preserve Jewish identity is uncertain, but Kurtzman and other young thinkers believe that rejecting liberal conceptions of fluid identity will only serve to further alienate the already alienated younger generation that the Reform movement needs to attract. New approaches are essential but will be ef-

28. Rabbi Rick Jacobs reading Torah at his installation as the president of the Union for Reform Judaism, with Rabbi Judith Schindler and Rabbi Eric H. Yoffie. Rabbi Jacobs has committed the Reform movement to dramatically expanding the URJ's presence on the Internet, deepening an involvement begun by Rabbi Yoffie. *Photo by Clark Jones. Courtesy of the URJ.*

fective only if the underlying concepts resonate emotionally with those being reached out to.

The Virtual Congregational Experience

Partly in response to the needs of this younger generation, Rabbi Rick Jacobs, as president of the Union for Reform Judaism (URJ), has committed the Reform movement to dramatically expanding its presence on the Internet. People looking for information about Judaism should encounter it immediately without first having to wade through pages and pages of material from Chabad, Aish HaTorah, and other Orthodox outreach groups. In his URJ presidential installation sermon, he reminded those in attendance that

> there are many authentic ways to live Jewish lives, including the Chabad way. But today on college campuses and in the public square, Chabad is working with little competition. No more. When

Jewish seekers Google Shabbat or the weekly Torah portion, we are what they're looking for but cannot find. For this next era of Jewish life, the Reform Movement will create a robust presence in digital media, on campus, across town and around the world so that all who are hungry for inspiring spirituality, passionate prayer, probing study, and social justice can find their way to us.[4]

Rabbi Jacobs is following up on an initiative originally proposed by Rabbi Eric H. Yoffie. At the 2009 URJ Biennial in Toronto, Yoffie called for experimentation with a wide range of creative technological approaches, to reinforce communal ties. Will the Internet undermine the synagogue? "Some fear yes—that it will lure Jews away from the old ways of connecting that require us to be in the same physical space." The pessimists fear that it "will become a substitute for in-the-flesh contact, and that if people start getting their needs met in the virtual world, they will have no need for the real world."

Yoffie reassured the three thousand delegates that "from the time of Ezra, who rewrote the Bible in a new script, we Jews have always adapted to our environment and taken advantage of the latest technologies." He reminded the leaders that Jews have always been quick in adapting to new systems of communication: "To encode our conversations and sacred texts, we moved with ease from stone tablets to parchment to paper, and we will move with equal ease to the electronic word."

Yoffie explained that the extensive use of computers as a vital part of congregational life is essential in contemporary society. "Our members do not have the time they once had. We are working more and sleeping less, and we can't get to the synagogue as much as we once did." In addition, "the web does what Judaism has always aspired to do: it opens up the vast treasury of Jewish knowledge to everyone." This is perfectly fine because "Judaism is not a religion of elites." Finally, "the web—potentially at least—empowers our members and democratizes our synagogues. The synagogue is the grassroots address of the Jewish world, and the web gives us an instrument to involve and include Jews as never before."[5]

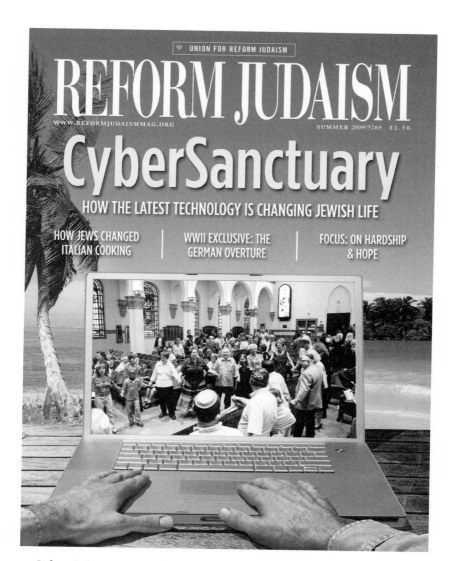

29. *Reform Judaism* magazine featured a cover story on the cyber sanctuary in their summer 2009 issue. As the magazine explained, "The way we communicate our sacred tradition has changed radically since the days of the oral tradition, quills and parchment, and the invention of the printing press." *Cover photo illustration by James Porto. Temple Israel of Greater Miami Erez Shabbat service photo by Robert Glazier. Courtesy of Reform Judaism magazine.*

"The synagogue of the future is a synagogue without walls," proclaims Rabbi Joshua Hammerman of Temple Beth El in Stamford, Connecticut, the author of *thelordismyshepherd.com: Seeking God in Cyberspace*. He argues that a substantial segment of the Jewish community, most of whom are not affiliated with actual Jewish institutions, will engage with virtual congregations. Riffing off of the often-repeated mantra "If you build it, they will come," Hammerman quipped, "If you stream it, they will come."[6] This is true only to a degree. There are many people who do not search the Internet for a virtual congregation and never will. But if only 1 percent of 1 percent do, that is a substantial number of people looking for religious community.

The introduction of virtual congregations is an innovation with the potential to transform American Jewish religious life. As it becomes more popular, it may pose a challenge to the status quo, potentially upsetting certain existing Jewish institutions. Futurists predict that all congregations will have to establish a program to webcast services, as well as adult education programs and other activities. This may seem an unlikely scenario, but remember that not long ago only a few congregations had websites. Then it became essential for every congregation to build a website, but most of them were poorly designed and only sporadically updated. Today, the norm is for congregations to have state-of-the-art websites that are constantly updated. The same pattern will hold true for "shulcasting."

The first time I heard about a congregation trying to use the media to reach out to people who might not be able or willing to physically come to their synagogue was in Miami, where Temple Israel had long broadcasted their Friday night service on radio. When they first started doing this, it must have seemed like a revolutionary idea. Imagine being able to listen to the complete Kabbalat Shabbat service from one's own apartment without having to go to temple! What a wonderful thing for elderly shut-ins, who might not be able to leave their homes at any time, as well as for others who might not be able to make it to services but still want to listen to the choir singing the Friday night prayers and perhaps hear the rabbi's sermon.

Religious broadcasting must be well done if it is to attract a significant audience. During the 1960s a number of rabbis began broadcasting religious programming on public television, but the production quality was frequently below expectations. I remember watching a few of these broadcasts in the 1970s produced by the Jewish Theological Seminary, which were rather conventional, even by the standards of the time. Despite my intense interest in Judaism, I quickly turned to another station.

The precedent for situating a spiritual community in a Web 2.0 environment has been established by a number of Christian virtual congregations. VirtualChurch.com brands itself as "Church wherever you are." On the top of its home page it asks in red print: "When was the last time you went to church?" The text goes on to ask four more questions: "Have to work? Can't get to church? Just don't feel like going? Need to hear the Word more?" On the right side of the home page, there is a green button labeled "Start Service," allowing the virtual congregant to begin praying with the community at any point he chooses. Since the online participant can choose the order of service, the website brags that no two virtual services are the same, allowing for over 365 billion possibilities!

With the widespread accessibility of Internet connectivity, it has become feasible to offer the live streaming of religious services through the computer. Afterward, the service can be archived and available for later viewing. However, the true potential of live streaming would be realized through the active participating of the worshiper at home. She would not just be watching but would become part of the congregation.

Over the past several years, a limited number of congregations have begun streaming their services, particularly on the High Holy Days. The original concept was that a temple could help housebound congregants to see the worship services. What has changed is that online congregations can now reach way beyond their local membership. Some, like OurJewishCommunity.org, are sponsored by a congregation in a particular place and draw a significant number of participants from their own membership while reaching out to many people elsewhere. Others, such as the synagogues on the website Second Life, are situated entirely in the virtual world and have no connection with any actual congregation in a specific location.

While live webcasting of services is only one aspect of the virtual congregation concept, it is primarily of interest to the non-Orthodox because halachically observant Jews would not use electricity on Shabbat or holy days. When *New York Jewish Week* journalist Steve Lipman researched an article on webcasting congregations, he found that "most of the congregations offering worship services online are Reform." Nevertheless, Yoffie expressed reservations as to its effectiveness: "Sinai is not something that happened by computer."[7]

As with so many new ideas, some have embraced the possibility of offering services and programming online much more than others. Not surprisingly, those who have pushed the limits in other ways are frequently more open to alternative forms of community. Rabbi Robert Barr, founder of Congregation Beth Adam in Cincinnati, has been one of the most enthusiastic. Barr became known throughout the Reform movement as the leader of a humanistic congregation that wanted to join the Union of American Hebrew Congregations (see chapter 7).

A number of years ago, I had just finished writing a short section on that controversy when I met Barr at a CCAR gathering. I could immediately see why he had been willing to put himself in such a potentially vulnerable situation—he was bold and confident, intellectually serious and on the far left end of the movement theologically. In an interview with *Soapbox* magazine in Cincinnati, Barr explained that the congregation's online activities were a logical extension of their progressive philosophy, "If the world is changing, and culture is changing, and ideas are changing, then we should be changing, as well."[8]

Barr began by doing podcasts. He recorded more than one hundred of them, made available for free through the Beth Adam website as well as through iTunes. The congregation then hired Rabbi Laura Baum to launch OurJewishCommunity.org, which is Beth Adam's online congregation. It calls itself "the world's first progressive online synagogue." On its home page, Baum has a three-minute video enthusiastically greeting new visitors: "We were so thrilled to have people not only watching the services but having conversations with each other online. It's a truly remarkable new model of Jewish community."

In an e-mail to me, Baum bluntly explained why there was a need for such a congregation. "The bottom line is most liberal Jews aren't coming to services." For that majority, the virtual experience "provides them something in their own time, in their own place." The idea, she claims, was greeted with great enthusiasm. In their first four months, they had sixty-two hundred visitors from forty-nine states and sixty countries. Now that they are established, they have ambitious plans to expand their programming. They have already launched a number of innovative training programs, including an online bar and bat mitzvah preparation course that was launched in January 2010.

Some of the people who frequent the online congregation are members of Beth Adam who live in Cincinnati but cannot come to services on a particular week. Others are people who used to live in Cincinnati but have moved away and want to keep in touch with the congregation. Some are elderly people who may live anywhere but have found Beth Adam's online congregation and like the contents as well as the presentation. Others are young and active but find they are too busy to regularly attend a physical synagogue. Baum told *Soapbox* magazine that one guy in England took his laptop with him to a soccer game so that he could watch both the services and the game at the same time.

Some had argued that offering free alternatives to paid congregational membership reduces the incentive to join a temple. The Beth Adam staff argues that insisting on payment first is counterproductive. Barr explained, "This is not giving away free samples—we are looking to create a new model—which also means exploring new financial models as well." Baum added, "It's also not about proving its value so much as it is a way to engage people . . . for people to feel like they have a community and a rabbi and that they can ask questions and learn about things that maybe they haven't felt comfortable asking about in the past."[9]

There was also the concern that "online communities" are an oxymoron since they are not communities at all. According to this way of thinking, watching a Rosh Hashanah service on a computer monitor is an entirely one-way experience. The viewer can see the service in the sanctuary and the backs of people's heads, but no one in the congregation—including the rabbis—can see the online viewer. While there is no question that a virtual community is quite different from direct per-

30. Rabbis Robert Barr and Laura Baum webcast a Friday night service for OurJewish Community.org. Appealing to those interested in Judaism and technology, it provides a place for people who may not have a progressive synagogue located nearby or prefer to access a congregation through their computer. *Photo by Alan Brown.*

sonal involvement, Baum argues that community is increasingly found online. A new generation of Jews is redefining what organized Judaism will look like. While old models speak to some Jews, they do not speak to everyone. The use of discussion boards, blogs, and even video responses can generate a great deal of meaningful interaction—perhaps more than what is normally found in a typical congregational building. "The hundreds of e-mails I've received and comments on the site . . . prove that people are engaging in a conversation. This is not a monologue from the pulpit. It's a conversation starter," says Baum.

As a rabbi, I was concerned for the staff of OurJewishCommunity.org. Running an online congregation can be incredibly time-consuming as well as emotionally draining. Many people from all over the world may write in, sending long e-mails describing their lives and hoping for a personal response. While it is certainly possible to build a warm and caring connection through e-mail, the rabbi will not be able to do that by just quickly perusing her inbox and zipping off a series of quick responses.

Rather, people are hoping to find a rabbi who will take the time to look carefully at what they have revealed and have the sensitivity to make a detailed and nuanced response.

There is certainly a market for an online community that can give people something they are not getting from the brick-and-mortar Jewish community. Baum claims that while 85 percent of the Jews in Cincinnati say that they would like a connection with the Jewish community, only about 50 percent are actually affiliated. According to Baum, many Jews under thirty-five find synagogues to be bland on one hand and coercive on the other. For both of these reasons, they avoid connecting Jewishly. She hopes that an inclusive online congregation can provide a more flexible and fluid solution.

Whereas OurJewishCommunity.com appears to be a standard website with links and streaming content, Second Life is a virtual world. Launched by Linden Lab in June 2003, a client program called Second Life Viewer allows participants, which they call residents, to interact with each other through avatars. Residents can explore different terrains while participating in all types of different activities depending on their virtual interests.

In 1999 Philip Rosedale, known in Second Life as Philip Linden, formed Linden Lab. He originally had hoped to create a computer hardware system that would allow the computer user to become fully immersed in a virtual world experience. The technicians actually built a prototype that was a cumbersome steel contraption with several computer screens set up at different angles that could be worn on the user's shoulders. Known as "the Rig," the prototype proved excessively unwieldy and was deemed to be commercially unviable. Rosedale then focused on creating Linden World, a virtual environment in which users could play task-based games and socialize in a three-dimensional online realm. During a 2001 meeting with investors, Rosedale revised his plans for the virtual world because he realized that participants were drawn to the collaborative, creative aspect of virtual world more than the original objective-driven gaming focus. And so he reworked what would become Second Life to allow for users to create their own community-driven experiences.

Beth Odets is credited with constructing Temple Beth Israel, the first permanent virtual synagogue. She recounts that there was an earlier synagogue, Congregation Or Atid (meaning "light of the future"), "but there was no building, or evidence of anything actually being there."[10] In the fall of 2006, she listed Temple Beth Israel in the Second Life directory and users began arriving asking for programming. She then decided to create a Second Life synagogue group so that she could communicate with those interested. The fledgling congregation held a small event for Sukkot and then began celebrating all of the subsequent Jewish holidays regularly.

Second Life has a plethora of Jewish institutions and activities. In addition to Temple Beth Israel, there is a Torah learning center, a Holocaust memorial museum, a Judaic gift shop, a mikvah, and Ir Shalom, a Jewish city. The user can enter into a fantasy world of kosher cafes and Talmudic study centers, but it can be much more than an entertaining video-game experience. For example, for those looking for real educational programming, the Second Life Hebrew School offers online courses that have been developed by users and can be expanded and revised by others.

Second Life can also be useful for those interested in visualizing various Jewish religious spaces, some of which users may be able to recreate in real space. For example, users can visit Second Life sukkot during the Sukkot holiday. If they like, they can participate in the sukkah building contest that is held there every year in the fall, shortly before the holiday itself. Since a sukkah must conform to specific halachic standards, users can observe how the various edifices handle the requirements while meeting the expectations of the virtual inhabitants. Some may then take this inspiration and knowledge to build their own physical sukkah at their local synagogue or in their backyard.

What is truly amazing about the Second Life and other virtual synagogues is that Jews and people interested in Judaism all over the world can gather in one (virtual) synagogue at the same exact time. Their avatars can put on yarmulkes and tallitot and join together in prayer, standing and sitting as the service progresses. They can take their virtual Torah out of the ark and conduct a full Torah reading if they choose,

31. The Hussey family studying prayer book Hebrew with Behrman House's Shalom Uvracha Interactive software, which uses a cartoon character named Professor Gimmelstein to teach students of all ages to identify the Hebrew letters and vowels. *Courtesy of Eleanor Crichton Hussey.*

allowing the real people to follow in Hebrew or in the local vernacular from either text on the screen or from a hard copy.

Tom Boellstorff, the author of *Coming of Age in Second Life: An Anthropologist Explores the Virtually Human*, told the *Washington Post* that contrary to what one might expect, the virtual world is quite similar to real life. "The surprising thing is when it's not surprising." As the newspaper noted, "Much like in real life, religion in cyberspace is prone to interfaith conflicts and internal schisms."[11] If Second Life is indeed remarkably similar to the real world, it could become a laboratory for both religious experimentation as well as pilot projects to revitalize congregational life.

Rabbi Hayim Herring, former director of Synagogues: Renewal and Transformation, blogs that "I realized that synagogues on Second Life respond to some of the critiques leveled at [real] synagogues." Herring, who has devoted his career to trying to find ways to make the synagogue experience more spiritually rewarding, explains that virtual life synagogues have, intentionally or not, incorporated many of the recommendations of synagogue renewal specialists. "You don't have to pay dues to belong, you can participate regardless of whether you have a denominational preference, you can experiment and practice Jewish behaviors in a supportive environment without fear of judgment—you can express and experience Judaism the way you would like it to be!"[12]

The boundary between serious religion and parodies or spoofs is potentially blurry. Some Second Life religious sites are clearly intended to be tongue-in-cheek, including the Church of Burgertime (which is based on an old video game called Burgertime). There is a stone tablet mock-up that instead of having the Ten Commandments chiseled into its face, says "Thou shalt not take us seriously." But what about the Church of Elvis? It is certainly not high church, but it may accurately reflect what is going on in Las Vegas.[13]

Noreen Herzfeld argues that while Second Life is good at reflecting the external face of religion, which includes ritual practice, codes and creeds, individual religious identity, and community organization, it is much less successful at fostering the internal face of religion, the daunting prospect of encountering the divine presence. Although the avatars can put on any sort of ritual item and assume the pose necessary to pray, Herzfeld does not believe that very many users will be able to actually experience spirituality through the computer. Pepper Laxness, the Second Life name of the founder of the Buddhism Listening and Discussion Group on Second Life, says that people ask him whether virtual meditation is the same as real-life meditation. "Are you kidding me? I don't know anyone who meditates in front of a computer."[14]

It is hard to tell if an online congregation can build significant relationships with substantial numbers. Some sociologists suggest that the Net generation, also referred to as "digital natives," is creating its own culture in a virtual space. Expressing different attitudes, values, and behaviors than the previous generation, they see digital friends and online communities as being real in a way that most older people do not. Even if we accept this idea as true, it still remains uncertain whether an online synagogue can draw people in and keep them connected.

Rabbi Niles Goldstein wrote a column for *Newsweek* back in 1998, describing his experience as rabbi of what he called a cybersynagogue.

It was not a fully functioning virtual congregation but rather an MSN forum called "Ask the Rabbi." In contrast with his early experience in a conventional Reform pulpit at Temple Israel in New Rochelle, New York, Goldstein found his cybersynagogue experience to be positive and stimulating. "While you can't perform a *bris* or conduct a funeral over the Internet, for many people that lack of focus on ritual is itself an enticement. Those turned off by organized religion but open to spiritual issues often find themselves drawn to our section of cyberspace."

While Goldstein found that his "congregants" were much more diverse than what he would have encountered in his pulpit in Westchester, in other ways "my work is surprisingly similar to that of a conventional cleric." Despite the vehicle for communication being different, he found he was still preaching sermons, teaching about Jewish tradition, and counseling individuals one on one. And in some ways, he found the virtual environment to be preferable. In his physical congregation, some wealthy members might try to bully the congregational leadership into doing things their way, or aggressive individuals might intimidate others in order to stifle dissent. "But in a virtual congregation, where distinctions between congregants don't exist and where boundaries between clergy and laity are more relaxed and less intimidating, I received a great deal of feedback and have been able to adjust my rabbinate accordingly."

Goldstein found that most of the users in his newsgroup had issues with religion. They were usually completely nonobservant and had not been successful in finding personal meaning in ancient rituals. They found the liturgy of the synagogue, even when it was translated into English, to be indecipherable. They came to the newsgroup to give Judaism another chance. In a safe environment where no one was going to judge them (because nobody could see them!), they wanted to explore spiritual possibilities that might help them to connect with God. Goldstein stressed that his virtual synagogue was only a first step. "We may all be created in the image of God, but only the shadows of those images will be visible online." The Internet, he said, draws people together at the same time that it distances them. "It expands the horizons of religion while collapsing its moorings and traditions."[15]

Yoffie understood these limitations. Nevertheless, he believed that the Reform movement had to engage in virtual community building. At the 2009 URJ Biennial, he spoke passionately about how "the Internet and cyberspace are changing all the rules of Jewish interaction, and we need to be at the forefront of these changes." Yoffie's concept is not just to serve the members of Reform congregations but to engage them. "The idea is not only to inform but also to inspire and create community. The idea is to see the Web not as a bulletin board for announcements but as an act of communal collaboration."

Integrating Meditation and Eastern Philosophies

Whereas religion used to be seen as an ascribed part of identity, it is now an achieved status. Until recent times, you were what your parents were. If they were white Presbyterians, then you were a white Presbyterian. If you came home from school one day and announced you were going to become a Sufi, your family would have looked at you in utter disbelief. You could just as easily have become a Martian. It was not considered possible to alter your religious identity, any more than it was possible to change your gender or skin color.

By the mid-1980s a Gallup poll found that fully one out of every three Americans was no longer practicing the religion in which they had been raised. Many Americans had switched religions not just once but two, three, or four times. Even those who told Gallup they were still practitioners of the same religion as their parents' were not necessarily looking at that faith in the same way. They may very well have developed radically different theological perspectives, and even if the theology had not changed much, their practice had very likely evolved significantly.

There were many reasons for the new fluidity in religious identity. Many Americans were marrying across previously impenetrable religious and ethnic boundaries. Until the recent housing crisis made it more difficult to sell one's home, Americans were moving frequently. Not only were they selling their homes and moving to new neighborhoods, but they were frequently traveling halfway across the country in search of better job opportunities and a more affluent and enjoyable lifestyle. In specific terms, large numbers left the Northeast and Midwest for the South, the Southwest, and the West. In their new habitats, these nuclear families had attenuated or severed their connections with their relatives, including the grandparents.

Because of these and other changes, Americans have become more open to the concept of spirituality. Whereas the term *religion* suggests a specific theological approach and a specific institutional response, the term *spirituality* implies an open-ended response to the inspiration and awe that are part of the human condition. Rabbi Lawrence Kushner, the Reform rabbi who has pioneered the concept of spirituality in the Reform movement, defines it as the immediacy of God's presence.

In order to feel God's presence, you do not necessarily have to join a synagogue or even participate in an organized prayer service. It may be enough to simply close your eyes and spend several seconds striving to connect with God, however you envision the divine presence. In a country in which most people have been able to satisfy their immediate material and materialistic needs, we yearn for something more. We are uncertain what this might be, but we know that it is an intangible concept that cannot be grasped in our hands but that must be experienced.

Many American Jews have become interested in Buddhist spiritual practices. Perhaps because they did not find what they were looking for in Judaism, many have sought a spiritual path through Buddhism and other Eastern philosophies. But while many regarded themselves as Buddhists, an increasing number have now begun to identify as Jubus, devoted Jews as well as practicing Buddhists. This is the formulation popularized by Sylvia Boorstein, author of *That's Funny, You Don't Look Buddhist: On Being a Faithful Jew and a Passionate Buddhist*.

Boorstein writes that in the middle of a Buddhist meditation retreat, "My mind filled with a peace I had not known before—completely restful, balanced, alert, joyous peace—and I said, '*Baruch Hashem*' (Praise God)." The next thing she did was say the Shehechiyanu, the Hebrew blessing of thanksgiving, for having lived long enough, for having been sustained in life, and being allowed to reach that day. "The blessings arose spontaneously in my memory rather than a habit, but the blessings felt entirely natural."[16]

Some of Boorstein's friends were surprised at her renewed interest in

Judaism. Having found a measure of mindfulness through Buddhism, why did she need to complicate her life with the challenge of integrating Judaism into her Buddhist practice? But she found this question puzzling because, she wrote, "It's not a question, for me, of *deciding* to complicate myself with Judaism. I *am* complicated with Judaism. I have too much background in it not to be. More important, though, is that the complication nourishes me. I love it."[17]

Boorstein, born in New York City in 1936, was an only child and an only grandchild. Her parents both worked at full-time jobs, so her grandmother was her principal caretaker when she was small. "I think of my grandmother as my first Buddhist teacher." She was "sensibly philosophical" about Boorstein's moods. "Sadness didn't worry her." When Boorstein told her grandmother that she was unhappy, her grandmother would gently ask, "Where is it written that you are supposed to be happy all the time?" Looking back, Boorstein thinks of it now as her introduction to the first of the Four Noble Truths of the Buddha. "Life is difficult. Just because it is. Because things change. Because change means loss and disappointment. Because bodies and relationships are, from time to time, painful."[18] While pain is a given in life, people can learn to end suffering through their own spiritual practice.

Boorstein had spent several years preoccupied with the idea that life was tragically flawed and had not found a way to relieve her obsession with this negative thought. What finally helped her was the first of the Four Noble Truths, the wisdom that she retroactively attributed to her grandmother. "Life is fundamentally unsatisfying because of its fragility, its temporality. Nothing lasts. I was relieved to hear this as the starting point for practice." It was Buddhist teachings that helped her realize that in reaction to her pain, she could cultivate wiser responses.

Over the past two or three decades, increasing numbers of American Jews who had been involved in Buddhism have been returning to Jewish practice, bringing with them wisdom learned from Eastern sources. Some feel free to integrate Eastern traditions into their Judaism while others prefer to focus exclusively on Jewish meditation. Nan Fink Gefen, the author of *Discovering Jewish Meditation: Instruction and Guidance for Learning an Ancient Spiritual Practice*, speaks about Jewish meditation as "spiritual practice found within the Jewish tradition." She argues that Jewish meditation has existed alongside other aspects of Jewish observance for a long time.

Jewish meditation, according to Gefen, "aims toward exploring the silence within." This is consistent with other meditative traditions that urge meditators to let go of their everyday concerns and open their senses to noncerebral spiritual experiences. In traditional Judaism, the goal of meditation is to bring the individual closer to God. Personal meditation's goal is to reduce the distance between oneself and the divine presence, and prayer in its various forms is one of the primary methods for attempting to do this. Contemporary Jewish meditation continues as tradition but adds other goals, including mindfulness and simple relaxation in a stressful world. In addition, Jewish meditation can help focus the worshipers on tikkun olam, to repair the world.[19]

Meditation in a Jewish context sometimes uses the same mantra technique used in transcendental meditation, where the individual repeats a simple word or expression. In Jewish meditation, a Hebrew word or phrase is used, helping the worshiper experience the divine presence. A number of Hebrew prayers are used as mantras, most notably the Shema, the classic prayer that is included in every Jewish prayer service. *Sh'ma Yisrael, Adonai Eloheinu, Adonai Echad*! (Hear, O Israel, Adonai is our God, Adonai is One!) The Shema, regarded as the central credo of Judaism, is a proclamation originally spoken by Moses to the children of Israel to urge them to remember that the source of all creation is the one God.

In most Reform temples, the prayer is read in Hebrew and English and many times sung by the cantor or choir. Although there is an attempt to put a special emphasis on it, repeating the words does not usually generate any special spiritual connection. There have been, however, a number of innovative groups that sought to bring a special spirituality to their recitation of this prayer. Yonasan Gershom, an early follower of Reb Zalman, the founder of the Jewish Renewal movement, remembers how it was at the B'nai Or Fellowship in the late 1960s. During prayer, the worshipers recited the Shema "with a full breath for each word, and our voices blending together in a crescendo which felt as if it pierced the very gates of Heaven."[20]

Tirzah Firestone, a Jewish renewal rabbi who went through a difficult spiritual evolution, found Reb Zalman's leading of the Shema to be "different than anything I had ever experienced in a Jewish context, and much more akin to the in-depth meditations that I was used to from the world of Arica," a psycho-spiritual practice in which she had formerly been involved. Reb Zalman asked the worshipers to recite the Shema four times, each time with a specific intention in mind. The first time, Reb Zalman told them, they should feel as if they were hearing it personally from Moses himself. The second time, he continued, they should feel as if the prayer was addressed specifically to each person, and say the words of the prayer through the voice of their own higher self. Firestone began this version of the prayer "Hear, O Tirzah . . . " Suddenly, she realized that it was "a personal reminder of our inclusion in the wholeness of the higher power."

The third time, the congregation recited the Shema by each inserting the name of a person with whom they had a fractured relationship. This would hopefully lay the foundation for eventual healing and wholeness. They paused to feel the power of what they were doing spiritually. Finally, they recited the Shema as if they were on their own deathbeds, preparing for their final transition from this world into the world where all is one. Firestone was so shaken by her exposure to this new approach to prayer that she began to reevaluate "the narrow view I had previously held of Jewish traditions."[21]

While most Reform congregations are unlikely to embrace Reb Zalman's approach in its entirety, many have already integrated a bit of the spirit of what he and other like-minded individuals have been doing. As Gefen explains, "It used to be that meditation was seen as inappropriate in Jewish settings, but that has mostly changed. The American Jewish community increasingly recognizes that people have spiritual needs, and that one way of meeting them is through meditation." In a relatively short time, meditation has gone from borderline unacceptable to mainstream. Many American Jews are spiritually hungry and are demanding new approaches to religiosity. "Judaism is enough settled in this country that it can take the risk of opening itself up."[22]

Kushner emphasizes humility, which he defines as "the joyful awareness that I am a creature of God and so is everyone else. It's the 'so is everyone else' that makes up humility, transforming the ecstasy into an abiding sense of gratitude." Humility, Kushner explains, is founded on creatureliness. "I have been created to do something that only I can do, just as you have been created to accomplish something that only you can do. It is founded on the notion that each life has a sacred, unique and never-recurring possibility." It does not matter "who I meet or how beneath me she might 'appear' to be intellectually, socially and finan-cially, spiritually, she has a job that only she can do and it is an honor to meet her . . . or him."

Kushner adds, "The basis of all humility is realizing that you're not [God], and no one else is either, and that as creatures, each with unique tasks, we revere one another's spiritual assignments." The reason for "our lack of humility is that human beings, as part of the human condi-tion and struggle, have this proclivity for falling into thinking that they're God."

We begin to think we are God because "we forget that we're going to die. That's it, in a nutshell. We get to thinking that we're going to live forever." And if we are going to live forever, "all bets are off, all rules are gone, and we can do whatever we like." But then something hap-pens; it might be "as devastating as an appointment with our physician who has bad news." Hopefully, this alarm will be just a scare. "I was on a plane last week that was hit by lightning, and I was reminded again." Kushner recalls that the greeting of the monks is *memento mori*, "Re-member, you're dying." He emphasizes that this is not said in "a morose or depressing way, but [rather] in a grateful and enlivening way. It's a reminder that you are a human being." Franz Kafka, after all, had said that "the meaning of life is that it ends."[23]

Creative Expressions of Spirituality through Art, Music, and Dance

In his 1954 book, *Man's Quest for God*, Abraham Joshua Heschel wrote that "the purpose of ritual art objects in Judaism is not to inspire love of God but to enhance our love of doing a mitzvah; to add pleasure to obedience, delight to fulfillment." The purpose "is achieved not in direct contemplation but in combining it with a ritual act; the art objects have a religious function but no religious substance." Heschel was most probably thinking of the synagogue ritual art objects such as the crown and breastplate used to adorn the Torah, but his comment can be understood in a broader context.

Over the past few decades, American Jews have begun to expand the accepted boundaries of how to express spirituality. This has been most obvious among the non-Orthodox, including many Reform Jews, who have begun incorporating various types of art, music, and dance into their worship services. These innovations are not being done by all congregations and are not necessarily being used on a regular basis, but the quantity of innovative services is substantial.

Reform services were quite rigid until relatively recently. The rabbi read certain prayers and led the congregation in responsive readings. An organist played the works of great Jewish composers such as Sulzer and Lewandowski and later Janowski, Binder, Helfman, Fromm, and Freed while a choir sang. But what had once been awe-inspiring sounded merely depressing to ears that had become accustomed to the Beatles and other types of modern music. Musical innovation began in youth groups and summer camps and eventually filtered its way into mainstream services. Guitars were heard more and electric keyboards frequently replaced the organ.

Israeli folk songs and Hassidic *nigunim*, tunes without words, became more popular, a consequence of the greater role that the State of Israel and the eastern European Jewish heritage began to play in Reform consciousness. The introduction of new prayer books in 1975, 1994, and 2007 helped create the environment in which musical change was encouraged. The question remains, what else can be done to stimulate Reform Jews to build a rich spiritual life and a personal relationship with God? There have been a tremendous number of innovative ideas that have been explored over the past decade or so. They are not necessarily ideas that originated from within the Reform movement; indeed, the focus in this section is on some of the ideas that can be fruitfully copied from outside sources.

By the 1970s many Jewish communities were changing demographically as well as religiously, and those demographic changes have continued to impact congregations of all types, including Reform temples. If there were not enough interested Jewish people in the area, the synagogue might even be forced to close. In a more favorable environment, they might be able to completely reorganize and reorient in the way that Congregation B'nai Jeshurun did in Manhattan in the mid-1980s. Other congregations were not necessarily declining numerically, but they felt the need to bring a new sense of excitement into their services.

In contrast to the typical suburban synagogue where congregants sat passively listening to the rabbi read and the cantor or choir sing, the B'nai Jeshurun experience emphasized participation. Worshipers—and hundreds began to come every Friday night and Saturday morning—joined with the song leaders in the exuberant singing of soulful *nigunim* (plural of *nigun*, a melody with repetitive sounds such as "bim-bim-bam" or "ai-ai-ai" instead of formal lyrics). They joined in celebratory song to the accompaniment of a band that included a mandolin, a cello, percussion, and keyboards. The congregation, which had been founded in the mid-nineteenth century and had been affiliated with the Conservative movement for many years, meshed traditional Conservative liturgical music with neo-Hasidic melodies, including songs by Shlomo Carlebach. Other songs drew from folk music (with artists such as Bob Dylan), Israeli pop songs, and even gospel and reggae.

When I attended Congregation B'nai Jeshurun a number of times on visits to New York, I did not see any of the rabbis, or if I did, I could not identify them as such. This is deliberate. The congregation has rejected hierarchical models of leadership, preferring an egalitarian approach in which not only men and women are equal but clergy and lay people as well. They did not use any responsive readings but preferred to sing virtually the entire service together as a congregation.

While this entire approach worked beautifully at B'nai Jeshurun, it requires a congregation that is sufficiently knowledgeable or at least willing to learn the tunes and the Hebrew words to the songs. This is by no means an impossible task. In my former congregation in Georgia, Mary Owens, a woman from a Christian background who married a Jewish man, was able within a few months to use transliterations to learn the

Hebrew words to songs we sang and become one of the most active participants in our Friday night services. But many Reform Jews are hesitant to engage with Hebrew words, whether in reading or song, and may not appreciate an aggressive retraining effort. Nevertheless, many of the approaches used at B'nai Jeshurun, Temple Sinai in Los Angeles, and elsewhere have been successfully used in Reform congregations, even temples located far from the centers of Jewish religious innovation. All it takes is a well-thought-out strategic plan and a leadership cohort that is willing and able to work diligently toward implementation.

While changes in music have been the most dramatic element of transformation in worship services, there has also been an interesting trend toward using different types of dramatic arts to bring the stories of the Torah to life. In traditional congregations, the Torah reading can go on for at least forty-five minutes on a typical Saturday morning. Many congregants look forward to this time to catch up with friends, enthusiastically jabbering away while the Torah reader *layns*, chanting the weekly portion in the traditional *nusach*, using Torah *trope*. But talking during services was never acceptable in Reform temples, which put greater stress on proper decorum. Partially as a consequence, the rabbi in the Classical Reform congregation would take the Torah from the ark, read a few lines, and then return it. While he (this is referring to before 1972 when all rabbis were men) might translate the text or devote his sermon to the subject of the Torah reading, the biblical text was not seen as being particularly exciting, to put it mildly.

That has all changed now. The Torah has come alive in recent years. Many cutting edge innovations are emerging every day, literally as you read the pages of this book. G-dcast.com, for example, is a website that has put up fifty-five four-minute animated cartoons in full color, one episode for each of the weekly *parshiot*. This dramatization brings to the Internet a trend that has been germinating for more than a decade in a person-to-person context. The series begins with Rabbi Lawrence Kushner talking about the "curious anomaly" in *parsha bereshit*—that light was created on the first day, but the sun, moon, stars, and heavenly luminaries were created on the fourth.

Peter Pitzele has pioneered a methodology of psychodrama called Bibliodrama that draws on an individual's own experiences to act out family stories from the Bible. Pitzele developed an interest in this area as a consequence of a long quest for spiritual meaning. The search "for a credible spirituality began for me as a solitary quest. It began in response to a few scattered moments of transcendent, almost hallucinatory, insight that had moved and troubled me as a young man." Pitzele experimented with a variety of spiritual approaches but did not find any of them permanently satisfying. "I often sampled and studied these but found I could not stay. I seemed unable or unwilling to conform my ideas about God and the meaning of life to any existing tradition or school of thought."

Eventually, he developed his own theological system, "an eclectic system of ideas, Eastern and Western, shamanic and poetic, classic and romantic." When he reached his midforties, he reconnected with Judaism through the study of the book of Genesis. He demonstrated the relationship between myth and experience through the imaginative retelling in a psychodramatic format. Others have developed similar styles of presenting the portion of the week, calling their systems Pop-up Torah, Open-Bible Play, Experiential Bible, or Modern Midrash. What they all have in common is the use of dramatic devices to open up personal insights into ancient sources.[24]

Storahtelling is a New York–based organization that focuses on personal growth via the arts. They offer five program models: Maven, which revives the Torah service for audiences of all denominations and ages; StorahLab, a teacher training institute to enhance supplementary school programming to promote creativity via the arts; Raising the Bar, reinvigorating the tribal art, ritual, and skill of storytelling as the vehicle for the bar and bat mitzvah; RitualLab, alternative worship experiences in which "personal access to the sacred" is facilitated through interactive liturgy; and StorahStage, fully staged theatrical performances that focus on biblical narrative through a modern lens.[25]

Amichai Lau-Lavie, who founded Storahtelling in 1999, explained that "We use edu-tainment. We make them laugh. It's 95 percent humor, culture, radical fun and 5 percent meaning." The program is part psychodrama and part psychotherapy. The Storahtelling participants utilize the stories in the Torah to engage worshipers. When I attended

32. Storahtelling is a Jewish educational program that uses theatrical performances to teach the stories of the Torah. Founded by Amichai Lau-Lavie, Storahtelling sees itself as continuing the tradition of *targum*, having the Torah translated as it was being read. *Photo by Shahar Azran.*

the regional conference of the Union for Reform Judaism in Savannah, Georgia, the attendees were visibly excited by the dramatic presentation put on by several Storahtelling actors. The group of musicians and actors have produced over five hundred presentations and educational programs—many of them multimedia shows combining drama, music, and comedy.

One of their new programs is called "Raising the Bar," which refers to the preparation of a Storah-style bar or bat mitzvah. Reform temples have long struggled with how to best prepare thirteen-year-olds for a ceremony that had been long rejected in favor of confirmation. With the trend toward greater reliance on tradition, virtually all Reform congregations have reintroduced the bar mitzvah, adding the bat mitzvah as well. Yet all is not well, with many children finding the preparation dull and the ceremony meaningless. Storahtelling has taken on the challenge, attempting to "raise the bar."

In order to revitalize the bar and bat mitzvah process, the "Raising the Bar" program involves about thirty hours of collaborative learning with a Storahtelling trainer working with the youth to translate, interpret, understand, and question ancient and modern Judaic texts. Together they relate those texts to the young person's personal experiences through dramatic exercises, creative writing projects, and person-to-person discussions, and then create a theatrical, audio, or visual ritual presentation for the bar or bat mitzvah ceremony itself.

The Liz Lerman Dance Exchange focuses on using dance to connect students with the emotional components of Jewish text and history through movement. The Dance Exchange has a number of different performances, including "Small dances about big ideas." They also run workshops called "embodying text." Choreographer Shula Strassfeld explains that their dance exercises help worshipers to sensitize themselves to prayer. "The more physical we get in prayer, using our whole body to experience a text, the more complete the experience."[26]

Right before the High Holy Days, Liz Lerman came to Temple Sinai in Washington DC to help the congregation prepare for the Days of Awe. She turned her hand toward her body and then away, prompting a reporter for *Washington Jewish Week* to remark, "The gesture is innocuous, something so mundane as to be barely noticeable." But Lerman repeated the gesture, asking, "What is more like Selichot—turning away or turning toward yourself?"[27]

Selichot are the penitential prayers recited in the weeks leading up to Rosh Hashanah. Traditional Jews may recite selichot very early in the morning or even late at night. The Hebrew word "selichot" is in the plural form, deriving from the singular "selicha," Hebrew for forgiveness. When Lerman moves her hand toward and then away from her body, she is suggesting that the process of repentance involves both internal and external interactions. Marissa Albert, a fifteen-year-old dance student at the Maryland Youth Ballet and DC Dance Collective, explained that she understood the pushing of her palms away from her body as meaning "this is pushing away all your sins."

Lerman, who received a MacArthur Foundation "genius grant" in 2002, has been able to explain in conceptual terms the contribution that dance can make to Jewish religious life. When she came to Temple Sinai, she reassured those in attendance that she did not have unreasonable expectations. "I know everybody doesn't want to get up and dance." Nevertheless, she felt that her program could help provide balance. "It feels to me that sometimes Jewish people in particular are afraid to get into our bodies for fear we will lose our minds." Lerman's workshop was designed to help temple members to overcome that fear. Blythe Albert, Marissa's mother, explains, "It was really remarkable how you just feel the tension slipping away . . . the body-mind connection—this is a really deep truth." Such an approach "forces us to slow down and to become aware, to feel. It's the first step in acknowledging that being quiet and listening to the physicality of that is a real vehicle for change."[28]

The easiest way to change Jewish attitudes toward dance and physicality in general is through summer camp programs. Children are much more open to innovative ideas, particularly when they are introduced to them along with all their friends over a sustained period of several weeks. Retreats are also effective, particularly for slightly older American Jews interested in expanding their spiritual horizons. At one experimental program in north Georgia, a dozen young actors are standing in a circle on an outdoor stage. Their task is to show each other movements and gestures that symbolize words and concepts from the *tefillah*, the standing prayer that forms a central part of Jewish liturgy. Actors demonstrate their assigned ideas by moving their bodies in different ways and using all their imaginative energy to convey a religious message without opening their mouths.[29]

Adventure Religion and Wilderness Judaism

Ellen Bernstein, the founder of a Jewish environmental organization called Shomrei Adamah (Guardians of the Earth) that was active between 1988 and 1996, had to "back into" Judaism because "no one taught me that the wilderness experience was so fundamental to my tradition." She had been active in outdoor sports since she was quite young. "Growing up, I paddled, biked, skied, and meandered through the New England countryside." Her desire to be outdoors and her need to journey determined many of the choices she would make throughout her life. As she grew older, she understood that her experiences in the outdoors resembled a religious quest.

She believed it was in the wild that she was able to encounter life's mysteries. "It would usually take several days on the trail to leave behind the weight of my ego, my self-consciousness and all that is familiar and routine." Freeing her mind, she could feel the world opening up to her, leaving her with a feeling of intimacy with the earth. Her entire mentality changed, and she was able to appreciate the world that was so frequently unseen in her normal daily life.[30]

Despite the fact that so much of Judaism was formulated during the desert experience or as a result of contemplating the desert experience, it took Bernstein a long time to make a connection between her interest in wilderness spirituality and Judaism. As a teenager, she rebelled against what she saw as an archaic tradition followed by hypocritical suburbanites, and she preferred the universal spirituality of the New England transcendentalists.

She certainly did not expect to find models for her wilderness spiritual journey in the Jewish tradition. But once she was able to move past her blind rejection of Judaism, she began to see that the Jewish tradition embodied extensive spiritual teachings about wandering. "Being a Jew is being a wanderer. Somehow what appears so obvious now took years for me to notice." The patriarchs and matriarchs of the Torah, as well as Moses and other personalities in the Hebrew Bible, were all called upon by God to forsake their homes and communities.

Many of those who were called upon wandered in the desert, where they encountered God and discovered their sense of purpose in life. As she understood it, the entire congregation of Israel was called upon to embark on a spiritual journey through the desert, where they spent forty years wandering. Bernstein saw the wilderness experience described in the Torah as "a metaphor for the journey we must all take to confront the unknown side of our soul and gain self-knowledge."

A number of pioneering Jewish guides have built Jewish spirituality programs based on an encounter with nature. Because this approach is counter to the values of institutional Judaism, they have had to surmount multiple difficulties. While many were raised in the Reform movement and still have strong associations with Reform Judaism, they believe in teaching Torah to everyone regardless of denominational affiliation. They are, therefore, part of the emerging trend toward postdenominationalism. Yet they have much to teach those of us still entrenched in the denominational framework.

The connection that pioneering spiritual guides make between natural world and spiritual world is critical for helping Americans connect to Jewish religious wisdom. While some people can relate to words on a page or ideas from a lecture, many others need to experience religion through physical activity. If the activity can be both physically exhilarating and aesthetically inspiring, there is a chance that the person can emerge transformed.

Bernstein insisted that her approach was different from that of other wilderness-focused thinkers, including Rabbis Michael Comins and Jamie Korngold. "My interest—different from Mike and Jamie's—is to bring the ecological dimensions of Judaism into synagogue life. I try to illuminate the God of Creation (which has been eclipsed by the God of History/Salvation/Liberation) everywhere in Judaism. I believe that many BuJews and outdoor Jews and others that have abandoned Judaism can relate much easier to the image of the God of Creation, the universal dimension of God; the God of the Present."[31]

Rabbi Michael Comins founded TorahTrek Spiritual Wilderness Adventures while leading the Jackson Hole Chaverim in Wyoming. The author of *A Wild Faith: Jewish Ways into Wilderness, Wilderness Ways into Judaism*, he objects to the idea that the Israelites understood God as being beyond the one world we all inhabit. The Greek idea of a separate, purely spiritual realm at odds with material reality infiltrated into Judaism after the biblical period. In contrast to the distorted understanding of many moderns, ancient Israelite religion focused mainly on the natural world. "The reason was simple: the Israelites needed to eat."

Unlike the Egyptians and Mesopotamians, who could count on irrigation from the Nile or the Euphrates, the Israelites were constantly exposed to drought and starvation. They offered sacrifices and prayed to God, urging Adonai to let it rain so that the seeds they had planted would grow. The pilgrimage holidays—Pesach, Shavuot and Sukkot—

celebrated the three harvest seasons that sustained the people (barley, wheat, and fruits). The ancient Israelites were religious innovators in several critical areas, including the monotheistic character of divinity and the divine character of ethics. But unlike the first several generations of modern biblical scholarship, recent studies emphasize the commonalities between pagan and Israelite religion rather than their differences.

Comins grew up backpacking with his family in the Range of Light, the Sierra Nevada Mountains of California. As a rabbinical student in Jerusalem, he spent his weekends—which in Israel is only Saturday—praying in synagogue. After a decade apart from nature, Comins felt "suffocated from books and buildings." He realized that he needed to change his entire lifestyle. He writes, "I returned to the source of my first spiritual feelings, to wilderness. It was like jumping into an alpine lake, a wake-up call that soothes the spirit by shocking the system."[32]

He began hiking through the desert in Israel in order to stop thinking about theology. So when he found God in the wilderness, it caught him completely by surprise. "Before then I had been a wannabe when it came to God." He studied in an Orthodox yeshiva and in the Reform movement's rabbinical program. Yet he failed to build a personal relationship with God. This did not worry him too much at first. After all, he rationalized, Jewish religious life is primarily communal. And then he began hiking in the desert, discovering a personal relationship with God for the first time.

Comins developed a curriculum to connect "inner and outer geography." Drawing on a variety of teachings and traditions, TorahTrek programs highlight the difference between being in the wilderness and being *mindfully* in the wilderness. The goal is not to rush through a hike at top speed but rather to train ourselves to listen in silence, to hear the words of the *siddur* in our heads as we take in the physical beauty of the natural surroundings, to see with "eyes remade for wonder." Leading a variety of spiritual wilderness adventures, Comins teaches "Torah-from-the-heart" with great passion. His HaMakom Soul-O solitude retreat, patterned on the Native American vision quest, focuses on connecting to God through immersion in the natural world.[33]

33. Adventure Rabbi participants hold the Torah while reading the story of Exodus under the Corona Arch outside Moab, Utah. Adventure rabbi Jamie Korngold found her niche in combining outdoor sports with Judaism, taking groups mountaineering, skiing, hiking, or nature walking in pursuit of Jewish spirituality. Korngold advocates for a Judaism that is connected to rather than divorced from the natural world. *Photo by Jeff Finkelstein.*

Rabbi Jamie S. Korngold was inspired by Abraham Joshua Heschel, who taught that "awe rather than faith is the cardinal attitude of the religious Jew." Korngold, like Comins, had long been involved in nature activities. After graduating from HUC-JIR, she tried a traditional congregational career but found that it was too constricting for her. While she was playing around with the idea of creating a "synagogue without walls," she was asked to officiate at the conversion and naming ceremony of an adopted baby, which was held in a beautiful natural setting. Korngold was struck with the sudden revelation that this could become her life's work. In November 2001 she founded "A New Kind of Synagogue: The Adventure Rabbi Program."

Her goal is to show how Jewish religiosity can enrich people's lives, infusing spiritual meaning into natural adventures. Korngold takes her congregation on holiday retreats to a ranch in the Rocky Mountains, providing them with "experiential teaching of Jewish ritual, practice, and theology." She takes groups on mountain minyan hikes, backpacking treks through the desert, and peak climbs, scaling a snow-covered Atlantic peak in Colorado in early June. "There are so many people whose religion is the outdoors, who really experience their spirituality outside of the synagogue. So what I do is say, 'You're going to be outdoors, you say it's a spiritual experience. Let me show you how it's Jewish.'"[34] She has devoted herself to this mission, helping those who want to understand what "adventure Judaism" can mean.

Many Jewish people had told Korngold how they found the Judaism they had been raised with no longer had any meaning for them. "My heart aches when I hear words like these. And I hear them often. There are too many Jews who have inherited a Judaism that is void of meaning or relevance. There are too many Jews who don't know of a Judaism that is fulfilling, interesting, and joyful. There are too many Jews with no idea that our own religion is rich with opportunities to deepen our relationships with ourselves, with our community, and with our Creator."[35]

Rabbi Niles Goldstein, the founding rabbi of the New Shul in Manhattan, has become known for his advocacy of "Gonzo Judaism," in which he urges American Jews to reclaim their rebel roots in order to create a celebratory Jewish life. He differentiates between extreme and extremist religion. Adapting the expression from extreme sports, Goldstein explains that while an extremist approach to religion closes a person's mind, an extreme approach is "about keeping one's mind *open*, about experimenting with bold and unconventional techniques for transmitting spiritual knowledge and for reshaping souls." Goldstein loves pushing the limits by doing things and going to places that few others would have the nerve to do. He certainly does not project the image that one would expect from a typical rabbi.

Extreme religion, Goldstein claims, can lead to self-empowerment, freeing individuals from the shackles of conformity. Suddenly, they no longer feel that Judaism is something they have to do to please their parents but rather something they want to do or even need to do. Through a series of unique group experiences, they become involved in intense community-based spirituality. "Extreme religion is lean and mean. It offers challenge rather than comfort, risk rather than conservatism. It is about pushing boundaries, not constructing them." One might think such an approach would be enthusiastically embraced by the Jewish establishment, but Goldstein has an explanation for why that has not happened. "Extreme religion scares the crap out of normative religion. Why? Because it calls into question, by its sheer existence, the supposed value of the comfort and security that is offered by a more conventional, bourgeois approach to religious life."

As one example of how to break out of the normal humdrum, Goldstein organized an Alaskan trip to practice "religion in the raw," going backcountry hiking, sea kayaking, and camping while studying biblical, Talmudic, and mystical texts. On the North Slope of the Arctic National Wildlife Refuge, they set up camp late on Friday, preparing to welcome Shabbat. They were standing on Icy Reef, a band of small islands that sit between the Alaskan mainland in the Arctic Ocean, with subzero winds from the Beaufort Sea blowing toward them. "The winds weren't gale force, but they were strong enough to make striking my matches nearly impossible. And with the midnight sun hanging like a dim bulb directly in front of us, it was hard to determine what exactly constituted a genuine sunset."

34. Rabbi Niles Goldstein demonstrating a spiritual warrior principle to soldiers at Fort Belvoir, Virginia. Goldstein told the Jewish Book Council blog in 2009: "When I earned my black belt in karate just after rabbinic ordination, I had learned not only a specific set of combat skills but a wide array of tools that would help me in my vocation as a religious teacher and counselor—commitment, patience, humility, the power of repetition and practice, empathy, the ability to channel my strength in positive ways, self-sacrifice." *Courtesy of Niles Goldstein.*

Goldstein went with his brother to northwestern Mongolia, traveling throughout the region mostly on horseback. After passing herds of yaks, camels, and goats, they came to a community celebrating the upcoming marriage of one of the young men of the tribe. Relatives and friends had come together to build him a *ger*, a circular tentlike structure that he and his future wife could live in. Goldstein was struck by the communitarian ethos that compelled everyone in the area to help construct a home for the new couple. He realized that it was due as much to necessity as to affection. No one could survive without the help of the group.

He connects this experience with the story of Abraham and Sarah welcoming passersby into their tent. They did it because it was the right thing to do but also because if they did not, travelers would not be able to survive. Pure necessity created a society in which selflessness was valued over individualism. Jews come from a nation of nomads, who follow a tribal religion with tribal roots. Being part of a tribe means that our behavior should "be grounded, not necessarily in what we *want* to do, but in what we *ought* to do." In order to achieve that goal, Judaism has to return to a more primal form of religion. A tribal experience can create the dynamics where external rituals reinforce internal values such as generosity and compassion. "A raw, rowdy, barrel-chested reservoir of energy and exuberance" can help us build an interdependence that can revitalize "the desiccated Judaism of our own day."[36]

Conclusion

The Promise of Reform Judaism

Shortly before the publication of this book, I wrote an opinion piece that appeared in the *Forward*, titled "Losing Zuckerberg: Why Did Facebook King Move Away from Reform Judaism?" At the time, there was considerable concern over what was popularly seen as a disastrous initial public offering of stock in Facebook. Many of the articles in financial publications expressed concern that the fall in the Facebook stock price would deepen investor distrust of stocks in general. Hilary Kramer, a stock analyst, told me, "The investors thought they'd be able to make a quick round-trip like in the Internet days, when stocks would rise 100 percent within seconds of commencing trading." That did not happen, and Facebook stock went down instead of up. Fortunately, I had not bought any.

What concerned me as a Reform rabbi was not Mark Zuckerberg the social networking genius or Mark Zuckerberg the entrepreneur or Mark Zuckerberg the CEO, but Mark Zuckerberg the Reform Jew. Facebook's presence in the news—and Mark Zuckerberg's skyrocketing prominence—got me reflecting on the long-term impact of the Reform Jewish religious experience on our youth. From what we know about Zuckerberg's religious beliefs and current orientation, it would seem that he is another alienated graduate of the Union for Reform Judaism alumni club.

I explained that I was not criticizing Zuckerberg personally. Individuals can do whatever they want, and Zuckerberg is no exception. Plus, there was absolutely no indication that he was rejecting the Reform Judaism of his youth because of any malice or vindictiveness. Rather, if—and I stressed, if—he had lost interest in Judaism, it was more a reflection on us than it was on him. For those in the Reform movement and for those who are committed to non-Orthodox American Judaism generally, I argued, we need to see the sudden interest in Zuckerberg's personal life as an opportunity to perform *cheshbon hanefesh*—to take an accounting of our accomplishments and, as in this case, our failings.

In the *Forward* article, I recounted how Rabbi David Holtz of Congregation Beth Abraham in Tarrytown, New York, had described the Zuckerberg family as highly involved in the synagogue. Coincidentally, I was the scholar in residence at this very same congregation a few years ago and had found it to be a well-run synagogue filled with serious-minded people. So how does a devoted Jewish family attending an exemplary Reform synagogue have an earnest young man emerge from that experience with no discernible interest—not even to speak of commitment—to the Judaism with which he had supposedly been raised?

As we are discovering—and we had better realize this quickly, before all the Mark Zuckerbergs in all our temples are chased away—concern and involvement are not enough. We need to have a clear religious faith that we can convey to our young people in a way that is compelling and convincing. As Rabbi Eric H. Yoffie points out in his foreword, I have long believed that a liberal theology overemphasizing personal autonomy is a recipe for disaster. So, too, is the opposite, an exclusive focus on Jewish ethnic identity at the expense of Jewish religious belief.

Even if Zuckerberg becomes a super-Jew over the next couple of decades, it still will not change the fact that we are losing huge numbers of young people who have gone through all the educational and religious requirements set down by their Reform temples. Clearly, the expectations we have had of these young people were not enough.

We failed Zuckerberg and will continue to fail young people like him because the pluralistic theologies of Reform Judaism articulated since the 1960s make it difficult to grasp what we Reform Jews believe about the big issues. Our faith is too amorphous. Math and science nerds, in particular, may be the type most likely to bolt. This is ironic because one raisons d'être of Reform Judaism was to create an approach to Judaism that would be scholarly and scientific. But we have lost our way, ignoring scholarship in favor of any type of "spirituality," no matter how vacuous.

We need to urgently reevaluate the worldview we are inculcating and whether it is in the best interest of keeping our form of belief and practice alive. A bright young man like Mark Zuckerberg, raised in a serious Reform synagogue, should be a devoted Jew today. We need to ask ourselves why he is apparently not committed to the God of his ancestors, and then we need to take big steps to rebuild our religious "ecosystem."

Our concern with creating a serious religious experience that can motivate commitment is not new. In 1983 Rabbi Alexander Schindler issued a prophetic warning. "Our numeric burgeoning can excite our hopes and ambitions, but our efforts will sink into nothingness unless we perceive and embrace Judaism as a serious religious enterprise." What he said thirty years ago remains true today. We need a strong and compelling theology that can motivate us to be totally committed to our religion and willing to sacrifice for our God.

The pluralistic theologies of Reform Judaism make it difficult to reach consensus on what we Reform Jews believe on any given issue. The liberal approach to observance makes it impossible to set and maintain high expectations in terms of communal participation. Without an omnipotent God who can compel believers to practice a prescribed pattern of behavior, religious consumerism becomes the movement's dominant ethos. As members focus on what they want rather than what they can contribute, it becomes increasingly difficult to build committed religious communities.

While Classical Reform Judaism emphasized the clear theological formulations of ethical monotheism and the mission of Israel, the neo-Reform approach, which became dominant beginning with the Columbus Platform of 1937, allowed for a greater degree of religious pluralism. This was a good thing in that it permitted divergent religious subgroups to practice Jewish ceremony in the manner they found most meaningful. But it also weakened the central theological core that had constituted the essence of Reform Judaism.

35. The cover of *Reform Judaism* magazine, heralding Rabbi Rick Jacobs as "the cata-lyst for change." In the interview, Jacobs argued that "a major restructuring of the URJ is required to meet these new realities of Jewish life." He listed five overarching imper-atives: "We need to create a URJ culture of excellence"; "we must think and act like a movement, instead of functioning as separate silos"; "we need a covenantal partnership between the URJ's lay leaders and staff"; "the URJ needs to see itself and be seen in the context of a relational culture instead of an all-knowing big brother"; and "we need to understand and harness the power of new technologies." *Courtesy of the URJ.*

By 1975 there was so much theological disagreement that the committee responsible for putting together the movement's official prayer book, *Gates of Prayer*, had to create ten different Friday night services, eight of which reflected alternative and sometimes contradictory theological perspectives. For example, while Service 1 spoke of the all-powerful God who reigns in the heavens above, Service 2 described the Divine Presence as the still, small voice of conscience within each human being. Both are touching and may stimulate spiritual feelings. However, one does not have to be a theologian to see the potential problems that arise in the face of so much obvious contradiction.

One can argue—with total sincerity and with a good deal of conviction—that this contradiction is a healthy part of postmodern pluralism. Nevertheless, this situation cripples us theologically because we become unable to articulate what we believe religiously. In a religious community setting, what we believe has an impact on how we behave. Every religious group needs a strict theology in order to make serious demands on their adherents. These demands, in turn, are what makes a religion more compelling. As one of the commentators on my article "Losing Zuckerberg" put it, "A religion that demands nothing is worth nothing."

Since a liberal theology leads to an emphasis on the autonomy of the individual, personal choice is inevitably promoted at the expense of the authority of God. In the absence of a strong theological basis for making religious demands, the members lose interest and wander off. This is what has happened in American Reform Judaism and in other non-Orthodox movements as well.

One might think that most people would prefer a congregation that allows each member to find his or her own comfort level rather than one that requires all sorts of obligations, in theology as well as in ritual. This is not necessarily true.

Yes, many potential members are deterred by high upfront demands. But for those who join, the commitment is much greater. Since most of the members in a demanding congregation are deeply committed and religiously active, the collective religious experience is much more fulfilling.

As the Reform movement has increasingly emphasized religious autonomy and the importance of choosing what each person finds spiritually meaningful, it has become impossible to compel members to come to services regularly, study Torah seriously, and contribute to the vibrant well-being of their congregation. Instead, they are allowed to come twice a year and call on the rabbi whenever they need a life-cycle ceremony. Whether you call it salad bar religion or a filling-station synagogue, the imagery is not pleasant.

There is a devil's bargain being made between an often self-satisfied leadership and an apathetic laity. Many Reform synagogues have large numbers on the books but few active participants. We are now seeing the consequences of the benign neglect that has been plaguing Reform Judaism for many years.

While Jewishness is an important component in contemporary culture, Judaism itself is in danger of being regarded as increasingly irrelevant. Arguments that convinced earlier generations to identify with Judaism will not be nearly as effective on those coming of age in the twenty-first century. Increasingly multicultural, the new generations have multiple identities and are open to multiple commitments.

We Reform Jews have been riding a rollercoaster for the past three decades. At one moment, it seems that our movement is in crisis, perhaps on the verge of collapse, only to make a seemingly remarkable recovery, becoming the model for not only other Jewish streams but other American religious and ethnic groups as well. In the 1980s and early 1990s, we enjoyed our moment in the sun, repeating like a mantra the often-quoted demographic fact that we had become the largest Jewish denomination in the United States. We watched as the children of many longtime members of Conservative synagogues joined Reform congregations, frequently after intermarrying. Everything seemed to be going great. But that moment of supremacy was short-lived.

We increasingly recognize that the differences between Reform Judaism and the other types of non-Orthodox Judaism—whether Conservative Judaism, Reconstructionist Judaism, Jewish Renewal, or any of several other variations and permutations—are superficial and unlikely to retain their intellectual coherence in the long-term. This realization

36. Campers at Camp Coleman in Cleveland, Georgia. Reform movement camping and immersive Israel experiences play a vital role in the formation of a strong and proud Jewish identity. According to the URJ website, children who attend a Jewish camp or participate in youth group have more Jewish friends, are more inclined to raise a Jewish family when they become adults, and are more likely to stay actively engaged members of a Jewish community. *Courtesy of URJ.*

frightens us because we identify as Reform Jews, believe in Reform Judaism, and look forward to a future that is distinctly denominational. Nevertheless, we must cope with a reality that minimizes Reform distinctiveness in what many are calling a postdenominational future.

No one in 1844 or 1885 or 1936 or even 1967 would have been able to predict that the Reform movement would have as many affiliated synagogues and as many programs and activities as it does today. If Rabbi Isaac Mayer Wise or Rabbi Kaufmann Kohler or Rabbi Stephen Wise were to come to a Biennial of the Union for Reform Judaism today, they would be amazed at the sheer numbers present, not to mention the vitality and enthusiasm.

But the movement faces tremendous challenges in the years ahead. We will need to develop new and convincing justifications for maintaining the Jewish people as a separate ethno-religious group in an era where boundaries and borders of all kinds are fading, if not disappearing. We will need to clarify our theology and communicate these religious beliefs with conviction.

From a sociological perspective, the Reform movement is an anomaly; it does not fit into the standard categories generally used to evaluate American religious groups. We are—despite forty years of intensive involvement in bringing in proselytes—still an ethnic-based religious group. Many of us do not hold strong religious beliefs and a significant number of us do not hold any religious beliefs at all.

We affiliate because we want to be part of the Jewish people, and we choose to show that ethnic solidarity through the vehicle of Reform Judaism. Others of us are deeply committed to spirituality but balk at any type of authoritarian approach to religion. We might even define ourselves as spiritual but not religious, although we are perfectly comfortable with Jewish ceremony so long as it is focused on personal spiritual needs.

As I write these words, the Union for Reform Judaism is undergoing yet another reorganization. This includes the laying off of numerous employees, many of whom were bright and conscientious, indisputably assets to the organization. We realize that social trends are now moving at such a rate that all organizations need to be fast and nimble, quick to adjust to the rapidly changing religious environment. But we cannot help asking, When will it all settle down? When can we go back to having a stable structure that we can rely on? When can we feel confident that the future will bring more of the same, only better? Unfortunately, we know that that day is unlikely to ever return.

The Judaism of the future will most likely bear little resemblance to the Judaism that we are familiar with today. As Americans continue to reimagine how their social institutions should look, they are distancing themselves from the sort of traditional organizational structures that the denominations embraced—and continue to embrace despite the obvious need for radical change.

Virtually all Reform temples have invested tremendous sums in their physicality. They have bought large plots of land and erected massive structures with huge sanctuaries and classroom complexes, much of which is used only a few hours a week. The payroll runs into the hundreds of thousands of dollars for highly trained professionals who are, in many cases, vastly overeducated for the primarily social work function that they perform.

The synagogue of the future may be much lighter on its feet. We may focus on developing strong emotional bonds among members who share certain common religious beliefs and social goals. The organization may be led by volunteers, with smaller numbers of rabbis and cantors rotating among a large number of congregations that function well without any full-time professional leadership. Our organizational structure may become very different, but if we can preserve the central tenets to our approach to Judaism, Progressive Judaism can have a tremendous future.

Religion in the United States has a very promising future, but that future may be so different from the present that we may not recognize its potential. We see a profound shift in the way that Americans—and particularly younger Americans—relate to organized religion. Large numbers are refusing to join organizations, preferring to "bowl alone." Growing numbers of young people network through virtual groups or in informal settings of their choosing. But this extreme individualism is going to make it nearly impossible to mobilize people. Can the Reform movement come up with a successful postmodern strategy for building community?

We need to create a liberal Judaism that can provide a personal experience that speaks directly to each individual. Rather than focusing on the importance of loyalty to community, we need to determine how to engage the individual in a search for existential meaning.

To be a significant religious influence on American society over the next fifty or one hundred years, the Reform movement must have a clear theological message. It cannot continue to be a "big tent" for virtually every type of Jew in the country, excluding a small number of still-forbidden heresies that fall outside the generous boundaries drawn by the intellectual leaders of the movement. Young people are continually asking the question, Why should I care? The answer is less important than the passion with which the answer is conveyed.

I believe that Judaism is the best means for developing a deep understanding and appreciation of God and our world. Rabbi Isaac Mayer Wise, the founder of the Reform movement in America, wrote that "Israel's religion . . . is the true religion, because its doctrines are taken from the revelations of God in His works and words." Not every Reform Jew finds that formulation acceptable, but I would argue that we need to develop a focused theological approach that we can truly believe in. Pluralism is a wonderful concept, allowing us to be united in our diversity. But it is no substitute for having religious conviction.

Reform Judaism, I would argue, is the best representation of Judaism. The reason is simple: there have been serious intellectual challenges to religion in general, and to the divine nature of the Bible in particular, over the past three hundred years. Reform Judaism is well-suited to integrate these scholarly studies that have been generally accepted as valid, including the most contemporary variations of the documentary hypothesis, which sees the Torah as consisting of at least four separate texts that were redacted over a long period. Reform Judaism moves us to a critical, scholarly understanding of the Hebrew Bible and then helps us emerge with multiple perspectives suitable for a postmodern world.

While finding room for these many perspectives, Reform Judaism should focus on what the nineteenth-century reformers called ethical monotheism, the idea that there is one and only one God, and that God demands ethical behavior. Properly understood, liberal Judaism can help us live our lives both ethically and joyfully. It can help us to understand how the ancient world molded our most cherished religious traditions and how we can approach complex contemporary social problems.

Can we make our faith both emotionally intense and intellectually honest at the same time? That is the central challenge for Reform Jews, a challenge inherent in any theology that stresses individual autonomy and critical thought. The key is to cultivate greater devotion to the values at the heart of Reform theology and build communities around a common and passionate commitment to these principles. This may mean moving away from the Reform movement's current focus on pluralism and looking more toward building a committed core, but it can be done.

Earlier in this book, I cited Rabbi Maurice Eisendrath: "God is a living God—not a God who revealed Himself and His word once and for all time at Sinai and speaks no more." His words are key for understanding the crucial role that Reform Judaism has to play in the coming decades. We Reform Jews believe that God gave us the Torah and that the Torah contains timeless religious truths of tremendous importance, not only to Jews but to the entire world. Every time we study Torah and incorporate its lessons into our lives, we are participating in the process of bringing God's revelation to us. That is Reform Judaism's mission. It has been a compelling mission for over two hundred years and it remains a truly compelling one.

Afterword

RABBI RICK JACOBS

Judaism is at a crossroads. Throughout our people's history there have been many times when internal and external forces have pushed the status quo to transform itself. For Reform Judaism, which was created precisely to foster continual change and innovation, such times are filled with great opportunity. And now is just such a time.

Can you imagine what Yahoo might look like next year? If so, you are a few steps ahead of Yahoo's new CEO. After a brilliant career at Google, thirty-seven-year-old Marissa Mayer comes to Yahoo at a pivotal time. Worldwide, about seven hundred million people visit Yahoo's site, available in thirty different languages, every month. Marissa Mayer's new job is to figure out what Yahoo will be in the coming months and years.

The Reform movement is not Yahoo, but we have a very similar challenge. After having grown steadily over the past 140 years, we are the largest and most vibrant movement in Jewish life today, with nearly nine hundred congregations and more than one and a half million people. But the landscape of Jewish life has changed dramatically, forcing us to redefine who we are and where we are going. What is required is nothing less than a reimagining of Jewish life.

For those who remain unconvinced that we need to make sweeping changes, consider the following: while 80 percent of American Jews affiliate with a synagogue at some point in their lives, their engagement tends to be temporary and tenuous. No more than 50 percent of North American Jews are members of synagogues at any one time. Our post–

World War II models of dues-based membership are less relevant to a generation that values variety and flexibility in its spiritual engagement. Add to these challenges the fact that technology has radically changed how we access Jewish knowledge and experience community. These new realities require a radical response, not just little tweaks or more of what has already been done.

One of the hallmarks of our movement is that we have had remarkable, and yes, radical leaders—people who faced the challenges of their day with wisdom and creativity. In these pages, Dana Evan Kaplan thoughtfully documents the bold responses of my three predecessors, Rabbis Maurice N. Eisendrath, Alexander M. Schindler, and Eric H. Yoffie.

Rabbi Eisendrath created three new pillar institutions of our movement that continue to endow us with incalculable strength. He oversaw the formation of our national youth movement, NFTY; the establishment of the first UAHC (now URJ) summer camps; and the remarkable Religious Action Center in Washington DC. Rabbi Schindler transformed Jewish life by pushing open the tent flaps of the Jewish community with his trailblazing outreach initiatives to interfaith families, redefining Jewishness to acknowledge and include patrilineal descent. Most recently, Rabbi Yoffie tackled the need for serious lifelong learning with Torah at the center and encouraged deeper spiritual engagement in our congregations. These courageous visionaries led us to widen our tent and stake out a position of centrality within the greater Jewish community.

Dana Evan Kaplan offers some useful conceptual and historical frameworks to better understand Reform Judaism. While providing overviews of the movement's history, theology, and dilemmas, Rabbi Kaplan invites his readers to struggle with the future of Reform Judaism. He points to its lack of a unifying theology or ideology as a binding force amid the dramatic changes underway. I am not convinced that we need one overarching ideology for Reform Judaism to thrive in the coming decades, but he is right to pose this serious question.

Today's Reform prayer books and rabbis offer a variety of theologies that enable growing numbers of individuals to deeply engage in the core commitments of Jewish life. In the late nineteenth and early twentieth centuries, Jewish theology and practice were more narrowly defined, leaving many North American Jews outside rigid walls. Currently, an ever-widening series of Jewish offerings within our movement enables those from more traditional backgrounds, those who have no experience with Judaism, and all those in between to find their place within our communities. Rabbi Kaplan wisely focuses on those communities that challenged our deliberately open boundaries: Jews for Jesus and Humanistic Judaism, which were deemed to be outside the bounds, and many other religious variations that have taken root within our broad tent.

Rabbi Kaplan joins with many who proclaim this age to be postdenominational. Not long ago, people sought out denominational labels when searching for a synagogue. Today, many are less concerned with labels, seeking Jewish communities defined instead by values. Our people want, and deserve, communities that are engaging, dynamic, and nourishing. And the values matter: serious, open, inclusive, spiritual, passionate, and substantive. No denomination is an end in itself; the larger entity is the Jewish people. We need to ensure that the Reform movement's expression of Judaism includes responsibility for and connection to those who do not identify with the Jewish community as it has traditionally been defined.

I am confident that we will be as imaginative as previous generations of Reform Jews in shaping our Reform community. But there are many questions before us. Will the Reform community of the future still be located in its own synagogue building? Will virtual communities outnumber actual ones? Will clergy and educators still have central roles? It is too soon to say, but the Jewish future will surely need communities of learning, spirituality, connection, and social justice. Those eager to understand and participate in this exciting new chapter in Jewish history will find extensive background and stimulation in *The New Reform Judaism: Challenges and Reflections*, a valuable contribution to this evolving discourse.

Timeline of Significant Events

1781   Christian Wilhelm Dohn publishes *Concerning the Amelioration of the Civil Status of the Jews*, arguing that once the Jews are given equal rights as citizens, they will abandon their more restrictive religious practices.

1810   Israel Jacobson dedicates the first Reform temple as part of a boys' school in Seesen, Westphalia. He conducts the first confirmation service that same year.

1818   Rabbi Eliezer Liebermann publishes *Nogah Ha-Tsedek* (The Radiance of Justice) and *Or Nogah* (Radiant Light), which argue in favor of specific liturgical and ritual reforms.

1824   Forty-seven congregants in Charleston, South Carolina, petition Kahal Kadosh Beth Elohim for minor changes in the worship service. Their request is refused by the trustees. Under the leadership of Isaac Harby, the dissident group sets up an independent body, the Society of Reformed Israelites, the first Reform congregation in the United States.

1842   Har Sinai Congregation in Baltimore is founded as an ideologically Reform congregation.

1844   A Rabbinical Conference is held in Brunswick, Lower Saxony, convened by Rabbis Levi Herzfeld and Ludwig Philippson.

1845   The second meeting of the "Conference of the Rabbis of Germany" takes place at Frankfurt am Main with Rabbi Leopold Stein as president.

1845   Congregation Emanu-El of New York City is founded.

1846   A third Rabbinical Conference is held in Breslau at which the Sabbath question is debated.

1846   Isaac Mayer Wise immigrates to the United States from Bohemia.

1847   Rabbi Isaac Mayer Wise prepares a manuscript of a prayer book, entitled "Minhag America," which he intends for use by all U.S. congregations.

1848   Rabbi Isaac Mayer Wise issued a call to Jewish ministers and other Israelites to come together to begin planning a national union of Jewish congregations.

1850   Rabbi Isaac Mayer Wise is fired from Congregation Beth-El in Albany, New York. His supporters found a new congregation, which becomes one of the earliest Reform-oriented synagogues in the United States.

1857   Isaac Mayer Wise edits the first American siddur, *Minhag America*.

1869   Thirteen mostly radical Reform rabbis meet in Philadelphia, passing what becomes known as the Philadelphia Principles, which stress the universal mission of Israel.

1869   Rabbi Isaac Mayer Wise and other colleagues introduce the late Friday evening service in response to waning attendance on Saturday mornings.

1873   The Union of American Hebrew Congregations is founded by lay leaders inspired by Rabbi Isaac Mayer Wise.

1875   Hebrew Union College is founded by Rabbi Isaac Mayer Wise in Cincinnati.

1885   A small group of rabbis meet in Pittsburgh, passing a set of principles called the Pittsburgh Platform, which becomes the basis for Classical Reform Judaism.

1889   The Central Conference of American Rabbis is founded by Rabbi Isaac Mayer Wise.

1892   The Central Conference of American Rabbis votes to allow conversion without circumcision or immersion in a mikveh.

1892   The Union Prayer Book is published by the Central Conference of American Rabbis and then is recalled.

1895   The first edition of the Union Prayer Book is published, replacing the 1892 version. It is revised in 1922 and 1941.

1897   The Central Conference of American Rabbis passes a resolution opposing Zionism seven weeks before the First Zionist Congress is convened in Basel.

1909   The Central Conference for American Rabbis passes a resolution stating that mixed marriages are contrary to the tradition of the Jewish religion and should be discouraged by the American rabbinate.

1922   Judith Kaplan becomes the first bat mitzvah at the Society for the Advancement of Judaism in New York City.

1922   Reform Rabbi Stephen S. Wise establishes the Jewish Institute of Religion in New York City.

1926   The World Union for Progressive Judaism is founded in London.

1937   The Central Conference of American Rabbis adopts a new platform at their annual meeting in Columbus, Ohio, which becomes known as the Columbus Platform.

1939   The North American Federation of Temple Youth is founded.

1943   Rabbi Maurice Eisendrath becomes executive secretary of the Union of American Hebrew Congregations. He becomes president in 1951.

1946   Rabbi Joshua Loth Leibman publishes *Peace of Mind*, which becomes a best seller.

1946   The Central Conference of American Rabbis issues a statement entitled "Judaism and Race Relations," which calls for an end to racial discrimination.

1947   Jacob Rader Marcuz founds the American Jewish Archives on the campus of Hebrew Union College in Cincinnati.

1948   The State of Israel is founded, ending most internal debate within the Reform movement over Zionism.

1950   Paula Ackerman, widow of Rabbi William Ackerman, begins serving Temple Beth Israel of Meridian, Mississippi, as its unofficial rabbi.

1950   Hebrew Union College in Cincinnati and the Jewish Institute of Religion in New York City merge.

1953   Rabbi Eisendrath advocates for the creation of an Israeli Reform movement.

1954   Hebrew Union College–Jewish Institute of Religion opens a prerabbinic program at the Wilshire Boulevard Temple in Los Angeles, supplementing a part-time College of Jewish Studies program that had been opened in 1947.

1959   The Union of American Hebrew Congregations passes a resolution opposing capital punishment.

1963   Followers of Rabbi Mordecai M. Kaplan begin concrete plans to create the Reconstructionist movement as a fourth denomination in American Judaism.

1963   The government of Israel offers Hebrew Union College–Jewish Institute of Religion a ninety-nine-year lease on a two-acre site in Jerusalem close to the King David Hotel.

1963   Seventy Reform rabbis take part in the March on Washington for Jobs and Freedom in August 1963, during which Dr. Martin Luther King Jr. delivers his "I Have a Dream" speech.

1963   Rabbi Nelson Glueck, president of Hebrew Union College, is put on the cover of *Time* magazine for his archaeological accomplishments.

1964   Albert Vorspan and fourteen rabbis are arrested for praying in an integrated group in front of Monson's Restaurant, and two others are arrested for sitting down at a table with three African American youngsters in Chimes Restaurant.

1965   Rabbi Abraham Joshua Heschel marches for civil rights with Martin Luther King Jr. in Selma, Alabama.

1965 Rabbi Eisendrath urges delegates from the Union of American Hebrew Congregations to protest against the Vietnam War, calling it a transgression of "every tenet of our faith."

1967 Facing Arab threats to annihilate her, the State of Israel launches a preemptive attack, conquering the West Bank and Gaza Strip in the Six-Day War.

1967 The board of Temple Emanu-El of New York City temporarily resigns from the Union of American Hebrew Congregations in protest against Rabbi Eisendrath's radical rhetoric.

1968 Havarut Shalom is founded in Somerville, Massachusetts, and serves as a model community for the Jewish counterculture.

1968 The Reconstructionist Rabbinical College is founded by Rabbi Ira Eisenstein in the Philadelphia area.

1968 The World Union for Progressive Judaism Biennial Conference is held for the first time in Israel.

1970 A new building in Los Angeles is constructed for Hebrew Union College–Jewish Institute of Religion, adjacent to the campus of the University of Southern California.

1970 Olin-Sang-Ruby Union Institute in Oconomowoc, Wisconsin, hired a then unknown Debbie Friedman as a song leader.

1971 Rabbi Alfred Gottschalk is appointed president of Hebrew Union College–Jewish Institute of Religion.

1971 Rabbi Joseph B. Glaser is appointed executive vice president of the Central Conference of American Rabbis.

1971 The Israel Movement for Progressive Judaism is incorporated under Israeli law.

1972 Rabbi Sally J. Priesand is ordained by Hebrew Union College–Jewish Institute of Religion.

1972 The CCAR Sabbath Committee, a successor to the Sabbath Observance Commission, publishes *A Shabbat Manual: Tadrikh l'Shabbat*.

1972	Theodore Lenn publishes a study entitled *Rabbi and Syna-gogue in Reform Judaism*, which found that fully 42 percent of rabbis felt that there is a "crisis" in American Reform Judaism.
1972	Leonard Fein publishes a study of UAHC membership entitled *Reform Is a Verb*, in which he finds that most Reform congregants have little emotional investment in their temple.
1973	The Central Conference of American Rabbis reaffirms its opposition to mixed marriage, first passed in 1909, while urging its members to encourage raising children of mixed marriages as Jewish.
1973	Rabbi Eisendrath dies of a heart attack in his hotel room hours before his final address to the UAHC Biennial. Rabbi Alexander M. Schindler becomes his successor.
1973	The Yom Kippur War takes place in the Middle East.
1973	The World Union for Progressive Judaism moves its headquarters from London to Jerusalem.
1975	*Gates of Prayer* is published by the Central Conference of American Rabbis, replacing the *Union Prayer Book*, which had been the primary Reform prayer book for about eighty years.
1976	The Central Conference of American Rabbis adopts "Reform Judaism: A Centenary Perspective" in San Francisco.
1976	Yahel, the first Reform kibbutz, is established in the Arava Valley.
1978	The Reform movement establishes ARZA, a Reform Zionist organization.
1978	Rabbi Alexander M. Schindler, president of the Union of American Hebrew Congregations, urges the UAHC board of trustees to warmly welcome non-Jews in interfaith marriages into Reform congregations, as well as to begin to openly proselytize.
1980	Rabbi Mordecai (Moti) Rotem is ordained as the first Israeli Reform rabbi.

1981   *The Torah: A Modern Commentary*, edited by Rabbi W. Gunther Plaut, is published by the Union of American Hebrew Congregations.

1983   The Reform movement accepts that patrilineal as well as matrilineal descent determine Jewish status of offspring born to intermarried couples.

1983   *Seder P'reidah*, a ritual of release written by Rabbi Simeon J. Maslin to provide a Reform ceremony following divorce, is published by the Central Conference of American Rabbis.

1983   Kibbutz Lotan, the second Reform kibbutz, is founded in the Arava Valley near Kibbutz Yahel.

1985   President Ronald Reagan visits the German military cemetery at Bitburg containing the graves of forty-seven members of the Waffen ss.

1988   A new manual for rabbis is published by the Central Conference of American Rabbis.

1990   Gay and lesbian candidates are allowed to apply for admission into the rabbinical program at Hebrew Union College–Jewish Institute of Religion.

1991   Beit Daniel is built in North Tel Aviv.

1991   The Union of American Hebrew Congregations passes a resolution at its Biennial in Baltimore calling on the American and Canadian governments to take measures to protect the environment.

1991   Rabbi Schindler tells delegates at the UAHC Biennial that a membership application from Congregation Beth Adam in Cincinnati, which is humanist in orientation, will open a debate on what beliefs, if any, should be required of a UAHC congregation.

1993   Rabbi Schindler supports the right of gay and lesbian couples to adopt children, to file joint income tax returns, and to be eligible for health and death benefits.

1997   On the occasion of the centenary of the first World Zionist Congress, the Central Conference of American Rabbis adopts the Miami Platform.

1999   The Central Conference of American Rabbis passes a new Pittsburgh Platform, the "Statement of Principles for Reform Judaism," which calls for greater ritual observance.

2000   The Central Conference of American Rabbis passes a resolution supporting rabbinic officiation at same-gender rituals of union, while recognizing the diversity of opinion within their ranks on this issue.

2000   Mercaz Shimshon, the cultural center of the World Union of Progressive Judaism, is opened in Jerusalem, adjacent to Hebrew Union College–Jewish Institute of Religion.

2001   David Ellenson becomes president of Hebrew Union College–Jewish Institute of Religion.

2001   *Dibrei Giur: Guidelines for Rabbis Working with Prospective Gerim* is accepted by the CCAR at its annual conference in Monterey, California.

2002   Hebrew Union College–Jewish Institute of Religion in Los Angeles begins ordaining rabbis.

2003   The Union of American Hebrew Congregations changes its name to the Union for Reform Judaism to better reflect its actual mission.

2005   Rabbi Paul Menitoff resigns as executive vice president of the Central Conference of American Rabbis after an audit reveals missing funds.

2006   Rabbi Steven A. Fox is appointed as executive vice president of the Central Conference of American Rabbis. His title is later changed to chief executive.

2007   A new Reform prayer book, *Mishkan T'filah*, is published by the Central Conference of American Rabbis.

2007   Ben Gamla Charter School, the first Hebrew-language charter school in the United States, opens in Hollywood, Florida.

2007   *The Torah: A Women's Commentary* is published by the Union for Reform Judaism.

2008   Congregation Sha'ar Zahav, a San Francisco synagogue with an emphasis on outreach to the LGBT community, publishes their own prayer book, *Siddur Sha'ar Zahav*.

2008   United States Immigration and Customs Enforcement raids Agriprocessors, a kosher slaughterhouse in Postville, Iowa.

2008   The Conservative movement publishes guidelines for a Hekhsher Tzedek kashrut certification, outlining ethical requirements that need to be met, in addition to the traditional ritual requirements, for a food product to be certified by them as kosher.

2008   Jewish organizations of all kinds begin to feel the effects of the October 2008 stock market crash, as well as a number of Ponzi schemes that disproportionately affect the Jewish community.

2008   The Society for Classical Reform Judaism is established by Rabbi Howard A. Berman, the longtime leader of Chicago Sinai Congregation.

2009   The Union for Reform Judaism announces a major restructuring of its organization, closing all fourteen regional offices and opening four administrative centers.

2009   Hebrew Union College announces that it may close two of its three campuses in the United States.

2009   Rabbi Eric H. Yoffie announces a URJ Biennial initiative called "Just Table, Green Table," a commitment to ethical eating.

2012   Rabbi Richard Jacobs assumes his position as the new president of the Union for Reform Judaism.

2012   The Israeli government agrees to begin paying some non-Orthodox rabbis and to recognize them as community leaders in response to an Israeli Supreme Court lawsuit. The non-Orthodox rabbis will receive their salaries through the Culture and Sports Ministry rather than the Religious Services Ministry, which funds Orthodox rabbis, in order to prevent the resignation of minister for religious services Yaakov Margi of the Haredi Orthodox Shas party.

2013   *Mishkan T'filah for Children: A Siddur for Families and Schools* edited by Michelle Shapiro Abraham is published. This full-color illustrated prayer book for kindergarten through second grade includes a family Shabbat Service and a weekday service for religious schools.

2013   HUC-JIR begins a discussion under the leadership of Rabbi Michael Marmur to consider allowing intermarried candidates to apply to rabbinical school. A heated debate begins in the pages of the *Forward* and on blogs.

2013   The URJ Biennial is held in San Diego featuring the three major URJ priorities—catalyzing congregational change, expanding our reach, and engaging the next generation.

2014   The Central Conference of American Rabbis anticipates publication of a new rabbis' manual entitled *L'kol Eit—For Every Moment*, edited by Rabbi Don Goor.

2014   *Mishkan T'filah for Youth: A Siddur for Families and Schools* is anticipated to be published. This full-color illustrated prayer book for third through fifth grade includes a family Shabbat Service and a weekday service for religious schools.

2015   *Mishkan HaNefesh: A Machzor for the Days of Awe* edited by Rabbis Edwin Goldberg, Sheldon Marder, Janet Marder, and Leon Morris is anticipated to be published. This High Holy Day prayer book promises to provide meaningful liturgy for those who pray regularly as well as for those new to Jewish spirituality and practice. It will hopefully bridge the personal and the communal, the ritual and the ethical dimensions of the Yamim Ha-Noraim, embracing the rich liturgical voices of the Jewish past and the aspirations of our people today.

Notes

1. In Search of Reform Jewish Theology

1. Robert Goldenberg, *The Origins of Judaism: From Canaan to the Rise of Islam* (New York: Cambridge University Press, 2007).
2. Michael L. Satlow, *Creating Judaism: History, Tradition, Practice* (New York: Columbia University Press, 2006), 3.
3. Maurice Eisendrath, *Can Faith Survive? The Thought and Afterthoughts of an American Rabbi* (New York: McGraw Hill, 1964), 243–44.
4. Samuel Cohon, "Report on the Guiding Principles of Reform Judaism," *CCAR Yearbook* 36 (1936): 104.
5. Chaim Stern, ed., *Gates of Prayer: The New Union Prayerbook* (New York: Central Conference of American Rabbis, 1975), 122, 143.
6. W. Gunther Plaut and David E. S. Stein, eds., *The Torah: A Modern Commentary*, rev. ed. (New York: Union for Reform Judaism, 2005), 107–8.
7. Julian Morgenstern, *As a Mighty Stream* (Philadelphia: Jewish Publication Society of American, 1949), 87–88.

2. Brief History of American Reform Movement

1. Michael A. Meyer, *Response to Modernity: A History of the Reform Movement in Judaism* (New York: Oxford University Press, 1988), 17.
2. Sylvan D. Schwartzman, *Reform Judaism Then and Now* (New York: Union of American Hebrew Congregations, 1971), 141, 151.
3. "Rabbi Maurice N. Eisendrath, UAHC President, Dies at 71: Leader of Reform Judaism Was to Have Present [sic]," November 12, 1973, Jewish Telegraphic Agency, http://archive.jta.org/article/1973/11/12/2966741 /rabbi-maurice-n-eisendrath-uahc-president-dies-at-71-leader-of -%20reform-judaism-was-to-have-presented-speech-sharply-critical-of- nixon-administration-us-%20jews-who-gave-uncritical-support-to -president%20.
4. David J. Meyer, "Fighting Segregation, Threats, and Dynamite: Rabbi William B. Silverman's Nashville Battle," *American Jewish Archives Journal*

60 nos. 1 and 2 (2008): 104–5; William B. Silverman, *Basic Reform Judaism* (New York: Philosophical Press, 1970), 14, 171–72.

5. Michael A. Meyer, *Response to Modernity: A History of the Reform Movement in Judaism* (New York: Oxford University Press, 1988), 369.

6. Eugene B. Borowitz, *Reform Judaism Today*, vol. 1: *Reform in the Process of Change* (New York: Behrman House, 1983), xii.

7. Jacques Steinberg, "Rabbi Alexander Schindler, Reform Leader and Major Jewish Voice, Dies at 75," *New York Times*, November 16, 2000, http://www .nytimes.com/2000/11/16/nyregion/rabbi-alexander-schindler-reform -leader-and-major-jewish-voice-dies-at-75.html?pagewanted=all&src=pm.

8. John Dart, "More Emphasis on Religion Urged for Reform Judaism," *Los Angeles Times*, November 3, 1985, http://articles.latimes.com/1985-11-03/ news/mn-3969_1_reform-judaism.

9. Eugene J. Lipman, "*Tanu Rabbanan*: Our Masters Have Taught Us," in *Tanu Rabbanan, Our Rabbis Taught: Essays on the Occasion of the Centennial of the Central Conference of American Rabbis*, ed. Joseph B. Glaser (New York: Central Conference of American Rabbis, 1990), 67.

10. Rabbi Rick Jacob's Speech to the Consultation on Conscience, May 2, 2011, http://weareforisrael.org/2011/05/03/rabbi-rick-jacobs-speech-to-the -consultation-on-conscience/.

11. Elaine Woo, "Alfred Gottschalk Dies at 79: A Leader of Reform Judaism," *Los Angeles Times*, September 13, 2009, A46.

12. Debra Nussbaum Cohen, "Alfred Gottschalk, a German Refugee Who Became a Reform Movement Leader," *Forward*, September 25, 2009, http:// www.forward.com/articles/114206/.

13. "The New Reform: Reform Judaism and Jewish Authenticity, Yale University, April 24, 1983, Rabbi Alfred Gottschalk, PhD," American Jewish Archives, Folder No. c5-c50, Box A2c-3.

14. "First Woman Rabbi in U.S. Ordained; She May Be Only the Second in History of Judaism," June 4, 1972, http://select.nytimes.com/gst/abstract.html ?res=F20F11F83A5910738DDDAD0894DE405B828BF1D3.

15. "Opening Session Welcoming Remarks, Exploration and Celebration Symposium, January 31, 1993, Dr. Alfred Gottschalk, Hebrew Union College–Jewish Institute of Religion, New York, New York," American Jewish Archives, Folder No. 10-10d, Box A2c-3.

16. Mira Avrech, "Israel's First Native-Born Reform Rabbi Challenges Rigidity and Sexism in His Faith," *People*, August 11, 1980, http://www.people.com/ people/archive/article/0,,20077169,00.html.

17. Jane Eisner, "Rabbi Yoffie to Retire as President of Union for Reform Judaism," December 13, 2011, http://www.haaretz.com/jewish-world/rabbi -yoffie-to-retire-as-president-of-union-for-reform-judaism-1.401152.

18. Howard A. Berman, correspondence with author, October 24, 2009.

19. "Our Mission Statement," *Reform Advocate* 1, no. 1 (Autumn 2008): 12.
20. Pauline Dubkin Yearwood, "Camp Spirit: Olin-Sang-Ruby Union Institute Celebrates a Half-Century of Bringing Judaism Out of Doors and into the Hearts of Reform Jewish Kids," *Chicago Jewish News*, July 21–27, 2000, 11.
21. Hank Bordowitz, "Singing unto God," *Reform Judaism* 30, no. 4 (Summer 2002): 65.
22. Margalit Fox, "Debbie Friedman, Singer of Jewish Music, Dies at 59," *New York Times*, January 11, 2011, http://www.nytimes.com/2011/01/11/arts/music/11friedman.html.
23. Adam Dickter, "Downsizing Reform," *Jewish Week*, March 11, 2009, http://www.thejewishweek.com/features/downsizing_reform.
24. Eric H. Yoffie, "Rabbi Yoffie's Remarks to the URJ Executive Committee March 2010," March 15, 2010, http://urj.org/about/union/leadership/yoffie/?syspage=article&item_id=37320.
25. Richard Jacobs, "At the End of Two Years," RJ.org: News and Views of Reform Jews, http://blogs.rj.org/blog/2011/12/18/at-the-end-of-two-years/.

3. To Observe or Not to Observe?

1. Eugene B. Borowitz, *Liberal Judaism* (New York: Union of American Hebrew Congregations, 1984), 324. Italics in the original.
2. Richard N. Levy, *A Vision of Holiness: The Future of Reform Judaism* (New York: URJ Press, 2005), 134.
3. "Just Table, Green Table," URJ Initiative, http://urj.org/life/food/.
4. Bernhard Felsenthal, *Kol Kore Bamidbar: Ueber jüdische Reform* (A voice calling in the wilderness: on Jewish reform) (Chicago, 1859), reprinted in *The Growth of Reform Judaism: American and European Sources to 1948*, ed. W. Gunther Plaut (New York: World Union for Progressive Judaism, 1965), 274.
5. W. Gunther Plaut, ed., *A Shabbat Manual* (New York: Central Conference of American Rabbis Press, 1972), 5–6.
6. Mark Dov Shapiro, ed., *Gates of Shabbat: A Guide for Observing Shabbat* (New York: Central Conference of American Rabbis, 1991), 49–59.
7. Mark Washofsky, *Jewish Living: A Guide to Contemporary Reform Practice* (New York: UAHC Press, 2001), 84.
8. Peter S. Knobel, ed., *Gates of the Seasons: A Guide to the Jewish Year* (New York: Central Conference of American Rabbis, 1983), 15–33.
9. Simeon J. Maslin, ed., *The Gates of Mitzvah: A Guide to the Jewish Life Cycle* (New York: Central Conference of American Rabbis, 1979), 29.
10. W. Gunther Plaut, *The Rise of Reform Judaism: A Sourcebook of Its European Origins* (New York: World Union for Progressive Judaism, 1963), 217–18.
11. Washofsky, *Jewish Living*, 154.
12. Simeon J. Maslin, "Yes, There Is a Reform Divorce Document," *Reform Judaism*, Spring 2000, 47.

13. David Polish, ed., *Rabbi's Manual* (New York: Central Conference of American Rabbis, 1988), 97.

4. Worship and Practice

1. Beth Sampson Bauer, letter to the editor, "Is It Time to Chart a New Course for Reform Judaism? Reactions," *Reform Judaism*, Spring 1999, 4.
2. Henry A. Fribourg, letter to the editor, "Is It Time to Charge a New Course for Reform Judaism? Reactions," *Reform Judaism*, Spring 1999, 8.
3. David Davidson, "The UAHC Board Comments," *Reform Judaism*, Spring 1999, 17.
4. David Van Biema, "Back to the Yarmulke," *Time*, June 7, 1999, 65.
5. Stacy J. Willis, "Reformed Reform? Jewish Leaders Say Platform Misunderstood," *Las Vegas Sun*, June 14, 1999.
6. *New York Jewish Week*, May 28, 1999.
7. Harry K. Danziger, "Between You and Me," *Temple Israel of Memphis Voice*, Midsummer 1999, 1.
8. Michael A. Meyer, *Response to Modernity: A History of the Reform Movement in Judaism* (New York: Oxford University Press, 1988), 358, 369.
9. Theodore I. Lenn, *Rabbi and Synagogue in Reform Judaism* (West Hartford: Central Conference of American Rabbis, 1972), 91, 138, 187.
10. Eric H. Yoffie, afterword to *American Reform Judaism: An Introduction* by Dana Evan Kaplan (New Brunswick NJ: Rutgers University Press, 2003), 262.
11. Leonard J. Fein et al., *Reform Is a Verb: Notes on Reform and Reforming Jews* (New York: Union of American Hebrew Congregations, 1972), 83–84, 140–41.
12. Fein, *Reform Is a Verb*, 140–52.
13. Morton Berman, "Report to the 1950 General Assembly of the Union of American Hebrew Congregations," American Jewish Archives, Morton M. Berman Papers, collection number MS-314.
14. W. Gunther Plaut, "The Sabbath in the Reform Movement," *CCAR Yearbook* 75 (1965): 189.
15. Alfonso A. Narvaez, "Solomon Freehof, 97, Dies, Leading Interpreter of Jewish Law," *New York Times*, June 13, 1990, http://www.nytimes.com/1990/06/13/obituaries/rabbi-solomon-freehof-97-dies-leading-interpreter-of-jewish-law.html.
16. W. Gunther Plaut, quoted in "Religious Discipline and Liberal Judaism," *CCAR Yearbook* 85 (1975): 193–94
17. W. Gunther Plaut, introduction to Maslin, *Gates of Mitzvah*, ix.
18. Quoted in Knobel, *Gates of Seasons*, vii–ix.
19. Eric H. Yoffie, "Realizing God's Promise: Reform Judaism in the 21st Century," address, Sixty-Fifth UAHC Biennial Convention, Orlando FL, 1999, 2–3, http://www.urj.us/orlando/speakers/ysermon.shtml.
20. Stern, *Gates of Prayer*, 766–79.

21. Laurie Goodstein, "In New Prayer Book, Signs of Broad Change," *New York Times*, September 3, 2007, http://www.nytimes.com/2007/09/03/us/03prayerbook.html.

22. Elyse D. Frishman, ed., *Mishkan T'filah: A Reform Siddur* (New York: Central Conference of American Rabbis, 2007), 165.

23. Lawrence A. Hoffman, ed., *Gates of Understanding* (New York: Central Conference of American Rabbis, 1977), 206n243.

24. Stern, *Gates of Prayer*, 152, 325.

25. Frishman, *Mishkan T'filah*, 276.

26. Ben Harris, "Reform Siddur Revives Resurrection Prayer," JTA, September 24, 2007, http://www.jta.org/news/article/2007/09/19/104226/reformprayerbook.

27. Vanessa L. Ochs, *Inventing Jewish Ritual* (Philadelphia: Jewish Publication Society, 2007), 167–86.

28. Hank Bordowitz, "Singing unto God," *Reform Judaism* 30, no. 4 (Summer 2002): 65.

29. Debbie Friedman, "Mi She-be-rach," http://www.allthelyrics.com/lyrics/debbie_friedman/mishebeirach-lyrics-204248.html; Frishman, *Mishkan T'filah*, 252–53.

30. Lawrence Hoffman, *Rethinking Synagogues: A New Vocabulary for Congregational Life* (Woodstock VT: Jewish Lights, 2006), 103.

5. Values and Ethics

1. Michelle Alperin, "America's First Female Rabbi: 40 Years Later," *Joint-Media News Service*, May 7, 2012, http://www.algemeiner.com/2012/05/07/americas-first-female-rabbi-40-years-later/.

2. Sally Priesand, *Judaism and the New Woman* (New York: Behrman House, 1975), xiii–xiv.

3. Francie Grace, "Nation's First Female Rabbi Retiring," *CBS News*, June 9, 2006, http://www.cbsnews.com/stories/2006/06/09/national/main1696701.shtml.65.

4. Alperin, "America's First Female Rabbi."

5. Alperin, "America's First Female Rabbi."

6. Alperin, "America's First Female Rabbi."

7. Grace, "Nation's First Female Rabbi Retiring."

8. Borowitz, *Liberal Judaism*, 386.

9. Borowitz, *Liberal Judaism*, 387.

10. Borowitz, *Liberal Judaism*, 289.

11. Leo Baeck, *God and Man in Judaism* (London: Vallentine Mitchell, 1958), 56–57.

12. *The Union Prayer Book for Jewish Worship, Part 1* (New York: Central Conference of American Rabbis, 1940), 71.

13. Albert Vorspan and David Saperstein, *Tough Choices: Jewish Perspectives on Social Justice* (New York: UAHC Press, 1992), 9.

14. David Saperstein, "Mandate for Social Justice," in *Where We Stand: Jewish Consciousness on Campus*, ed. Allan L. Smith (New York: UAHC Press, 1987), 386.

15. *Where We Stand: Social Action Resolutions Adopted by the Union of American Hebrew Congregations* (New York: UAHC Press, 1980), 43–46.

16. Richard Jacobs, "*Aloh Na'aleh*—Let's Get Going to That Better Tomorrow: URJ Presidency Acceptance Speech as Delivered by Rabbi Jacobs," *News and Views of Reform Jews*, June 12, 2011, 10 Sivan 5771, http://blogs.rj.org/ blog/2011/06/12/rabbi-rick-jacobs/.

17. Bernard Lazerwitz, J. Alan Winter, Arnold Dashefsky, and Ephraim Tabory, *Jewish Choices: American Jewish Denominationalism* (Albany: State University of New York Press, 1998).

18. Ephraim Tabory, "The Legitimacy of Reform Judaism: The Impact of Israel on the United States," in *Contemporary Debates in American Reform Judaism: Conflicting Visions*, ed. Dana Evan Kaplan (New York: Routledge, 2001), 221.

19. Matthew Gutman, "New Campaign for Jerusalem Pol: Religious Pluralism," *Forward*, May 31, 2002, http://www.forward.com/issues/2002/02.05.31/ news10.html.

20. Nathan Jeffay, "The Heart of Israel's Reform Judaism: The Country's Largest Reform Congregation Turns 25," January 12, 2011, *Forward*, http://www .forward.com/articles/134639/#ixzz1jqbFj6We.

21. Hillary Zaken, "In First, Non-Orthodox Rabbis to Receive State Funding," *Times of Israel*, May 29, 2012, http://www.timesofisrael.com/state-will-pay -non-orthodox-rabbi-salary/.

22. Rick Jacobs, "A Commitment to Israel Will Be Hard to Maintain If Equality Is Not Upheld," *Haaretz*, May 30, 2012, http://www.haaretz.com/opinion/a -commitment-to-israel-will-be-hard-to-maintain-if-equality-is-not-up- held-1.433216.

23. Frishman, *Mishkan T'Filah: A Reform Siddur*, 40.

24. "Civil Marriage for Gay and Lesbian Jewish Couples," resolution adopted by the General Assembly of the Union of American Hebrew Congregations, Dallas TX, November 2, 1997, http://urj.org//about/union/governance/ reso//?syspage=article&item_id=2000.

25. Lynn Townsend White Jr., "The Historical Roots of Our Ecologic Crisis," *Science* 155, no. 3767 (March 10, 1967): 1203–7.

26. Tamara Cohn Eskenazi and Andrea L. Weiss, eds., *The Torah: A Woman's Commentary* (New York: Women of Reform Judaism, 2008), 8.

27. Rachel Cohen, correspondence with author, April 8, 2010; also "About Carbon Offsetting," Religious Action Center of Reform Judaism, http://rac .org/Articles/index.cfm?id=3716.

28. Walter Jacob, ed., "Judaism and the Environment," in *Contemporary American Reform Responsa* (New York: Central Conference of American Rabbis, 1987), 17.

29. "Environment," resolution adopted by the 101st Annual Convention of the Central Conference of American Rabbis, Seattle WA, June 1990, http://data.ccarnet.org/cgi-bin/resodisp.pl?file=environ&year=1990.

6. Who Is a (Reform) Jew?

1. Laurel Snyder, *Half/Life: Jew-ish Tales from Interfaith Homes* (Brooklyn NY: Soft Skull Press, 2006), 4.

2. Snyder, *Half/Life*, 4.

3. Laurel Snyder, "My Faith: Raising Religious (But Not Too Religious) Children," *CNN*, April 13, 2012, http://religion.blogs.cnn.com/2012/04/13/my-faith-raising-non-kosher-jewish-kids/.

4. Washofsky, *Jewish Living*, 135.

5. Eric H. Yoffie, "The Importance of Outreach in Maintaining Reform's Autonomy, Diversity, and Pluralism," in *Contemporary Debates in American Reform Judaism: Conflicting Visions*, ed. Dana Evan Kaplan (New York: Routledge, 2001), 150.

6. Julie Wiener, "Reform Set to Approve Conversion Standards," *Jewish Telegraphic Agency*, June 19, 2001, http://www.jta.org/news/article/2001/06/19/7278/Reformsettoapprov.

7. Alexandra J. Wall, "Reform Rabbis Adopt Conversion Blueprint in Monterey," *j.*, July 13, 2001, http://www.jweekly.com/article/full/15974/reform-rabbis-adopt-conversion-blueprint-in-monterey/.

8. Wiener, "Reform Set to Approve Conversion Standards."

9. David Polish, ed., *Rabbi's Manual* (New York: Central Conference of American Rabbis, 1961), 112.

10. "The Status of Children of Mixed Marriages," Report of the Committee on Patrilineal Descent, March 15, 1983, http://data.ccarnet.org/cgi-bin/resodisp.pl?file=mm&year=1983.

11. Debra Nussbaum Cohen, "Reform Conference to Re-examine Controversial 'Patrilineal' Policy," *Jewish Telegraphic Agency*, June 16, 1998, http://archive.jta.org/article/1998/06/17/2889873/reform-rabbis-to-reexamine-controversial-patrilineal-policy.

12. "Participation of Non-Jews in a Public Service," *American Reform Responsa: Jewish Questions, Rabbinic Answers* (New York: Central Conference of American Rabbis, 1983), reprinted in *Defining the Role of the Non-Jew in the Synagogue: A Resource for Congregations* (New York: Union of American Hebrew Congregations, 1990), 57–59.

13. "Guidelines for Rabbis Working with Prospective Gerim," adopted by the Central Conference of American Rabbis, June 2001, http://ccarnet.org/

rabbis-communities/professional-resources/guidelines-for-rabbis-working
-with-prospective-gerim/.

14. Eric H. Yoffie, "Biennial Sermon 05, Sermon by Eric H. Yoffie at the
Houston Biennial, Union for Reform Judaism 68th General Assembly,"
November 19, 2005, http://urj.org/about/union/leadership/yoffie/
biennialsermon05/.

15. "Inviting Conversion—A Biennial Initiative: A 68th Biennial Initiative,"
n.d., Union for Reform Judaism, http://urj.org/cong/outreach/conversion/
inviting/.

16. Samuel N. Gordon, "A Rabbi's Response to Eric. N. Yoffie's Conversion
Message," n.d., http://www.interfaithfamily.com/news_and_opinion/
synagogues_and_the_jewish_community/A_Rabbis_Response_to_Eric_H_
Yoffies_Conversion_Message.shtml.

17. Michael Luo, "Reform Jews Hope to Unmix Mix Marriages," February 12,
2006, http://www.nytimes.com/2006/02/12/nyregion/12convert.html?scp
=9&sq=Luo+Reform+Jews+Hope&st=nyt.

18. Rick Jacobs, "Op-Ed: Synagogues Must Reach Out to 'the Uninspired,'"
Jewish Telegraphic Agency, March 28, 2012, http://www.jta.org/news/
article/2012/03/28/3092388/op-ed-synagogues-must-reach-out-to-the
-uninspired.

7. On the Boundaries of Reform

1. Rob Patterson, "To Moishe Rosen: 'Was Jesus Really Jewish?'" http://www
.lincolnnewsmessenger.com/detail/91393.html.

2. Ruth Rosen, ed., *Jews for Jesus* (San Francisco: A Messianic Jewish Perspective, 1987), 1–11.

3. Moishe Rosen, "Moishe Rosen's Testimony," Jews for Jesus website, May 2,
2006, http://www.jewsforjesus.org/about/headquarters/moishe/testimony.

4. "An Apostate Proselyte," Responsum 71, in *American Reform Responsa: Jewish Questions, Rabbinic Answers*, ed. Walter Jacob (New York: CCAR Press,
1983), 242.

5. "An Apostate Proselyte," 242.

6. Walter Jacob, "Status of a 'Completed Jew' in the Jewish Community," Responsa 68, in *Contemporary American Reform Responsa* (New York: Central
Conference of American Rabbis, 1987), 109–12.

7. Walter Jacob, ed., *American Reform Responsa: Collected Responsa of the Central Conference of American Rabbis, 1889–1983* (New York: Central Conference of American Rabbis, 1983), 471–74.

8. Washofsky, *Jewish Living*, 52–53.

9. Mark Washofsky, correspondence with author, November 11, 2009.

10. Larry Kaufman, comment on William Berkson, "Strengthening Reform, 7:
JuBu Is Not the Way," July 24, 2008, http://blogs.rj.org/blog/2008/07/24/
strengthening_reform_7_jubu_is/.

11. Larry Rohter, "On the Road, for Reasons Practical and Spiritual," *New York Times*, February 24, 2009, http://www.nytimes.com/2009/02/25/arts/music/25cohe.html?_r=1&8dpc.

12. Rodger Kamenetz, *The Jew in the Lotus* (San Francisco: HarperSanFrancisco, 1994), 7.

13. Sylvia Boorstein, *That's Funny, You Don't Look Buddhist: On Being A Faithful Jew and a Passionate Buddhist* (San Francisco: HarperSanFrancisco, 1997), 25.

14. Boorstein, *That's Funny, You Don't Look Buddhist*, 21-22.

15. Louis Sahagun, "At One With Dual Devotion," *Los Angeles Times*, May 2, 2006, http://articles.latimes.com/2006/may/02/local/me-jubus2.

16. Akiva Tatz and David Gottlieb, *Letters of a Buddhist Jew* (Southfield MI: Targum Press, 2004), 11.

17. W. Gunter Plaut, "Reform as an Adjective: What Are the Limits?" in *The Jewish Condition: Essays on Contemporary Judaism Honoring Rabbi Alexander M. Schindler*, ed. Aron Hirt-Manheimer (New York: UAHC Press, 1995), 357-60.

18. Leo Baeck, *The Essence of Judaism*, rev. ed. (New York: Schocken Books, 1948), 60.

19. Jeffrey W. Goldwasser, "How Compatible is Buddhism with Judaism?," About.com, n.d., http://judaism.about.com/od/interfaithquestions/f/budjud.htm.

20. William Berkson, "Strengthening Reform, 7: JuBu Is Not the Way," July 24, 2008, http://blogs.rj.org/blog/2008/07/24/strengthening_reform_7_jubu_is/.

21. Karen Kissel Wegela, *The Courage to Be Present: Buddhism, Psychotherapy, and the Awakening of Natural Wisdom* (Boston: Shambhala Publications, 2009).

22. Robert Barr, correspondence with author, May 2009.

23. "Humanistic Congregation," Responsum 5751.4, CCAR Responsa, http://data.ccarnet.org/cgi-bin/respdisp.pl?file=4&year=5751. The responsum was originally published in W. Gunther Plaut and Mark Washofsky, *Teshuvot for the 1990s: Reform Judaism's Answers for Today's Dilemmas* (New York: CCAR Press, 1999), 9-16.

24. Lawrence Bush, "Focus On: The God Debate—Can We Accept a Congregation That Does Not Worship God?" *Reform Judaism*, Winter 1994, 25.

25. "Beth Adam's Concept of God," *Beth Adam: Judaism with a Humanistic Perspective*, http://www.bethadam.org/about_liturgy_conceptofgod.htm.

26. "Cincinnati, Ohio—Beth Adam (Congregation for Humanistic Judaism Records, Manuscript Collection No. 696," American Jewish Archives, http://americanjewisharchives.org/collections/ms0696/.

27. Jack Wertheimer, "What Does Reform Judaism Stand For?," *Commentary*, June 2008, http://www.commentarymagazine.com/viewarticle.cfm/what-does-reform-judaism-stand-for—11393.

28. Mark Washofsky, correspondence with author, November 11, 2009.

29. Wade Clark Roof, *Spiritual Marketplace: Baby Boomers and the Remaking of American Religion* (Princeton: Princeton University Press, 1999), 4.

8. Seeking the Spiritual

1. Jessica Ravitz, "'New Jews' Stake Claim to Faith, Culture," CNN, October 30, 2009, http://www.cnn.com/2009/LIVING/10/28/new.and.emergent.jews/.

2. PunkTorah, http://www.punktorah.org.

3. Joey Kurtzman, "The End of the Jewish People," *Jewcy*, June 11, 2007, http://www.jewcy.com/dialogue/2007-06-11/joey1.

4. Rick Jacobs, "Shelach Lecha: A Glimpse of the Future," URJ Presidential Installation Sermon of Rabbi Rick Jacobs, June 9, 2012, http://urj.org/about/union/leadership/rabbijacobs/?syspage=article&item_id=90580.

5. Eric H. Yoffie, Shabbat Sermon, URJ Biennial, Toronto, Canada, November 7, 2009, http://urj.org/about/union/leadership/yoffie/?syspage=article&item_id=27481.

6. Steve Lipman, "'If You Stream It, They Will Come,'" *Jewish Week*, September 16, 2009, http://www.thejewishweek.com/viewArticle/c37_a16768/News/National.html.

7. Lipman, "'If You Stream It, They Will Come,'" http://www.thejewishweek.com/features/%E2%80%98if_you_stream_it_they_will_come%E2%80%99_0.

8. Jonathan DeHart, "Congregation Beth Adam: Progressive Judaism Coming to a Computer Near You," *Soapbox Cincinnati*, December 9, 2008, http://www.soapboxmedia.com/features/43bethadam.aspx.

9. Robert Barr and Laura Baum, correspondence with author, February 4, 2009.

10. "2Life Investigates: What Was the First Synagogue in Second Life?," *2Life: The Jewish Magazine in Second Life*, no. 6, September 2007, 6, http://www.2lifemagazine.com/downloads/2Life_06.pdf (no longer accessible).

11. Shona Crabtree, "Finding Religion in Second Life's Virtual Universe," *Washington Post*, June 16, 2007, http://www.washingtonpost.com/wp-dyn/content/article/2007/06/15/AR2007061501902.html.

12. Hayim Herring, "Second Life: Resurrecting Jewish Community Online," *Co-Star Blog: Sharing Insights about Synagogue Life*, October 16, 2007, http://www.starsynagogue.org/blog/second-life-resurrecting-jewish-community-online/24.

13. Cathy Lynn Grossman, "Faithful Build a Second Life for Religion Online," USA Today, April 1, 2007, http://www.usatoday.com/tech/gaming/2007-04-01-second-life-religion_N.htm.

14. Crabtree, "Finding Religion in Second Life's Virtual Universe."

15. Niles Goldstein, "My Online Synagogue: The Internet Draws People Together but There's Still No Substitute for Human Contact," *Newsweek*, September 14, 1998, http://www.highbeam.com/doc/1G1-21117768.html.

16. Sylvia Boorstein, *That's Funny, You Don't Look Buddhist: On Being a Faithful Jew and a Passionate Buddhist* (San Francisco: HarperSanFrancisco, 1997), 1.

17. Boorstein, *That's Funny, You Don't Look Buddhist*, 41.

18. Boorstein, *That's Funny, You Don't Look Buddhist*, 14.

19. Nan Fink Gefen, *Discovering Jewish Meditation: Instruction and Guidance for Learning an Ancient Spiritual Practice* (Woodstock VT: Jewish Lights, 1999), 7–9.

20. Yonassan Gershom, "What B'nai Or Was Like in the Old Days . . . ," from the introduction to *Forty-Nine Gates of Light: Kabbalistic Meditations for Counting the Omer* (self-published, 1987).

21. Tizrah Firestone, *With Roots in Heaven: One Woman's Passionate Journey into the Heart of Her Faith* (New York: Dutton, 1998), 225.

22. Debra Nussbaum Cohen, "From 'Om' to 'Shema': Up Close; Long on the Margins, Jewish Meditation Is Now Emerging in the Mainstream," *New York Jewish Week*, February 2, 2001, 16, 18.

23. Mary NurrieStearns, "Being a Joyful Servant: An Interview with Lawrence Kushner," Personal Transformation website, http://www.personaltransformation.com/Kushner.html.

24. Peter Pitzele, *Our Father's Wells: A Personal Encounter with the Myths of Genesis* (San Francisco: HarperSanFrancisco, 1995).

25. Storahtelling, http://www.storahtelling.org.

26. "Teaching through Movement: Liz Lerman Dance Exchange Brings Text Alive," JESNA, http://www.jesna.org/pd-notes/fall-2008/288-teaching-through-movement-liz-lerman-dance-exchange-brings-text-alive.

27. "Dancing Your Sins Away: Liz Lerman Helps Temple Sinai Congregants Prepare for Holidays," *Washington Jewish Week*, September 16, 2004, http://www.highbeam.com/doc/1P3-845603511.html.

28. "Dancing Your Sins Away."

29. Julie Wiener, "Using Dance and Nature, Fellows Bring Judaism into Summer Camp," JTA, June 14, 2001, http://www.highbeam.com/doc/1P1-79386652.html.

30. Ellen Bernstein, "How Wilderness Forms a Jew," in *Ecology and the Jewish Spirit: Where Nature and the Sacred Meet*, ed. Ellen Bernstein (Woodstock VT: Jewish Lights Publishing, 1998), 51.

31. Ellen Bernstein, correspondence with author, April 29, 2010.

32. Mike Comins, *A Wild Faith: Jewish Ways into Wilderness, Wilderness Ways into Judaism* (Woodstock VT: Jewish Lights, 2007), 2–3, 11, http://www.awildfaith.com.http://www.torahtrek.com/.

33. TorahTrek, Center for Jewish Wilderness Spirituality, http://www
.torahtrek.com.

34. Rachel Silverman, "Judaism Finds Its Niche in Great Outdoors," JTA, July
7, 2006, http://www.jewishjournal.com/travel/article/judaism_finds_its_
niche_in_great_outdoors_20060707.

35. Jamie Korngold, *God in the Wilderness: Rediscovering the Spirituality of the
Great Outdoors with the Adventure Rabbi* (New York: Random House, 2007),
http://www.adventurerabbi.com/jamie-personal-statement.htm.

36. Niles Elliot Goldstein, *Gonzo Judaism: A Bold Path for Renewing an Ancient
Faith* (New York: St. Martin's Press, 2006), 21–23, 81–84, 101.

Glossary

Adonai. One of the names for God used in the Torah.

aggadah. A Jewish legend, also used to refer to the body of work consisting of nonhalachic (nonlegal), homiletical material.

agunah (agunot, pl.). A woman whose husband cannot or will not grant her a divorce.

aliyah (aliyot, pl.). Being called up to bless the Torah before and after each reading. Alternatively, to move to Israel.

amma. A measurement used in the Talmud.

aron hakodesh. Ark. The sacred space where the Torah scrolls are kept in the synagogue, usually at the front of the sanctuary.

atid. The future.

av Aram. As Abram, he was the father of Aram, the country from which he came. As Abraham, he became the father of many.

av hamon. God gives Abraham this name signifying his new status as father of a multitude, meaning the progenitor of many nations.

avot melacha. The thirty-nine categories of work prohibited on Shabbat.

baal teshuvah. A term applied to Jews who have turned to traditional observance and embraced Orthodox Judaism.

baal taschit. Translated as "do not destroy" and used as a concept to teach that one should not be wasteful.

bark mitzvah. A pseudotraditional observance and celebration of a dog's coming of age.

bar mitzvah. Coming of age ceremony for boys at age thirteen, at which the young man is called up to read from the Torah.

Baruch Hashem. Blessed be the Name of God.

bat mitzvah. Coming of age ceremony for girls at age twelve or thirteen. The ceremony itself varies depending upon the denomination. It usually includes the reading of the Torah.

beit din. Rabbinical court.

beit midrash. A house of study.

bocher. Yiddish, for a young, unmarried man.

brit *or* **bris.** The covenant between God and Israel. The term is frequently used to refer to the circumcision ceremony. The word is pronounced, and sometimes spelled, "bris" in Ashkenazic Hebrew.

Central Conference of American Rabbis (CCAR). The professional organization of Reform rabbis.

Chabad. Hebrew acronym for Chochmah, Binah, and Daat, meaning Wisdom, Understanding, and Knowledge. An organization, alternatively called Lubavitch Hasidism, that believes in intensive religious outreach to Jews of all backgrounds.

daat. Biblical Hebrew word for religion.

daven (davenology, the science of daven). The act of praying, usually referring to traditional prayer.

diaspora. The dispersion of the Jews.

eco-kashrut. A contemporary Jewish concept that expands the idea of fitness to everything consumed and includes ideas of sustainable agriculture, fair labor practices, and ethical treatment of animals.

erusin. Formal betrothal ceremony at which the groom gave a ring to the bride and recited the traditional words that constituted kiddushin, the sanctification of the relationship.

frum. Committed to obey the major laws of Judaism.

galut. Exile.

gemara. Extensive legal debates on the contents of the mishnah, brief rabbinic legal statements. The mishnah and the gemara together form the Talmud.

gemilut hasadim. The giving of loving-kindness, a fundamental social value in the everyday lives of Jews.

ger (gerim, pl.). A convert to Judaism. Alternatively, circular tentlike structure used for housing in Mongolia.

get (gittin, pl.). A religious document of divorce.

giur. Conversion to Judaism.

Haggadah. The liturgy for the Passover seder.

halacha. Jewish law.

Hanukkah. Eight-day festival of lights celebrating the victory of the Maccabees over the Hellenizers in the second century BCE.

Haredi (Haredim, pl.). Fervently Orthodox Jews, as distinct from the Modern Orthodox. Technically, it refers to either "Lithuanian" non-Hasidic Jews of Ashkenazic descent, Hasidic Haredim of Ashkenazic descent, or Sephardic Haredim.

Haskalah. The Jewish enlightenment, which developed in the aftermath of the emancipation.

hatafat dam brit. The drawing of a drop of blood to symbolically indicate that a circumcision is being performed to bring the man into the covenant.

havdalah. A ceremony to mark of the end of Shabbat and holidays and to usher in the new week. It includes blessings over wine, spices, and the light from a multiwick candle.

havurah (havurot, pl.). A small group of like-minded Jews, usually young and liberal-leaning, who assemble for the purpose of facilitating Shabbat and holiday prayer services.

hazzan. A cantor or a musician trained in the vocal arts who leads the congregation in songful prayer.

Hebrew Union College–Jewish Institute of Religion (HUC-JIR). Academic institution serving the Reform movement of North America and throughout the world with campuses in Cincinnati, New York, Los Angeles, and Jerusalem.

Hekhsher Tzedek. A Justice Certification, formally attesting that food is produced in a way that meets halachic standards for workers and animals. Later renamed Magen Tzedek, a Shield of Justice.

herem. A communal ban.

hovah. Requirement or obligation.

huppah. A wedding canopy.

Kabbalah (kabbalistic, adj.). A discipline concerned with the mystical aspect of Judaism, dealing with the ideas of creation and concepts of a spiritual nature.

Kabbalat Shabbat. Service for welcoming the Sabbath.

kaddish. Mourner's prayer for the dead.

kadosh. Holy

Karaites. A medieval Jewish sect that rejected the Oral Law. A small number exist today, most of whom live in Israel. There are, however, some Karaites in California and elsewhere in the United States.

kasher. To make kosher.

kashrut. Jewish dietary laws.

k'dushah. Holiness.

kehillah (kehillot, pl.). Community.

ketubah (ketubot, pl.). A Jewish marriage contract.

kiddushin (kedushah). The betrothal ceremony that constitutes part of the Jewish wedding service.

kinyan. The halachic category of acquisition where a man gives a ring to his betrothed in a Jewish wedding ceremony to concretize the marriage.

kippah. A head covering traditionally worn by males to remember the existence of God above. In Classical Reform Judaism, the wearing of head covering was abolished and all worshippers went bareheaded. This practice has largely been reversed, although few Reform temples require male worshipers to cover their heads. Many women now wear a kippah during services as well.

klal yisrael. The unity of the Jewish people. THIS expression is used by those who wish to speak on behalf of the entire Jewish people.

Kohen (Kohanim, pl.). A priest who served in the temple in Jerusalem. In modern times, a Jewish person of priestly descent.

Kohen Gadol. The high priest in the Jerusalem temple.

kosher. Ritually "fit," usually used to refer to food.

layn. The chanting of the Torah using trope.

Lecha Dodi. A Hebrew-language liturgical song recited Friday at dusk in synagogues to welcome Shabbat prior to the evening services.

Levi (Leviim, pl.). A member of the tribe of Levi who assisted the Kohanim in the Temple.

li-kavod Shabbat. In honor of the Sabbath.

Lubavitch. A Hasidic movement in Orthodox Judaism.

mamzer (mamzerim, pl.). A child born of an adulterous or incestuous union. Mamzerut is the state of having been born under such circumstances.

matzah ball. A matzah-meal ball eaten in chicken soup.

menuchah. Sabbath rest.

mezuzah. Small parchment scroll of Torah verses affixed to doorposts.

midrash (midrashim, pl.). Classical rabbinic biblical interpretations dating from second to fifth centuries CE.

mikveh (mikveot, pl.). A body of running water in which one is immersed in order to achieve ritual purity.

mincha. The afternoon prayer service.

minhag (minhagim, pl.). An accepted tradition or group of traditions. Alternatively, a style of worship.

minyan (minyanim, pl.). A quorum of ten adult Jewish males (and now females in all non-Orthodox streams) required for public worship.

Mi Sheberaich. Literally, the one who blesses. A prayer offered during the Torah reading in honor of the person called up to bless. In Reform Judaism, it is a healing prayer popularized in songwriter Debbie Friedman's version.

mishnah. A compilation of brief rabbinic legal statements edited by Rabbi Judah the Prince around the year 200 CE.

mitzvah (mitzvoth, pl.). A commandment (in religious terms) or a good deed (in popular terminology).

mitzvot aseh she-ha-zman gumrah. Positive, time-bound commandments.

m'nuchah. Rest.

mussar. A particular approach to ethics.

nigun (nigunim, pl.). A melody with repetitive sounds such as "bim-bim-bam" or "ai-ai-ai" instead of formal lyrics.

nisuin. The nuptials of a Jewish marriage ceremony that traditionally took place one year after the erusin (betrothal).

Nogah Ha-Tsedek. The Radiance of Justice, a collection of responsa on Reform innovations collected near the end of the 1920s.

nusach. The style of a prayer service or the melody of the service, depending on when the service is being conducted.

oneg. Joy.

Or Nogah. Radiant Light, Eliezer Liebermann's manuscript in which he argues that some prayers should be recited in German.

parsha (parshiot, pl.). The "portion" of the week, that is, the section of the Torah read in synagogues on Saturday morning and in some congregations on Monday and Thursday mornings as well. Also called sidra.

parshat bereshit. The story of creation in the first book of the Hebrew Bible.

Passover hagaddahs. Stories containing the Israelites' exodus from Egypt read at the Passover Seder meal. A ritual book used in Passover.

Pesach. Passover. Jewish festival celebrating the exodus of the Israelites from Egypt.

Pirkei Avot. A classic work, often translated as "Ethics of the Sages" or "Sayings of the Fathers."

posek (poskim, pl.). Rabbinic legal scholar with sufficient halachic expertise to make policy decisions.

Purim. A Jewish holy day or festival commemorating deliverance from the massacre by Haman in ancient Persia.

rachamim. Mercy, one of the most important Jewish values.

Rashi. Eleventh-century biblical and Talmudic commentator.

rebbetzin. A rabbi's wife.

rehem. Womb.

responsum (responsa, pl.). A legal response to a halachic question.

Rosh Hodesh. First day of every month in the Hebrew calendar.

Rosh Hashanah. Jewish New Year, observed by Jews around the world by attending synagogue services and undergoing a process of repentance and forgiveness.

Seder. The ritual meal conducted on the first (and in traditional homes on the second) night of Passover.

Seder P'reidah. A Reform Jewish document of religious release issued at the time of divorce.

selichot. Prayers said in the period leading up to the High Holy Days and on fast days.

Sephardi (Sephardim, pl.). Descendants of the Spanish Jews exiled in 1492.

Shabbat. The Sabbath, the seventh day of the Jewish week and a day of rest. Shabbat is observed from sundown Friday until sunset Saturday.

Shavuot. Jewish holiday commemorating the day God gave the Torah to Moses at Mount Sinai.

shechitah. The ritual of slaughtering a kosher animal for the purpose of eating.

Shehechiyanu. Hebrew blessing of thanksgiving.

Shema. The Shema Yisrael is the central prayer of Judaism, encapsulating the religious concept of ethical monotheism. The text begins with the words "Hear, O Israel, Adonai is our God, Adonai is One!," taken from Deuteronomy 6:4.

Sheva Berachot. The Seven Benedictions that form part of the Jewish wedding ceremony.

shiduchin. The engagement in a Jewish marriage.

Shlomo Carlebach. Jewish religious teacher known as the "Singing Rabbi" during his lifetime.

sh'mirat Shabbat. The observance of Shabbat.

shochet. A person who performs the ritual slaughter of kosher animals for the purpose of eating.

shofar. A ram's horn that is blown one hundred times as part of the Rosh Hashanah liturgy and at the conclusion of Yom Kippur.

shtetl. A small Jewish village in eastern Europe.

shul. A Yiddish term for a synagogue, almost always used to refer to a traditional congregation.

shulcasting. Taking the congregation into the cyber world by "webcasting" Shabbat services.

Shulchan Aruch. Also known as the code of Jewish law, this is the most authoritative legal code, which traditional Jews see as binding to this day. The work was written by Rabbi Yosef Caro in Safed in 1563 and published in Venice in 1565. The legal rulings follow Sephardic law and customs, thereby necessitating a commentary to explain how Ashkenazic customs would differ. This commentary, written by Rabbi Moses Isserles, almost always is printed alongside the code of Jewish law itself, thereby providing Jews from both backgrounds with a comprehensive set of laws and customs.

siddur. Prayer book.

simcha chochma. Literally, the joy of wisdom. A new ceremony conducted for those who reach a certain age.

s'micha. To rely on or to be authorized. Generally refers to the ordination of a rabbi.

sukkah (sukkot, pl.). A booth built to celebrate the holiday of Sukkot.

Sukkot. Festival of tabernacles, one of the three pilgrimage festivals.

tallit (tallises and tallitot, pl.). A rectangular, fringed prayer shawl.

Talmud. The oral law that consists of the Mishnah and the Gemara. It is a vast compilation of legal discussions divided into six orders and sixty-three tractates.

Tanakh. The three parts of the Hebrew Bible, including the Torah, the Prophets, and the Writings.

tefillah (tefillot, pl.). Prayer.

tefillin. Phylacteries.

tenaim. A legal contract stipulating the obligations of the two parties to a marriage and the penalty for the violation of the terms set forth.

teshuva. Repentance. Can also refer to a responsum (see teshuvot).

teshuvot (pl). Responsa literature.

tikkun olam. A Hebrew phrase meaning "repairing the world" or "perfecting the world," usually referring to the Jewish imperative to work for social justice.

Torah. The first five books of the Bible.

treif. Nonkosher food. Also called trefa, as in the "Trefa Banquet."

trope. A Yiddish word referring to the cantillation notes used for the ritual chanting of the Torah and haftarah (Prophets) portions. These notes are a set of symbols that appear above and below the Hebrew text to indicate how the word is to be chanted. The Hebrew word for trope is teamim.

Tu B'Shevat. A minor Jewish holiday that marks the "New Year of the Trees."

tum'ah. Ritual impurity.

Union of American Hebrew Congregations (UAHC). The original name of the Union for Reform Judaism, the organization of Reform congregations in North America.

Union Prayer Book (UPB). The prayer book published by the Central Conference of American Rabbis in 1894-95 and used as the authoritative prayer book by the Reform movement until 1975.

Union for Reform Judaism (URJ). The organization of Reform congregations in North America, formerly called the Union of American Hebrew Congregations.

Yahadut. Modern Hebrew word meaning the Jewish religion.

yarmulke. Skullcap for men and, in the liberal movements, for women, too. The yarmulke traditionally indicated humility before God. Also called kippah.

Yeshua. Usually translated as Jesus. Also a common name among Jews of the Second Temple Period.

Yiddish. A Jewish language based on German, written with the Hebrew alphabet.

Yom HaAtzmaut. National independence day of Israel.

Yom HaShoah. Holocaust and Heroism Remembrance Day.

Yom Kippur. Day of Atonement. The central themes of this High Holy Day are atonement and repentance. Jews pray and fast from one evening to the following nightfall before the gates of heaven close and their destiny is determined.

Zionism. The political movement to establish and support a Jewish country in the historic land of Israel.

Index

Page numbers in italic indicate illustrations.

Abraham, 40–41, 43, 174, 212–13, 218
Abrahamic covenant (*b'rit*), 7, 33, 40–46, 115, 120–21
Abram. *See* Abraham
acculturation. *See* assimilation
Ackerman, Paula, 326
activism. *See* political activism
Adland, Jonathan, 226
admonishment, 28
Adoration (Alenu) prayer, 175
adultery, 128
Adventure Rabbi Program, 302, 303
adventure religion, 298–306
agnosticism, 243, 262, 264
Agriprocessors (kosher slaughtering facility), 113, 331
Akiva, Rabbi, 53
Albert, Blythe, 298
Albert, Marissa, 297
Aleph, Patrick, 270–71
Alkabetz, Shlomo Halevi, 159
Allen, Morris, 113
American Council for Judaism (ACJ), 72, 89
American Israelite (newspaper), 65
American Jewish Cavalcade, 73
American Reform Judaism (Kaplan), 138

Amos, book of, 171
animal cruelty, 113
Anshe Emeth (Albany NY), 65
anthropocentrism, 202
antisemitism, 54, 80, 220
apathy in congregations, 2, 83, 139, 149, 312, 328. *See also* participation
apostates. *See* conversion
Appel, Batsheva, *164*
Aravah, Michael S., 270
archaeology, 75, 326
arguments, determining boundaries with, 268–69
art, 291–92
Asher, Judith Sherman, 265
"Ask the Rabbi" (online forum), 285
assimilation: change and, 85, 269; dietary laws and, 107; in the digital age, 274; Leviticus prohibition, 99; in Reform Judaism, 31, 97–98
Associated Press, 134
Association of Reform Zionists of America (ARZA), 191, 328
atheism, 262, 264, 266
Aub, Joseph, 125–26
Augsburg Synod (1871), 61–62, 125–26
authority, religious, 3, 5, 8–9, 20, 101–2, 151–52
autonomy, personal: CCAR policy positions, 82; as a challenge, 315–16; con-

autonomy, personal (*continued*)
version and, 229; dangers of, 308-15;
dietary laws and, 109; halacha
and, 101, 102; interdependence and,
306; opposition to authority, 3; personal meaning and, 10-11, 147-48,
259; progressive revelation and, 46;
Sabbath observances, 123; in spirituality, 81, 123, 157-58, 160
avot melacha (prohibited work categories), 116

baal taschit (do not destroy), 206, 207
Baeck, Leo, 171, 257
bar mitzvah, 141-43, 152-53, 279, 295-
97
Barr, Robert, 260-64, *261*, 266, 278-
81, *280*
Barre Center for Buddhist Studies, 253
Bar Yochai, Shimon, 203
Basic Reform Judaism (Silverman), 79
bat mitzvah, 142-43, 279, 295-97, 325
Baum, Laura, 278-81, *280*
Baxter, the Pig Who Wanted to Be Kosher
(Snyder), 211
Beit Daniel (Tel Aviv), 191-92, 329
Beit Shmuel (Jerusalem), 189, 191
Ben Gamla Charter School (Hollywood
FL), 330
ben Hiyyata, Levi, 203
Ben Zakkai, Yochanan, 159
Bergman, Elihu, 127
Berkowitz, Henry, 225
Berkson, William, 258-59
Berman, Howard A., 89, 331
Berman, Morton, 144-45
Bernstein, Ellen, 298-99
Beth Adam (Cincinnati OH), 260-61,
263-66, 278-81, 329
Beth-El (Albany NY), 64-65, 324
Beth Elohim (Charleston SC), 62-63,
63, 323

Beth Israel (Atlantic City NJ), *69*
Beth Israel (Meridian MS), 326
Beth Israel (virtual synagogue), 282
Bibliodrama, 294-95
birds, dietary restrictions on, 106
blessings, 160-61, *164*, 196, 287
B'nai Israel (Albany GA), *110*, 143, 223-
24
B'nai Jeshurun (Manhattan NY), 293
Boellstorff, Tom, 283
Boorstein, Sylvia, 254-55, 287-88
Borowitz, Eugene B., 37, 81, 101-2,
169-70
Breslau Conference (1846), 58, 117
b'rit. See Abrahamic covenant (*b'rit*)
British Liberal movement, 60
British Reform movement, 59-62
broadcasting programs, 276-77
Buddhism, 16-18, 253-60, 287-91
Bu-Jews. See Jubus

calendars, ancient, 59
Camp Coleman (Cleveland GA), *313*
camp programs, 89, 90-92, *178*, 298,
313
CAN!!CAN (punk band), 270
CCAR. *See* Central Conference of
American Rabbis (CCAR)
Centenary Perspective (1976), 37
Central Conference of American Rabbis (CCAR): civil rights activism, 78-
79, 179-81, 325; Columbus Platform
(1937), *35*, 36, 325; on conversion,
225-27, 237, 325; on divorce, 130, 329;
environmentalism, 205-6; founding
of, 324; gay rights, 199-201, 330; on
interfaith marriages, 128, 325, 328;
membership growth, 72; on non-
Jews in synagogue life, 235-36; on
patrilineal descent, 222, 227, 230,
231; Pittsburgh Platform (1885), 69-
70, 324; Pittsburgh Platform (1999),

111, 131–35, 329; Sabbath guidelines, 120–23, 121–23, 146–48; theological diversity, 81–82, 144–45; on the Vietnam War, 79; on Zionism, 71, 325. *See also* Responsa Committee (CCAR)

Central Synagogue (Manhattan NY), *105*

ceremonies. *See* rituals

ceremony, defined, 11–12

Chabad (organization), 273

Chavez, Cesar, 84

Chen-See, Nigel, *214*

Christianity: compared to Judaism, 28, 175; conversion to, 54–55, 220, 223, 246; environmentalism and, 202–3; fringe Jewish groups, 242–45; history of, 24–25, 245–46, 247; interfaith ceremonies, 39; Jewish proselytization and, 218–19, 221; participation in Jewish life, 235; virtual congregations, 277

circumcision: Abrahamic covenant and, 44–46; conversion and, 218–19, 225, 226, 325; Rabbi Geiger on, 58

citizenship. *See* emancipation

civil rights movement, 78–79, 80, 179–81, 325, 326

classical rabbinic tradition, 22–24

Classical Reform Judaism, *105*; on bar/bat mitzvahs, 141–43; emphasis of, 68–69, 158, 308; *misheberach* (blessing), 160–61; rejection of traditional rituals, 89–90, *132*, 139; shift away from, 137–39, 150–51

clean foods. *See* dietary laws

Cohen, Judah, 92

Cohen, Leonard, 253

Cohen, Rachel, 203

Cohon, Samuel S., *35*, 36

Columbus Platform (1937), *35*, 36, 325

Coming of Age in Second Life (Boellstorff), 283

Comins, Michael, 300–301

Commission on Social Action of Reform Judaism, 113

Committee on Jewish Law and Standards (CJLS), 269

Committee on Reform Practice (CCAR), 144–48

Concerning the Amelioration of the Civil Status of the Jews (Dohn), 54, 323

Confederate Underground, 79

confirmation, 55–56, 141–43, *142*, 152

congregational boards, 151–52

Conservative Judaism: Congregation B'nai Jeshurun, 293; gender inequalities in, 141–43; membership growth in, 77; prohibitions in, 82; split from Reform Judaism, 67–68; Trefa Banquet, 66–67, *67*; weaknesses of, 267, 269

conversion to Christianity, 246; role of clergy in, 237–41

conversion to Judaism: converts in rituals, 44; declines in, 229; *giur* process, *214*; historical, 218–20, 233; Jewish fringe groups, 248–49; in Reform Judaism, 213–15, 223, 325; traditional requirements for, 225

covenant theology. *See* Abrahamic covenant (*b'rit*)

Crane Lake Camp (URJ), *178*

creation, biblical account of, 32

Cronbach, Abraham, 81

cyber synagogues, 275, 284–85

dairy products, dietary restrictions, 107

dance, 292, 297–98

Daniel Centers for Progressive Judaism, 192

Danziger, Harry, 135

davenology, 158

David (Buddhist Jew), 256
Davidson, David, 133
Dead Sea Scrolls, 22
decision-making processes, 5
Dennis, Geoffrey W., 4
denominations, xi, 56–57, 158, 321. *See also individual denominations*; post-denominationalism
Desbois, Patrick, *95*
Deuteronomy, book of, 174, 176, 207–8
Dibrei Giur (CCAR), 226, 330
dietary laws: alternative approaches, 112–13; kitchen policies, *110*; kosher foods, 104–7; reasons for not observing, 107–9, 111–12, 211; religious basis for, 103–7
digital natives, 284. *See also* technology
Discovering Jewish Meditation (Gefen), 288–89
D'Israeli, Isaac, 59
divine presence, 284, 287, 289–91. *See also* God
divorce, 128–30, 329
Divrei Giur (CCAR), 237
Dohn, Christian Wilhelm, 54, 323
dramatic arts, 294–98
Dresner, Israel, 180

Eastern philosophies, 286–91
Ecclesiastes, 204, 206
eco-kashrut, 112–13
economic justice, 177
educational programs: confirmation and bar/bat mitzvah, 141–43; conversion, 224, 237; family-focused, 97; Jewish literacy, 88; online, 282; Seesen academy, 55–56
Einhorn, David, 49, 129
Eisendrath, Maurice N., 73–75, 79, 179, 181, 190, 316–17, 325, 327
Eisenhower, Dwight D., 76
Eisenstein, Ira, 327

Eisner Camp (URJ), *178*
Eliezer, Rabbi, 51–52
Ellenson, David, 84, *95*, 156, 168–69, 226–27, 330
e-mails, 280–81
emancipation, 6, 24–25, 54–55, 61, 85, 323
Emanu-El (New York City), 74, *95*, 324, 327
Emergent Jews, 271
emotional needs, 135–36, 137, 140, 145, 151, 161
environmentalism, 113–14, 201–8, 298, 329
equality, 125–26, 175, 179–81, 198–201, 293.
erusin (betrothal ceremony), 124, 125
essentialism, 25–26
ethical behavior: biblical view of, 170; dietary laws and, 112–14; religious laws and, 102–3, 130; ritual observance and, 29, 172–73, 174–75; social justice and, 79
ethical monotheism, 8, 27–28, 49, 68, 171, 316
ethnicity. *See* identity, Jewish religious
European Reform movement, 10, 54–62, 220
extreme religion, 304
extremist religion, 304
Ezra (prophet), 219

Facebook, 307
Fein, Leonard, 139, 328
Felsenthal, Bernhard, 117–18
feminism. *See* women
financial issues, 93–95, 97, 314–15
Finkel-Peltz, Doris, 265
Firestone, Tirzah, 290
Flaum, Gabrielle, *178*
flexibility: challenges due to, 3–6, 7, 8–11; historical examples, 51–52, 159–60; in prayer books, 153–55; pro-

gressive revelation and, 46–47. *See also* halacha; pluralism

food restrictions. *See* dietary laws

Four Noble Truths (Buddhism), 288

Fox, Steven, 128, 330

Frankel, Zacharias, 58

Freedman, Joseph H., 143, 181

freedom, 101–2, 121, 267–68

Freehof, Solomon B., 71–72, 135–36, 145–46

Freestone, Orville, 244

Free the Soldiers Rally, *178*

Friday night services, 118–19, 154–55, 311, 324

Friedman, Debbie, 92–93, 161–63, *162*, 327

Frishman, Elyse D., 156–57

Gamaliel, Rabban, 159

Gates of Mitzvah (CCAR), 122, 147, 148

Gates of Prayer (CCAR), 37–38, 81–82, 153, 154–55, 311, 328

Gates of Shabbat (CCAR), 122–23

Gates of the Seasons (CCAR), 122, 124, 147–48

gay rights, 84, 195, 198–201, 329, 330

G-dcast.com (website), 294

Gefen, Nan Fink, 288–89, 290

Geiger, Abraham, 58, 117

gemara (legal debates), 23

Generation X, 271, 272

Generation Y, 271, 272

Genesis, book of, 32, 40, 124, 174, 202–3

gentiles. *See* non-Jews

gerim (Judaist convert). *See* conversion

German Liberal movement, 60

German Reform movement, 55–58, 62, 323, 324

Gershom, Yonasan, 289

Gittelsohn, Roland, 191

Glaser, Joseph B., 84, 327

Glueck, Nelson, 75, 77–78, 165, 326

God: authority of, 311; Classical Reform concept of, 161; connecting with, 285, 287, 301; ethical behavior and, 170–71, 172–73, 174; Humanistic Judaism concept of, 262–64, 265–66; image of, 27, 175, 176, 200; Noahide Laws, 233; Reform concepts of, 7, 32–40, 42, 83, 154–55. *See also* Abrahamic covenant (*b'rit*); theology

Gold, Miri, 193–94

Goldstein, Niles, 284–85, 303–6, *305*

Goldwasser, Jeffrey W., 258

Gomorrah (city), 174

Gonzo Judaism, 303–4

Good Night, Laila Tov (Snyder), 211–12

Goor, Don, 332

Gordon, Samuel N., 238–39

Goren, Shlomo, 87

Gottschalk, Alfred, 84–87, 165, 327

Grafman, Milton, 180–81

Greenfield, Gail, 15–19

Greenwood, Dru, 231

Grotell, David, 256

guidance. *See* authority, religious

Ha'Am, Ahad, 114

halacha (Jewish law): in early Reform movement, 100–103; ethical behavior and, 174–75; history of, 23–24, 52; Jewish identity, 213; in Reform Judaism, 5, 9–11, 29, 146, 234–35; traditional understanding of, 57–58; women under, 130, 169–70

Half/Life (Snyder), 210

Halstead, Stan, *39*

Hammerman, Joshua, 276

Hanif, Salahuddin H., *39*

Harby, Isaac, 323

Haredi Jews, 188, 193, 194

Har Sinai (Baltimore MD), 323

hatafat dam brit (drawing of blood), 225, 226

Havarut Shalom (Somerville MA), 327

havurot (small groups), 158

Hay, Louise L., 16

healing services, 92–93, 160–61, 161–64

Hebrew language, 2, 100, 152–53, *283*, 330

Hebrew Union College (HUC): American Jewish Archives, 325; founding of, 66–67, 324; Jerusalem campus, 191; under Rabbi Glueck, 75–76; Trefa Banquet, 66–67; women at, 167

Hebrew Union College-Jewish Institute of Religion (HUC-JIR): budget cuts, 94–95, 331; Jerusalem campus, 77–78, 326; Los Angeles campus, 77, 87, 326, 327; merger, 70, 326; New York City campus, 87; soup kitchen, *182*

Hekhsher Tzedek (Justice Certification), 113, 331

Heller, James G., 72

Henriques, Ainsley, *12*

Herring, Hayim, 283–84

Herzfeld, Levi, 323

Herzfeld, Noreen, 284

Heschel, Abraham Joshua, 154, 291–92, 303, 326

Highland House, 66–67

Hinchin, Martin, 143

Hineni Ministries. *See* Jews for Jesus

Hirsch, Emil G., 28

Hirsch, John, 265–66

Hirsch, Richard, 188

Hiyya bar Abba, 235

Hoffman, Anat, 188, *192*, 193

Hoffman, Lawrence, xi, 163

Holdheim, Samuel, 117, 129

Holocaust, 70, 71, 160

Holtz, David, 308

homosexuality, 126, 198–99

hovah (obligation), 146

HUC. *See* Hebrew Union College (HUC)

HUC-JIR. *See* Hebrew Union College-Jewish Institute of Religion (HUC-JIR)

Humanistic Judaism, 260–67

humility, 290–91

Hussey, Eleanor Crichton, *283*

identity, Jewish religious: alternative approaches to, 270–72; assimilation and, 85; changes in, 286–87, 308–15; conversion and, 217–27, 237–41; defining, 212–17; essentialism and, 25–26; in Humanistic Judaism, 262–66; keeping kosher and, 111; lineage and, 227–32; under polythetic understanding, 6; Sabbath observance and, 121

idolatry, 208, 255–56

immersion, *214*, 225, 325

inclusivity, 9, 194–201, 234, 248, 265

individualism. *See* autonomy, personal

Insight Meditation Society, 253

intellectualism. *See* rationalism

interdependence, 305–6

interfaith families: acceptance of, 83, 127–28, 325, 328; conversions, 220–25, 238–39; Jewish identity and, 213, 236; Laurel Snyder, 209–12; non-Jews in synagogue life, 233–34; patrilineal descent, 227–32, 328; wedding ceremonies of, 82

Internet, 273–86, 294. *See also* technology

Isaiah, book of, 172–73

Islam, 28, *39*, 235

Israel (ancient kingdom), 21

Israel, State of: American Jewish connections to, 80; commemoration days, 160; formation of, 70–72, 326;

as part of Jewish identity, 271–72; Reform movement in, 185–94, 331; support for, 96–97, 178–79

Israel, Temple (Miami FL), 276

Israelite (newspaper), 65

Israelites, 21–22, 33, 213, 300–301

Israel Movement for Progressive Judaism (IMPJ), 186, 191, 327

Israel Religious Action Center (IRAC), 189

Jacob, Walter, 235, 250

Jacobs, Richard: installation service, x, *273*, 331; social justice work, 84, 96–98, 185; support of Israeli Reform movement, *192*, 193–94; technological innovations, 273–74; on the uninspired, 240–41; on URJ restructuring, *310*

Jacobson, Israel, 55–56, 323

Jeremiah, Rabbi, 52

Jerusalem Holy Temple, 56

Jesus, 243–44, 245–46, 247

"Jew by choice," 223, 229

Jewcy (website), 272

The Jew in the Lotus (Kamenetz), 254

Jewish Buddhists, 16–18, 253–60, 287

Jewish Christian groups, 246–47

Jewish Daily Forward (newspaper), 307–8

Jewish identity. *See* identity, Jewish religious

Jewish Institute of Religion (JIR), 70, 325. *See also* Hebrew Union College-Jewish Institute of Religion (HUC-JIR)

Jewish Living (Washofsky), 216, 248–49, 252

Jewish Religious Union (JRU), 60

Jewish Renewal movement, 112, 158, 259, 289–90

Jewish Telegraphic Agency (newspaper), 240–41

Jews Against Divisive Leadership, 96

Jews for Jesus, 242–45, 247–48, 267

JIR. *See* Jewish Institute of Religion (JIR)

Jonas, Regina, 197

Joshua, Rabbi, 52

Jubus, 253–60, 287

Judah (ancient kingdom), 21

Judah the Prince (rabbi), 23

Judaism: compared to Christianity, 175; defined, 5–6, 20–22, 25–26; as ethno-religious identity, 76, 213; historical discrimination, 246; history of, 20–24; Humanistic Judaism, 260–67; Jubus, 253–60; Messianic Jewish groups, 245–52

Judaism and the New Woman (Priesand), 165–67

justice: ethics and, 8, 171, 173–75, 175–85; in Reform movement, 28, 67, 69, 78–80; tied to Jewish identity, 84. *See also* political activism

Justice Certification (*Hekhsher Tzedek*), 113, 331

"Just Table, Green Table," 113–14, 331

Kabbalat Shabbat service, 118, 159

Kafka, Franz, 291

Kamenetz, Rodger, 254

Kant, Immanuel, 102

Kaplan, Dana Evan, *39*, *164*

Kaplan, Judith, 325

Kaplan, Mordecai M., 142–43, 145, 326

Karff, Samuel E., 83

kasher (to make kosher), 106–7. *See also* dietary laws

kashrut (dietary laws). *See* dietary laws

Kaufman, Debra, 197

k'dushah (holiness), 122

Kehilat Birkat Shalom (Kibbutz Gezer), *190*

Kehilat Har-El (Jerusalem), 190

ketubah (marriage contract), 125–26

Kibbutz Gezer, *190*

kiddushin (betrothal ceremony), 125, 200–201. *See also* marriage

King, Martin Luther, Jr., 180–81, 326

kippah (head covering), 135

kitchen policies, *110*

klal yisrael (unity of the Jewish people), 70, 215

Klein, Edward, 1, 168

Knobel, Peter S., 153

Kohler, Kaufmann, 68

Kol Ami (Flower Mound TX), *4, 45*

Korngold, Jamie, 300, *302*, 303

kosher practices. *See* dietary laws

Kramer, Hilary, 307

Kurtzman, Joey, 272

Kushner, Lawrence, 287, 290–91, 294

labor rights, 69, 84, 113, 177

Larchmont Temple (Westchester County NY), 239–40

Lau-Lavie, Amichai, 295–97

law. *See* halacha (Jewish law)

Law of Return, 187

Laxness, Pepper, 284

Lazarus, Moritz, 62

L'chah Dodi (poem), 159

Leibman, Joshua Loth, 325

Lelyveld, Arthur, 180

Lenn, Theodore, 137, 328

Lerman, Liz, 297–98

Letters of a Buddhist Jew (Tatz), 256

Levy, Richard N., 111–12, 131–34, *132*

liberalism, 8, 68, 176, 186, 267, 309–11

Liberal movement, 59–60

Liberman, Marc, 254

Liebermann, Eliezer, 99–100, 323

li-kavod Shabbat (in honor of the Sabbath), 123

Linden, Philip, 281

Linden Lab, 281

lineage, 227–32, 329

Lipman, Steve, 278

liturgy. *See* worship services

Liz Lerman Dance Exchange, 297

L'kol Eit (CCAR), 332

logic. *See* rationalism

Los Angeles campus (HUC-JIR), 77, 87, 326, 327

Lotan (Reform kibbutz), 329

Lubavitch Hasidic, 157

Luo, Michael, 239–40

Magen Tzedek (Shield of Justice), 113

Maimonides, 44

mamzerim (children from adultery), 102–3, 128

Man's Quest for God (Heschel), 291–92

mantras, 289–90

Marcuz, Jacob Rader, 325

Margi, Yaakov, 193

marriage: ceremonies, 86, 125–28, 250; children as mitzvah, 126; history of, 124–26; sanctification of, 129. *See also* interfaith families

Maslin, Simeon J., 130, 329

matrilineal descent, 222, 227, 329

Mayer, Marissa, 319

media, 134–35

meditation, 257, 288–91

membership in synagogues: criteria for, 260; declines in, 93–94, 139–49; fees, 279; growth in, 72–73, 76, 77, 136–37

men in Reform Judaism, 196, 198

Menitoff, Paul, 330

Mercaz Shimshon (Jerusalem), 189, 330

messiah, Jewish concept of, 219, 244, 248, 251

Messianic Judaism, 242–45, 245–52

Metro Toronto Convention Centre, 204

Meyer, Michael A., 80, 137
mezuzah (doorpost scroll), 24
Miami Platform (1997), 330
Micah, book of, 29, 49–50, 171, 172
Mihaly, Eugene, 146
mikveh (running water), 225
millennial generation, 271, 272
minhag (tradition), 65
"Minhag America" (prayer book), 65, 324
Miriam's Tambourine, 157
misheberach (blessing), 160–61
Mi Sheberaich (healing blessing), 92–93, *162*
Mishkan T'filah (prayer book), 153–57, 196, 330
mishnah (rabbinic positions), 23
Mitzvah Day, 148, 183
mitzvoth (commandments), 111, 146, 148, 195–96, 232
m'nuchah (rest), 122
Moab (biblical nation), 272
monotheism, 20, 33. *See also* ethical monotheism
Montagu, Lily, 60
Montefiore, Claude G., 60
Morgenstern, Julian, 7, 47–48
Moses (prophet), 53
music: camp programs and, 91–92; in New Reform movement, 151; in worship services, 89, 92–93, 99, 292–93
mussar (ethical approach), 174

Nashville Jewish Community Center, 79
Nathan (prophet), 172
National New Congregations Committee (UAHC), 265
negative freedom, 101
neo-Reform Judaism, 11, 74, 144, 151, 309

Net generation, 284
New Jews, 271
New Reform Revolution, 135–36, 148–57
news media, 134–35
New York City campus (HUC-JIR), 87
New York Jewish Week (newspaper), 135
New York Times, 134
NFTY. *See* North American Federation of Temple Youth (NFTY)
nigunim (melodies), 292, 293
nisuin (nuptials), 124, 125
Nixon, Richard Milhous, 74
Noah, 232–33
Noahide Laws, 233
Nogah Ha-Tsedek (Liebermann), 99, 323
non-Jews, 215, 217, 221, 232–37, 247
normative statements, 25–26
North American Federation of Temple Youth (NFTY), 2, 89, 90–91, 325
Numbers, book of, 176

Obama, Barack, 201
Ochs, Vanessa L., 157
Odets, Beth, 282
Ohabai Sholom (Nashville), 79
Olin-Sang-Ruby Union Institute (OS-RUI), 91, 327
oneg (joy), 122
ordination, 65–66, 85–87, *95*, *166*, 197
Or Nogah (Liebermann), 99–100, 323
Orthodox Judaism: categorization of people in, 194–95; conversion and, 219–20, 230–31; definition of Jewish identity, 213–15; as a denomination, 57; early Reform movement and, 57–58, 61; ethics under, 173; family dynamics in, 126; gender inequalities in, 141–43; on halacha, 101, 278; in Israel, 186–94; on lineage, 227–28; monopoly on religious status, 86–87, 109; Shabbat observance, 116
orthodoxy, defined, xi

orthopraxy, defined, xi
OurJewishCommunity.org, 261, 278–81, 280
Outreach campaign, 217, 221–23
Owens, Mary, 293–94

pacifism, 69–70
Palestine, 71, 187, 189
pancultural Jews, 271
participation: benefits of, 93, 151–52; declines in, 319–20; in online communities, 279–80; pluralistic theology and, 308; in virtual congregations, 277. See also apathy in congregations
patrilineal descent, 83, 215–16, 222, 223, 227–32, 329
patriotism, 76–77
peace, 67, 69–70, 122
Peace of Mind (Leibman), 325
Pesach pilgrimage festival, 59–60, 300–301
pet blessing ceremony, 164
Pharisees, 22–23
Philadelphia Rabbinical Conference (1869), 129, 324
Philippson, Ludwig, 323
pilgrimage festivals, 59–60, 300–301
Pirkei Avot (Ethics of the Sages), 23
Pittsburgh Platform (1885), 34, 68–69, 109, 324
Pittsburgh Platform (1999), 38–40, 111, 131–35, 329
Pitzele, Peter, 294–95
Plaut, W. Gunther, 121, 145–47, 264, 267, 329
pluralism: challenges of, 32; in confirmation ceremonies, 142; dangers of, 137–38, 308–15; growing acceptance of, 38, 109; in Reform movement, 6; strengths of, 86–87
podcasts, 278, 294
Polish, David, 191

political activism: of rabbis, 70–71, 74–75, 84; in the Reform movement, 8, 79–80, 176–85; for the State of Israel, 186. See also justice
polythetic approach, 6, 26
pork, dietary restrictions, 104, 112
positive freedom, 101–2
post-denominationalism, xi, 13, 300, 313, 321
Poznanski, Gustavus, 63
prayer: healing power of, 92–93; language of, 100, 152; in meditation, 289–90; transliterations, 153; women and, 195
prayer books: gender equality in, 196; in Humanistic Judaism, 263–66; importance of, 65, 90; language of, 100, 153–57; problems with, 81–82; resurrection of the dead prayer, 155–57
Priesand, Sally, 85–86, 165–69, 166, 327
Progressive Judaism, 60–61, 109, 186–94
progressive revelation, 46–53, 269
prophetic Judaism, 68, 171
prophets, 27–29, 49–53, 170–73, 175–76
proselytization. See conversion
psychodrama, 294–95
PunkTorah.com, 270–71

Rabbi and Synagogue in Reform Judaism (Lenn), 137
Rabbinical Assembly, 82
rabbinical schools, 66, 70, 77–78, 87
Rabbi's Manual (CCAR), 130
The Radiance of Justice (Liebermann), 99
Radiant Light (Liebermann), 99–100
radio programs, 276
Raising the Bar program, 295–97
Ramaz School (Manhattan NY), 1–2
Rashi (Talmudic commentator), 203–4

rationalism: commitment to, 30, 33; Kant and religion, 102; limits of, 145, 163; ritual practices and, 108, 135–36, 151

Reagan, Ronald, 329

rebbetzin (rabbi's wife), 167

Reconstructionist Judaism, 33, 142, 158, 326, 327

Reformed Society of Israelites, 62

Reform Is a Verb (Fein), 139, 328

Reform Judaism: during the 1960s, 79–80; boundaries of, 8–11, 242, 245, 248, 265–66, 267–69; challenges of, 3–6, 312–16; change in, 11–13, 30–32, 85; criticisms of, 31; defined, 1, 13–14, 26; early American, 62–69, 70–81; future of, x, 319–21; in Germany, 54–58, 62, 323, 324; in Great Britain, 59–62; in Israel, 186–94; under Rabbi Jacobs, 96–98; under Rabbi Schindler, 81–88, 127; under Rabbi Yoffie, 88–96; strengths of, xi; timeline of events, 323–32. *See also* neo-Reform Judaism

Reform Judaism (magazine), 88, *132*, *133*, *275*, *310*

Reform Progressive movement, 59–60

Reform rite, 12–13

Religious Action Center (RAC), 177–79, 205

religious authority, 3, 5, 8–9, 20, 101–2, 151–52

responsa, 99–100

Responsa Committee, (CCAR): Beth Adam application, 264; on Buddhism, 256–58; establishment of, 9–10, 100; Messianic Jews, 249–51

responsa literature, 268–69

resurrection of the dead prayer, 155–57

retreats. *See* worship retreats

revelation, ix, 27, 30, 46–53, 147–48, 269

Ritual Committees, 151–52

rituals: under Classical Reform, 68–69; creation of new, 157–64; defined, 11; ethics over, 29, 172–73, 174–75; guidance on, 131–35, 144–48; history of, 99–103, 135–44; modern return to, 30–32; under Reform Judaism, 133, 140, 148–57; rejection of obligatory practices, 57–58. *See also* dietary laws

Rodef Shalom (Pittsburgh), 131

Roman Empire, 218–19

romanticism, 135–36

Roof, Wade Clark, 269

Roosevelt, Franklin Delano, 70

Rosedale, Philip, 281

Rosen, Ceil (née Starr), 242–45

Rosen, Moishe, 242–45

Rosh Hashanah, *45*, 297

Rosh Hodesh, 157–58

Rotem, Mordecai (Moti), 86–87, 328

Ruth (biblical), 218

Sabbath: current views on, 114; *li-kavod Shabbat* (in honor of the Sabbath), 123; need for guidance in, 145–48; origins of, 114–16; prohibited activities, 116; purposes for, 121–22; in Reform Judaism, 117–24; Saturday services, 88, 119, 123–24, 143–44; Sunday services, 119–20

Sabbath Committee (CCAR), 146–48, 327

Sabbath school, 119

Sacred Survival (Woocher), 271

Safdie, Moshe, 78, 191

sages: history of, 22–24; interpretation of Torah, 4, 51–53; recreating Jewish practice, 159–60; Sabbath observances, 116

Saperstein, David, 175

Sarna, Jonathan D., 156, 240

Satlow, Michael L., 6, 25–26

Saturday services, 88, 119, 123–24, 143–44

Schachter-Shalomi, Zalman, 112–13, 158, 259, 289–90

Scheuer, Richard J., 78

Schindler, Alexander M.: on commitment, 308; Congregation Beth Adam, 264, 266, 329; on conversion, 221, 237–38; gay rights, 200, 329; interfaith families, 127, 328; as leader, 74, 82–84, 87–88, 328; on lineage, 222, 228

scholarship: in early Reform movements, 58; of halacha, 100–101; need for spirituality in, 155, 156–57; in Reform Judaism, 308, 316; religious beliefs and, 7–8; of revelation, 47–48; scientific explanations, 30, 75

Schwartzman, Sylvan D., 62

seafood, dietary restrictions, 104–6, 107, 112

Second Life (virtual world), 281–84

Second Life Hebrew School, 282

Second Temple Period, 22, 246

Seder P'reidah (ritual of release), 130, 328

Seesen school, 55–56, 323

segregated congregations, 65

self-determination. See autonomy, personal

selichot (prayers), 297

Seltzer, Sanford, 141, 143

Sha'ar Zahav (San Francisco), 331

A Shabbat Manual (Plaut), 121–22, 146, 327

Shalom Uvracha Interactive software, 283

Shapiro, Richard, 226

Shas party, 188, 193, 332

Shavuot pilgrimage festival, 55, 59–60, 300–301

shechitah (ritual slaughtering), 106

Shema (prayer), 289–90

shiduchin (engagement), 124–25

Shield of Justice (Magen Tzedek), 113

sh'mirat Shabbat (Sabbath observance). See Sabbath

shofar (ram's horn), 45

Shomrei Adamah (Guardians of the Earth), 298

Siddur Sha'ar Zahav (prayer book), 331

Silver, Abba Hillel, 70–71

Silverman, William B., 79

simcha chochma (celebration of wisdom), 92–93, 161

Simlai, Rabbi, 50

Sing unto God (album), 92

Sirkman, Jeffrey J., 239–40

Six-Day War, 80, 327

Six Points Sports Academy, 91

Skirball, Jack, 77

slaughter methods, 106, 113

s'micha (ordination). See ordination

Snyder, Laurel, 209–12

Soapbox (magazine), 278

social justice. See justice

societal changes: halacha and, 101–3; non-Jews and, 233; patrilineal descent and, 229–32; as reason for New Reform movement, 150–51; ritual practices and, 135–37, 140–41

Society for Classical Reform Judaism (SCRJ), 89–90, 331

Society for Humanistic Judaism (SHJ), 260–65, 267

Society for the Advancement of Judaism, 142–43, 325

Society of Reformed Israelites, 323

Sodom (city), 174

soup kitchens, 182

spirituality: alternative expressions of, 148, 154, 270–71, 291–98; ceremony creation and, 158–59; concept of, 287; creating one's own, 15–19; healing in, 163–64; Jewish Buddhism, 253–55, 259; in online environments, 284; ritual practices and, 68–69, 109–10, 139, 140; Sabbath observances, 123; in scholarship, 155, 156–57; societal changes and, 13–14; spirituality programs, 299–306. *See also* autonomy

spiritual wilderness adventures, 298–306

"Statement of Principles for Reform Judaism" (CCAR), 38, 111, 131–35

Stein, Leopold, 323

Stephen Wise Free Synagogue, 168, 177

Stern, Shira, 201

Storahtelling programs, 295–97

Strassfeld, Shula, 297

Strauss, Charles, 253

Sukkat Shalom (Wilmette IL), 238–39

Sukkot pilgrimage festival, 59–60, 282, 300–301

synagogue, x–xi, 55, 240–41, 270–71. *See also* worship services

Tabory, Ephraim, 188

Talmud, 10, 20, 23–24, 57, 100, 249

tambourine, 157

Tanakh, 173–74

Task, Arnold S., 249

Tatz, Akiva, 256

technology: e-mails, 280–81; Internet, 273–86, 294; online programs, 279; podcasts, 278, 294; webcasting, 277–78; websites, 276

temple, historic use of term, 56

temple cult, 172

tenaim (marriage contract), 124–25

Ten Commandments, 115–16, 255

teshuva (repentance), 249

That's Funny, You Don't Look Buddhist (Boorstein), 254–55, 287–88

thelordismyshepherd.com (Hammerman), 276

theology: ambiguity in, 155–57; changes in, 6–8; clarification of, xi, 308–15; Classical Reform, 68–69; disagreements on, 81–82; Jewish Buddhism, 253; ritual requirements and, 27–30, 137–38, 140. *See also* God; pluralism

tikkun olam (repairing the world), 181–83, 208

Time, 134

timeline of events, 323–32

Torah: anthropocentrism in, 202–3; conversion in, 218; ethics in, 170, 171, 173–74; on homosexuality, 198–99; interpretation of, 4; justice, 176

Torah (oral): dietary laws, 106; history of, 23; interpretation of, 46–53; in Reform Judaism, 27; traditional understanding of, 57–58

Torah (written): dietary laws, 103–7; history of, 23; interpretation of, 46–53; in Reform Judaism, 27; traditional understanding of, 57–58

The Torah: A Modern Commentary, 41–43, 329

The Torah: A Woman's Commentary, 17, 203, 331

Torah readings, 119, 160–61, 294–95

TorahTrek Spiritual Wilderness Adventures, 300–301

tradition, concept of, 11

traditional Judaism: categorization of people, 194–95; dietary restrictions in, 103–7; fear of returning to, 134; meditation, 289; Reform movement and, 30, 57–58, 89; women in, 195–98. *See also* Orthodox Judaism

translations, 81, 153, 156

Trefa Banquet, 66–67

Truman, Harry S., 70–71

UAHC. *See* Union of American Hebrew Congregations (UAHC)

unclean foods. *See* dietary laws

Union for Reform Judaism (URJ): camp programs, 89, 90–91, *313*; on conversion, 328; environmentalism, 204–5, 329; gender-related initiatives, 198; membership requirements, 260; prevention of animal cruelty, 113–14; restructuring of, 94, *310*, 314–15, 331; URJ Press, 88–89

Union of American Hebrew Congregations (UAHC): Biennial Convention (1999), 149–50, 151–52; camp programs, 91; conversion education programs, 237; environmentalism, 205, 207–8; founding of, 65, 324; gay rights, 199–200; Los Angeles campus, 77; membership growth, 72–73, 76, 77, 136–37; membership requirements, 260, 263–66; social justice advocacy, 176–79, 326; on Zionism, 191. *See also* Religious Action Center (RAC); Union for Reform Judaism (URJ)

Union of Messianic Jewish Congregations (UMJC), 248

Union Prayer Book, 148, 175, 325, 328

The Union Prayer Book-Sinai Edition (SCRJ), 90

United Jewish Appeal, 271

United Jewish Communities, 271

United Synagogue of Conservative Judaism, 77

unity of the Jewish people, 70, 215

universalism, 71

URJ. *See* Union for Reform Judaism (URJ)

values: environmental responsibility, 201–8; gender equality, 165–70; social justice, 175–85; value of inclu-sivity, 194–201; Zionism, 185–94. *See also* ethical behavior

Vietnam War, 79, 327

VirtualChurch.com, 277

virtual congregations, 275, 276–86

virtual worlds, 281–84

Vorspan, Albert, 75, 175, 180, 326

Washington Post, 283

Washofsky, Mark, 123, 126, 216, 248–52, 268–69

webcasting, 277–78

websites, 276

Wegela, Karen Kissel, 259

Weidhorn, Peter, 94

Weinstein, Yehuda, 193

Wertheimer, Jack, 267, 272

West London Synagogue of British Jews, 59–60

White, Lynn Townsend, Jr., 202–3

Wiener, Julie, 226

wilderness spirituality, 299–306

A Wild Faith (Comins), 300

Willis, Stacy J., 134

Wine, Sherwin T., 262–63

Wise, Isaac Mayer, 64–70, 69, 103, 118–19, 167, 221, 315–16, 324

Wise, Stephen, 70, 177, 325

women: Augsburg conference (1871), 61–62; bar and bat mitzvahs, 142–43; ceremonial innovations and, 157–58; conversion and, 223; dietary laws and, 108; in leadership roles, 85–86, 165–70, 198, 327; prayer books, 81; in Reform Judaism, 196; in traditional Judaism, 195–96, 196–97

Woocher, Jonathan, 271

workaholism, 114

worker's rights, 69, 84, 113, 177

World Union for Progressive Judaism (WUPJ), 60–61, 71–72, 186, 189–91, 325, 327

Other Works by Dana Evan Kaplan

Contemporary American Judaism:
Transformation and Renewal
(2009, 2011)

The Cambridge Companion to
American Judaism
(2005)

American Reform Judaism:
An Introduction
(2003, 2005)

Platforms and Prayer Books
(2002)

Contemporary Debates in American
Reform Judaism: Conflicting Visions
(2001)

World War I, 69–70

World War II, 71–72

worship retreats, 152, 298

worship services: creative expression in, 292–93; early European reforms to, 55; under New Reform, 88–90, 149, 151–55; ritual practice changes in, 140–44; Sunday worship services, 119–20

WUPJ. See World Union for Progressive Judaism (WUPJ)

Yahadut Mitkademet movement. See Progressive Judaism

Yahel (Reform kibbutz), 328

yarmulkes (head coverings), 89, *132*, 135

Yehuda, Rabbi, 53

Yeshua. *See* Jesus

Yoffie, Eric H.: on challenges in Reform movement, 87–88, 148–52, *149*; on conversions, 237–38; on environmentalism, 113–14, 205, 331; on-line environments, 274, 286; Outreach campaign, 217; reaching Reform youth, 90–91; restructuring of URJ, 94–96; on Shabbat observance, 88, 123–24; on social justice, 183–85; on theological consistency, 138

Yom HaAtzmaut, 160

Yom HaShoah, 160

Yom Kippur War, 80, 328

youth: approaches to religion, 272–73, 315–16; connecting with, xi, 86–87; Jewish identity of, 236–37; programming for, 90–91; theological generation gap, 138–39, 307–9

Zalman, Reb. *See* Schachter-Shalomi, Zalman

Zion Collegiate Association, 66

Zionism: beginning of movement, 61; opposition to, 72; Reform stance on, 56, 70–71, 188–89, 325; support for, 80, 185–86; taught in schools, 2

Zuckerberg, Mark, 307–9